China and the Barbarians

China and the Barbarians

Resisting the Western World Order

by

Hendrik Schulte Nordholt

LEIDEN UNIVERSITY PRESS

English translation: John Eyck
Editor: Jonathan Earl

Cover design: Geert de Koning
Cover image: Mao Zedong's mausoleum in Tiananmen square, Beijing, China (AP Photo/Elizabeth Dalziel)
Lay-out: TAT Zetwerk

ISBN   978 90 8728 278 3
e-ISBN   978 94 0060 289 2 (ePDF)
e-ISBN   978 94 0060 290 8 (ePub)
NUR   692

Original title *China en de barbaren*
© 2015 by Henk Schulte Nordholt
First published in 2015 by Em. Querido's Uitgeverij, Amsterdam

© Hendrik Schulte Nordholt / Leiden University Press, 2018

This book is distributed in North America by the University of Chicago Press (www.press.uchicago.edu).

Contents

Note on Spelling   vii
Prologue   ix

Introduction   1
1 – The Lofty Classical Order   15
2 – The Century of Humiliation   45
3 – A New Beginning   71
4 – Xi Jinping Has a Dream   91
5 – The Eternal Party   113
6 – An Alternative to the Party?   143
7 – The Experience of History: From Supremacy to Shame   177
8 – Foreign Policy under Mao and Deng: From Rebellion to Harmony   207
9 – The New Nationalism   233
10 – The Party on a Dead-End Street   261
11 – The Third Way   275
12 – The World of the Great Harmony   293
Epilogue   309

Acknowledgements   311
Chronological overview of dynasties in China   313
Chairmen and Party Secretaries of the People's Republic of China   315
Notes   317
Works Consulted   349
Illustration Credits   354
Index of Persons   355

Note on Spelling

For the transcription of Chinese words I have used the pinyin-transcription, commonly used in mainland China. This goes for names as well, unless it concerns a name which is know in the West by another transcription. I have therefore not changed – by way of example – the name of Sun Yatsen into Sun Zhongshan.

As to the capital of China, I have used both 'Peking' and 'Beijing'. The former when describing the pre-1949 history of China, that is before the founding of the People's Republic of China. The latter for the period thereafter. 'Beijing' can, moreover, refer to either the physical presence of that city, or to the government of the People's Republic of China. The context should make it clear which of these two meanings is applicable.

I also use the pinyin-transcription for that other (former) capital of China: Nanjing. I only use 'Nanking' in the context of the 1842 'Treaty of Nanking'.

Overview of China's administrative divisions (2011)

Prologue

An unnatural glow lights up the warm summer night. At the Southern Gate of the Forbidden City, right under the six-metre-tall portrait of Mao Zedong, a tank has been set ablaze. Flames leak out and shoot way up into the air, giving the bloated countenance of the Great Helmsman a sinister glare. Screaming feverishly, an enraged mob circles the steel skeleton shimmering in the heat – as if they mean to exorcise the evil that is bound to come. Though this one tank has been rendered harmless by the demonstrators on Tiananmen Square, everybody knows that more of them will follow.

Then, all of a sudden, panic sets in, rage turns abruptly into fear. 'The army's coming, they're coming from the west, from Mengtougou!' Rudderless, the mob starts to drift, unsure what to do next. The flower-power mood of the previous weeks has dissipated, evaporated into the threatening glow of the muggy night. For just a moment, cheerfully crackling fireworks break the spell, but my Chinese friends realise more quickly than I that it is something completely different. 'Take cover, they're shooting!' Screaming, thousands of people run in every direction, taking cover behind trees and low walls at the edge of the square.

In one long sprint I run in the direction of the Peking Hotel and hide behind a planter. The intensity of the fireworks increases, as if gigantic firecrackers were being shot from every rooftop in Beijing. The immeasurably large square catches all the sounds and throws them back: The ra-ta-tat of shots, the cries of fear and rage, the dull rumble of the tanks that come rolling in from the west. My next sprint brings me into the lobby of the Peking Hotel. Recovering my breath, I look around and see it is deserted, but in the corner I spot a couple of public telephones. It is three o'clock in the morning, and I have been on the move since the evening started. In a world without cell phones, I had virtually disappeared from the face of the earth – it was high time to tell my wife that I am still alive.

I drop a coin into the phone, dial the number and wait for it to start ringing. At that very moment, from out of nowhere, a small man with an enormous pair of shears looms into view. Silently he cuts through the line, as matter-of-factly as a gardener cutting flowers. Enraged, I push him up against the wall. He does not resist, and stares at me with cold, expressionless eyes – as though the absurdity of his action has become the new normal for the world after 4 June 1989.

Introduction

*One merely feels she is there, a tremendous exist-
ence somewhat too big for the human mind to
encompass, a seemingly inconsequential chaos
obeying its own laws of existence ...*

Lin Yutang

In the years when my intellectual hunger seemed insatiable, I read many books on philosophy: General introductions like *The History of Philosophy* by Hans Joachim Störig, but also the works of the great thinkers themselves. My favourite philosopher was Friedrich Nietzsche. His poetic way of writing, and surprising use of metaphors, made his thinking more accessible than the often elaborately-phrased thoughts of Kant and Hegel. In Nietzsche's writing, fiction and philosophy seemed to merge effortlessly. Growing older, I am less susceptible to the charms of the 'Philosopher with the Hammer', but one of his observations has guided me through the years: 'It (i.e. philosophy) always creates the world in its own image; it cannot do otherwise; philosophy is this tyrannical impulse itself... In the philosopher, on the contrary, there is absolutely nothing impersonal; and above all, his morality furnishes a decided and decisive testimony as to WHO HE IS...'[1]

What are my 'images' of China? Which 'morality' has shaped those images? For ten years I have studied sinology at Leiden University. I have been a China expert at the ministry of Economic Affairs, and from 1985 I lived for twenty years in Beijing: First as a banker, then as a businessman. I have travelled through all the provinces and autonomous regions of this continental state; I slept in creaky tents, dirty guesthouses and five-star hotels. I have climbed the huge mountains of Tibet and swam in the Li river, which shaped the surreal Karst mountains of Southern China which have inspired countless Chinese painters. Observing carefully, I have experienced China to the bone, but as a sinologist I have also tried to make intellectual sense of what I saw. I read hundreds of books and thousands of articles; yet never reached the point that I fully came to understand the shapeless mass of what is being called 'China'. By studying sinology, I have been put on a road of discovery that knows no end.

This short summary of my resumé is not meant to convince the reader that this book is 'authoritative' – but to clarify where I come from and which experiences have shaped my images of China. It is harder to define the 'morality' which has processed these images into ideas and convictions. I believe that nothing is impossible, but I am also conscious of human fallibility. Romanticism and realism have (I suspect) 'tyrannically' shaped my Chinese world.

The romantic impulse already manifested itself at a tender age. Hendrik Bos, the neighbour of my parents, was a sinologist who as an interpreter and diplomat had been living in China before the Second World War. I have no memories of Hendrik (he died when I was two years old), but I do remember the things that he had left behind: Rooms filled with blue-white porcelain vases and long scrolls depicting bamboo sheds reduced to insignificant dots against the background of magnificent, misty mountain ranges. From then on it dawned on me that one day I must make my own journey to the east, and see these magical lands with my own eyes.

When studying sinology, I came to realize that the 'China' I had been dreaming of as a child did not bear any resemblance to the China that had been created by the Communist Party after 1949. Mao was still alive, and the country was in a state of disruption owing to the 'Great Proletarian Cultural Revolution' that the Great Helmsman had launched in 1966. Many western intellectuals believed that Mao had created a better and happier society than ours. I was sceptical. I felt a profound resistance to the bombastic slogans predicting the inevitable victory of the proletariat, the propaganda posters depicting happy peasants collecting bumper harvests year after year. Truly revolutionary books such as *Chinese Shadows* by Simon Leys, and Fox Butterfield's *Alive in the Bitter Sea*, confirmed that Mao had created a hell rather than a heaven on earth. When Deng Xiaoping came to power in 1978, this was admitted in China as well – albeit using different wording, because the Cultural Revolution that had destroyed millions of lives was being dismissed as a 'mistake' attributable to the 'Gang of Four', the clique headed by Mao's wife Jiang Qing that had supposedly misled the Great Helmsman.

The position of the Communist Party itself could not be questioned. That became manifestly clear in the spring of 1989, when the mass demonstrations held in Tiananmen Square were crushed with excessive violence. I was working at the time for the AMRO Bank in Beijing, and saw with my own eyes how the dramatic events unfolded. That was perhaps my most defining China experience: The sight of millions of people who had for weeks called on their government for a more humane society, only to be supressed when the tanks of the People's Liberation Army violently cleared the Square of Heavenly Peace. The memories of that Beijing spring[2] have been carved in my mind forever: The thrill of a new dawn that filled the air, the feelings of desperation and disgust when the Party started shooting at its own people.

Cultural Revolution

The *Wuchan Jieji Wenhua Dageming* ('Great Proletarian Cultural Revolution', better known as the 'Cultural Revolution') was launched by Mao Zedong in May 1966. Its purpose was 'to destroy the old and create the new'. Temples, monasteries and city walls were destroyed all over the country. Opera, theatre, music, sculptures, dance, film, poetry and literature were also targeted, because many of these artistic expressions were regarded as 'feudal' and 'immoral'. The class struggle against the representatives of the old order – teachers, musicians, factory directors and high officials – killed or mutilated millions of people. Behind the ideological façade of 'attacking the old', almost all of the Party's leading officials were purged: In Mao's view, these people were guilty of 'revisionism' and 'bourgeois thinking'. In 1969 the worst excesses had ended; but only with the arrest of the Gang of Four, following Mao's death in September 1976, did the Cultural Revolution officially come to an end.

Patriotic Education

The importance of 4 June 1989 was truly monumental. It showed that great political movements seem to come out of nowhere, and are (as the Chinese saying goes) like 'sparks turning into a prairie fire'. It almost meant the end of the Party's grip on power, so once that threat had disappeared its policies were all the more surprising. Almost all the China experts in the West (genuine or self-proclaimed) were convinced that Beijing's gerontocrats would close the door to the West – just as Leonid Brezhnev had done in 1964 after his coup d'etat – but the opposite happened. Deng Xiaoping, the 'Supreme Leader' nearing ninety years old, launched a vigorous renewal of the 'Open Door' policy which put the country on a two-track approach: Support for economic reforms, while supressing calls for political reforms. This policy of 'one-legged development' resulted in an unprecedented economic boom that transformed China within 25 years from an impoverished agricultural giant into a high-tech superstate that has become a crucial player in the world economy.

But the Party felt that more was needed than creating economic prosperity. A new ideological base had to be found to re-affirm its right to rule. The sight of hundreds of thousands of young people singing and dancing in Tiananmen Square was felt to be deeply unsettling. How was it possible that the protest movement's leaders were trained at China's top schools such as Peking University and Qinghua University? How could China's future leaders have had the audacity to erect the 'Goddess of Liberty' on Tiananmen Square – symbol of power of the communist state? The Party was unequivocal in its conclusion. Its work had fallen short in one of the key areas supporting communist power: Propaganda. With this grave omission, the time had come to launch a major counter-attack, positing the Party as saviour of the nation and symbol of patriotic fervour. Its major tool was the Patriotic Education Campaign, which set out to rewrite the country's history textbooks.[3] The so-called Century of Humiliation (1839–1949) – when foreign imperialist powers colluded to dismember the old empire – received a disproportionate (given the length of Chinese history) amount of attention. Chinese children were henceforward being taught that only thanks to the Party had this imperialist aggression been brought to an end, and that only thanks to the Party had the creation of a 'New China' been made possible.

Takeover of the South China Sea

In 2012 the Chinese navy took possession of the Johnson South Reef in the South China Sea by lifting millions of cubic meters of sand from the ocean floor, and turning the virgin reef into an artificial island that could be used for docking ships and landing planes. No violence was used (not against humans, at least), no people displaced, and no international protest was submitted. The necessary ingredients for 'breaking news' were absent and so no attention was paid to it by the western media. In the Spratly Archipelago alone, China has since then built seven artificial islands and militarized them.[4] Beijing's barely concealed aim is to transform the entire South China Sea into a Chinese lake – an area that is five times the size of France, rich in oil and gas, and whose waters act as a highway over which more than a third of the world's trade is being shipped. Littoral states such as Vietnam and the Philippines, who also have territorial claims to (some of) the islands in the South China Sea, have been protesting against their huge neighbour's policy of land reclamation for years. Former president Aquino of the Philippines even compared Beijing's actions in the South China Sea with Hitler's annexation of the Sudetenland in 1938.[5] Brushing off these criticisms, China is taking possession of existing islands and creating new ones – thus making it clear who is the regional boss, and preparing itself for what many strategic thinkers in China see as inevitable: A military clash with the United States.

Seen from an ideological perspective, Beijing's actions are harder to explain: No country in the world proclaims as loudly as China that non-interference in the affairs of other countries is one of the basic norms that govern relations between states, and that disputes must always be solved peacefully. Even more, Beijing uses this argument as a defensive weapon against Western thinking that in certain situations the international community has the right, even the duty, to violate the sovereignty of other states – when, for instance, that state has committed genocide or other crimes against humanity. According to Beijing, intervention in other countries is always forbidden.

Foundations of Nationalism

Why does Beijing in the South China Sea violate its own core principle of non-intervention? Political opportunism is one of the reasons. To stay in power, the Party needs a rallying cry to unite the people behind its banner. 'Preserving the territorial integrity of the motherland' has in the early twenty-first century become a key mission that justifies the Party's right to rule China. But there are other reasons as well, drawn from deeper sources than the daily-felt need to keep the party in power.

The People's Republic of China has not yet turned seventy – no more than a fleeting moment in the endless stream of Chinese history. When Mao Zedong ruled (1949–1976), China's pre-modern history was seen as a dark period of feudalism and oppression that, according to the laws of historical determinism, only served as a kind of preliminary phase for the more developed eras of capitalism and socialism. At the beginning of the twenty-first century, ideology no longer restricts Beijing's historical thinking: The imperial era is now seen as a glorious time when China reigned supreme, and the foreign barbarians humbly acknowledged Beijing's supremacy. Inspired by a same sense of pride, President Xi Jinping frequently talks about the 'Great Rejuvenation of the Chinese Nation', but what makes present-day nationalism complex and at times difficult to read is that other source of historical consciousness: The Century of Humiliation. China is not only proud of its magnificent historical achievements; it is also brittle and prone to fits of bad temper when sensitive issues (such as its historical relations with Britain or Japan) are brought up.

With these observations I touch upon some key questions that this book seeks to answer: What feeds Chinese nationalism at the beginning of the twenty-first century, and what are its most important manifestations? And even more important: How serious is the threat it poses for peace and security in East Asia and the rest of the world? To give a brief answer to that last question: Extremely serious. Beijing's assertiveness in the South and East China Seas has led to structural tensions with Japan, the Philippines and Vietnam. For their defence, these first two countries are leaning more and more on the United States, and even Vietnam is intensifying the military relationship with its former adversary. This increases the risk that a local conflict will turn into a global war – even more so because Washington will not sit idly by and let its major geo-political rival take over sea routes vital to world trade. The two major powers communicate through various channels on economic, political and military matters, but that does not necessarily lead to an increase in trust. On the contrary: Mistrust seems to be the name of the game. Perhaps this is inevitable. Writing in the fifth century BCE on the conflict between Athens and Sparta, the Greek historian Thucydides already claimed that war between an upcoming and existing power cannot be avoided. In the case of the United States and China, this risk seems even greater because their different political systems result in a fundamental lack of trust. Mistrust runs deepest on the Chinese side: Beijing is convinced that Washington is secretly plotting to change China's political system.

The End of History?

Can the two major powers escape Thucydides' historical determinism? Are they 'free' to avoid a major conflict? Clear-cut predictions on how China will behave are usually off the mark, but I am convinced that that there is less risk of conflict if Beijing were to choose a different system than 'socialism with Chinese characteristics'. Will this happen? In his essay 'The End of History and the Last Man', political historian Francis Fukuyama argues that the global victory of political and economic liberalism is inevitable. Fukuyama made his prediction, significantly, in 1989 – the year of the fall of the Berlin Wall. 'What we may be witnessing is not just the end of the Cold War, or the passing of a particular period of post-war history, but the end of history as such: That is, the end point of man's ideological evolution and the universalization of Western liberal democracy as the final form of human government'.[6] Fukuyama leans heavily on the German philosopher Hegel, who saw history being propelled forward by a kind of universal 'Mind' that manifests itself through great individuals in the realms of religion, art, culture, politics and philosophy, and has one overriding aim: The establishment of a free and equal society where reason reigns. Hegel's dialectical world view inspired Karl Marx, although the founder of communism did not see the 'Mind', but rather the materialistic relations between classes as moving history forward.[7] In the end, Marx predicted, history will be completed by the establishment of the classless society. As to China: Who will be the true, and who will be the false prophet? Hegel or Marx?

Some thirty years after *The End of History* was published, China's cities have unmistakably become part of the globalized world that Fukuyama saw coming into being. Shanghai is not only an integral part of the new globalized economy; it leads the way. In the city's countless coffee shops, latte-sipping youngsters are continuously online. The concentration of software and design start-ups is higher than in any other city in China. A CNN travel documentary has difficulty in limiting the reasons why Shanghai is 'the best city in the world' to only fifty attractions. From its rich historical legacy, its bars and entertainment to its magnetic bullet train which connects the city with the airport: The buzz and excitement can be felt everywhere.[8] Shanghai has always been a pioneer in China's modernization drive, but in the early twenty-first century the whole country has rejected the pallid uniformity that characterized Maoist China. At the Berlin Film Festival of 2014, the film *Black Coal, Thin Ice* won the prestigious Black Bear Award. Painters like Zhang Xiaogang sell their works for millions of dollars, and the 2008 opening ceremony of the Olympic Games dazzled the world through its extravagance and creativity. China's participation in the global world of 'leisure and lifestyle', however, does not mean that its government allows a convergence with Western political culture as well. On the contrary: The Party's resistance to Western thought in general is becoming stronger. The Chinese citizen can choose what he wants to wear or what music he wants to hear, but does not have a say in which leaders govern him. This clashes fundamentally with the western idea of the 'consent of the governed' – an idea that was originally crafted by the English philosophers Hume and Locke, and adopted by America's Founding Fathers as one of the core principles in the Declaration of Independence: 'We hold these truths to be self-evident: that all men are created equal; that they are endowed by their Creator with certain unalienable rights; that among these are life, liberty, and the pursuit of happiness. That to secure these rights, Governments are instituted among Men, deriving their just powers from the *consent of the governed*.'[9] The Universal Declaration of Human Rights, adopted in 1948, elevates sovereignty of the people to an international norm and links it to democratic elections: 'The will of the people shall be the basis of the authority of government; this will shall be expressed in periodic and genuine elections which shall be by universal and equal suffrage and shall be held by secret vote or by equivalent free voting procedures.'[10]

China signed the Universal Declaration of Human Rights, as well as the International Covenant on Civil and Political Rights (though it did not ratify the latter), but that does not mean that ideas on individual freedom and representative government are deeply rooted in the Chinese mind. The resistance to these typical 'western' ideas is not only fed by Party propaganda; also among Chinese intellectuals there is a deeply felt reluctance to accept western political thought as universal. Rather instinctively, many of the country's leading intellectuals feel that China's sophisticated philosophical tradition is too old, too unique and too superior to fit into western models of thought. As the prominent intellectual Gan Yang phrases it: 'China's very existence creates a problem for Western accounts of world history. The Bible didn't say anything about China. Hegel saw world history starting with primitive China and ending in a crescendo of perfection with German civilization. Fukuyama's "end of history" thesis simply replaces Germany with America. But suddenly the West has discovered that in the East there is this China: A large empire, with a long history and glorious past. A whole new world has emerged.'[11]

It is more difficult to gauge the political views of the Old Hundred Names (the people) – the last time that free elections were held in China was in 1912. This has given rise to the somewhat condescending view (often heard in the West) that 'the Chinese' are not interested in politics, and are only interested in making money. I strongly disagree. When in the spring of 1989 the shackles of authoritarian rule were temporarily removed, people from all walks of life expressed their political views with great detail and nuance. I will never forget the old man who grabbed my hand and said with tears in his eyes 'Two hundred years ago you had the French Revolution in the West; now it is our turn!' Just as we do, Chinese people value 'life, liberty and the pursuit of happiness' – no matter how different their cultural and historical background may be. The many years that I lived in China have, however, also left a less hopeful impression: It is not man (to quote the Greek philosopher Protagoras), but the *Chinese* man who is the measure of all things. Hence the saying *hua yi zhi bian* – there is a difference between China and the barbarians. This generally-held view provides the Party with a fertile ground for planting its seeds of nationalism. A Chinese friend of mine once praised in exalted terms the glories of the Song dynasty (960–1279). I suggested that Europe's contribution to world civilisation had at that time also been substantial, witnessed by the many magnificent cathedrals built in the twelfth and thirteenth centuries. He did not believe me: 'in those days you people were still going around in bear skins!'

A New Model?

Can the Party continue to limit the freedom of its citizens? Many western politicians and intellectuals believe that is impossible. Former Secretary of State Hillary Clinton is typical in this conviction. When asked in 2011 about Beijing's defensive reaction to the Arab Spring, she said: 'They're worried, and they are trying to stop history, which is a fool's errand. They cannot do it. But they're going to hold it off as long as possible.'[12]

This statement articulates America's long-held conviction that the global march towards liberty is irresistible and that the 'manifest destiny' of the United States lies in spreading the gospel of freedom. Fukuyama's claim that 'The triumph of the West, of the Western idea, is evident first of all in the total exhaustion of viable systematic alternatives to Western liberalism'[13] is treated in Beijing with derision and condescension. In 2011, twenty years after the demise of the Soviet Union, *The People's Daily* crowed that China's economic success showed that Fukuyama's thesis of the 'end of history' was nothing more than an illusion created by the West. Why did the Soviet Union fall apart while China stayed strong and united? 'Because Moscow was not capable of carrying out genuine economic reforms.'[14]

This is a telling statement: The Party thinks it can not only *escape* from the tide of history, it can even *write* history by creating a model that is more successful than the Western one, and that can serve as an example to those countries who are fed up with the West taking the high moral ground. Seen from that perspective, the bloody crackdown of 4 June 1989 on the demonstrators on Tiananmen Square was not the final convulsion of a doomed regime, but the violent birth of a new order which

Harvard professor Larry Summers calls 'authoritarian mercantilism': Export-driven growth, state-guided capitalism, nationalistic and anti-democratic.[15] Through a combination of economic reforms, sophisticated repression and ideological flexibility, the Party has up to now managed to escape the fate of its sister party in the Soviet Union. Can she keep it up? And if not, which system will replace 'authoritarian mercantilism'? Will Fukuyama's economic and political liberalism indeed prove to be invincible? Or will we see something of a 'third way' taking shape, the creation of a system that is more receptive to the voice of the people, but also draws its inspiration from Confucianism – China's dominant ideology before the empire fell in 1911? These are the second set of questions being raised in this book, although I must immediately add that 'big questions' can seldom be met with 'big answers'. Certainly not if the subject of our inquiry concerns China – a country (as every Chinese intellectual is fond of reminding his Western counterpart) which is actually too big and too complex to comprehend. Books such as *The Coming Collapse of China* or *When China Rules the World* unfortunately confirm what the simplicity of their titles suggest: A one-sided explanation of a country that Lin Yutang calls a 'tremendous existence somewhat too big for the human mind to encompass'.[16] The good thing about asking big questions, however, is that it forces us to look at developments which tend to disappear from view through the daily stream of news on natural disasters, political turmoil and terrorism. Giving clear-cut answers on what will happen is pretentious at best, but we can try to make an educated guess on a possible direction.

To encourage the reader to continue reading: The chance that China will follow the 'third way' is by far the biggest possibility. The repressive one-party state is doomed because it is not equipped to solve the endemic corruption that has pervaded it; the introduction on the other hand of a western-style parliamentary democracy is also unlikely: On top of feelings of cultural exceptionalism, China simply does not have the institutional framework to make democracy a success. Certainly not in the short term. Chaos would likely rule.

As a consequence of this probable domestic development, I expect China's foreign policy to follow the 'third way' as well. Beijing will reassert its 'natural' position in East, Central and South-East Asia. It is already doing this now, but the legitimacy of the new regime will depend first of all on clean and effective domestic government, not on seeking confrontation abroad. Old Confucian virtues such as the *Zhong Yong* (moderation, seeking the middle ground) will prevail once more, and, just like in the imperial days, the barbarians will feel compelled to pay their respects to the emperor in Beijing – not because they are forced to, but by the irresistible pull of Chinese civilisation. Tu Weiming, a famous professor of Chinese philosophy at the university of Harvard, sees modern China as a battlefield of three 'ism's: Socialism, Liberalism and Confucianism.[17] I think he is right. The China that we now see coming into being is a complex cocktail of ideologies and ideas to which various ingredients have been, and still are being, added. But in the end, I expect the heavy, time-tested taste of Confucianism to prevail. In his book *The Clash of Civilisations*, Samuel Huntington, Fukuyama's great intellectual opponent, predicts more or less the same: China's course in the twenty-first century will be set by the rediscovery of its own civilisation, not by western ideas on liberalism and socialism.[18]

The Past Determines the Present

George Orwell's 1984 is forbidden in China, but the communist regime has meticulously put one of its maxims into practice: 'Who controls the past controls the future. Who controls the present controls the past.' History is an important tool for the Party to legitimize her hold on power: Only *she* has been able to liberate China from its domestic and foreign oppressors, without *her* there would have been no modern China, and only the *Party* can restore the country's territorial integrity by recovering the lands that were lost at the end of the imperial age. To truly understand what motivates the Chinese leadership and intellectuals, one has to look back – to the long history of supremacy, but also to the Century of Humiliation (1839–1949). History therefore makes up an important part of this book – not by summing up the dry facts, but by analysing several big ideas and major events which are the reference point of China's elite when looking at the past. Unavoidably, the use of these facts to frame the present will also be described in this book. 'Who controls the past… .'

The Party's obsession with the past, however, cannot be explained only by its wish to stay in power or the chauvinistic feelings it harbours on the glories of the empire. It also has to do with the perception of time. From the dawn of Chinese history, time has been perceived to move in circles, not in a linear direction like in the West. The eternal interaction between *Yin, Yang* and the *Wuxing* – the five elements of fire, water, wood, metal and earth that feed and destroy each other – does not only drive nature forward, but also the human world. Individuals, families and kingdoms rise and fall in an endless line of unbroken, natural rhythms. There is no narrative of creation, no founding myth that explains why man exists or where he comes from. The Western calendar era begins with the birth of Christ, while in the Islamic world time is set into motion by Mohammed's flight from Mecca to Medina. To the Chinese, these are strange stories. Time, after all, knows no beginning. With the accession of each new dynasty, time simply starts anew – just like spring replaces winter.

The notion that time and dynasties always repeat themselves entails certain risk for the historical profession, because the presented facts can easily be read as a mirror of the present. In 1965 the historian Wu Han wrote the play *Hai Rui Baguan* ('Hai Rui is dismissed from office'). It tells the story of the virtuous sixteenth century official Hai

Rui, who had the courage to criticize the emperor for his mistakes. After first having praised the play, Mao Zedong later read in it an implicit attack on his own rule. Wu Han was arrested and died in prison in 1969.[19]

Dynasties must fall, but each imperial family will still try to extend its rule as long as possible. The regime that now rules China is no exception; but unlike its predecessors, the Party is guided by Marxism, an ideology that predicts progress leading towards perfection, not decay. Karl Marx saw time as a sequence of historical phases which lead to the final phase of the classless society. History is then fulfilled, and time completed. Is the end of history nigh in China? At the 19th Party Congress of October 2017 Xi Jinping predicted that 'a new era' is at hand – albeit not the end of history. By the middle of the century China will be 'prosperous, strong, democratic, culturally advanced, harmonious and beautiful'. And yes, socialist as well, but Xi did not mention the classless society that according to Marxist futurology is the key characteristic of a truly 'socialist' society. In fact, nobody in China believes in the communist ideal anymore. Marx and Mao are still revered in name, but behind the façade of their outdated thought a grand ideological reorientation is taking place. A key element of the new narrative is that the Party (in spite of all its ideological twists and turns) is a 'necessary' historical movement that represents the fundamental interests of the people and protects the essence of Chinese culture. A Party that is capable of fulfilling the mission of the 'Great Rejuvenation of the Chinese Nation' by being non-corrupt and providing excellence of governance.

In the West we are justifiably concerned about Chinese nationalism and its side-effect of rapid militarization; but the true challenge lies in China's *domestic* project: If the world's second economy delivers higher growth and is more successful in solving environmental and social problems, then the 'China Model' would receive an even greater acceptance than it already does now. Not only by dictators in Africa and the Middle East, but also by many in the West who believe that democracy is a broken system, incapable of taking major and necessary decisions.* The risk of a conflict between the United States and China then also increases, because the Peloponnesian War that Thucydides wrote about was more than a battle of hard power: It was also a battle of ideas – between the democracy of Athens and the oligarchy of Sparta. After winning a few initial victories, Athens lost the war: The citizens of that city state were not united and determined enough to fight for their freedom. Sparta won the war, and Athens' democracy perished.

---

* The Party has always been reluctant to present China as an example for other countries, but during the 19th Party Congress of October 2017, Xi Jinping called China's socialist model 'a new option for countries who want to accelerate their development while preserving their independence'.[20]

The Great Harmony

China and the United States are both nuclear powers with large conventional armed forces. A war between these two would be a disaster of apocalyptic proportions. I don't think it will happen. Wishful thinking may guide my optimism, but there is a more rational reason as well: The perfection of autocracy that Xi Jinping is now engaged in cannot succeed. In the 'New China' that will arise after Leninism has failed, the voice of the people will carry more weight. Legitimacy will be derived from a cleaner environment, less inequality and better health care – not from protecting China's 'territorial integrity'. Nationalism will no longer determine foreign policy to the extent that it does now, thus substantially lessening the risk of an armed confrontation with the United States. This does not mean that China will (or should) disregard its own cultural and philosophical heritage. That is also not desirable, as one of China's finest minds in the early twentieth century, the reformist writer Liang Qichao, noted: 'What is our duty? It is to develop our civilisation with that of the West and to supplement Western civilisation with ours so as to synthesize and transform them to make a new civilisation.'[21] This journey already started, certainly in intellectual circles. Chinese thinkers are coming up with original and valuable ideas on finding a new balance between freedom, solidarity and responsibility for the wellbeing of nature. This is not only important for China, but also for the world at large. Perhaps, through China's contribution, we will even see the dawn of a new order that will signify the end of history. Not Fukuyama's liberal world order, and certainly not Xi Jinping's 'Socialism with Chinese Characteristics for a New Age' – but rather the World of the Great Harmony that was described more than two thousand years ago in the Book of Rites, and which is being given a new meaning by philosophers such as Tu Weiming. At the end of this book I share some thoughts with the reader of how this 'Chinese Dream' could look like.

A Realistic Check on my Romantic Vision

Some thirty years have passed since the spring of 1989, when millions of people called for freedom and a representative government. Especially under the rule of Xi Jinping (since 2012), China has moved in the opposite direction: Scores of activists have been jailed, meaningful policy debate in the top of the Party has been replaced by stultifying declarations of loyalty to the Great Leader, and the Party has retaken control of all levels of society – be it companies, religious organizations, local government, schools, universities or the army. As Xi Jinping succinctly phrases it: 'Government, the military, society and schools, north, south, east and west – the party leads them all.'[22]

The liberal intellectuals in China I spoke to are divided on how to read these developments. Some point out that the Party leadership is actually more divided than it appears to be, and that changes to the present hard-line policies are bound to be made. Their optimism is also based on the wisdom of that old Taoist maxim *wu ji bi fan* – when things get too extreme, a reaction must follow. Others are less hopeful. They are astonished to see that forty years after Deng Xiaoping launched the 'Open Door' policy, that same door is (mentally at least) being closed again. The abovementioned Liang Qichao remarked that as long as the Chinese only care about themselves and their family, and not as *citizens* take responsibility for the affairs of state, then tyranny would have a good chance of prevailing: 'As the government seeks repeatedly to eradicate opposition, the resistance gets steadily weaker, more despondent, and melts away until eventually the rigorous and intoxicating consciousness of rights comes increasingly under control and is increasingly diluted, to the point that any hope of its restoration is lost and the people come to accept repression.'[23]

As in the early twentieth century, China is once again at a crossroads. But this time, its political choices not only affects the wellbeing, peace and stability of the country itself, but also that of the world at large.

History

In China the past always serves the present. When establishing a new dynasty, the emperor immediately instructed his historians to write the history of its predecessor. Without exception the former rulers were always portrayed as morally depraved – thus giving justification to the new, virtuous dynasty to take over the reins of the realm. The People's Republic of China presents itself as the 'New China' that has left the corruption and chaos of the Republic of China (1911–1949) behind it, and has opened a new shining chapter in the nation's history. Devastating events such as the Great Leap Forward and the Cultural Revolution, which were directed by the state and cost millions of Chinese their lives, do not fit into the narrative of the virtuous renewal that the new regime has supposedly brought about. They are therefore retold to fit into the Party line, or put away as 'mistakes'.

CHAPTER 1

The Lofty Classical Order

Our dynasty's majestic virtue has penetrated unto every country under Heaven, and Kings of all nations have offered their costly tribute by land and sea.

Emperor Qian Long

The history of China is long, and it is monumental. In the middle of the second millennium BCE, in the central basin of the Yellow River, a culture arose that lived in large, walled cities, wrote in pictographs, waged war in chariots, and venerated its ancestors. Later known as the Shang dynasty, this political entity viewed the surrounding peoples as barbarians. In the eleventh century BCE, the Shang was replaced by the Zhou dynasty, which rapidly fell apart into warring states. Even so, each of these kingdoms felt it was part of a shared and superior culture. In 221 BCE, the kingdom of Qin united the country, and an empire emerged that in its prosperity and military might rivalled that of the Romans, simultaneous in its ascendancy ten thousand kilometres away. The king of Qin was a despot. But in his reign, he standardised weights and measures, unified the writing system, connected the country with roads, and kept the northern barbarians at bay through a series of defence works that would, after subsequent dynasties, become known as the Great Wall. He called himself Qin Shi Huangdi – the first emperor of the Qin – and boasted that his bloodline would rule for 'ten thousand generations'. Qin Shi Huangdi governed the country with an iron fist: Countless peasants were drawn into slavery by threat or deceit to carry out major public works, and legislation was executed in cold-blooded terms. A man failing to report a family transgression was hacked in two. After the death of the first emperor in 210 BCE, major peasant rebellions arose, and the Qin was soon replaced by the Han, a dynasty with a greater capacity for endurance: It did not fall until four hundred years later. The Han set the trend for the two thousand years that followed. It elevated Confucianism to a political doctrine and introduced the principle of meritocracy: The country's administrators were not selected for their family background, but for their knowledge and virtue.

To this day, the Qin and the Han have fundamentally influenced political thought. The unification of the country by the Qin has been exalted as a sacred achievement that every ruler of China should adhere to. *Yingxiong* ('Hero'), the epic 2002 film directed by Zhang Yimou, reinforces this point. The assassination attempt on the first emperor delivers a political message: At the last moment, the assassin forgoes the murder, realising that despite all the spilt blood, only the emperor can bring peace and stability: 'Only the King of Qin can stop the chaos by uniting All-Under-Heaven.' The emphasis on law and punishment – a legacy of the school of Legalism that emerged in the third century BCE – is a legacy of the Qin as well. China remains extraordinarily bureaucratic to this day, and no other nation executes as many of its citizens.

The greatest contribution of the Han dynasty consists of the introduction of Confucianism – a doctrine placing morality above laws, virtue above violence, and humanism above religion. In the words of its founding philosopher: 'When a prince's personal conduct is correct, his government is effective without the issuing of orders. If his personal conduct is not correct, he may issue orders, but they will not be followed.'[1]

The Riddle of Longevity

What continues to astonish is the vitality of the Celestial Empire. The highly civilised empires of Egyptian pharaohs, Babylonian kings, Roman Caesars, and Ottoman sultans have all risen only to fall again. China alone has been able to endure into the twenty-first century as a political and cultural entity. Three characteristics of the Chinese political system help to explain the riddle of its longevity: The dynastic cycle, the status of the emperor, and the Mandate of Heaven. Despite the tumultuous and bloody history of peasant rebellions, palace coups, and barbarian invasions, the pre-eminence of the state remained unchanged: It formed the cornerstone of an empire that knew no equal – certainly not in the world familiar to China at that time. The result was not only an unprecedented political continuity, but also an aversion to change: One so deep-seated that for two thousand years there appeared no need to learn from, let alone adapt to, other countries in any profound way.

The Dynastic Cycle

History never repeats itself, yet China's millennia-old history does have something of an 'eternal return' about it. The lifespans of China's five major dynasties – the Han, Tang, Song, Ming, and Qing – bear witness to this. They follow the same pattern: First a period of violence in which the dynasty is established: Then a flourishing era when the economy and the culture reach their high-water mark, and finally, a period of decay leading to a major peasant rebellion or foreign invasion (and often a combination of the two) that culminates in the dynasty's downfall. At which point, the process begins anew. The sinologist J.K. Fairbank speaks of the 'dynastic cycle': 'that oft-repeated pattern of initial vigour, subsequent stability, slow deterioration, and eventual collapse'.² The Chinese at that time experienced this cycle in precisely this way. A commentary on the *Book of Changes* (the *Yijing*) reads: 'When the sun stands at mid-day, it begins to set; when the moon is full, it begins to wane. The fullness and emptiness of heaven and earth wane and wax in the course of time. How much truer is this of men, or of spirits and gods!'³

No wonder the Chinese experienced time not as linear, but as circular. They also expressed it as such, for with every emperor's reign time began 'anew'. For example, the eighteenth-century edict for giving the Dutchman Van Braam Houckgeest good treatment (an imperial decree mentioned later in this book) begins as follows: 'Edict issued on the 1st day of the 12th month of the 59th year of the reign of the Qian Long emperor of the great Qing dynasty.' The Republic of China, now seated in Taiwan, still employs this imperial dating method. But its point of reference is no longer the administration of the sitting president, but the founding of the Republic. Thus 2018 is the 107th year of the Republic of China.

The five major dynasties spanned more than two thousand years in total, but there were long periods of division in between (the longest such period lasted from 220 to 581). Each of the five major dynasties took roughly three hundred years to work through its dynastic cycle. The Han dynasty even lasted for four hundred years.

The Han dynasty set the wheel of dynastic history in motion. It was administered by an elite class of officials (who became known in the West as 'mandarins') and was the first dynasty to embrace Confucianism as a political doctrine. Its domain covered a large part of present-day China, had a population of nearly sixty million people, and produced clothes from a material that amazed all who encountered it: Silk.

By way of the great trade routes of Central Asia, the 'wool combed off [the leaves of] trees'⁴ (as Pliny the Elder observed) reached even the Roman Empire. It became hugely popular among rich Roman ladies; silk garments constituted a statement of haute couture. The moralistic philosopher Seneca took offence at this shameless custom: 'I can see clothes of silk, if materials that do not hide the body, nor even one's decency, can be called clothes... Wretched flocks of maids labour so that the adulteress may be visible through her thin dress, so that her husband has no more acquaintance than any outsider or foreigner with his wife's body.'⁵ The Senate issued various edicts to forbid the wearing of silk – for economic reasons, too, since the large imports led to a considerable export of gold – but to no avail. The Romans supposed that silk was made by the Seres, the inhabitants of Serica – 'the country where silk comes from' – but they had no idea where that country was. Pliny the Elder placed it in the neighbourhood of the Caspian Sea.

Despite several missions, the Roman Empire and the Han Empire knew virtually nothing of each other. The distance separating them was simply too big, but the *Hou Hanshu* (*The annals of the later Han dynasty*) provide another reason: 'They [the Romans] trade with *Anxi* [Parthia] and *Tianzhu* [Northwest India] by sea. The profit margin is

Fresco of Roman women wearing silk, Pompeii, ca. 60 CE

ten to one. [...] The king of this country [the Romans] always wanted to send envoys to Han, but *Anxi* [Parthia], wishing to control the trade in multi-coloured Chinese silks, blocked the route to prevent [the Romans] getting through [to China].'[6]

By far the most important foreign country for China was in the north, in the area populated by tribes known as the *Xiongnu* in the Han era. To the civilised mandarin, these bellicose nomads had all the characteristics of barbarians: They ate raw meat, drank koumiss (fermented mare's milk), did no farming, and could not write. The *Xiongnu* – who, like the Huns (to whom they were perhaps related), used the skulls of their vanquished enemies as drinking cups – regularly invaded China with their agile cavalry. Given their unwieldy armies, the Han could not easily defend itself against these raiding expeditions. The Han began a practice, maintained well into the nineteenth century, of keeping the nomads at bay by building long defensive walls. They also appeased the barbarians by weakening their virility, and in this context, the advice of a Chinese official living two thousand years ago is timeless. He counselled '[t]o give them... elaborate clothes and carriages in order to corrupt their eyes; to give them fine food in order to corrupt their mouth; to give them music and women in order to corrupt their ears; to provide them with lofty buildings, granaries and slaves in order to corrupt their stomach... and, as for those who come to surrender, the emperor [should] show them favour by honouring them with an imperial reception party in which the emperor should personally serve them wine and food so as to corrupt their mind. These are what may be called the five baits.'[7]

The Emperor as a Gateway Between Heaven and Earth

As with the Romans, the Han were led by an emperor who stood at the head of the state. But in the context of Chinese history, it would be misleading to identify this emperor with a 'Caesar': Though the emperor did possess secular power, and would sometimes lead his armies against the barbarians, his spiritual role was more important. He was called *Huangdi* – 'August Sovereign' – a name that also alluded to the first mythical forefather of the Chinese race. The veneration of one's ancestors is an essential component of Chinese culture: In Chinese thought, those who have died are transformed into spirits actively involved in the lives of their descendants. This is why there were ancestral shrines in every household. Common mortals venerated their ancestors and asked for their advice, but the emperors venerated 'Heaven' – a kind of primordial force that guides nature, yet is also the source of our sense of morality, and cares about the fate of the people. To keep this power attuned the emperor had to carry out numerous rituals, the most important of which took place in the Temple of Heaven in the southern part of Peking. There, around the time of the solstice, the emperor carried out the 'three prostrations and nine kowtows' – a ritual in which he knelt deeply three times in a row, bent his upper body forward, and 'kowtowed' (from the Chinese *ke tou* – 'to knock the head' against the ground) three times with each successive bow. The correct execution of the rites was crucial for preserving the cosmic order: If the emperor failed to fulfil his duty, dikes burst, harvests failed, and barbarians ravaged the empire. Chaos, in other words, ruled the earth. The emperor's crucial role as the mediator between heaven and earth was also clear from his other title: The *Tianzi*, 'Son of Heaven'. The emperor was – to extend the analogy with Ancient Rome – not only an *imperator* but also a *pontifex maximus* (the Romans' highest priest).[8]

The Mandate of Heaven (Tianming)

The emperor's power was absolute: He decided over the life and death of his subjects, just as a father did over the life of his child. Yet the obedience owed him was not unconditional; in exchange, he had to provide for virtuous governance in the form of reasonable taxation, a spotless administration, and a secure country. The philosopher Meng Zi (Mencius, 372–289 BCE) was the most important advocate of the view that the emperor is appointed to serve the people: 'The people are the most important element in a nation; the spirits of the land and grain are the next; the sovereign is the lightest [i.e. of least import].'[9] If the prince no longer served his people, natural disasters occurred by way of a warning, for the people's suffering did not remain unnoticed: 'Heaven sees according as my people see; Heaven hears according as my people hear.'[10]

If the emperor remained deaf to his father's voice, then the peasants who were driven to despair had the right to rise up and replace the Son of Heaven with a new favourite. In their final days, all dynasties had to deal with this feared phenomenon of the *liumin* – literally, the 'flowing people', the drifters. Major peasant rebellions constitute a bloody constant in Chinese history: The rebellion of the *Taiping Tianguo* (the 'Heavenly Kingdom of Great Peace'), from 1850 to 1864, completely disrupted the country and, according to some estimates, cost twenty million people their lives.[11]

A successful revolt proved that Heaven had washed its hands of the incumbent house, whilst a revolt's failure showed that the 'Father' still supported his 'Son'. As the Chinese proverb goes: 'The winner becomes king, the loser a bandit.' The idea that a virtuous heavenly power appoints the prince – the so-called Mandate of Heaven – has been embedded in the country's essence for three thousand years: As far back as the eleventh century BCE, it was used to justify the ascendancy of the Zhou dynasty. Because renewal was not only possible but also justified, this way of thinking provided the political system with enormous resilience. In the West, the divinely appointed prince was a comparable phenomenon, though different in concept and execution. Absolutist seventeenth-century kings like Louis XIV of France and Charles II of England derived their legitimacy from *le Droit Divin*, the divine right to rule, but their power was unconditional – the approval of the people was not important.

In the officially atheist People's Republic of China, the will of Heaven is still feared. In July 1976, an earthquake destroyed the city Tangshan, leaving more than 200,000 people dead. Many held Mao Zedong responsible (even though no one dared to say it openly) because the country's economy was in a deplorable state as a result of the Cultural Revolution. Six weeks after one of the deadliest earthquakes in the history of humanity, the first 'emperor' of the People's Republic of China died.

No Nation-State

When hearing the word 'country', we tend to think of a fixed territory, permanent borders, and a native population. China did not fulfil this modern definition – which makes the permanence of its classical order even more puzzling. The land area increased or decreased depending upon the strength of the dynasty, the borders were fluid, and there was no notion of a 'Chinese' people.

No Fixed Territory

The Chinese call their own country *Zhongguo* (conventionally called the 'Middle Kingdom'), but this name stems from the beginning of the twentieth century, when China followed the example of the modern Western nations by declaring the people and the territory it ruled over.[12] For thousands of years before this, the Chinese experience was fundamentally different. Certainly, for the elite, 'China' stood for an unparalleled level of civilisation. That status gave those who represented this culture – the emperor and his civil servants – the right to rule. This rule extended not only over 'China', but over *Tianxia*, 'All-Under-Heaven' – all the areas on earth that had converted to Chinese culture.

The concept of the *Tianxia* makes the universal pretensions of the emperors clear, yet the territory where they exercised jurisdiction originally was in fact quite limited: The core area of Chinese civilisation extended from the North China plain to the central basin of the Yellow River. The Shang dynasty that had developed there in the second millennium BCE was in many ways the cradle of Chinese culture. The scribes of the Shang described the world around them with symbols that, over the centuries, would be transformed into the current system of writing in characters. As the Chinese experienced it, the art of writing constituted the greatest distinction between the Celestial Empire and the barbarian world. The emperor's appointment by 'Heaven' was not translated *per se* into secular power: The Shang and Zhou dynasties ruled only a small part of the present China, while the rest was controlled by continually warring states. From a spiritual perspective, though, the supremacy of the Shang and the Zhou was undisputed. The sovereignty granted by Heaven was not divisible: There could only be one emperor on earth.

In the third century BCE, one of the warring states, the Qin, built up a powerful army, eliminated its rivals and united the country. The Qin took over the Mandate of Heaven from the Zhou, and set in motion the wheel of imperial history that lasted for two thousand years. Mao Zedong was a great admirer of Qin Shi Huangdi, and rejected the criticism that the first emperor had murdered many scholars during the process of unification: 'Qin Shi Huangdi killed the scholars... only because they got in the way of his efforts to unify China and build the Chinese empire. ... Where was the great tragedy in that? One ought not, in looking at Qin Shi Huangdi, exaggerate the trivial and ignore the great.'[13]

The Qin and its dynastic successors expanded the territory of China step by step. Until approximately 1000 CE, the core area did not extend beyond the North China plain. The capital of these dynasties was Chang'an ('Perpetual Peace'), later renamed Xi'an ('Peace in the West'), a city that was to become world-famous in the 1970s with one of the greatest archaeological finds in history: The discovery of the mausoleum of the first emperor of the Qin, the despot who boasted that his house would rule for 'ten thousand generations', yet whose dynasty was swept away just

Detail of the terracotta army

three years after his death. His soldiers 'survived' him, however. Arranged in their battle positions, the life-size archers, spearmen, charioteers, generals, and infantrymen stare intensely at the twenty-first century visitors. No statue is a copy of another one. In their thousands, they bring the war machine of the Qin back to life; frozen in time, the terracotta army seems to be waiting for the drum roll giving the signal for the attack.

I first visited the mausoleum at the end of the 1980s, before the buses of tourists began streaming in and out. At the entrance, an old farmer was sitting on a stool, humming contentedly. When Yang Zhifa was digging a well to irrigate his parched land in 1974, he struck upon broken pottery shards. Curious, he dug further, and soon headless bodies and bronze weapons appeared at the surface. Yang put the torsos and heads in his wheelbarrow, but after he arrived in the village the old women hastily lit incense sticks to ward off the evil. What if the disturbed ancestors wanted revenge? Arriving there rapidly, the archaeologists put the villagers at ease: A world-renowned discovery had been made on their land, which would attract droves of well-paying tourists.[14] Since then, Yang's fame has been secured; he passes his days signing books and posing for photos.

I asked Yang to put his signature in my book about the *bingmayong* ('statues of horses and warriors'). While his brush elegantly flicked over the paper, I studied his weathered face, graced with high cheekbones: The same elegant nose and squinting eyes as the generals beneath the ground – facial features that you only encounter in

North China. What was his bloodline? For how many generations had his ancestors been connected to this land? Was it coincidence that he had found the grave?

In the steadily expanding territory of the North China plain lived the *Hua-ren* (People of Hua). *Hua* is the ancient name for China, but it means 'radiant' as well: The light of civilisation had shone upon the *Hua-ren*. Ethnicity was of no significance: All-Under-Heaven made no distinction between yellow, black, or white. From an historical perspective, the sense of having a global reach was not unique. The philosopher Seneca contended that the '[Romans] measure the boundaries of our nation by the sun', and at the height of Roman power, in the second century CE, the emperor Antoninus Pius even took on a new title: Dominus Totius Orbis (Lord of All the World).[15] Just as in Rome, though, the reality gap between *Dichtung und Wahrheit* was considerable.

The Xiongnu nomads who ravaged the Han dynasty were followed by peoples of Turkic stock, Mongols, and Manchus – races who had one thing in common: An agile cavalry which, through its superior battle tactics, largely prevailed over the Chinese armies. China stood up to this perpetual threat in two ways. The best-known still ranges across the North China landscape: The Great Wall, which runs from the Yellow Sea to the heart of Central Asia. This biggest engineering project in human history only reached its greatest extent in the seventeenth century and has many branches. It is therefore difficult to measure, though the Chinese speak of the *wanli changcheng* (the 'Wall of 10,000 *li*', one *li* being 500 metres).

The other defence mechanism proved to be much more efficient over the long term: The vastly superior numerical strength of the Chinese. 'Barbarian dynasties' dominated China regularly, but in the end the barbarians behaved *plus chinois que les chinois* – the demographic dominance and cultural allure of the Middle Kingdom were too overwhelming to resist.

China's last dynasty is a good example of that attraction. In 1644, the Manchus conquered the ancient empire and founded the Qing dynasty. Determined to avoid the fate of other barbarian peoples, interracial marriages were forbidden, Manchu was used as the official language in addition to Chinese, and every Chinese man was required to wear the hairstyle known as the *queue*. The homeland of the Manchus (now the three north-eastern Chinese provinces of Heilongjiang, Jilin, and Liaoning) was off limits to the Chinese; to emigrate there was strictly forbidden. The Great Wall no longer served to keep the barbarians outside but, rather, to keep the Chinese *inside*. Over the course of the nineteenth century, the weakened Qing dynasty could no longer maintain this policy: Manchuria was inundated by Chinese emigrants and just one century later the language and culture of this once mighty people had all but disappeared. Nowadays only a few hundred people still speak Manchu and no-one (aside from a small number of academics) can read the splendid, elegant script that adorns countless stone steles.[16]

No Fixed Borders
The borders of the empire ebbed and flowed with the power of the kingdom. While militant dynasties like the Han and the Tang led their armies over the mountain chains of the Hindu Kush into present-day Afghanistan and Uzbekistan, the more defensively-minded Ming and Song guarded the borders of what from the nineteenth century was called 'China Proper': The areas in the east and south of today's People's Republic, where the majority of the population had been speaking Chinese and following Chinese cultural practices for centuries.

The myth of sovereignty over everything in All-Under-Heaven did not preclude border treaties with foreign powers. Even at the time, the Chinese were too pragmatic for that. A good example is the treaty with Tibet from 821. To westerners that name evokes the beatific image of peaceful monks and a Dalai Lama: But in the era before the country converted to Buddhism, the reality was different. During the Tang dynasty (618–907), the 'Land of Snows' was the main Central Asian power to clash regularly with the Chinese empire. Tired of conflict, however, the countries made peace with each other at the beginning of the ninth century. The stone column on which the statement of peace is chiselled still stands in Lhasa's Barkhor Square.

'Tibet and China shall abide by the frontiers of which they are now in occupation. All to the east is the country of Great China; and all to the west is, without question, the country of Great Tibet. Henceforth on neither side shall there be waging of war nor seizing of territory. [...] Between the two countries no smoke nor dust shall be seen [as a sign of approaching armies]. There shall be no sudden alarms and the very word "enemy" shall not be spoken. Even the frontier guards shall have no anxiety nor fear and shall enjoy land and bed at their ease. All shall live in peace and share the blessing of happiness for ten thousand years. [...] This solemn agreement has established a great epoch when Tibetans shall be happy in the land of Tibet, and Chinese in the land of China. So that it may never be changed, the Three Precious Jewels of Religion, the Assembly of Saints, the Sun and Moon, Planets and Stars have been invoked as witness [...].'[17]

On the eve of the 1951 occupation of Tibet, the *People's Daily* wrote: 'The Chinese People's Liberation Army must liberate the whole territory of China, including Tibet, Sinkiang [Xinjiang] and so forth. Even an inch of Chinese land will not be permitted to be left outside the jurisdiction of the People's Republic of China.'[18] The Century of Humiliation (1839–1949) and the fever of nationalism that went with it had completely changed the Chinese mindset.

No Distinction Between 'Native' and 'Non-Native'
A people touched by the light of civilisation became 'Chinese', and that is why in Ancient China no ethnic distinction existed between 'native' and 'non-native'. At least three major dynasties were of non-Chinese origin: The Tang was Turkic, the Yuan

(1279–1368) Mongol, and the Qing (1644–1911) of Manchu origin. Founded by Kublai Khan (grandson of Genghis Khan, Mongol conqueror of the world), the Yuan was the odd one out, being the only 'barbarian' dynasty to resist the attraction of Chinese culture. The fact that the Yuan ruled for less than a century probably has something to do with this. The Yuan dynasty established its capital in Zhongdu (later known as Peking), yet it strictly adhered to Mongol customs: In the centre of the imperial palace, close to today's Forbidden City, was a grassy plain where *gers* (Mongol tents) were set up – the inhabitants of the steppe could not get used to sleeping under a roof. And because they did not trust the Chinese civil servant apparatus, the Mongols abolished the Confucianist state examinations and put the administration of the state into the hands of Persians, Uighurs, Koreans, and that one Italian – if this is true, at least, for Marco Polo is not mentioned in the Chinese annals, and there is even an historian who contends that the Venetian never ventured further than Constantinople. He supposedly created his own fantasy journey while listening to the tales of merchants in the bars of that erstwhile crossroads between East and West.[19]

Heavy drinking at court certainly contributed to the Yuan's rapid demise. During their many festivities, such enormous quantities of koumiss were consumed that soon the government was no longer functioning. William of Rubruck, the Flemish Franciscan priest who, as the envoy of the French king Saint Louis (Louis IX), visited the Mongol court during the 1250s, tells of a debate he had with a Buddhist and a Moslem to determine which of the three religions was the true one. The Mongols venerated the eternal heaven, but were tolerant towards those who thought differently. The dispute revolved around reincarnation, good and evil, and the eternity of the soul – yet the fine points of the theological argument blurred rapidly through the vast amounts of alcohol that the Mongol jury consumed after each round of the debate.[20]

Towards the end of the Yuan dynasty, major peasant rebellions broke out. To break the resistance, the counsellor Bayan advised his emperor to execute all the Chinese with the last names Wang, Li, Liu, Zhao and Zhang – a proposal that would have cost ninety percent of the population their lives.[21] That measure was too drastic, even for Toghon Temür, the last Mongol emperor. In 1368, he fled with his followers to the land of his ancestors, to what Rubruck described as 'the land of only heaven and earth'.[22]

The sledgehammer blows dealt by Western and Japanese imperialism in the nineteenth century led to deep introspection concerning what China actually stood for. How could these despised foreigners divide the country 'like a melon' (as evidenced by the anti-imperialist propaganda posters of the time)? What had caused the economic and military supremacy of the West?

The key answer to those questions ran as follows: The *Tianxia*'s ideal of civilisation could not embrace the modernisation necessary in the areas of education, economy, and defence. A change in direction was vital: Like the Western powers, China had to become a modern nation-state with a national anthem, flag, and fixed territory. That ambition also redefined the relationship with the peoples with whom China had previously coexisted amid shifting power dynamics. It is true that the eighteenth-century conquests of the emperors Kang Xi and Qian Long had brought large parts of Central Asia under Chinese authority, but Peking did not as a result exercise sovereignty in the modern sense of that word. By providing China with their symbolic submission, the peoples of these regions were able to preserve a large share of their autonomy. The Chinese emperors did not have exclusive jurisdiction.

Twentieth-century nationalism denied this historical reality. The Chinese constitution adopted in 1912 stipulated that '[t]he territory of the Chinese Republic consists of 22 provinces, Inner and Outer Mongolia, Tibet and Chinghai [i.e. Qinghai]'.[23] The constitution makes no distinction between Chinese and non-Chinese inhabitants: according to the simple wording in Article 1, 'The Republic of China is composed of the Chinese people'. The development from a classical, *Tianxia*-like mentality towards a modern, nation-state identity, however, was anything but straightforward. Later constitutional revisions, such as the one of 1923, simply state that 'the sovereign territory of the Republic of China continues to be the same as the domain of the former Empire'.[24] It is important to note that the Chinese word for domain ('*lingyu*') also means 'territory', but it has a vaguer meaning than '*lingtu*', which only means 'territory'.

From 1916 onward there even appeared semi-official 'Maps of National Shame', which indicate in detail which areas China has 'lost' to the imperialist powers. On a map of 1938, even Indochina, Korea, and the largest part of Central Asia were claimed as former territory of the empire.[25] The yearning for the glorious past also spoke to China's weakness at the beginning of the twentieth century: Tibet and Xinjiang were de facto independent, and the government of the Republic of China that was declared in 1912 exercised only a limited degree of authority in the rest of the country. The more the Republic weakened, the more extravagant its claims on 'lost' areas became.

Unlike its predecessor the Republic of China, the People's Republic of China that began ruling in 1949 saw itself as a 'multi-ethnic state'. Together with the Han Chinese (the dominant ethnic group), the so-called 'peoples of the small numbers' (*shaoshu minzu*) make up part of the country's 56 ethnicities. On paper, this wording is an improvement on the Republican concept of absorbing minorities into one uniform Chinese culture. Today's ethnic minorities, however, still have little or no say in their own affairs. The legislative authority of 'autonomous' regions like Tibet and Xinjiang is more limited than that of a Chinese province, and the Party Secretary (the highest position, and more important than that of governor) is always a Han Chinese. According to the constitution, secession is strictly forbidden: '[A]ny acts that undermine the unity of the nationalities or instigate their secession are prohibited [...] All the national autonomous areas are inalienable parts of the People's Republic of China.'[26] Beijing's oft-repeated declaration of the principle of sovereignty is explained by its fear that the minorities in its own state wish to establish their own states. That

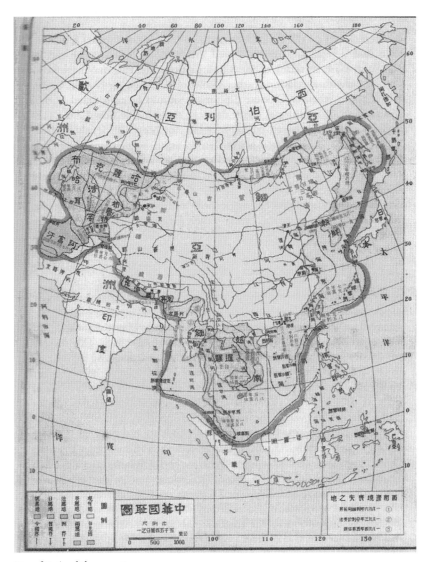

Map of National Shame, 1938

is understandable, but Beijing's position is double-edged: Just like the Republic of China, its precursor, the People's Republic publishes its own 'Maps of National Shame', marking lost imperial territories – especially after 1994, when the Patriotic Education campaign was supposed to create a new sense of history amongst the country's youth. Is it justified to claim the territories of other states (even if this is not done officially) while declaring its own territory as inviolable?

Eternal China?

Li Hongzhang (1823–1901) was an extraordinary man, the prototype of the virtuous mandarin who devoted a life of service to his country with a religious fervour. He lived during a period that shook the two thousand-year-old structure of the Confucianist state to its foundations. The Western powers were trampling upon China's sovereignty, and major domestic rebellions ravaged the country. Amidst all this chaos, Li preserved his dignity and serenity. At the end of his life he was able to temper the strict demands that the Western powers had imposed on China after the Boxer Rebellion. It was his final achievement: Exhausted from a life of continuous crisis management, he died at the age of seventy-eight.

His life was not only dignified, however, but sad as well: Despite his unequalled dedication, Li could not keep pace with the rapid changes in the world around him. He looked through the same lens as an official from the Han dynasty of two thousand years before: The emperor and his mandarins rule the empire, Confucianism is the state doctrine, and foreign countries are populated by barbarians. Li could not deviate from that vision, even though his world was already imploding on all sides. Mandarins like Li Hongzhang have exemplified the Western myth of *la Chine Eternelle*, the never-changing Celestial Empire spinning around in circles of self-satisfied autarky. Such an image, however, is not wholly accurate: As far back as the Song dynasty (960–1279), dynamic changes were taking place in the Chinese economy and society that nearly led to an industrial revolution – long before James Watt's steam engine made that revolution possible in eighteenth-century Europe.

Some scholars sink their teeth into one subject for their entire lives. The English-man Joseph Needham is an example. He devoted his life of nearly a century (1900–1995) to studying scientific knowledge in Classical China, and the influence of that learning on its society. The result of these assiduous labours is the monumental, seven-volume *Science and Civilization in China* (its first volume was published in 1954). Needham demonstrates that before the explosion of the scientific revolution in Europe in the seventeenth century, China led the West in areas such as shipbuilding, farming, irrigation, ceramics, and civil engineering. That fact is a source of pride in today's increasingly nationalistic China. Every child in China learns about the 'four great inventions': The compass, movable type printing, papermaking, and gunpowder. In doing so, they do not fail to mention that these inventions were made centuries earlier than in the West.[27]

China's oldest book, the *Diamond Sutra*, was printed around the year 868, nearly six hundred years before the Gutenberg Bible. The seventeenth-century philosopher and scientist Francis Bacon realised the importance of these inventions when he wrote – without referring to China – that 'these three [printing, gunpowder, and the magnet] have changed the whole face and state of things throughout the world;

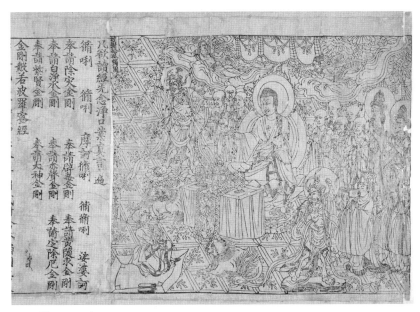

Cover of the Diamond Sutra, ca. 868

the first in literature, the second in warfare, the third in navigation; whence have followed innumerable changes, insomuch that no empire, no sect, no star seems to have exerted greater power and influence in human affairs than these mechanical discoveries'.[28]

The Open Empire

Not only the mind of the empire opened up, its doors opened too. In the heyday of Classical China – between the years 600 and 1200 – Persians, Arabs, Jews, and Indians (as well as now forgotten races like the Sogdians, from the border region of today's Uzbekistan, Afghanistan, and Tajikistan) came to China to do business by way of the Silk Road or the sea. Many settled in major communities like the harbour city of Canton, or the capital Chang'an. In the seventh and eighth centuries, with its population of one million and a surface area of 80 square kilometres, Chang'an was by far the world's largest city, twice as great as Constantinople and vastly larger than Aachen, the tiny European capital of Charlemagne. Foreigners were free to spread the word of Islam, Judaism, and Nestorian Christianity, while even the mystical Manichaeism from Persia, which saw life as an eternal struggle between Light and Darkness, gained a firm foothold. This openness of belief contrasted sharply with medieval Europe (and especially that of the later Middle Ages), which saw those who thought differently burned at the stake as heretics. In fact, one could say (somewhat anachronistically) that China entered into dialogue with other religions. In the seventh century, for example, the monk Xuan Zang travelled to India to study the foundational texts of Buddhism. His *Great Tang Records on the Western Regions* – the account of his 'Journey to the West', as it popularly became known – tells of large kingdoms, since disappeared, in the heart of Asia; of crossing the Himalayas in sandals, and of the wonders of Nalanda in India, the site of the largest university in the world at that time.

This spirit of openness, however, was limited to merchants, sailors, monks, and scholars. China did not conduct foreign policy in order to learn from other countries or trade with them. On the contrary: Merchants were often prosecuted, the governing doctrine of Confucianism teaching that the hard-working farmer was virtuous, and the merchant a non-productive parasite. On the other hand, officials were not averse to levying customs duties on the merchandise from the thousands of foreign ships calling annually at the ports of Guangzhou, Quanzhou, and Ningbo. This filled the nation's coffers – as well as the pockets of the inspectors, who stipulated with whom the foreign merchants were allowed to trade. The only exception to this indifference to the outside world was in 'defence technology'. As far back as the second century BCE, China's first great explorer, Zhang Qian, had journeyed to the Far West to bring war horses back from Central Asia. His destination was the domain of the Yuezhi, located in contemporary Tajikistan, where 'heavenly horses' galloped around in great numbers. After a rigorous expedition lasting fourteen years, Zhang returned with a small number of horses: But lacking nutritious fodder, these could not be bred for offspring. It was not until the seventeenth century that the bow and arrow succumbed to gunpowder, and the military balance of power in Central Asia tilted in China's favour. Until then, the North China plain was the playground of barbarian raiding expeditions.

The combination of technological superiority and the size of the domestic market ensured that, for centuries, China was stronger in economic terms than the fragmented West. Even in the year 1830, when China's old order was on its last legs, its national product amounted to 30 percent of global production. At that time, the United States constituted only 1 percent.[29]

The highest economic growth was recorded under the Song dynasty (960–1279), when the population doubled from fifty to one hundred million people through the combination of a strong expansion of agricultural acreage, new crops, and better irrigation. Surplus goods in the production of silk, porcelain, and iron found their way abroad, causing prosperity to rise further. Economic growth accompanied the issuing of paper money and the rise of large businesses which – in a very modern way – created divisions between ownership and management. Foreign trade flourished as never before: The Song traded with more than fifty countries, including even the kingdoms of East Africa.[30]

Visiting the Southern Song capital of Hangzhou in the middle of the thirteenth century, Marco Polo could barely describe his amazement at the wealth of the city, known to him then as Kinsai: 'The city of Kinsai is about 100 miles in circumference, because its streets and watercourses are wide and spacious. [...] There are said to be 12,000 bridges, mostly of stone, though some are of wood. Those over the main channels and the chief thoroughfare are built with such lofty arches and so well designed that big ships can pass under them without [striking] a mast. [...] There are ten principal market-places, not to speak of innumerable local ones. [...] All ten squares are surrounded by high buildings, and below these are shops in which every sort of craft is practised and every sort of luxury is on sale, including spices, gems, and pearls. [...] in each of these squares, three days in the week, there is a gathering of forty to fifty thousand people, who come to market bringing everything that could be desired to sustain life.'[31]

Marco Polo's account of Hangzhou continues in this lyrical vein, full of astonishment. The Travels of Marco Polo initiated the West's fascination with China's unprecedented riches, as well as the inexhaustible commercial possibilities that were there for the taking. Christopher Columbus was a great admirer of the book, and his well-thumbed copy has been preserved, including all his notes.[32] Without this book, America would not have been discovered – at least not by Columbus, his goal being to find a western route to the Venetian traveller's 'Cathay' (as Marco Polo called China).

Many scholars have wracked their brains as to why the economic revolution of the Song did not lead to an industrial revolution, as happened in the West. All the ingredients were present: Capital, technology, energy, and major markets. This riddle has even acquired a name of its own: 'The Needham Question', after the eminent Englishman who was the first to wrestle with it. Needham places the blame upon Confucianist ideology, which mistrusted independent thinking and rejected trade and investment as 'impure' economic activities (farming was deemed the noblest business). The economist Justin Lin elaborates this argument further by pointing to the state's stifling influence on public debate and the exchange of information – two qualities essential for developing scientific knowledge to its maximum potential. Moreover, the personal right to benefit from an invention was never guaranteed: The all-powerful state could nationalise any form of private property at any moment.[33] In seventeenth-century Europe, precisely the opposite effect took place: The church no longer used the yardstick of theological dogma against invention, and nations that competed with one another positively encouraged independent research. The consequence was the start of a scientific revolution that we are still a part of today.

Social reasons have also been offered for the lack of a great leap forward for China's industry: The money earned by company heads was not invested in research and development, but in the studies their sons undertook to pass the state examinations –

which sometimes lasted dozens of years. The membership of the mandarin elite provided prestige and wealth; yet it also protected the mandarins against the prosecutions to which merchants were regularly exposed. Yet another argument points to the enormous supply of cheap labour, efficient production methods, and well-developed trade networks: supply and demand were so well attuned, that there were no incentives for mechanising production. The historian Mark Elvin calls this the 'high-level equilibrium trap'.[34] The last argument points to the significant distances between economic centres in the middle of the country (the central and lower basin of the Yangtze River) and the coal mines in the north. In England, the cradle of the industrial revolution, the mines and factories were much closer to one another, and transporting energy considerably cheaper.

Whatever the merits of these arguments, it is certain that the Chinese lacked that essential characteristic that drove both the voyages of discovery and the scientific revolution in the West: A curiosity for the world beyond their own civilisation. Foreign languages were barely studied, and there was no Chinese equivalent of Joan Blaeu's *Atlas Maior*. Foreign countries had a certain exotic value – as well as an economic one, as in the case of the export of porcelain from the seventeenth century – yet they were not the subject of any serious and systematic studies. In Japan, by contrast, this interest did exist: The *Rangaku* ('Holland studies' – so-called because merchants from Holland, in settling on the island of Dejima, were the most important suppliers of Western knowledge to Japan) led, from the seventeenth century onwards, to a transfer of information and technology from the West. This marked divergence in attitudes to the outside world meant that, during the nineteenth century, China and Japan would react to Western gunboat diplomacy in radically different ways.

Three Schools of Thought

Chinese civilisation was sustained by a doctrine that the West has come to call 'Confucianism', though in China itself the teachings are known as the *Rujia*, the '*Doctrine of the Scholars*'. This was an extensive body of canonical texts that originated before the Christian era, and defined the thinking of the elite. Its focus was on political issues. As one expert on Chinese philosophy, Karel van der Leeuw, succinctly puts it: 'Nearly every Chinese philosophical school – certainly those from the earliest period – tries to provide a solution for contemporaneous political problems.'[35] *Zhengzhi* (politics) literally means 'rectifying' or 'making things straight', implying that society has to be shaped in accordance with political ideals – a normative connotation that is barely present in our word 'politics' (derived from *polis*, the Ancient Greek word for city-state). Modern Chinese thought is still permeated by this concept: It is not concerned with finding the proper balance between the forces that shape society but, rather, with establishing an ideal social order. That is why knowledge of Confucianism is essential for a good understanding of modern China. Chinese philosophy, though, is richer than the sometimes-rigid moralism of Confucius: More subtle and less dogmatic, though certainly no less profound, two other original thinkers have also had an impact on the collective consciousness – Master Lao and Master Sun.

Confucianism

Before the country was united in 221 BCE, many principalities were fighting for domination. Some were as large as four of today's Chinese provinces combined; others were as small as a city-state. To eat or be eaten was the Darwinian order of the day, and in the process not only the continued existence of the state was at stake, but also that of the ruling house. If the vanquished prince was accused of treason or rebellion, he ran the risk that his immediate family and friends would also be executed. In those days of uncertainty, a special role was set aside for the political counsellor. He advised the prince on how to rebuff attacks from other states, and expand the power of his own.

Kong Zi (Master Kong), later known as Confucius, was that kind of person. He was born in Lu, a small principality in today's Shandong province, and he roamed through the four quarters of China to try to find a prince who would put his teaching into practice. That effort came to nothing, and so, when he was nearly seventy years old, he gave up the search: 'At seventy, I could follow what my heart desired, without transgressing what was right.'[36] He returned to the land of his birth and shared with his disciples a series of aphorisms that have become as well-known in the Chinese cultural sphere as the New Testament in the West: The *Lun Yu* (*The Discourses* or *Discussions*, often translated into English as *The Analects*).[37]

Confucius supposedly also compiled the *Five Classics*, the most sacred books in the land, but historically speaking that is untenable. After his death, his name and fame spread. In the second century BCE his teachings were elevated to the level of state doctrine, a position that was not undone until the downfall of the empire in 1911. Matteo Ricci – the Jesuit who, at the end of the sixteenth century, had been charged with the impossible task of converting China to Christianity – Latinised the name of Kong Zi into Confucius. Together with his chief follower Meng Zi (Mencius), Master Kong is the only Chinese who has been granted this distinction.

Five Classics

These consist of *The Book of Poetry*, *The Book of Documents*, *The Book of Rites*, *The Book of Changes* and the *Spring and Autumn Annals*. The precise authorship of the *Five Classics* is impossible to ascertain, though some texts originate from the beginning of the first millennium BCE. The *Five Classics* were required

'Saint' Confucius

material for the state examinations institutionalised from the seventh century forwards. During the Song dynasty (960–1279 CE), the *Four Books* were added to these five: *The Analects, The Works of Mencius,* and two chapters from *The Book of Rites,* i.e. *The Great Learning* and *The Doctrine of the Mean.*

Many shoots have grown from the stem of Master Kong's thought over the course of twenty-five hundred years: Countless scholars have provided commentary on the foundational texts, and that is why it is difficult to determine what the original teaching actually consisted of. Yet certain core concepts did survive the ravages of time (as well as the filleting of philologists), and can be regarded as purely 'Confucianist'. I mention five of them here: A selection based above all on their vital relevance to modern day China.

– *Perfection.* Every person can become a perfect human being, if he practises the five virtues: *Ren* (humaneness), *yi* (sense of duty), *li* (proper ritual conduct), *zhi* (wisdom) and *xin* (sincerity). These five virtues are frequently supplemented with *shu* (reciprocity) and *zhong* (loyalty). The spirit of *shu* is expressed in perhaps the most famous aphorism of Confucius: 'Zi Gong asked, saying, "Is there one word which may serve as a rule of practice for all one's life?" The Master said, "Is not reciprocity [*shu*] such a word? What you do not want done to yourself, do not do to others."'[38] The third virtue, *li* (proper ritual conduct) is seen in the West more as outward behaviour than an inner quality, but in Chinese thought these two are inseparable. As the philosopher Jan Bor states: 'The mature inner self can only be shaped through its external form.'[39] Through the interaction between inner cultivation and external civilisation, people can realise their human potential and achieve the status of a *junzi* (a noble person), who serves as an example to his less virtuous fellows: 'The relation between superiors and inferiors is like that between the wind and the grass. The grass must bend, when the wind blows across it.'[40]
Chinese culture is rightly described as a family culture, but the aspirations of Confucius and his followers stretched further: Not only family but also society, and even the cosmos, must be illuminated by the light of virtue. As the philosopher Mencius exquisitely put it, human beings are, after all, *tianmin* (citizens of the universe). By *ordering* it in ever-expanding circles, the Universe is brought to perfection. In *The Great Learning* (which enjoyed high regard similar to *The Analects* of Confucius), this concentric effect of virtue is eloquently expressed: 'Things being investigated, knowledge became complete. Their knowledge being complete, their thoughts were sincere. Their thoughts being sincere, their hearts were then rectified. Their hearts being rectified, their persons were cultivated. Their persons being cultivated, their families were regulated. Their families being regulated,

their States were rightly governed. Their States being rightly governed, the whole kingdom was made tranquil and happy.'[41]

– *Humanism*. Man is the centre of the universe. The love of nature that characterises Taoism and the compassion for all living beings in Buddhism are initially absent from Confucianism: 'On one occasion when, as Confucius was returning from an audience at the palace, he heard that his family stable was on fire, his first question was: "Has any man been injured?" He did not ask about the horses.'[42] Unlike the Ten Commandments of Moses, the teachings of Kong Zi were not dictated from above; there was no room for metaphysical speculation: 'While you do not know life, how can you know about death?'[43] The source of moral nature is in man itself, and that is why the first line of *The Great Learning* says: 'What the Great Learning teaches is to illustrate virtue; to renovate the people; and to rest in the highest excellence.'[44] Under the influence of Buddhism and Taoism, Confucianism would in subsequent centuries replace this anthropocentric thinking with a cosmological system, in which nature was assigned a value as great as humanity.

– *Harmony*. Life – both in nature and in the character of man – consists of opposites. This is as inevitable as it is natural. Day and night, man and woman, life and death are inseparable; they define each other in the continuous interaction of *yin* and *yang*. Society works in the same way. The art of ruling consists of the capacity to direct societal relationships in such a manner that opposites do not degenerate into *oppositions*. In that process, a special role is set aside for the 'Sage King': Only he can bring about the 'Great Harmony' – a society that, according to Confucius, had actually existed in the early years of the Zhou dynasty (1046–256 BCE), and which could be restored through exemplary leadership and correct moral behaviour.

Great Harmony

The Great Harmony has fascinated Chinese thinking through the centuries. In *The Book of Rites*, the records tell us what this kind of society looks like: 'When the Great Way prevailed, the world belonged to all. They chose people of talent and ability whose words were sincere, and they cultivated harmony. Thus people did not only love their own parents, not only nurture their own children... In this way selfish schemes did not arise. Robbers, thieves, rebels and traitors had no place, and the outer doors were not closed. This is called the Great Harmony.'[45]

– *Inequality*. Equality – one of the three ideals of the French Revolution – is seen in Chinese thought as unnatural: A lower-ranking person must obey someone of higher rank, especially in the context of family. That is why a harmonious society can only develop if the 'Five Relationships' named by the philosopher Mencius are observed with due respect: The relationship between father and son, older and younger brother, man and woman, emperor and subject, and friend and friend. Only friends stand on equal footing – though not entirely, either: For there is no absolute balance between doing and returning favours (upon which friendship in China is based). The Five Relationships explain the age-old deep respect in China for authority: For the father, the teacher, and the emperor. For centuries, the most important primer in Chinese schools was the *Xiaojing* ('The Book [or Classic] of Filial Piety'), which was supposedly written by Zeng Zi, a disciple of Confucius. The first lines immediately set the tone: 'Filial piety is the root of all virtue, and the stem out of which grows all moral teaching.'[46]

– *Meritocracy.* People must know their place, but – unlike the caste system in India or the estate-based society of medieval Europe – their social position is not carved in stone. The virtuous farmer's son has just as much right to become emperor as the mandarin's son. Confucius' clear instruction – 'In teaching there should be no distinction of classes'[47] – has always been a guideline in the selection of the civil servant apparatus. Already two thousand years ago, the Han dynasty tested the mandarins on their knowledge of Confucianism, and from the seventh century onwards formal examinations took place on three levels – district, provincial, and national. The candidate was expected to know the *Five Classics* and the *Four Books* from memory. Those who passed the national examination earned the title of *jinshi* ('presented scholar', i.e. a scholar brought before the emperor), and formed the country's rarefied elite of a couple of thousand men. In practice, the results were often tampered with, and the rank of an official could even be bought, but the principle that intelligence carried more weight than a good background was revolutionary, and was never dropped. In this fundamental embracing of meritocracy, China was centuries ahead of the West and other civilisations.

Taoism

Taoism stands in polar opposition to Confucianism. The legendary founder Lao Zi (the 'Old Master') supposedly lived during the same era as Confucius. Little else is known about his life, other than that towards the end of it, he went to the west riding an ox. Having arrived at the border, a guard stopped him, requesting that he write down his teachings. It was something the old master could not refuse; the result was a work of just five thousand characters called the *Tao Te Ching* (*The Book of the Way and of Virtue*, also sometimes translated as 'the way and inner strength'), which would profoundly influence Chinese culture. The first lines are as timeless as the first lines of the Bible:

The eternal *Tao*
cannot be expressed in words
The eternal name
cannot be named[48]

The *tao* is also a fundamental concept for Confucianists: But for them, following the right way (*tao* = way) consists of cultivating the self, behaving properly, and carrying out the rituals correctly. The Taoists mocked this because, as they saw it, that kind of behaviour led to a loss of spontaneity and denial of the true nature of humanity. In a fictitious dialogue, Lao Zi explains to Confucius what moves the 'perfect man': 'Look at the spring, the water of which rises and overflows; it does nothing, but it naturally acts so. So with the perfect man and his virtue; he does not cultivate it, and nothing evades its influence. He is like heaven which is high of itself, like earth which is solid of itself, like the sun and moon which shine of themselves; what need is there to cultivate it?'[49]

The way can only be followed 'step-by-step'; putting down stakes or border markers denies the nature of reality, which cannot be captured in dogma and doctrine. There is no underlying truth in the continually changing world; the only reality is change itself. The favourite character in Taoist stories is the sage who renounces worldly fame, the rebel recluse. The best-known among them is Zhuang Zi (fourth century BCE), who lived two hundred years after Lao Zi, and whose collected works are as familiar and beloved as the *Analects* of Confucius in the Chinese world.[50] One day, Zhuang Zi received an offer of sumptuous gifts from the king of Chu to become his minister. Zhuang Zi burst out laughing and said to the envoy: 'A thousand ounces of silver are a great gain to me, and to be a high noble and minister is a most honourable position. But have you not seen the victim-ox for the border sacrifice? It is carefully fed for several years, and robed with rich embroidery that it may be fit to enter the Grand Temple. When the time comes for it to do so, it would prefer to be a little pig, but it cannot get to be so. Go away quickly, and do not soil me with your presence.'[51]

Taoism stands for cheerfulness, spontaneity and, with its scepticism towards proper behaviour, a certain degree of boorishness. In its desire for reuniting with nature, it is the source of the ancient and rich Chinese tradition of *shanshui* ('mountain and water') poetry. The country's poets were not hippies or dropouts, however, but successful officials who regularly retreated to their mountain cabins to sing the praises of nature's beauty. Even the emperors composed poetry – doing so constituted proof of their being men of letters, but it was also a diversion from the daily concerns of governance. The tone of Taoist poetry is timeless:

The Autumn wind blows white clouds
About the sky. Grass turns brown.
Leaves fall. Wild geese fly south.
[...] I dream of
That beautiful face I can
Never forget. [...]
(Emperor Wu of the Han dynasty, second century BCE)[52]

'Three Laughs at Tiger Brook': A Confucian, a Taoist, and a Buddhist

Fierce the west wind,
Wild geese cry under the frosty morning moon.
Under the frosty morning moon
Horses' hooves clattering [...]
We are crossing its summit,
The rolling hills sea-blue,
The dying sun blood-red.
(Mao Zedong, 1893–1976)[53]

The desire for reuniting with nature went hand in hand with a quest for immortality. Taoism has many stories of saints who reached a venerable old age through strict diets and meditative practices, gradually becoming purely ethereal beings.[54] The quest for immortality also led to substantial investigations into the elixir of life. These were not without risk, and some Taoists paid for their experiments (such as swallowing lead) with their lives. Less harmful was their contribution to medicine – the classic Taoist notion that everything is connected led to a profound, holistic knowledge of the body, and the development of practices like acupuncture.

Writing in the 1930s, the well-known cultural philosopher Lin Yutang observed that Taoism responds to a part of the Chinese character which Confucianism cannot satisfy, because Taoism 'stands for the return to nature and the romantic escape from the world, and revolts against the artificiality and responsibilities of Confucian culture'.[55] That is not to say that a Confucianist cannot also be a Taoist; one could even say that the literate mandarin of yore united the country's *three* great spiritual traditions in himself. As the saying goes, 'Confucius is for the state, Buddha for the mind, and the *tao* for the body.' Taoism is the oldest religion of China, which – despite being persecuted by Confucianism and, subsequently, Maoism – has come vibrantly back to life: Monasteries are being built again, and Taoist priests perform as soothsayers, and as attendants at rituals for birth and death. Even the tradition of hermits is experiencing a genuine revival, although that may not be so strange in view of the hectic nature of modern life. After his business went bankrupt, Zhang Baoyi retreated to Wangwu Mountain where, according to legend, the Yellow Emperor made offerings to heaven five thousand years ago. Zhang now spends his days meditating, cleaning temples, and practising calligraphy. Instead of being 'selfish, bad-tempered and greedy', hermits like Zhang now opt for living a simple life.[56]

The thinking of Lao Zi influences politics, too. Deng Xiaoping's decision in 1978 to privatise the economy and to eliminate Maoist ideology from daily life was a textbook example of *wu wei* ('non-action') – one of the most important virtues of Taoism. 'Non-action' does not mean *doing nothing* but, rather, not forcing nature to do what you want. Whoever practises this wisdom realises the goals he sets for himself in an almost magical way. After Deng's decision, the Chinese people started to act in keeping with their nature: Everyone became entrepreneurs, businesses were started, and prosperity increased by leaps and bounds. In this way Deng achieved his goal of establishing China as an economic superpower almost automatically.

Yet the most lasting legacy of Taoism lies in the words of Lao Zi himself: 'Reversal is the movement of the Tao'. The succession of the seasons is inevitable, winter will always be followed by spring. This heritage – to quote Feng Youlan, China's best known twentieth century philosopher – gives the Chinese a 'psychological weapon': The inner certainty that even the darkest period comes to an end.[57] This results in an indestructible kind of optimism, one that strikes and impresses every Westerner who works with the Chinese. There is no place for pessimism: Put your shoulder to the wheel, and trust in the good times that will inevitably come.

Master Sun
Literate Chinese – whether they are politicians, business people, or intellectuals – enjoy using *chengyu*, four-character proverbs proclaiming everyday, practical wisdoms. They range from the banal *Shi shi qiu shi* ('Seek truth from facts') to the more poetic *Hua she tian zu* ('drawing a snake, adding a foot', meaning to add something superfluous). Relations with friendly countries are often labelled as *Feng yu tong zhou* ('wind rain, same boat') – that is, they can weather a storm together. As for joint ventures with foreign businesses which fail as a result of cultural differences, the saying *Tong chuang yi meng* ('same bed, different dreams') applies. Once, my Chinese business partner walked in with a worried look on his face; we had been working a long time on securing a big order, but the client was hesitant to sign the contract. I asked my partner what his greatest concern was. *Ye chang meng duo* ('night long, dreams many') he answered,

by which he meant that if the client would hesitate too long in taking a decision, then he would start thinking about another supplier. Politicians often draw from preachy, morally pompous texts. Practising calligraphy, President Xi Jinping's wife Peng Liyuan wrote *Hou de zai wu* (literally, 'strong virtues, carry things'; i.e. 'Only people of great virtue are suited to undertake great things') during Michelle Obama's visit to Beijing in 2014 – whereupon a blogger immediately wondered whether the United States ought to behave more properly.[58]

The frequent yet subtle use of *chengyu* demonstrates the erudition of the speaker, who is aware of being part of the oldest uninterrupted culture on earth. Many of the texts quoted stem from the Warring States period (475–221 BCE) – an era that, more than any other in Chinese history, is characterised by treachery, manipulation, and raw power. Perhaps this is also the reason that *chengyu* are again so popular: In the Darwinian climate of modern China, many people are waging a daily battle to survive financially and emotionally.

One of the most famous texts from this chaotic early era is *The Art of War* by Sun Zi (Master Sun). Living in around 500 BCE, this political advisor worked in the service of the king of Wu, a state in the south of China. Not much is known about his life, but in the chronicles of the historian Sima Qian – the 'Herodotus of China' – there is a hair-raising anecdote about Master Sun's modus operandi. King He Lu of Wu wanted to appoint Sun Zi as his military advisor, but to test his capacities, the king first asked Sun Zi to arrange for one hundred eighty of his ladies from the palace to conduct a military exercise: The underlying notion presumably being that it is more difficult to discipline women than soldiers. Sun took up the challenge, put a spear in each woman's hand, and said: 'When I say "turn toward the left", you turn toward the left. 'When I say "turn toward the right", you turn toward the right. Is that clear?' The ladies from the palace nodded, but when to the sound of drums, he gave the order, they burst out laughing. After the order was ignored a second time, Master Sun said quietly: 'If the words of the general are clear, but his soldiers do not follow them, then it is the fault of the soldiers.' On that, he gave the order to execute two 'officers' from amongst the troops of ladies.

Alarmed, the king – who had been watching from above – sent a messenger to Master Sun: 'If I am to miss these two concubines, my meat and drink will lose their flavour. It is my wish that they not be beheaded.' Sun remained tranquillity itself: 'Because I am appointed to be general of His Majesty's troops, there are certain instructions I cannot follow.' The two women were then immediately beheaded. When Sun gave the command to resume the exercise, the ladies from the palace marched seamlessly in close order, without uttering a sound. Sun sent a message back to the king: 'Your soldiers are now drilled and disciplined. They can be deployed for whatever you want. Ask them to go through water and fire, they will obey.' The king perceived the inestimable value of Sun, and appointed him general. Following this, one neighbouring state after the other was conquered: But after Sun's death his lessons were forgotten. In 473 BCE the kingdom of Wu suffered a crushing defeat and was swept from the map.[59]

Yet *The Art of War* is more subtle than simply a Chinese variation on von Clausewitz's description of the blind obedience of the Prussian corps: '[T]o fight and conquer in all your battles is not supreme excellence; supreme excellence consists in breaking the enemy's resistance without fighting.'[60] Any means are allowed in doing so: Espionage, deception, treachery, and diversionary tactics. That is why Sun Zi also says 'All warfare is based on deception.' Sun Bin – a descendant of the master, as well as counsellor to the king of Zhao – is associated with the most famous story of deception. When Zhao was attacked by its much stronger neighbour Wei, Sun Bin gave his prince the remarkable advice of surrounding the capital of Wei with the help of Qi (another state that felt similarly threatened). This proved a master stroke. In a panic, the king of Wei commanded his generals to quit the attack on Zhao, and to return immediately to rescue the capital. This made the Wei army vulnerable to the guerrilla operations of Sun Bin, who ultimately lured his weakened opponent into a fatal ambush. Since then, the saying 'Besiege Wei to rescue Zhao' has become proverbial for a successful diversionary manoeuvre.[61]

The best-known representative of ruthless opportunism is Cao Cao, a general from the *Romance of the Three Kingdoms*. Everyone in China knows his name. During the siege of a town, the merchant responsible for supplies reported that there were food shortages. 'Reduce the rations,' said Cao Cao. 'That won't be well received,' said the merchant. 'I have a solution,' said Cao Cao, 'I want to borrow something that will keep the men quiet.' 'What's that?' asked the merchant, curious. 'Your head, sir,' said the general. 'I hope that you won't mind. I've made arrangements for your family.' Before the stunned man could recover from the shock, he was dragged outside and beheaded. His head was stuck on a pike, from which a sign hung: 'Merchant Wang Hou, responsible for supplies – punished for stealing grain and rationing the troops.'[62]

The Three Kingdoms

Running to over 800,000 words, the *Romance of the Three Kingdoms* is a fourteenth-century novel written by Luo Guanzhong. The story concerns the kingdoms of Wei, Wu, and Shu, which fought one another by all possible means after the fall of the Han dynasty (206 BCE – 220 CE). Based on historical fact, the novel is hugely popular in the Chinese cultural sphere – everyone knows the key players. Cao Cao, advisor to the last emperor of the Han dynasty, has come to symbolise a treacherous and merciless tyrant. Zhuge Liang, chancellor of the kingdom of Shu, is regarded as one of China's greatest strategic geniuses, comparable with Sun Zi. Ultimately, all three kingdoms would meet their downfall at the end of the third century.

Stories like these possess not only literary value. In today's China, they still constitute a frame of reference for taking political and military action. Mao Zedong was known to be a great admirer of the *Romance of the Three Kingdoms*. When Xi Zhongxun, the father of the current president, was able to sap the 1950s Tibetan rebellion of its strength through talks instead of using force, Mao compared him with Zhuge Liang, the famous strategist from this novel.[63] Henry Kissinger compares the foreign policy of the People's Republic of China with *Weiqi*, a game that looks like chess, yet in which the opponent is slowly strangled instead of being put in checkmate.[64] Indeed, today's regime seldom opts for a frontal attack to achieve its goals. In recent years, the thumbscrews have gradually been applied to Vietnam, the Philippines, and to Japan in the East and South China Seas – by placing drilling platforms in disputed areas, for example, or by unilaterally declaring an 'Air Defence Identification Zone'. The opponent protests furiously but, for fear of China's economic and military might, does not dare to take harsher countermeasures. Once feelings have calmed down, Beijing takes the further step, and the scenario repeats itself. Master Sun would have greeted this modus operandi with a nod of approval.

The obsession of Chinese authorities and businesses with obtaining information is another example of the influence of *The Art of War*. A 2013 report by the US company Mandiant, for instance, states that a special unit of the People's Liberation Army is carrying out countless cyberattacks on Western governments and businesses from a nondescript building in Shanghai.[65] In this case it is not only about collecting intelligence, but also about corporate secrets and the technology employed by foreign businesses. For Master Sun, this would have also been a recognisable and legitimate means of waging war: Knowledge of the opposing party is crucial. 'If you know the enemy and know yourself, you will win a hundred victories in a hundred battles', he is supposed to have said. Even so, the People's Liberation Army has failed on another significant level: Their espionage came to light. 'In making tactical dispositions, the highest pitch you can attain is to conceal them; conceal your dispositions, and you will be safe from the prying of the subtlest spies, from the machinations of the wisest brains.'[66] Sun Zi always remained true to this core principle, even after his death. In an ancient text, there is a short passage about the Master's tomb: 'Outside the Wu Gate of Wu Hsieh (Soochow), at a distance of ten li, there was a large tomb which is that of Sun Tzu [Master Sun].'[67]

It has never been found.

CHAPTER 2

The Century of Humiliation

The imperial powers descended on China like a swarm of bees, looting our treasures and killing our people.

Inscription for 'The Road to Rejuvenation', a permanent exhibit at the new National Museum of China in Beijing

The unimaginably long-lived imperial order finally collapsed in 1911. That fate did not just come out of the blue, though. The powerful emperor Qian Long reigned for a good sixty years (1736–1796), but his successors were of another calibre entirely. After his death, the unmistakeable signs of dynastic decay therefore manifested themselves one by one: Corruption, peasant rebellions, natural disasters, and foreign aggression. China had the misfortune that this time the barbarians did not invade on horseback – as in the previous two thousand years – but by sea, and with gunboats. The elite were not prepared for their arrival. They viewed the threat from Western imperialism through the lens of their time-tested policy towards barbarians: By seducing them, the enemy would inevitably conform to Chinese mores, and recognise the supremacy of the highest civilisation on earth – just as the *Xiongnu*, Turkic, and Manchu invaders had done. That was a fatal miscalculation, however: The ancient empire did not recognise the new world order it was facing, let alone adapt to it, and was downgraded by the Western powers and Japan to a semi-colonial status. While nothing remains to be seen of what later came to be called the Century of Humiliation (1839–1949), the memory of the destruction of railways, factories, and cities continues to fester. That memory explains the prickly responses of the Beijing regime when its former aggressors do something it does not like, as well as its continual suspicion that the West is again setting out to colonise China – this time not with violence, but with ideas.

The Sun at its Zenith

In the middle of the eighteenth century there was still little that pointed to the impending doom. The sun stood at the zenith of its dynastic trajectory. Economic growth, political stability, and the introduction of new crops from America – sweet potatoes, corn, peanuts – led to a spectacular increase in population: From 138 million in 1700 to at least 430 million in 1850, according to some estimates.[1] As protector and guardian of the written word, Qian Long had all the key literary and philosophical works of the country collected, edited, and re-published. The result was the *Siku Quanshu* ('The complete books of the four treasuries'), a compilation of 36,000 volumes, employing 15,000 writers and scribes.[2] Just as in today's China, this attention to the written word went hand in hand with political repression: The authorities burnt any work that contained politically sensitive passages (for example, praise for an earlier dynasty was read as criticism of the current house). In some cases, the owners of such works were beheaded, or cut into a thousand little pieces – a gruesome but customary punishment in ancient China. Yet Qian Long was more than a paranoid despot. The *yin* of the repressive side of his character was complemented by the *yang* of his religious and artistic refinement. The emperor was a painter, poet, and calligrapher, as well as protector of the teachings of Siddhartha. In many Buddhist temples in China, one still finds steles with inscriptions written by him.

Expansionary Foreign Policy

The foreign policy of Qian Long was expansive, if not violently aggressive. He led his armies deep into Central Asia and Tibet, Mongolia, and East Turkestan (renamed in the nineteenth century as Xinjiang, the 'New Border Area') came more firmly under Chinese authority. In doing so, the emperor doubled the territory of the previous dynasty, the Ming, from 6.5 million to more than 13 million square kilometres.[3] But this did not mean that China satisfied the prerequisite for sovereignty under international law – that is, the exercise of effective authority: In exchange for their ritual recognition of the emperor as the supreme prince on earth, the peoples at the margins of Chinese civilisation were de facto independent. This is an important point to make, for Beijing claims that these areas have been an inseparable part of China for centuries. In fact, these regions were protectorates where the Qing dynasty intervened if China's position as the dominant power in Central Asia was endangered. Qian Long thus, for instance, rushed to the aid of the Tibetans in 1788 and 1791, when they were attacked by the Nepalese. The barbarians at the margins of Chinese civilisation were considered to be family members; they belonged to the clan, but they also had to know their place. That is why in official documents their princes are addressed as 'cousin' or 'younger brother', and why Qian Long made the distinction between *zhongnei yijia* and *zhongwai yijia* – family members *inside* the centre, and family members *outside* it – the people who lived in the core area of China and the people at its periphery.

Emperor Qian Long, attributed to Giuseppe Castiglione

The relationship with Tibet had yet another dimension. In exchange for exercising their secular protection, the emperors recognised the Dalai Lama as the highest spiritual authority on earth – a relationship recalling that between the pope and the Holy Roman Emperors in medieval Europe. The comparison goes even further: The emperors of the Qing dynasty claimed the right to approve the designation of the Dalai Lama – just as the Holy Roman Emperors frequently interfered in the appointment of the pope in Rome. In Europe, church and state are now separate: Yet in today's China, the atheist leaders of the Party still contend that they have the final say in designating the leaders of Tibet's theocracy.

Under Qian Long, the empire reached its greatest extent – even greater than present-day China. During the nineteenth century, large areas were lost to Russia, and Mongolia seceded at the beginning of the twentieth century. Qian Long's expansionary drives, though, did not lead only to success: The expeditions to subjugate Vietnam and Burma ended in catastrophes, costing the lives of tens of thousands of Chinese soldiers. After Qian Long's death in 1799*, the sun started to set, and the dynastic energy began to fade – even though the end would still be more than a hundred years in coming.

The Tribute System

Foreign peoples and states were not treated as equals – the deeply felt sense that Chinese civilisation was superior gave emperors after all the right to rule over the *Tianxia*, All-Under-Heaven. This was true not only for the surrounding vassal states, but for every non-Chinese state on the face of the earth. Starting with the Ming dynasty (1368–1644), foreign relations were officially cast in the mould of the tribute system: From time to time the foreign envoy would visit Peking to offer the emperor gifts such as precious stones, ivory, tropical hardwoods, incense, horses and pearls. In exchange, the envoy would receive coveted products like porcelain, lacquerware, and silk. In fact, this was a hidden form of foreign trade, but the fiction that the barbarian was being granted a 'favour' was maintained at all times. Its ritual expression consisted of the ceremonial of the *ke tou*, in which the envoy touched the ground with his forehead nine times in the presence of the emperor. In Western, egalitarian thinking to *kowtow* was soon seen as the equivalent of cowardly, spineless submission: But in ancient China's hierarchical and ceremonial society, this practice was seen in an entirely different way. Ritual submission to higher powers was considered completely

---

* Qian Long abdicated the throne in 1796, because it would be seen as unfilial to rule longer than his grandfather Kang Xi did (1661–1722). Qian Long remained however the actual ruler of China until his death in 1799.

normal – even the emperor prostrated himself before Heaven every year to pray for prosperity and good harvests. The implementation of the tribute system lay in the hands of the Ministry of Rituals, but those who profited most were the eunuchs – the castrated courtiers who as favourites of the emperor acted as intermediaries in the trade exchanges that accompanied the tribute process. In today's China, this custom is alive and kicking: Well-situated middlemen still exact ample payment in exchange for access to highly placed decision-makers.

Chinese Civilisation as the Norm

Acceptance of the tribute system was grounded in the normative effect of Chinese culture. The Japanese (who, for that matter, had stopped sending tributary missions to Peking in 1549) copied the character-writing system, and painted landscapes on which poems were written – just like the Chinese scholar-painters used to do. Nara, Japan's first capital, founded in the eighth century, was an exact albeit smaller copy of Chang'an, China's capital over many dynasties. The Korean court observed the Confucianist rituals of the Chinese court: The ritual dance and music used by Korea's Silla dynasty during official ceremonies were directly imported from China's Tang dynasty.[4]

The normative influence of the Celestial Empire was felt in even more remote areas. On one of his journeys the great fifteenth-century explorer Zheng He and his powerful fleet called at the south-western Indian state of Cochin. The local ruler was so impressed by this meeting that he wrote a lyrical letter to the Chinese emperor: 'How fortunate we are that the teachings of the sages of China have benefitted us. For several years now, we have had abundant harvests in our country [...]. Our old are kind to the young, and our juniors respectful to their seniors; all lead happy lives in harmony, without the habits of oppression and contention for dominance. The mountains lack ferocious beasts, the streams are free of noxious fish, the seas yield rare and precious things, the forests produce good wood, and all things flourish in abundance, more than double what is the norm. Violent winds have not arisen, torrential rains have not fallen, pestilence and plagues have ceased, and there have been no disasters or calamities.'[5]

Whether the prince truly wrote this letter is doubtful (its only source is Chinese), yet it does speak volumes about the self-image the Chinese had of the emperor as the intermediary between heaven and earth. Those who accepted his authority received the same blessings as China's inhabitants – every resident of the *Tianxia* was a child of the emperor, after all. This kind of world view could not be reconciled with the modern, Western concept of equality amongst states. China resisted this form of international relations for a long time: Until 1860, the country did not even have a ministry of Foreign Affairs. Foreign 'policy' came under the Ministry of Rituals, which was primarily responsible for formulating and executing the extremely refined court ceremonies – including the ceremonies regulating the reception of foreign tributary missions.

Zheng He

Between 1405 and 1433, China's most famous seafarer undertook seven major expeditions to India, Ceylon, the Arabic world, and even East Africa. His first fleet consisted of more than three hundred ships; the flagship was 127 metres long and 52 metres wide. The fleet numbered 28,700 – seamen, scientists, astronomers, linguists, physicians, soldiers, and even ladies of the court. The primary mission was spreading the power of the Chinese, and ensuring that the 'barbarians' recognised the emperor as the Son of Heaven. Zheng He brought exotic gifts back with him to Peking – even, from Malindi in Kenya, a giraffe, which unfortunately did not survive the city's cold winter. The great seafarer died in 1433, during his last expedition, and his body was entrusted to the waves. His death meant the end of China as a naval power. Chinese junks continued to sail the 'Western' (Indian) Ocean, but the state turned its gaze inward towards the land, and spent its money and energy on the threat of the Mongols in the North. In the late fourteenth century, construction began on the Great Wall in the form that we now know it – a project that would take more than three hundred years.

A New Sort of Barbarian

In the seventeenth century new barbarians appeared: Not from the surrounding lands that the Celestial Empire had known for centuries, but from across the seas. They arrived on three-masted vessels, hardened seamen with fair-coloured hair, blue eyes, and a strong body odour. The Dutch East India Company, or VOC (*Vereenigde Oost-Indische Compagnie*), and its British counterpart, the East India Company, had been sailing to China since the beginning of the seventeenth century, satisfying the ever-growing demand for porcelain in Europe. To gain a foothold on Chinese ground, the Dutch wanted to set up their own factory – just as they had done on Java. The only foreign visitors who had succeeded in doing that were the Portuguese: In 1557, the town they called Macau (Aomen in Chinese), located at the mouth of the Pearl River, fell into their hands. For the VOC, this Portuguese enclave was an attractive prize worth capturing. Securing it would give the Dutch not only a base of operations on the Chinese mainland, but would also mean yet another blow to their hated Catholic competitor, as the Dutch systematically set about robbing them of their Asian possessions.

In 1622 the attack was launched. The Portuguese made every effort to defend themselves, yet it seemed that they would have to submit to the army of eight hundred Dutchmen. In their distress they begged for the Almighty's help, and their prayers were immediately answered: From the city walls, the Jesuit priest Padre Jerónimo Rho landed a lucky shot in the Dutch gunpowder stores, killing many of the attackers. Spurred on by this lucky blow, the Portuguese commander Lopo Sarmento de Carvalho cried 'Santiago!' at the top of his lungs and began a counter-attack. The remaining Dutchmen resisted fiercely but bolted after their leader Hans Ruffijn was killed in action. According to Dutch sources, one hundred thirty-six of the VOC soldiers lost their lives, though the Portuguese contended it were at least three hundred. Having ordered the attack, Jan Pieterszoon Coen, the governor-general of the VOC who resided in Batavia (now Jakarta), was furious about 'this shameful manner [in which] we lost most of our best men together with most of the weapons'.[6]

After 442 years Macau again changed owner, this time voluntarily. In 1999 Lisbon transferred Macau to China, under the same terms as the pledge enshrined in the transfer of the British crown colony of Hong Kong (i.e. preserving its autonomous status for another fifty years).

The failed attack on Macau did not mean the end of VOC activities in North-East Asia. Cleverly capitalising on the fact that some countries barely maintained relations with one another, the Dutch became intimately involved in the inter-Asian trade. The VOC shipped, for instance, silk and cotton from China to Japan, and iron and silver in the other direction. And should such lawful trade fail to yield a sufficient profit, then the VOC was not averse to piracy. The Ming Shilu ('The Veritable Records of the Ming [Dynasty]') give convincing evidence of this practice: 'The Red-haired Barbarians will risk their lives in search of profit, and no place is too remote for them to frequent. [...] If one falls in with them at sea, one is certain to be robbed by them.'[7]

Taiwan in Dutch Hands

The attack on Taiwan (then still called Formosa) was successful, however: In 1624, the island came into Dutch possession, though its occupation brought the VOC little profit. Unlike the Dutch East Indies, few lucrative crops or spices could be cultivated there, and because Formosa was not at that time part of the Celestial Empire (like Macau), it did not act as a gateway to the Chinese market. In 1662 the Dutch were forced to leave. Driven off by the Manchus for his loyalty to the Ming dynasty, Zheng Chenggong (whose honorary title Guoxingye – meaning 'Lord of the Imperial Surname' – was bastardised by the Dutch as 'Koxinga') sailed with an army of 25,000 men to the

Dutch colony and laid siege to Fort Zeelandia. His superior forces overwhelmed the Dutch, and after a few months the fort was occupied. Koxinga proved himself to be conciliatory: He allowed the Dutch to sail back to Jakarta with their lives and some bottles of jenever intact. 'I realise that since the Dutch have come a great distance to carry on trade, it is their duty to do whatever they can to preserve their fortress. This devotion pleases me, and I see no misdeed in it.'[8] In that very same year Koxinga died unexpectedly from malaria. He was succeeded by his son Zheng Jing, who did not give up the dream of restoring the Ming dynasty. After various defeats, however, he died in 1681. In 1683, the seed was planted for one of the greatest geo-strategic problems of the twentieth century. From Fujian province, General Shi Lang of the Qing dynasty began a large-scale attack on Taiwan, ousted the descendants of Zheng Chenggong, and made the island part of the Chinese empire.

Historians of the Party maintain the fiction that Taiwan has always belonged to the mother country, yet before the Dutch occupation (or the Portuguese occupation for that matter), the island had never been part of China. The Qing dynasty occupied it out of security considerations: Taiwan could never become a base camp for Ming loyalists again, or be re-conquered by the Dutch.[9] Historical 'what if' hypotheses are by definition debatable (history always follows its own course), but had the island not then been annexed by China, Taiwan would probably have become a sovereign state recognised by the international community – just like Singapore, where the population is also of Chinese origin. That is why those favouring Taiwanese independence regret that the Dutch did not exercise a longer colonial rule: This would have given the island time to develop a stronger identity, and to fight for its independence during the global process of decolonisation in the twentieth century. In this case, the 'Taiwan question' would not exist as a source of structural tensions between China and America.

Restricting Foreign Trade

The Qing was an even more continental power than the Ming. Overseas trade was seen as superfluous, and even threatening to the security of the state, because of the increased contact with the barbarians that went with it: Foreign traders and pirates were frequently (and not entirely unfairly) lumped together. In 1760 Qian Long therefore decided that foreign trade could now only be conducted in the southern port city of Guangzhou (then known as Canton). This led to an increase in corruption and the abuse of power among the Chinese officials. The *Hoppo* (chief inspector for trade), for instance, stipulated how long a ship should lie at anchor, and via which *Hongs* (trading houses) goods could be sold or purchased. These practices contributed to a view of China that became widely spread in the West; the tirade by the eighteenth-century English captain George Anson offers a good example: 'Indeed, thus much may undoubtedly be asserted [...] that in artifice, falsehood, and an attachment to all kinds of lucre, many of the Chinese are difficult to be paralleled by any other people; but then the combination of these talents, and the manner in which they are applied in particular emergencies, are often beyond the reach of a Foreigner's penetration.'[10]

As long as China was economically and politically more powerful than Europe (let alone any individual European nation), the Emperor could impose his conditions without hindrance. Yet the world was changing quickly. Bristling with energy and self-confidence from its industrial revolution, Britain was avidly seeking out new markets for selling its products and importing raw materials. In the middle of the nineteenth century, the Celestial Empire would engage with the new world order the hard way – but the first signs of change became evident fifty years earlier, in the last decade of the eighteenth century, when a British earl paid his respects to the Chinese emperor.

The Macartney Mission

At the end of the eighteenth century, Great Britain was the most powerful maritime nation in the world – a position of supremacy it would maintain for more than a century. Unlike the Dutch, who were only interested in commerce, for the British, empire-building and the expansion of international trade went hand in hand. Free trade was not only good for making profit; it also contributed to the might of the British Empire. Protecting British merchants and opening up foreign markets therefore became one of the cornerstones of national policy during the nineteenth century – even though it was formulated in loftier terms. The ideological grounds for this policy were already laid out by Adam Smith in 1776, in his famous 'An Inquiry into the Nature and Causes of the Wealth of Nations': 'It is the maxim of every prudent master of a family, never to attempt to make at home what it will cost him more to make than to buy. ... What is prudence in the conduct of every private family, can scarce be folly in that of a great kingdom.'[11]

So Qian Long's move to restrict foreign trade to Guangzhou was a thorn in the flesh of the British. To rectify this situation, Earl George Macartney travelled with a delegation to Peking in 1793. The nobleman wanted to achieve two aims: The suspension of the monopoly position of Guangzhou, and the accreditation of an English ambassador in Peking. These petitions shocked the Chinese deeply. How deeply can be read in the letter the ancient monarch Qian Long gave Macartney to take home to his sovereign George III: 'As to your entreaty to send one of your nationals to be accredited to my Celestial Court and to be in control of your country's trade with China, this request is contrary to all usage of my dynasty and cannot possibly be entertained. [...] Hitherto, all European nations, including your own country's barbarian merchants, have carried on their trade with our Celestial Empire at Guangzhou. Such has been the procedure for many years, although our Celestial Empire possesses all things in prolific abundance and lacks no product within its own borders.'[12]

In terms of protocol, there were also clashes between East and West, for Macartney resolutely refused to kowtow before the Chinese emperor. After long negotiations, a creative solution emerged: The earl bowed before the emperor, but only under the condition that the portrait of the English king was hung up behind Qian Long. Unfortunately, this ceremonial creativity did not contribute to finding a substantive solution – the differences were simply too great to bridge for that. The parties were living on different planets. Qian Long resided in the static world of the uninterrupted supremacy of Chinese civilisation; Macartney in the dynamic world of industrial innovation and colonial expansion, which in the nineteenth century would culminate in a British Empire 'on which the sun never sets' – a proclamation supposedly coined by Macartney himself, in 1773.[13] With a forward-looking, if condescending, vision, the Engishman predicted that the days of the imperial order were numbered: 'The Empire of China is an old, crazy, first-rate Man of War, which a fortunate succession of able and vigilant officers have contrived to keep afloat for these hundred fifty years past, and to overawe their neighbours merely by her bulk and appearance. But whenever an insufficient man happens to have the command on deck, adieu to the discipline and safety of the ship. She may, perhaps, not sink outright, she may drift some time as a wreck, and will then be dashed to pieces on the shore; but she can never be rebuilt on the old bottom.'[14]

The Dutch Trade Mission of 1795

Two years later, in 1795, a Dutch delegation led by the ambassadors Andreas Everardus van Braam Houckgeest and Isaac Titsingh also went to Peking. Van Braam, a corpulent merchant of fifty-six and head of the Dutch factory in Guangzhou, initiated the mission. The company, consisting of a twelve-man entourage and three hundred coolies, travelled in the middle of winter from Guangzhou to the Chinese capital – a distance of nearly 2,500 kilometres. They covered the first segment by boat, but from Nanchang, capital of Jiangxi province, they journeyed overland. The two ambassadors were transported in sedan chairs, while the remaining dignitaries travelled on horseback. The hundreds of coolies followed on foot, loaded down by gifts such as musical clocks, golden watches, boxes inlaid with gold, coral, amber, telescopes, silver and gold thread, guns, Persian rugs, Western clothing, mirrors, lamps, sandalwood, nutmeg, and cloves. Van Braam was well aware that the Celestial Court only received barbarians who offered fitting tribute. The inconveniences of early modern travel –

poor roads, hostile local officials, and filthy inns – caused further delay, so it was by a minor miracle that on 9 January 1795, fifty days after departure, the company saw the high grey city walls of Peking looming before them. Weakened, the procession went through the *Xuanwumen* (the 'Gate of the [Manifestation] of Military Might') and prepared themselves for a meeting with the most powerful prince on earth.

Arriving in Peking did not mean that the mission was completed. Just like Macartney, the Dutch delegation fell into the hands of the Ministry of Rituals, which negotiated protocol for ten days before granting the delegation an audience. At the end of January, the time finally came. Van Braam and Titsingh were received by the emperor in the Hall of Preserving Harmony – one of the countless buildings in the imperial complex that in the West later came to be called the 'Forbidden City'. Unlike Macartney, the Dutch merchants eagerly prostrated themselves in the dust and banged their heads nine times on the ground. When, owing to his weight, Van Braam hit the ground too hard and lost his hat, Qian Long asked with a laugh whether he had hurt himself. *Bu dong* ('I don't understand') was the reply, whereupon the emperor laughed even harder, because a barbarian had said in Chinese that he understood no Chinese. John Barrow, who wrote the account of the Macartney mission, had nothing good to say about the behaviour of the Dutchmen: '[T]hese two ambassadors... cheerfully submitted to every humiliating ceremony required from them by the Chinese, who, in return, treated them in the most contemptuous and indignant manner.'[15]

This criticism is understandable, for the behaviour of the ambassadors was lowly indeed, if not obsequious. In the letter they wrote to the governor of Guangzhou to request permission for the delegation, they even stated that 'all far-flung regions have subordinated themselves to China's civilising influence'. Barrow, on the other hand, just like most Englishmen of his era, was no friend to the Dutch, and could not appreciate that the VOC was only driven by making money – the country's image was of secondary importance. In the end, the subservience of Van Braam and Titsingh made no difference, for their specific petition – the suspension of the Guangzhou monopoly – was not granted. On 15 February 1795, they left Peking empty-handed, though not in the literal sense: Court etiquette prescribed that the barbarian who had behaved properly should travel home showered with gifts. Van Braam retained a splendid collection from his mission: Silk, satin, fans, figurines, paintings, maps, and many more objects. We know exactly what, for his entire collection was auctioned by Christie's in London in 1799. An even greater and more practical gift was the letter that Qian Long gave to the Dutchmen to facilitate their trip back: '[O]rders are herewith given to transmit this Edict to all the Viceroys concerned, that in future, when the said Ambassador and his suite will pass their territory on their return journey, in accordance with the precedent of the treatment of the English ambassador, banquets shall be given in their honour.' They deserved this treatment, the imperial decree

A
Catalogue

OF A

CAPITAL, AND TRULY VALUABLE

Assemblage of Chinese Drawings,

PAINTINGS,

Natural and Artificial. CURIOSITIES,

THE PROPERTY OF

A. E. VAN BRAAM, ESQ.

Chief of the Direction of the Dutch East India Company at Canton,
and Second in the Dutch Embassy to the Court of Pekin, in the
Years 1794 and 1795, of which, Mr. VAN BRAAM will speedily
publish an Authentic Account.

The Whole of which

WILL BE SOLD BY AUCTION,

BY MR. CHRISTIE,

AT HIS GREAT ROOM, PALL MALL,

On FRIDAY, FEBRUARY the 15th, 1799,

AT ONE O'CLOCK.

Title-page of Christie's sales-catalogue

The auction of one of Van Braam's collections, as announced by Christie's, 1799 continues, by their 'desire to be civilised by Chinese culture'.[16] The letter worked wonders: The journey back proceeded smoothly, and every evening the most delicious feasts were set before them.

The Sun Begins to Set

At the end of Qian Long's long reign (1736–1796), the signs of dynastic decay were becoming increasingly visible. The country's administration fell into the hands of less competent, even downright corrupt figures such as He Shen, who in his position as 'Minister of Revenue' and later 'Minister of the Imperial Household' accumulated unprecedented riches. After Qian Long's death in 1799, the new emperor Jia Qing had He Shen arrested, and his possessions confiscated. The value of the assets he had accumulated over the years was equal to fifteen times the annual income of the state. Even the Party bosses now getting caught in the net of Xi Jinping's anti-corruption campaign cannot begin to match that level of wealth. He Shen was condemned to death by a thousand cuts, but this punishment was commuted to the more honourable and lenient alternative of suicide by silk rope. On 22 February 1799, the richest man in China hanged himself. In another act of imperial compassion, his family was spared the punishment of *miezu* ('the eradication of the clan'), but instead allowed to live.[17] He Shen's corruption was symptomatic of the dynasty's decay, as was the military's decreasing preparedness, the diminishing of tax revenues, and the major White Lotus peasant rebellion in south-western China. The sun of the Qing (or 'clear') dynasty was still high in the sky, but it was certain to set.

The Four Indignities of the Century of Humiliation

The Party's current propaganda division ensures that every Chinese schoolchild learns about the humiliations that the West and Japan put China through between 1839 and 1949. In three of these four narratives the West, particularly Britain, plays a leading role. It is the fourth, though – Japan's step-by-step campaign to subjugate totally the Celestial Empire – that leaps out. This story still evokes such fierce emotions that the resolving of every current problem between the countries seems to be held hostage by it. Those who want to understand why Beijing risks a war with Japan over five little islands in the East China Sea must therefore familiarise themselves with this history – as it is being told by the Party.

The Opium War

Fifty years after Macartney's delegation, the world had drastically changed. The industrial revolution, with Britain as the front runner, had burst forth and created radically different economic relations. Mass production had replaced local manufacturing and, supported by their governments, a new class of capitalists with unbridled energy went in search of new markets and suppliers of raw materials. With the emergence of new weapons like the gunboat and the rapid-fire rifle, the West acquired a level of military supremacy that fundamentally changed international relations. It forced every country or kingdom that resisted this new world order to its knees. The isolation of the Celestial Empire was thus no longer accepted – especially since the Chinese were exporting goods like porcelain and tea to Europe, while keeping their own market almost hermetically sealed. As a result, a major trade deficit emerged for Britain; though the balance would rapidly turn in their favour through the illegal export of opium from India, to which the British government turned a blind eye. Between 1810 and 1830, imports of opium into China increased tenfold.[18]

Chinese trade deficits became even larger with the growing production of tea on the hillsides of Darjeeling and in other parts of India, making the tea-addicted British less dependent on Chinese exports. Silver, the means of payment at the time, flowed out of the Celestial Empire by the ton. Social disruption was enormous: Millions of Chinese became addicted to opium and were reduced to the dregs of society.

The court in Peking decided to intervene. In 1838 Lin Zexu, a high official with a reputation for incorruptibility, was sent to Guangzhou to restrict the importing of opium. Lin vigorously destroyed the local distribution networks of the white poison. He did not stop there: Proper control of the barbarians demanded not only harsh measures, but an appeal to the barbarians' sense of justice – as a morally superior nation, China was compelled to act like this. Lin's letter to Britain's Queen Victoria is an exquisite example of that position: 'Let us suppose that foreigners came from another country, and brought opium into England, and seduced the people of your country to smoke it, would not you, the sovereign of the said country, look upon such a procedure with anger, and in your just indignation endeavour to get rid of it?'[19]

We do not know if the English monarch read the letter, though she certainly did not reply to it. Lin subsequently took harsher measures: He encircled the foreign factories and forced the traders to surrender their stores of opium, which he then burnt in public. Twenty thousand chests, each with fifty-five kilos of opium, went up in flames. It was a spectacular gesture, but also a senseless one: In weighing ethics against commercial interests, the government in London opted for the latter. Though the queen did not approve of the sale of opium, '[She] cannot' (in the words of Lord Palmerston, her Foreign Secretary) 'permit that her subjects residing abroad should be treated with violence, and be exposed to insult and injustice.'[20] The conflict escalated quickly, and the infamous Opium War broke out. Equipped with muskets and bows-and-arrows, the Qing army was no match for the armoured boats, heavy cannons, and repeating rifles of the British. In a series of field and naval battles, the Chinese suffered one defeat after the other. After taking Guangzhou, the British sailed up the Yangtze River and laid siege to a ship that was transporting tax revenues – a bold raid that showed that the barbarians could strike the empire at its core. In 1842, China quit the unequal fight.

Of the many concessions that Peking had to grant under the Peace Treaty of Nanking (August 1842), two core items stand out. First, the island of Hong Kong was ceded to Great Britain 'in perpetuity', and secondly, the Western powers acquired extra-territorial rights in five Chinese ports: They could apply their own legal system in certain parts of those ports, and Westerners could in general enjoy a high level of immunity in China.

According to some historians, the real reason why Palmerston had initiated the Opium War was Western rancour towards Chinese arrogance. John Quincy Adams, the sixth president of the United States, supported him in that respect: '[T]he cause of the war is the kowtow – the arrogant and insupportable pretensions of China that she will hold commercial intercourse with the rest of mankind not upon terms of equal reciprocity, but upon the insulting and degrading forms of the relations between lord and vassal.'[21] Adams certainly had a point, even though the word 'arrogant' was not well chosen. The Chinese did not consider themselves arrogant: Their policy was based on the self-evident inequality between the civilised and the uncivilised world. The first line from the aforementioned letter of 1793 from Qian Long to King George III clearly reflects this fundamental attitude: 'You, O King, live beyond the confines of many seas, nevertheless, impelled by your humble desire to partake of the benefits of our civilisation, you have dispatched a mission respectfully bearing your memorial. ...'[22] The English, for their part, felt no less lofty. John Barrow, the private secretary to Earl Macartney on his China mission, described his report as a travel account, 'in which it is attempted to appreciate the rank that this extraordinary empire may be considered to hold in the scale of civilized nations.'[23]

China and the West were each living on their own planets, whose orbits must one day collide. For centuries the West had been waging war against the Islamic world, but these two antagonists to some extent occupied the same planet. Like Christianity, Islam is a monotheistic religion, and from the early Middle Ages the two civilisations had shared an intense exchange of culture and knowledge. These points of contact were totally absent between the West and China. The Opium War was – to paraphrase Samuel Huntington's book, *The Clash of Civilizations and the Remaking of World Order* – the first clash of cultures on a global level. Given Beijing's current resistance towards 'hostile Western forces', one could say that the battle is still being waged, albeit with different weapons. But in their first engagement, the West was the clear winner, and could impose its world view on the Chinese. The Treaty of Nanking thus stipulated that, from now on, official correspondence between Britain and China was to remain free of terms like 'supplicating' and 'submitting a petition'. In a heavy-handed manner, it was made crystal clear that the new world order rested on equality among sovereign states.

The impact of the Opium War continues to reverberate. Beijing sees the Treaty of Nanking as the first in a long series of unfair accords that have humiliated the Chinese people. However, the forced opening of the ancient empire also had a positive effect. Without its separation from China, Hong Kong would never have developed into the financial centre that made the economic construction of the motherland at the end of the twentieth century possible. The contribution of Shanghai (the most important of the five treaty ports) is of even greater value – this twenty-first-century New York City is the harbour into which new ideas are sailing, where art is being renewed and foreign cultures embraced – a city where the cosmopolitan spirit of the Tang and Song dynasties has come back to life once more.

The Second Opium War

The Opium War signalled the start of a long and painful process of increasing foreign aggression and domestic decay. Less than twenty years later, the Arrow War broke out. The conflict was named after the illegal inspection (according to the British) of their ship *The Arrow*, but it is more generally known as the Second Opium War. The causes went deeper than the inspection of the ship: The foreign powers were dissatisfied with the execution of the Treaty of Nanking and demanded more concessions, including greater access to the domestic market and an increased number of treaty ports. The Chinese had no choice but to submit, yet resolutely refused to accredit a British envoy in Peking – in this regard, their stance had not budged one millimetre since the Macartney mission of 1793. A concession on this point would mean the end of the *Tianxia*, the admission that the Son of Heaven's sovereignty on earth was divisible.

The English sought a diplomatic way out, but their negotiating team was imprisoned, and several envoys even tortured and executed. Seeking revenge, an Anglo-French military force marched on Peking and, in October 1860, destroyed the imperial summer palace – the luxurious abode of the emperors embellished in the eighteenth century by the Italian architect Giuseppe Castiglione. To keep the memory of this barbarian plunder alive, the *Yuanmingyuan* ('Garden of Perfect Brightness'), as the palace is called in China, has deliberately not been restored. For the modern visitor it is a strange experience to walk past the chunks of the ruins, decorated with stone seashells and flowers. For a moment, you are deluded into thinking you are in Europe – but not for too long, for the surrounding park is once again typically Chinese, with its artificial hills, marble bridges, and subtle vistas.

The ruins of the Old Summer Palace, ca. 1920

This destruction of the 'Versailles of China' still evokes intense emotions. Chinese schoolchildren are taught: 'The invaders shouted: "We must have revenge without mercy! Occupy Peking and chase the emperor from his palace! Let us, Englishmen, rule over the Chinese!"' In 1860, the Anglo-French army attacked again. Everything in their path was burnt, looted, and murdered. The Anglo-French army destroyed the Yuanming palace and set it on fire.'[24] What stings the most is the theft of twelve bronze statues of the Chinese zodiac, which have seen various owners in the last one hundred fifty years. After the last owner, Yves Saint Laurent, died in 2009, the rat and rabbit figures were auctioned by Christie's. A Chinese businessman, Cai Mingchao, bid forty million dollars, but subsequently refused to pay, saying that it was his 'patriotic duty' to protest the auction. 'I think any Chinese person would have stood up at that moment,' Cai said of his bid, 'It was just that the opportunity came to me. I was merely fulfilling my responsibilities.'[25]

A spectacular finale followed in the spring of 2013, when François-Henri Pinault, the CEO of the Kering holding company (owner of Yves Saint Laurent and Christie's), donated the pair of bronze animals to China. Song Xiao, director of the State Administration of Cultural Heritage, responded approvingly: 'The Chinese side offers its high praise for this gesture and considers it to be in conformity with the spirit of relevant

S. Exc. Tchang.   S. Exc. Liu.   S. Exc. Shui-Tan.   Le prince Tching.   S. Exc. Shui.   S. Exc. Souane

ÉVÉNEMENTS DE CORÉE. — Le Tsong-li-Yamen, ou Conseil des ministres de l'Empire chinois.

D'après une photographie prise à Pékin, dans le jardin du Palais des ministres, par M. Vaporeau fils.

The Zhongli Yamen, ca. 1894

international cultural heritage protection treaties.'[26] The Pinault family was no less polite: 'We went to great efforts to retrieve these two significant treasures of China and strongly believe they are now back where they belong'.[27] Questions can be raised regarding these efforts (the Kering group is after all the owner of Christie's), but it is clear that the gesture was related to the major business interests of this French concern in China. It is a fine example too of Beijing's increasing capacity for manipulating not only states, but also private parties in such a way that they start behaving like 'friends of China' and take into account 'the feelings of the Chinese people'.

After the summer palace was burnt down, the Court was forced to concede to the accrediting of British diplomats in Peking. Based on the principle of 'most-favoured nation' (a concession to one applied as a concession to all), the other Western powers quickly followed the British example. As counterpart to these foreign delegations, the *Zhongli Yamen* was established, an abbreviation for *Zhongli geguo shiwu yamen* ('Office in Charge of Affairs of All Nations'). This Office preceded the Ministry of Foreign Affairs, but the fact that the Zhongli Yamen was created as a *temporary* body says a lot about the disinclination, or in any case uneasiness, towards the new world order. Once the crisis had blown over, ran the implication, foreign affairs could again be conducted as of old (that is to say, by means of the tribute system).

Institutionally speaking, the Zhongli Yamen did not have much power either: It operated under the auspices of the Grand Council (the highest imperial administrative body) and the members of the Zhongli Yamen belonged to other government agencies at the same time.[28]

China is presently much more closely interwoven with foreign countries than one hundred fifty years ago. Even so, the minister of Foreign Affairs still occupies a modest position in the bureaucratic hierarchy of the government. All major decisions are taken by the Party leadership on the recommendation of the so-called Foreign Affairs Leading Small Group. As well as the minister of Foreign Affairs, departmental ministers like the ministers of Commerce and Defence have a seat in this organisation. The general coordination of foreign policy is in the hands of the State Councillor for Foreign Affairs, a man who ranks higher both in the government and the Party hierarchy than the minister of Foreign Affairs.[29]

The Boxer Rebellion

Of the many domestic uprisings in Chinese history, the Boxer Rebellion is perhaps the strangest. The *Yihetuan* ('Society United in Righteousness', also the 'Righteous and Harmonious Fists') – which, owing to their preference for martial arts, became known in the West as the 'Boxers' – was a religious group which believed that by carrying out Taoist magic practices they became immune to rifle bullets. The target of their rage was not the court in Peking, but foreign missionaries and their converts, whom they suspected of sinister practices, such as using the eyes of Chinese orphans for making medicine. A pamphlet makes their feelings clear: '[T]he Catholics and Protestants have vilified our gods and sages, have deceived our emperors and ministers above, and oppressed the Chinese people below. [...] This forces us to practice the I-ho magic boxing so as to protect our country, expel the foreign bandits and kill the Christian converts, in order to save our people from miserable suffering.'[30]

From early 1900 thousands of Christians, both Westerners and Chinese, were murdered in an orgy of violence in the countryside around Peking. That June, the uprising expanded to the capital, with every unguarded foreigner vulnerable to attack. Its best-known victim, the German envoy Von Ketteler, was murdered in the street – a fate that the arrogant baron had called upon himself by beating up an innocent Chinese boy and subsequently executing him. In panic the Westerners took refuge in their embassies, which they had surrounded with hastily-erected barricades. Protection from the court could not be expected: After first waiting to see which way the wind was blowing, Ci Xi (the empress dowager in whose hands the real power lay) soon openly aligned herself with the rebels. Her words reflect the realization of every ruler that the people can make or break the dynasty. 'Today China is extremely weak. We have only the people's hearts and minds to depend upon. If we cast them aside and lose the people's hearts, who can we fall back on to save the country?'[31] The

Empress Dowager Ci Xi

rebels were so fanatical and numerically superior that it only seemed a matter of time before the diplomats and their small garrisons would be finished off down to the last defender. The mass execution in Shanxi province was a harbinger of what awaited the Westerners in Peking: Under the pretence that they could be better protected against the attacks from the Boxers there, the governor Yu Xian lured the foreign missionaries to the capital Taiyuan. Once they had arrived, he had all forty-four of them – men, women, and children – murdered.[32]

But the foreign powers did not sit still: England, France, Germany, Japan, the United States, Austria-Hungary, Russia and Italy hastily amassed an army of 20,000 men to deliver their embassies. On their way to Peking, the veteran journalist Thomas Millard noted: 'Every town, every village, every peasant hut in the path of the troops was first looted and then burned.'[33] On 14 August 1900 the foreign powers entered China's capital. The empress fled deep into the interior of the country and a few generals committed suicide – a common act in classical China to escape the loss of face caused by defeat. In their harshness, the peace terms recall the Treaty of Versailles signed nineteen years later. China was prohibited from importing arms for two years, was forced to accept permanent foreign guards at embassies, and was ordered to execute the most important Boxer leaders – including Yu Xian, the complicit governor of Shanxi. The Western powers also demanded an indemnity of 450 million taels

(1 tael was approximately forty grams [around 1.5 ounces] of silver), or 333 million US dollars at the prevailing exchange rate – an astronomical amount, equal to twice the annual income of the treasury. At an annual interest rate of 4 percent, the amount was to be fully discharged by 1940.[34] As with Germany nineteen years later, China was condemned to destitution.

The *baguo lianjun* (the 'Eight-Nation Alliance') has become proverbial for brutal and unsolicited interference in China's domestic affairs. While living in Beijing in the 1990s, my family and I would regularly make excursions to the Great Wall – preferably to those parts of the fortifications that had not yet been restored and were therefore not yet overrun by tourists. We regularly returned to one especially nice spot. The local farmers had also noticed it and suddenly a barrier had been installed across the access route. Passage was only possible after paying 50 *renminbi* per person, at that time still a substantial amount for nearly all Chinese. A female friend accompanying us got into a discussion with a farm girl and feelings soon ran high – so high, that our friend slapped the girl – or rather, lightly touched her cheek. The girl froze and pulled back as white as a ghost, screaming shrilly: 'Are you human?! Or do you come from one of the countries from the Eight-Nation Alliance?' Our denial of that final question did not make much of an impression; nor did the price initially go any lower. In the end, (as always in China) a negotiated solution emerged, and we were allowed to pass at a reduced group rate.

In 2006, the magazine *Bing Dian* (*Freezing Point*) ran an article by Professor Yuan Weishi that criticised historical propaganda that leads to oversimplification and deception: '[S]ince the "foreign devils" are the invaders, the Chinese are justified and praised in whatever they do – even the Boxers who cut down telegraph lines, destroyed schools, demolished railroad tracks, burned foreign merchandise, murdered foreigners and all Chinese who had any connection of foreign culture'. He argued for revising the ways of teaching, because otherwise 'our youth are continuing to drink the wolf's milk!' The Party cracked down hard: Li Datong, the *Bing Dian* editor who published the article, was fired, and the journal was suspended. To justify these actions, it was alleged that the article 'attempted to vindicate the criminal acts by the imperialist powers in invading China... [and that] it had seriously hurt the feelings of the Chinese people'.[35]

Japanese Aggression

The emotions evoked in today's China by the fourth story from the Century of Humiliation – that of Japanese aggression – reduce the first three stories to annoying, but trivial occurrences. Like China the 'Land of the Rising Sun' was broken open in the middle of the nineteenth century by the West, by US Commodore Matthew Perry in 1853. Yet unlike its larger neighbour, Japan modernised at a furious pace – militarily, politically, and economically. The position of the Japanese emperor was not affected by such change. On the contrary: Thanks to the so-called Meiji restoration of 1868, the monarch was freed from the marionette role that the shoguns (feudal rulers) had imposed on him for centuries, and under the motto *Fukoku Kyohei* ('make the country rich and the army strong') he became the symbol of a new and modern Japan. The difference with China was striking. After the death of the Xianfeng emperor in 1861, de facto power came to rest with the empress dowager Ci Xi. Although she carried out certain reforms like the modernisation of the army, the construction of railways, and some degree of industrialisation, she did not challenge the institutions of the state and the power of the conservative mandarins. The new oligarchy in Japan took a radically different course: It stripped power from the ruling samurai class, and modernised education. In Japan the emperor became the symbol of progress – in China one of stagnation. Until Ci Xi's death in 1908, the country stayed stuck in half-hearted reforms that would very soon signify the deathblow for the Qing dynasty.

In the years following the Meiji restoration Japan quickly expanded its influence in the region. In 1879 it annexed the Ryukyu Islands – a vassal state of China for centuries. The second target was Korea, a proud and ancient country that had, as the 'hermit kingdom', been independent during long periods of its history, but which like Poland had the misfortune of being caught between two major powers that regularly interfered in its domestic affairs. When in 1894 the Korean king was threatened by a domestic uprising, both Peking and Tokyo sent military forces to 'protect' him. The Japanese, arriving faster, defeated the Chinese armies that had rushed to the king's aid. Yet Japan did not stop there. In lightning-fast campaigns a portion of North-East China was occupied and the *Beiyang* Fleet ('Fleet of the Northern Ocean') annihilated. The Treaty of Shimonoseki imposed humiliating terms on the Celestial Empire: The complete 'independence' of Korea was to be respected; Japan gained access to four additional treaty ports in China; and Taiwan, the Pescadores (a group of islands located close to Taiwan) and the Liaodong region (in North-East China) were ceded to Japan 'in perpetuity'.

Ever since the First Opium War of 1839 the ancient empire had regularly been humiliated by the Western powers. But now it had been overpowered by a country familiar for centuries and dubbed disparagingly the 'Land of the Dwarves' – and moreover, a country greatly indebted to China for its culture, religion, and state institutions. Now the roles were reversed. At the signing of the Treaty of Shimonoseki the Japanese statesman Itō Hirobumi said to the Chinese minister Li Hongzhang: 'Ten years ago at Tientsin I talked with you about reform. Why is it that up to now not a single thing has been changed or reformed?' Li's answer succinctly summarises China's tragic history during the nineteenth century: 'The affairs in my country are too confined by tradition.'[36]

At the beginning of the twenty-first century, the loss of face from the 1894 war still rumbles on; the pain is so deep-seated that since 2012 Beijing has been agitating over a territorial dispute ignored for over a century.

Senkaku or Diaoyu Islands?

Fifty years after the Chinese defeat of 1895 the roles were reversed again: Japan was defeated in the Second World War and was forced to give up its conquests in Asia. On 27 November 1943, ahead of Japan's loss, US president Roosevelt, England's prime minister Churchill, and the Chinese leader Jiang Jieshi (known better by the Cantonese version of his name, Chiang Kai-shek) agreed in their Cairo Declaration that: 'All the territories Japan has stolen from the Chinese, such as Manchuria, Formosa, and the Pescadores, shall be restored to the Republic of China.'[37] At its capitulation in 1945, Tokyo recognised the legality of the Cairo Declaration, yet the question remained disputed as to whether the Senkaku Islands (*Diaoyu* in Chinese) made up part of 'all areas stolen by Japan', or whether they were already Japanese territory *before* the Sino-Japanese War of 1894.

In 1972 the United States transferred to Japan its administration, carried out since the end of the Second World War, over the Okinawa Prefecture (of which the Senkaku Islands were a part). And then, and only then, did Beijing challenge Japanese sovereignty over the islands.[38] The 1969 discovery of potentially large gas and oil reserves in the surrounding waters certainly played a role here. Maritime law says that states may create an 'exclusive economic zone' around their islands – granting the right to exploit the natural resources above and below the ocean floor to a distance of two hundred nautical miles from their coastlines.

International legal issues around the dispute are complex. China only protested in 1972 – nearly eighty years after the occupation of the Senkaku Islands, which (according to Tokyo) were already in Japan's possession even before the war of 1894. There is no established timeframe in international law that causes 'tacit agreement' with a specific situation to take effect, though eighty years of silence is certainly a strong indication of consent. Beijing counters that the Diaoyu Islands have been mentioned on Chinese maps for centuries, and that Tokyo has taken them from their rightful owner by force. We do not know how an international court would rule in this case, because China takes the fundamental position that territorial disputes must be settled by means of bilateral discussions. Yet Beijing is not talking; it is taking action by regularly sending 'research ships' and aeroplanes to the disputed area. The tensions arising have potentially dramatic consequences: According to Article 5 of their bilateral security treaty, Japan and the USA must come to each other's aid in the event of any armed encounter with a third power.[39] On his visit to Tokyo in February 2017 the US defence minister Jim Mattis confirmed that the Senkaku Islands fall within the scope of this treaty, thus maintaining the position held by the Obama administration.[40]

The Long Struggle against Japan

The crushing victory in the 1894 war constituted the first phase in Japan's long-term strategy of annexing the ancient empire step-by-step. The First World War then offered Tokyo a golden opportunity. Like Japan, China was on the side of the Allies and sent more than one hundred forty thousand workers to the French front. Yet its loyalty to the Allied cause could not prevent the Treaty of Versailles from being a disaster for Peking: The German concession in Shandong province was not returned to China, but transferred to Tokyo.

But even this rich prize could not sate the Japanese hunger for expansion. As a late-imperialist power Tokyo looked to China as a supplier of raw materials and labour to fuel the Japanese economy. Manchuria (home of the founders of the Qing dynasty) was an ideal springboard for achieving its large-scale aspirations. The area was vast, not far from Japan, and rich in resources like timber and oil. In 1931 it was conquered and renamed Manchukuo ('Land of the Manchu People'). Pu Yi, better known as the 'last emperor of China', became head of the new state. As a three-year-old boy this tragic figure was installed on the dragon throne in 1908, but had to abdicate when the empire fell in 1912. Xuan Tong (as he was known by his dynastic name) was again crowned emperor in 1932, though it was clear to everyone where the real power in Manchukuo lay. The League of Nations, precursor to the United Nations, attempted to mediate by setting up the Lytton Commission: But when this body stated that Japan must withdraw from the conquered areas, and with the League of Nations condemning that country as the aggressor, Japan simply cancelled its membership of the League. As a result, 'Manchukuo' not only became the symbol of Japanese aggression, but also signified the League's impotence at its decisions. Tokyo's 1932 recognition of Manchukuo as an independent state was not endorsed by any other country.

In July 1937 the Sino-Japanese dispute escalated dramatically. Japanese military exercises close to Peking's Marco Polo Bridge were construed by Chiang Kai-shek as an attempt to claim even more Chinese territory, and he attacked the Japanese by declaring that it would be an 'unforgiveable crime' to give up even 'one centimetre' of Chinese ground. In Japanese military circles the mood was no less bellicose: The calls for making short work of the government of the Republic of China were getting louder and louder.[41] Fighting quickly spread to other parts of the country. Better-organised and better-armed, the Japanese army pulled off one victory after another, but it was also guilty of large-scale atrocities against the civilian population. The countryside was ravaged by implementing the gruesome 'Three Alls Policy': 'Kill all, burn all, loot all.'[42] The more the Chinese resisted, the more ferocious the Japanese became. They were, as the historian Barbara Tuchman aptly puts it, 'Like a hyena of conquest, growing more ravenous by what it fed on'.[43]

The cities were not spared, either. After the bombing of Shanghai ensued what the Chinese have come to call the 'massacre of Nanjing'. In December 1937 an unknown number of civilians and soldiers were horrifically murdered in that city – a war crime commemorated every year in China on 13 December, and one recently elevated by the Party to the same level as Japan's attack on Pearl Harbor. Factually this is incorrect:

The Japanese attack on Nanjing was not a surprise assault designed to knock out an essential component of the Chinese military. Still, the comparison speaks to the depth of the suffering caused by the Japanese. The sinologist Jonathan Spence calls it 'a period of terror and destruction that must rank among the worst in the history of modern warfare'.[44]

Unfortunately, 'Nanjing' is also proof of Beijing's tendency to put the past at the service of the present: The massacre cannot be forgotten, because it keeps ethnic hatred of the Japanese alive, strengthens nationalism under the banner of the Party and puts the government in Tokyo under permanent moral pressure. The various numbers of victims demonstrate these motivations. Spence estimates the figure at less than 100,000, while the Tokyo Tribunal puts it at 200,000. At 300,000, the Chinese estimate is the highest. This is not surprising – in the Patriotic Education Campaign, other figures are being adjusted too. The number of Chinese killed in action during the 1931–1945 war with Japan, for example, has grown from ten million to at least thirty-five million.[45]

Downfall of the Empire

The four attacks on China's sovereignty – the four stories from the Century of Humiliation – accelerated the downfall of the two-thousand-year-old imperial order. There were other reasons too: Corruption grew rampantly, and the White Lotus Rebellion at the end of the eighteenth century was followed by even greater uprisings. By far the largest rebellion – the Taiping Tianguo (the 'Heavenly Kingdom of Great Peace') – lasted from 1850 to 1864 and overwhelmed half of China in a spiral of violence and reprisals. Certainly twenty million died in the process, making this civil war – when related to world population at the time – the second bloodiest conflict in history.[46]

In the 1860s progressive officials like Zeng Guofan and Li Hongzhang strove to save the dynasty from downfall. Under the motto Zhong Ti Xi Yong ('Chinese core, Western application'), these leaders of the so-called 'Self-Strengthening Movement' wanted to preserve the Confucian-based state structure, but also strengthen the country through Western knowledge and technology. Railways were built, the army modernised, and industries like shipbuilding and steelmaking created. But unlike in Japan, these reforms never really got off the ground – conservative resistance with its attachment to tradition was too strong. For example: Trains would supposedly disturb the spirits of the ancestors, while the tracks' straight lines were bad for feng shui, the doctrine that teaches how structures or objects attract good qi (energy) and repel bad qi.

Corruption posed another essential problem. Funds intended for modernising the army largely disappeared into the pockets of crooked eunuchs. Only after the catastrophic defeat to the Japanese in 1895 and the disastrous Boxer Rebellion of 1900 was there finally a change in direction. It was slowly recognised that Western domination in the areas of arms, science, and technology had not just come out of the blue, but was built upon different models of education and national administration. The elite came to comprehend that the ti (core) and the *yong* (application) could not be separated. As the reform-minded writer and publisher Liang Qichao succinctly put it, what China needed was 'a constitution, a parliament, and a responsible government'.[47] Just like those in power today, the Qing dynasty in its final days faced a catch-22 situation: Not reforming could delay the dynasty's fall, but it could not hold back its demise. But to reform was like jumping into the abyss: It could result in death, but perhaps the fall would be broken, and the dynasty could miraculously rise again. In 1905 the court chose the latter course of action. It enacted a series of reforms, the most dramatic of which was the scrapping of the Confucianist examinations. That measure turned out to be a jump too far. The mandarins were the glue that held the empire together, and their removal signified the dynasty's deathblow. The end was not long in coming now.

CHAPTER 3

A New Beginning

China is a civilization pretending to be a state.

Michael Ledeen

Empress Dowager Ci Xi, the remarkable woman who had ruled China with an iron fist since 1861, died in 1908. The three-year-old Pu Yi (whose tragic life story was told by the Italian director Bernardo Bertolucci in *The Last Emperor*) ascended the throne. This child emperor, though, was unable to breathe new life into the two-thousand-year-old dynastic skeleton. In 1911 the curtain fell: In the city of Wuhan, a group of Republican officers rebelled, and the revolution soon spread like wildfire. In 1912, Pu Yi abdicated the throne and Sun Zhongshan (known in the West as Sun Yatsen, his Cantonese name) was appointed the first president of the Republic of China.

The Three Principles of the People

Born in Guangdong province, Sun Yatsen and a few fellow revolutionaries set up the *Tongmenghui* (usually translated as the 'Chinese Revolutionary Alliance') with the goal of overthrowing the Qing dynasty. This alliance would later transform itself into the *Kuomintang* (the KMT, or 'National People's Party'), which would govern large parts of China from 1927 to 1949. After losing the civil war to Mao Zedong's Communists, however, the KMT had to flee to Taiwan. A Christian who had initially opted for a career as a physician, Sun saw his task as curing the Chinese people from their centuries-old feudal load. The ideological foundation of that pursuit was expressed in his famous *Sanmin zhuyi* ('Three Principles of the People'):

- Minzu ('nationalism' = 'boss in your own country'). Like many other Chinese, Sun saw the Qing dynasty as a foreign oppressor that must be driven out – even though the Manchus had been fully assimilated into Chinese culture since the dynasty's founding in 1644. Sun did not argue for ethnic cleansing, or a 'China for the Chinese': As a multi-ethnic nation, the new state was supposed to offer a home to various demographic groups. That is why the Republic of China's first flag displayed five horizontal stripes, each of which depicted one of China's key

Sun Yatsen with his wife Song Qingling (right)

nationalities: The topmost red stripe stood for the Han Chinese, the yellow for the Manchus, the blue for the Mongols, the white for the Hui, and the lowest black stripe (it is difficult not to see this as symbolic) for the Tibetans.

–   *Minsheng* ('welfare for the people'). This principle means that every person is entitled to the basic necessities of clothing, food, and shelter: Later this was adopted as a global tenet in Article 11 of the International Covenant on Economic, Social and Cultural Rights (ICESCR).[1] Here, Sun's inspiration was not Karl Marx, but the American economist Henry George, who argued for better utilisation of land. 'We must make land common property' argued George in his book *Progress and Poverty*, though the nationalised land could be administered by private parties through leasing. The tax that individuals paid was measured by the value of the land, but it could be reduced – or even waived – if the land was used productively. In this way, George hoped to counteract speculation and promote productivity.[2] Interestingly, the Party put George's thinking into practice in 1978: The land remained in state hands, but was leased to farmers who used it productively. This however is also where the similarity with George ends: In recent years many farmers have been driven off their land by the *kong-si** of local authorities and

* Kong-si, from the Chinese word *gongsi* (company), has in Western parlance obtained the meaning of a secretive alliance.

project developers, who compensate them poorly and prohibit them from sharing in the profits from the hotels and factories built on it. As a result, a situation has emerged in the People's Republic that is the opposite of what George had in mind: Greater inequality, and the impoverishment of segments of the rural population.

– Minquan ('power to the people'). This principle is an interesting mix of Western and Chinese political philosophy. The people's right to elect and depose its leaders is typically Western: Sun calls it zhengquan (the 'power of politics'). The exercise of this power (which Sun calls zhiquan – the 'power of governance') is carried out by a government consisting of five branches, or yuan. The first three branches derive from Montesquieu's trias politica: A legislative, executive, and judicial yuan. The last two – an 'examination' yuan and a 'control' yuan – are a continuation of the imperial tradition for monitoring the honesty and quality of the government.[3]

Kang Youwei

A period of chaos and violence often unleashes creative forces – for a while, the stifling authority of the central government lapses. In China it was no different. The division of the country between the fall of the empire in 1911 and the attack by Japan in 1937 liberated the minds of painters, actors, writers and political thinkers. There was a whiff of renewal in the air: An expectation that a modern nation could be founded that could preserve the best of Chinese tradition. The best-known political thinker was probably Kang Youwei (1858–1927), the scion of an ancient line of mandarins who emerged as a radical reformer. In 1898 Kang received the Guangxu emperor's mandate to save the Qing dynasty by fundamentally reforming China. His radical agenda proposed the founding of a constitutional monarchy, a free market economy and a new educational system in which the country's elite was chosen for their knowledge of current political issues. But after a hundred days a reactionary clique led by the empress dowager Ci Xi put an end to the reforms. Kang was condemned to death, but saved his skin by fleeing to Japan.

After this blow, Kang no longer occupied any official role, but developed into an intellectual with increasingly radical ideas. In his magnum opus, the Datongshu (The Book of the Great Harmony), Kang was inspired by what the ancient Book of Rites describes as a society in which 'people of talent and ability... were sincere, and they cultivated harmony. [...] Robbers, thieves, rebels, and traitors had no place, and thus outer doors were not closed.'[4] To achieve this world he dreamt of, inequality between men and women, races and clans must be abolished. In each field Kang presented specific proposals. States, for example, must prepare first for disarmament, then for forming alliances with other nations, and finally for assimilating into larger federations. Once nation-states have been disintegrated, no more wars will be waged, and a world government will automatically be established. Kang is no revolutionary: Like most Chinese thinkers he favours a gradual approach. To arrive at the final goal of Great Harmony, society must go through several phases: 'The Era of Disorder', 'the Era of Increasing Peace-and-Equality', 'the Era of Lesser Prosperity' and 'the Era of Complete Peace-and-Equality'. After these, the World of Great Harmony will dawn, though its realisation may take centuries. Thanks to an active policy of racial miscegenation, there is no longer any distinction between people in this utopian future. Everyone will be 'of the same color, the same appearance, the same size, and the same intelligence'.[5]

As we shall see later, today's intelligentsia is also fascinated by the notion of Great Harmony. According to some thinkers, it is already upon us – though they don't have Kang Youwei's egalitarian world without races in mind. They are rather thinking of a world order in which China regains its ages-old position of moral superiority. Even the Party makes use of this Confucianist futurology. President Hu Jintao (2002–2012) created the goal of achieving a 'moderately prosperous society' by 2020 (i.e. the 'Era of Lesser Prosperity', as conceived by Kang Youwei): The majority of the population will be better off, materially speaking; prosperity will be more equitably distributed, and the environment will be respected.[6] At the 19th Party Congress, held in October 2017, president Xi Jinping reiterated this target.

Yan Fu

At the opposite end of the scale to Kang Youwei's utopian idealism sits Yan Fu, a follower of Herbert Spencer – an English sociologist who contended that the survival of the fittest applied not only to species but to states as well. Yan, who lived from 1854 to 1921 and was the first president of Peking University, contended that in the beginning, species fight with species; but as people continue to evolve, there is also struggle among social groups. 'The weak invariably become the prey of the strong, the stupid invariably become subservient to the clever.'[7] In order to survive, China would need to become more intelligent, but above all stronger: 'the yellow race is in a "perpetual state of war" against the "superior" white race and "inferior" red, brown, and black races'. The strength of the race determines its 'national health' and its 'national spirit'.[8] This Chinese variation on social Darwinism was directly related to the existential crisis that the country went through. Could China survive the series of humiliations and the ever-growing threat to its sovereignty, or not? Was the weakness of the country not a direct consequence of the weakness of the race?

Today's China still searches for an answer to these questions. To prevent new 'humiliations' obsessive attention is given to the country's 'comprehensive national strength'. The Chinese Academy of Social Sciences has even developed a system that uses sixty-four indicators to compare the power of China with that of other countries[9] –

military, political, and economic, as well as other factors harder to measure, such as cultural appeal. Purity of race is not one of the sixty-four indicators, yet racist remarks are
heard more and more often. Black people are often called 'monkeys', even by highly educated Chinese, and the Japanese 'little devils'.[10] A television advertisement from May
2016 shows a black man having a packet of *Qiaobi* laundry detergent shoved into his
mouth by a young Chinese woman. He is then stuffed into a washing machine. While
the man is screaming, the machine goes to work. After some time, a young Chinese
man pops out of the washing machine, whom the woman greets with a smile.[11] The
Party does not openly support this increasingly racially-tinged nationalism, but it
does not denounce it either. While governor of Fujian province, the current president
Xi Jinping was involved in editing the book *Kexue yu aiguo* ('Science and Patriotism').
In it he wrote that 'Yan Fu's scientific and patriotic thought is still not out of date'.[12]

The Country Acquires a Name of its Own

Hand in hand with ideas about national renewal came the quest for a new name for the
country. Over the course of the nineteenth century, it had become painfully clear that
the lofty notion of China as a centre of civilisation provided no protection against the
rapacity of the English, French, and Japanese. The *Tianxia* order represented ancient
thinking, and thus no longer sufficed. In 1911 the name *Zhongguo* was chosen – as an
abbreviation of *Zhonghua Minguo* ('China Republic') – but this appellation also reached
back to much older times, to the eras of the *Spring and Autumn Annals* (771–476 BCE)
and the *Warring States* (475–221 BCE). This was the period when the opposing kingdoms
distinguished between the 'barbarian' states on the periphery of civilisation and the
one that embodied Chinese culture: *Zhongguo*, the 'central state', the ruler of which was
Heaven's appointed representative on earth. *Zhongguo* thus stands for both the modern
nation-state and an ancient tradition of lofty imperial governance. This is among other
examples demonstrated by the 'Maps of National Shame', which show not only the
borders of modern China, but also the purported extent of the realm during imperial
times. Founded in 1949, the *Zhonghua Renmin Gongheguo* (People's Republic of China)
continues this tradition. In abbreviated format, it also calls itself *Zhongguo* – and it
too publishes maps showing which areas have been stolen by the imperialist powers.

The General Elections of 1912

Politically, a new era appeared to have dawned with the fall of the empire. Sun Yatsen
was appointed provisional president, yet in a break with the past, the legitimacy of
the new regime was to be decided by the people. In 1912, the first – and to this day

only – general parliamentary elections took place in China. The Senate was chosen by the provincial councils, but the House of Representatives was elected directly by proportional representation. Any man who paid taxes, had a specified income and had received a primary school education could vote; women, illiterates, opium smokers, bankrupts, and the feeble-minded were excluded.[13] These criteria reduced the number of voters to forty million, approximately 10 percent of the population: Yet even these limited elections proved to be a unique, one-off experiment in the history of China. More than a hundred years later the members of the National People's Congress, China's parliament, are elected by the representatives of the Provincial People's Congresses. The candidates must be approved by the Party, however, and cannot exceed the number of available seats by more than 10 percent. In the 1912 elections, multiple parties competed for the voters' support – a completely inconceivable version of the 'Democratic Centralism' practised in the People's Republic.

The candidate for the Kuomintang was Song Jiaoren, a charismatic thirty-year-old politician who was hoping that the election results would curb the power of the military strongman Yuan Shikai (who had assumed the presidency from Sun Yatsen). After a whirlwind campaign the Kuomintang won nearly half the seats in the House of Representatives. Song toured the country triumphantly, and his victory speeches attacked the authoritarian aspirations of President Yuan Shikai. On 20 March 1913 the young victor stood on the platform of the station in Shanghai to board the train to Peking. Suddenly from the shadows a uniformed man moved forward, put a bullet in Song's back and fled. Mortally wounded, Song still managed to dictate a letter to President Yuan, the man who had probably contracted the assassin: 'I die with deep regret. I humbly hope that your Excellency will champion honesty, propagate justice, and promote democracy.' The investigation into Song's murder led to various arrests, but the suspects mysteriously disappeared or were themselves assassinated. Proof that President Yuan himself was behind the murder never emerged.[14]

Warlords

Song's dying wish went unheard: Yuan Shikai soon dissolved the congress, declared the Kuomintang an illegitimate party, and in 1915 even had himself crowned emperor. This conservative restoration was detested everywhere:* Mass demonstrations took

* When it was announced on 25 February 2018 that the term limit of two times five years for the presidency was to be removed from the constitution (thus paving the way for president Xi Jinping to continue his rule as long as he chooses), the Party censored many words and terms on social media which could indicate the public's displeasure. 'Yuan Shikai' and 'emperor' were among the words censored.

place, and the provinces of Yunnan, Guizhou and Guangxi went so far as to secede from the central government. In March 1916, Yuan found himself compelled to give up the imperial title, and in June of that year he died at the age of 56 from a kidney disorder: An affliction that, according to many, was aggravated by the humiliation of his forced abdication. After his death, some of the local warlords voiced their support for the Kuomintang government (which had fled to Guangzhou in 1920), but essentially, they did as they pleased – extorting farmers, trading in opium, and fighting one another. The most colourful amongst them was undoubtedly Feng Yuxiang, nicknamed the 'Christian general'. Just as in sixteenth-century Europe – when, according to the principle of *cuius regio, eius religio*, the prince determined the religion of his subjects – Feng ordered the large-scale conversion of his soldiers to Christianity. For baptisms, he reportedly even sprayed the converts with a fire hose at mass rallies.[15] The period of the warlords drove the intellectuals with their dream of freedom and democracy to despair. The progressive journalist and publisher Liang Qichao lamented that 'In China today only cunning, crooked, vile, and ruthless people can flourish.'[16]

The blow dealt to the 1912 elections, and the relapse into dictatorship that followed, contain two important history lessons. The positive conclusion is that the Chinese people are not afflicted with an autocratic gene that make them unsuited for democracy; less good news is that every movement that tries to give shape to the desire for freedom – from the 1912 elections to the 1989 demonstrations in Tiananmen Square – has always been followed by a violent reaction. The Australian sinologist W.J.F. Jenner draws the grim conclusion that the story of China comes down to a *history of tyranny* from which there is no escape.[17] That is perhaps too bleak, yet it is clear that China has not succeeded in following Japan, Korea, and Taiwan in their fruitful transformation from a Confucianist autocracy to a parliamentary democracy.

May 4th Movement

Such a development in China was entirely possible. In fact, the seeds for it were already sown, because in May 1919 another popular movement arose that could have put the country on a different, more pluralistic course. It was instigated by the Treaty of Versailles, which gave Japan (not China) sovereignty over the former German possessions in Shandong province. An infuriated reaction ensued. Just like seventy years later, thousands of students gathered in Tiananmen Square. They forced their way into the house of the minister of Trade – a man who maintained close ties to the Japanese government – and set it on fire. Impassioned pamphlets were handed out: 'China's territory may be conquered, but it cannot be given away! The Chinese people may be massacred, but they will not surrender! Our country is about to be annihilated. Up, brethren!'[18]

Protesting students, 4 May 1919

The May 4th Movement (as it later came to be called) was the first modern expression of public anger in China's history. The similarities with the movement in the spring of 1989 are striking: Student unions were set up, the movement spread rapidly to other towns and cities and there was strong support from the working class. In 1919, in Shanghai alone, 60,000 labourers in forty-three enterprises laid down their work. The May 4th Movement led to countless articles in newly-established magazines like *Shuguang* ('Dawn'), *Xin shehui* ('New Society'), and *Xin funü* ('New Woman'). Foreign intellectuals and writers were eagerly studied. The philosophers Bertrand Russell and John Dewey travelled across the country giving lectures; the Indian poet and Nobel Prize recipient Rabindranath Tagore publicly expressed his thoughts on aesthetics and non-violence, and in 1922 Albert Einstein visited the country *en route* to Japan, soon after publishing his ground-breaking theory of relativity. Norwegian Henrik Ibsen's *A Doll's House*, in which a woman leaves her husband to find her own way in life, was a smash hit amongst the country's young women seeking emancipation. Russell's companion, Dora Black, was dumbfounded when the young women from a girls' school in Peking asked her all kind of questions about marriage, free love, and contraceptives.[19] It was an unparalleled period of freedom in China's history – certainly unprecedented in the history of the People's Republic. Chang Ping, a well-known political analyst, describes it as follows: 'Chinese people in the late Qing and

Pro-Democracy Demonstration-Tiananmen Square 1989

early republican era were free to form political parties, publish newspapers and take part in rallies and strikes. Such forms of social protest are now not tolerated, no matter how unjust the social system is or how arrogant privilege and wealth becomes. Today's Communist party is thus the inheritor of a revolutionary tradition in an era in which revolution is banned.'[20]

June 4th: Another May 4th Nipped in the Bud

The impact of the student movement of 1989 was shorter, more violent and more dismal. Having started on 15 April, the demonstrations were already over by 4 June, when the soldiers and tanks of the People's Liberation Army cleared the square and hundreds – by some estimates thousands[21] – of people were killed. (By contrast, one student died on 4 May 1919 after being beaten by the police.) The cultural and political freedom that had flourished for six weeks in 1989 was soon restricted: A tsunami of propaganda contended that the student leaders were not acting as patriots or combating corruption (as they saw themselves, and as many in society saw them), but were counter-revolutionary troublemakers bent on 'undermining socialism'. Some of the student leaders were arrested, but the majority managed to escape abroad – a sign of the large-scale support they received from the people, for very few in China slip through the fine mesh of the Public Security Bureau's tracking network.

The hardliners within the Party believed that 'June 4th' was the consequence of a 'peaceful evolution' – a Western strategy that aims to undermine China's Socialist system and deviously conceals its hidden motives in the guise of cooperation and friendship.[22] The country's youth, with its dreams of freedom and democracy, is supposedly the specific target of this strategy. The Party's mistrust of the West's 'hidden motives' has since not diminished. When stepping down in 2012, President Hu Jintao warned that the West is extremely persistent in forcing 'peaceful evolution' upon China.[23] A century after the May 4th Movement, the uninhibited and curious stance towards the outside world has given way to suspicion and mistrust. Just like Master Sun, the author of *The Art of War*, the Party sees the world through a lens of conspiracy, concealment, and treachery.

Establishing the Communist Party

'The world under heaven, after a long period of division, tends to unite; after a long period of union, tends to divide. This has been so since antiquity.'[24] These first sentences from the *Romance of the Three Kingdoms* concisely reflect the oscillation between the forces of central and local authority during Chinese history. Periods of division invariably unleash forces that fight to reunite the country, producing individuals who feel religiously inspired to save China from its downfall. The 1920s are a good example of that kind of zeal. Driven to the country's south by the warlords, the Kuomintang pondered a strategy that would restore its control over the entire country. For support they looked to the Soviet Union – a young nation (it was founded in 1922) that advocated through its enticing vision that man must be liberated from his capitalist master. Armed with this idea, the Russian Communists had succeeded spectacularly in breaking the chains of tsarist despotism. For its part, the Soviet Union was glad to come to China's aid: With its gigantic population exploited by domestic and foreign capitalists, China constituted the logical springboard for realising Communism on a global level. This mission was entrusted to the Moscow-based Communist International (Comintern), which sent its delegate Mikhail Borodin to provide the Kuomintang with financial and organisational support.

In the meantime, however, the Kuomintang was not the only party carrying Sun Yatsen's revolutionary banner. On 23 July 1921, in a back room in Shanghai, fourteen revolutionaries gathered for the first congress of a political party that would become the largest and richest in the world: The Communist Party of China. The 27-year-old Mao Zedong was one of them, but the most striking co-founder was a barbarian with blond hair and a bushy moustache: Hendricus (Henk) Sneevliet from

Rotterdam, who had been sent by the Comintern in 1921 to help the Communists in
their organisational work. In Shanghai's Xingye Street, in the building where this
almost sacred Communist council took place, the patriarchs of the Party can still
be admired as life-size wax mannequins. Neatly dressed, Sneevliet sits somewhat
absent-minded at the table, as if as a foreigner he does not quite belong there – which
was probably the case, for in the annals of the Party he is barely mentioned. After his
departure from China in 1923 Sneevliet broke with the Comintern, though he remained
active as the leader of various left-wing splinter parties in the Netherlands. After the
Germans invaded, he joined the resistance; an act he would pay for with his life. The
Germans arrested him on 12 April 1942 and he was executed at Camp Amersfoort.
Sneevliet showed exceptional courage: Perhaps he even longed for a martyr's death.
Before he fell he sang 'The Internationale' at the top of his lungs.[25]

Break Between the Kuomintang and the Party

From the very beginning, the Comintern's primary goal was to create a 'United
Front' between the Communists and the Kuomintang – only then would the Chinese
revolution have any chance of winning. The collaboration initially seemed to be
successful, but after the death of Sun Yatsen in 1925 the relationship soon soured.
The new Kuomintang leader, Chiang Kai-shek, did not consider the Soviet model to
be suitable for his country and shifted more and more towards the right – or rather,
towards 'China', for left and right are Western political concepts that are of little use
in the Chinese context. Chiang was 'left-wing' in his social policy, which resulted in
widespread distribution of high-quality education in the country, but he was 'right-
wing' in his ties to the underworld and his preference for dictatorial authority. The
goal of his 'Northern Campaign', which he launched in 1926, was to bring the warlords
north of the Yangtze River under central authority. Militarily speaking, it was a big
success: In 1928, the country was united again for the first time since 1911. Yet the
common struggle did not bring the Kuomintang and the Party any closer together –
instead, it accentuated the ideological gap between the parties.
    Chiang Kai-shek's party was closely connected with individuals who had money
and power: The industrialists and merchants, as well as bosses of the secret societies
that dominated the trade in drugs and prostitution. The Communists were anti-
capitalist; just like the Bolsheviks in Russia, they believed in the historic role of the
Party as the 'Vanguard of the Proletariat' for realising the classless society. That did
not mean that the Party was kept on Moscow's leash: Already during the 1920's the
Chinese and Russian sister-parties had been at each other's throats. The core of the
dispute was tactical in nature: How could the classless society be made reality? The
Soviets advocated a revolution by the industrial proletariat, but Mao rejected that

Chiang Kai-shek and Mao Zedong

approach because China was barely industrialised at that time. The subsequent Great Helmsman (his omnipotence would only be confirmed at the Zunyi Conference in 1935) fixed his hopes on the hundreds of millions peasants, who – as serfs bound to the land – saw no chance of escaping a countryside ravaged by warlords' soldiers and bandits. The peasants' situation grew even more desperate when the dikes of the Yellow River broke in 1931 and 1938, with an estimated four million losing their lives in the first disaster alone.[26]

United Front

The strategy for the United Front was formulated by the Party for the first time in 1924. Its goal was to 'keep as many allies together as possible in order to beat the common enemy'. This strategy distinguishes between the arch-enemy (like Japan after 1931) and lesser enemies (the nationalists, or China's national minorities agitating for independence). Temporary alliances could be forged with these lesser enemies to beat the greater enemy together. The end goal, however, continued to be the absolute, indivisible victory of the Party. Deng Xiaoping breathed new life into this strategy in 1979 and the *Tongzhanbu* ('United Front Work Department', which sits immediately under the Party's Central Committee) is still responsible for relations between the Party and China's ethnic and political minorities today.

In 1927 the two revolutionary contenders finally clashed in Shanghai. Chiang Kai-shek had become convinced that Communist infiltrators wanted to take command of his party from within, and with the help of the mob boss Du Yuesheng (nicknamed 'Big-Eared Du') he attacked the labour unions that were controlled by the Party. The purge soon extended to other towns: In the days that followed an estimated 5,000 to 8,000 people died, though according to some sources it was even more.[27] The later premier of the People's Republic, Zhou Enlai, just barely escaped being arrested and executed. The massacre marked the beginning of the Chinese civil war that would last more than twenty years. In spite of the increasing threat from Japan, Chiang Kai-shek was determined to eradicate the *Gongfei* ('Communist Bandits'). The Japanese 'were a disease of the skin', Chiang declared, while the Communists 'were a disease of the heart'.[28] In a series of campaigns Chiang surrounded the Soviet republic Mao had established in Jiangxi province. But with an utmost effort Mao managed to break the siege in October 1934, and began his famous Long March. This expedition, which was later elevated to epic heights, led the Communist elite to Yan'an, a town located on the Loess Plateau in Shaanxi province. There Mao and his followers were safe from attacks by Chiang Kai-shek and could begin rebuilding the badly battered Party.

Long March

In the historiography of the Party, the Long March has taken on mythic proportions. The deprivations experienced, the march's length (ten thousand kilometres) and the number of victims – only twenty thousand of the hundred thousand who began the march survived – gave the Party a reputation for tenacity as well as a story of origin for the 'New China' that the country's youth could identify with. Many of them found their way to Yan'an and joined the Communists. Not just Chinese: The American journalist Edgar Snow spent some time there, and his subsequent bestseller *Red Star over China* describes the atmosphere of camaraderie and idealism. Those who survived the Long March formed the steely cadre of the Party, which supplied the first generation that were to rule the People's Republic of China. Occupying crucial positions in government and big business, their descendants still form the country's elite.

United Front against the Japanese

Chiang's stubborn refusal – even in the face of the Japanese threat – to do business with the Communists led to a rebellion within his own party. In 1936 he was arrested by the 'young marshal' Zhang Xueliang, who forced him to conclude an alliance with Mao*. This devil's pact accomplished little against the Japanese war machine that steamrolled the country in the years from 1937 to 1945: The parties barely cooperated, each leaving the other to do the dirty work. The stalemate that followed left the Japanese in control of the towns in the east, the Communists controlling the countryside, and the Kuomintang (with American aid) standing their ground in the south-west. Despite its military supremacy Japan could not conquer China as a whole. It ran into the same problem as the German *Wehrmacht* in Russia: The country and its population were simply too large to fully control. After the atom bomb laid waste to Hiroshima in August 1945, the Japanese withdrew from China, making the reconstruction of the country possible. For two years the American general George Marshall (famous for the 'Marshall Plan' that helped to rebuild post-war Europe) tried to persuade the parties to cooperate. But his mission was doomed to failure, for neither Mao nor Chiang was willing to share power. The fighting quickly flared up again but, unlike in the 1930s, the Communists now had the upper hand: Thanks to large-scale land reforms the Party had acquired the support of the poor farmers, and their army, recruited from peasants, was much more motivated than that of the Kuomintang.

In the end, support from the Soviet Union was the decisive factor. In the final days of the Second World War Stalin declared war on Japan, invaded Manchuria and handed its factories and military arsenals over to the Communists. The Kuomintang controlled the towns, but because of their economic mismanagement, inflation rose to unprecedented heights, reducing a large segment of the population to destitution. A large sack of rice costing 6.7 million yuan in June 1948 sold for 63 million yuan two months later. According to some historians, this was the key reason why the Kuomintang lost the Mandate of Heaven so soon after the victory over Japan.[29] After fighting a bitter civil war of four years the curtain fell: On 31 January 1949 the Communists occupied Peking and soon afterwards Chiang fled to Taiwan with a following of nearly two million people. The revolutionary adventure that had begun in a backroom in Shanghai on 23 July 1921, came to a triumphant apotheosis twenty-eight years later. On 1 October 1949, looking out over the sea of people assembled on Tiananmen Square, Mao declared in his shrill, high voice that '*Zhonghua renmin gongheguo jintian chengli le!*' ('The Chinese People's Republic is established today!').

A new dynasty had seized power, a new era had dawned.

---

* Chiang never forgave Zhang Xueliang this act of 'treason'. Soon after the Xi'an incident he had him put under house arrest, from which he was released only in the late '80's. Following ancient tradition, Zhang spent his long years of imprisonment as a scholar of literature and collector of fine arts.

Re-Evaluating the Republican Period

In the early years of the People's Republic, Communist propaganda disdainfully regarded the previous Republican period as a sinister time of division, corruption and impotence against foreign aggression. These attacks followed the customary pattern of dismissing the previous dynasty as morally depraved, for only then could the rise of the new imperial house be justified. Under the regime of the pragmatic Deng Xiaoping (paramount leader: 1978–1997), this criticism decreased, though in recent times it has grown again, undoubtedly as a result of the Party's uncertainty about its own legitimacy. In a recent article, the nationalistic newspaper *Global Times* vehemently raged against 'a small number of intellectuals' who contend that the earlier Republican period was one of '"democracy, freedom and respect for wisdom"'. According to *Global Times*, the Kuomintang Republican period was in fact 'rotten at the core, subject to foreign powers' and 'cannot be compared to present-day China in terms of national comprehensive strength, international status, level of livelihood and social security'.[30] Apart from the propaganda that colours every official description of the past, the Party does have a point: The clique surrounding Chiang was disgustingly wealthy, millions of peasants were impoverished, and the resistance towards Japan was half-hearted.

Even so, in what would later be called the 'Nanking Decade' (1927–1937), there were indeed economic and social advances. The increase in schools and universities was spectacular: The number of universities grew from 44 in 1927 to 108 in 1935, enrolling almost twice the number of students (from 25,198 to 41,922).[31] The total length of motorways doubled and there were 45,000 cars on the road in China in 1936 – nearly three times as many as ten years before.[32] The economist Gregory Chow even contends that it was on account of the liberal-economic success of the Nanking Decade that Deng Xiaoping dared to implement his own economic reforms in 1978.[33]

Even the foreign business community did well in those years. The annual reports of Unilever show that the highest revenues and profits were being made at the end of the 1930s – a striking statistic, given that Japan had invaded China in 1937. Sales of soap and margarine were evidently not impacted by the state of war that China found itself in.[34] In view of China's long tradition of censorship, the cultural freedom of the Nanking Decade was even more surprising. As a melting pot of many nationalities, Shanghai provided a safe haven to White émigrés from the Russian Civil War and Jewish refugees who had fled Nazi Germany. Life was lavish and decadent: Writers, poets, painters, and filmmakers who were persecuted in the rest of China flooded the 'Paris of the East'. Jiang Qing, the later wife of Mao Zedong, was one of these 'cultural refugees'. Ironically, she would, during the 1960s, become the high priestess of puritanical culture in China. In her Shanghai years she acted in romantic B-movies under her artistic name Lan Ping, and was said to have been entangled in various amorous scandals.

聯華畫報

第九卷

第三期

每冊一角

Jiang Qing

The People's Republic as the Successor of the Republic?

Rather than representing a break from the old regime, contemporary China is in many ways a continuation of the Republican period: The country's elite are exorbitantly rich, the gap between urban and rural incomes is widening dramatically, foreign business interests exert a powerful influence and government – especially local government – increasingly enlists mobsters to intimidate the people. In one regard, however, the difference is a major and continuous one: The Republic of China never succeeded in exercising its sovereignty over Chinese territory in its entirety – with the possible exception of the years 1928–1931, when Chiang Kai-shek had ended his Northern Campaign and the Japanese had not yet annexed Manchuria. The Western powers supported Chiang in his struggle against the Japanese, but the relationship was not one among equals: Not until 1943 were the last unequal treaties renounced. This led, for example, to the humiliating situation that during the 1940s British warships were still free to sail up the Yangtze River unhindered. After the defeat of Japan, the Kuomintang was finally sovereign in its own country, but its strength was soon sapped by the civil war with the Communists. Only with the establishment of the People's Republic in 1949 did a regime come to power that – for the first time since the 1839 Opium War – exercised undivided sovereignty. Mao could with good reason contend that the Party had brought the Century of Humiliation to an end.

Who is the Heir of Sun Yatsen?

If the Party has indeed begun to look more and more like the Kuomintang, who then is the heir to Sun Yatsen and his 'Three Principles'? This question is not only of academic interest, for both parties contend that the state they created resembles the society that Sun Yatsen envisaged. In the People's Republic of China, the principle of *Minsheng* ('welfare for the people') appears to have been realised. Most of the people have clothing, food, and housing, though the goal of a fair distribution of this prosperity remains a distant dream: China is one of the most inequitable countries in the world. Moreover, the side-effects of the economic boom – the gap between rich and poor, the environmental nightmare and the corruption – are so dramatic that 'welfare for the people' as a source of political legitimacy is increasingly less valid. The failure to bring *Minquan* ('power to the people') about is even more obvious, even if the Party wants us to believe that 'the people are the master of the state'. Sun Yatsen was certainly not convinced of the virtues of democracy (he initially promoted a transitional phase of military government to educate the people 'in wisdom and responsibility'), yet when the Qing dynasty abruptly fell, he did announce the general elections of 1912. That feat has not been repeated by the People's Republic, neither are there any plans to phase in democracy – certainly not under the current leadership.

As far as the principle of Minzu ('nationalism' = 'boss in your own country') is concerned, the Party's claim to being Sun Yatsen's true heir is better founded. The People's Republic of China is a powerful, independent country, free of foreign intervention. Strangely enough, the regime in Beijing sees this differently: China will not be free from foreign domination until the 'territorial integrity' of the country is restored. Until only a few years ago that meant reunification with Taiwan, but after the 2008 Olympic Games the scope of this mission statement has broadened: Sovereignty over the entire South China Sea has been elevated to a 'core interest' with the same political importance as the reunification with Taiwan; the dispute with Japan over the Senkaku (Diaoyu) Islands has been placed in the same dramatic light.[35] To justify the latter claim, the Second World War is dragged into the mix. 'China's will to defend its national sovereignty and territorial integrity is firm, and its resolve to uphold the outcome of the World Anti-Fascist War [standard Party speak for the Second World War] will not be shaken by any force.'[36] The reason for broadening the call for 'reunification' has everything to do with the shaky domestic legitimacy of the Party: 'Nationalism is to provide a new ideological basis for legitimacy on the one hand, and to serve as a new rallying force to develop a national aspiration around the leadership of the Party on the other' – as Professor Steve Tsang of the University of Nottingham rightly observes.[37]

With its base now in Taiwan, the Kuomintang has a stronger claim than the Party for seeing itself as the heir to the 'Three Principles': The political structure of the island is democratic, the people are more wealthy and equal than in China, and Taiwan is de facto independent. On paper, the Kuomintang pursues the reunification of the 'Two Chinas'; but in practice, the policy is oriented towards maintaining the status quo. The 'territorial integrity' of the island has therefore already been realised.

The Unshakeable Position of Sun Yatsen

There is one issue the parties on either side of the Taiwan Strait fully agree upon: The position of Sun Yatsen. The Kuomintang has elevated 10 October – the day in 1911 that Sun's Republicans rose up against the Qing dynasty – as a national holiday, and the banknotes of Taiwan still show his wise, paternal face. In China, every major town has a Sun Yatsen Square, Park, or Street, and on the national holiday of the People's Republic his ten-metre portrait hangs above Tiananmen Square. Until the end of the 1980s he was accompanied by Marx, Engels, Lenin, and Stalin, but these patriarchs of Communism – whom the people of Beijing derisively called the 'Gang of Four' after the clique surrounding Mao – are now no longer taken out of mothballs.

Criticising Sun Yatsen is simply *not done* in China; it is almost even more dangerous than criticising Mao himself. In 2011 – one hundred years after the Republican revolution – Chen Zhong, the president of the newspaper *Nanfengchuang* ('South Wind Window'), was demoted for approving an article that dismissed Sun Yatsen as a traitor to the country. In his struggle against the warlords, Sun was supposedly willing to cede Manchuria and Hainan Island to the Japanese in exchange for their military support. He even intended to give them control over collecting tax revenues in Beijing, Tianjin and Inner Mongolia. The censors who dealt with Chen Zhong said that the article was directed against the Party and that it constituted defamation of Sun Yatsen, the 'true revolutionary pioneer'.[38]

CHAPTER 4

Xi Jinping Has a Dream

Fight corruption too little and destroy the country; fight it too much and destroy the Party.

Chen Yun

When President Xi Jinping took office in March 2013, hopes were high that he would set out on a new, liberal course. The feats of his father Xi Zhongxun strengthened these expectations. As Party Secretary in the late 1970s of the southern province of Guangdong, the elder Xi had played an important role in setting up the 'Special Economic Zones' where foreign businesses were allowed to invest in China for the first time since 1949. Xi Sr was not only a reformer, but reputedly also a humanist. During the 1950s he was responsible in Qinghai province for relations between the Han Chinese and Tibetans. The land reforms introduced by the Communists had thrown the local economy into disarray and incited hatred towards the Chinese occupier, but Xi did not respond repressively. He mitigated the worst excesses, and even after the Tibetan uprising against these measures was beaten down, he showed a conciliatory attitude. His flexibility made an impression upon the young Dalai Lama, who in 1954 was staying in Beijing for a few months. The spiritual leader called the elder Xi 'very friendly, comparatively open-minded and very nice'. He even gave the elder Xi a wristwatch as a present. According to the Dalai Lama's brother, who met Xi Zhongxun at the beginning of the 1980s, he was still wearing the watch at that time.[1]

Xi Jr is reportedly cut from the same cloth, and would like to use the office of paramount leader to realise the dream of his father: A liberal and reform-minded China. For various reasons this argument amounts to wishful thinking. First, it is debatable whether the elder Xi was indeed as liberal as the annals would have us believe. The sinologist Frank Dikötter has uncovered how at the beginning of the 1950s Xi Zhongxun overtook Mao 'on the left' by pointing out to him that the number of victims of the anti-corruption campaign at that time was too low: In the north-west of the country alone, there should not be 340,000, but more than one million people detained.[2] Secondly, the son's character is not a carbon copy of his father's – not even in a country like China where filial obedience to parental authority is considered the supreme good. More than his father, Xi Jinping seems to be fascinated by power, and in order to grab it he has skilfully kept a low profile throughout his career. In

American embassy documents made public by WikiLeaks, an old childhood friend (now an academic) describes the president as 'supremely pragmatic and a realist, driven not by ideology but by a combination of ambition and "self-protection." [...] Xi has a genuine sense of "entitlement," believing that members of his generation are the "legitimate heirs" to the revolutionary achievements of their parents and therefore "deserve to rule China." [...] Xi was reserved and detached and "difficult to read," said the professor. He had a "strong mind" and understood power, but "from day one, never showed his hand."'[3]

Taking clear positions (which can become suddenly undesirable when the political winds shift) makes an individual vulnerable to his enemy's slings and arrows. That is why Chinese leaders carefully keep a low profile, rarely showing who they are or what they think. Xi is no exception to this rule – just like the strategist Sun Zi, he prefers to remain 'invisible' – though the flip side of this tactic is that policy lines are not clearly laid out, and the bureaucracy must guess at 'the emperor's will'. This may lead to paralysis, or (worse) to 'vigorous' measures that are supposedly in line with what the paramount leader stands for. The siting in 2014 of a Chinese oil platform in a maritime territory disputed by Vietnam (which led to deadly anti-Chinese riots in that country) is a good example: The decision was supposedly taken without Xi's approval.[4] In his dealings with foreign leaders the president also shows his imperial instincts. During a meeting of APEC (Asia-Pacific Economic Cooperation) countries in Beijing in November 2014, Xi left the Japanese leader Abe in limbo for a long time as to whether he would deign to see him. Foreign dignitaries visiting the court in imperial times were likewise (sometimes for weeks) kept in the dark whether the 'August Sovereign' would have time for an audience. The Party's mouthpiece, the People's Daily, also noticed similarities between the APEC conference and China's imperial era. The welcoming banquet for foreign leaders reminded the newspaper of China's glory days, when vassal states came to bring tribute to the emperor in Peking. Even the dinner service, the paper noted, was yellow – the colour that during feudal times was only allowed to be used by the emperor.[5]

But the clearest evidence that Xi Jinping is anything but a closet liberal is given by himself. His relentless march towards supreme authority seriously took off in 2015. In October of that year, a resolution was passed that thenceforth forbade Party members from making 'groundless comments on national policies'. Likewise, Party members 'who defame the nation, the Party and State leaders or distort the history of the nation and the Party will be held accountable'.[6] In a statement from January 2016, the official Xinhua ('New China') News Agency made it crystal clear that the 'leadership of the Party' consists of Xi alone: Party members should 'be aligned with the central leadership of the party led by Xi in actions and thoughts'.[7] Xi's unofficial ascendancy to the throne followed in October 2016, when a plenary session of the Party anointed him as 'core leader' – an honorary title his predecessor Hu Jintao never managed to acquire.[8] Not since the days of Deng Xiaoping as demigod of China (when he was in de facto control from 1978–1997) has one man been able to seize so much power.

The New Emperor of China

The Communist Party of China (CPC) held its first congress, in Shanghai, in July 1921. It was a minuscule affair: Only fifty-seven men took part in it, and for fear of arrest (the Party was still illegal at the time) the site for the gathering was changed halfway through the congress. The difference between the 1st and 19th congress, held in Beijing in October 2017, is one between day and night. As the country's only power broker, the Party itself now determines who is arrested, and the number of participants amounted to more than 2,300 members. As to the content, however, the Party congresses have not changed: The 'correct' doctrine is proclaimed, and the man approved by a handful of Party elders is 'elected' or 're-elected' as the Secretary General of the Communist Party. In a strange way (given that the country's doctrine is still atheist Marxism-Leninism), Party congresses are reminiscent of the councils of the Catholic church with their fixed script, liturgical repetitions of sacred words (i.e. Party jargon) and semi-religious rituals, such as the slow and deliberate stroll of the great leader to the platform where he will deliver his speech of 3.5 hours. And just as the word of the Pope was declared 'infallible' at the first Vatican Council of 1870, since October 2017 nobody is allowed to doubt the words of Xi Jinping, because as the 'core' of the Party he is the ultimate lawmaker, the source of orthodoxy.

In the run-up to the 18th Party Congress in October 2012, the signs of Xi Jinping's omnipotence were anything but clear. His three predecessors (Zhao Ziyang, Jiang Zemin and Hu Jintao) had all been designated by Deng Xiaoping. Deng's prestige was such that Hu was only appointed as Party Secretary five years after Deng's death in 1997, yet nobody dared to question Deng's decision. But who would succeed Hu himself? The two likely candidates were Hu Jintao's protegé Li Keqiang and Xi Jinping. The 86-year-old Jiang Zemin chaired an 'electoral commission' of Party elders that was to take a decision. Given the secrecy of the Party's inner proceedings, nobody (certainly in the West) knows exactly what went on, but what we do know is that various factions negotiated for months to reach a consensus. In the West we call these political groups for simplicity's sake 'conservative' or 'liberal', but their composition is determined first of all by family connections, and a shared history of attending the same schools and careers. Xi Jinping seemed to cruise to an easy victory, but then something remarkable happened: Right before the Party congress of November 2012 he disappeared from the face of the earth. Because no information was provided about his absence, rumours started flying around: Xi supposedly did not have the requisite support from the most senior members of the Party, and Li Keqiang had turned from a dark horse into a winning horse. Xi Jinping was even said to have had a heart attack.[9] After a few weeks, however, Xi resurfaced in apparently perfect health and was appointed Party Chairman.

'The rest is history', but the public was in for one more surprise. The National People's Congress (China's parliament) still had to ratify Xi Jinping as president, and in March 2013 it duly convened to do so. Since the People's Congress is in no way a representative assembly in the Western sense of that word, a wave of astonishment rippled through the hall when the results of the secret ballot appeared on a large monitor: 2,952 members of parliament had voted yea, three had abstained, and one parliamentarian had voted nay. On the internet, speculation about the identity of the solitary dissident immediately went into overdrive, but when search terms like 'nay-vote' were censored, the digital debate soon ended. Some bloggers recalled the fate of Zhang Dongsun – a philosopher and member of the government's highest advisory body, the Chinese People's Political Consultative Conference (CPPCC) – who had the audacity to vote against the elevation of Mao as the paramount leader in 1949. Accused of 'selling state secrets', he was thrown out of the Party and at the height of the Cultural Revolution, in 1968, arrested at the age of 82. Nothing more was heard of him, until his family got word in 1973 that he had died in prison.[10]

In 2018, any opposition (as far as we know) to Xi has dissolved into thin air, and he certainly isn't hiding anymore. On the contrary: The president is constantly making headlines, not only in the state-owned media, but also in the news outlets on social media. So it surprised no one that Xi Jinping was elected for the second time at the 19th Party Congress as Secretary-General of the Party – this time without any 'nay' vote. More surprising was the composition of the Politburo Standing Committee, the seven-man body representing the Party's (and therefore the country's) top leadership. Many China watchers had predicted that Xi would surround himself with his loyal followers – people like Chen Xi, the no. 2 in the powerful Organisation Division (responsible for the promotions and demotions of the Party cadre), with whom Xi shared a room at Beijing's Tsinghua University during the 1970s. Or with Cai Qi, the Party Secretary of Beijing, who held various high positions in Zhejiang province when Xi was Party Secretary there from 2002 to 2007. Even Wang Qishan, the widely feared chairman of the Central Commission for Discipline Inspection and Xi's ally since day one, was not included in the elite seven-man corps. In view of Wang's unconditional loyalty to the president, his 'successes' (depending upon how you see it) in the fight against corruption, but also his financial and economic expertise, many had expected this. However, the 69-year-old Wang faithfully observed the unwritten Party rule of *Qishang Baxia*: 'At 67 (or younger), you may stay; at 68 (or older), you are out'.

On the other hand, it surprised many observers that Premier Li Keqiang and Wang Yang (appointed in March 2018 as chairman of the Chinese People's Political Consultative Conference) did make it to the Politburo Standing Committee. Both politicians are (just like the former president Hu Jintao) associated with the Communist Youth League, which has been harshly attacked by Xi Jinping as being 'arrogant' and 'out of touch'.[11]

Another surprise were the appointments of Party ideologue Wang Huning and Shanghai Party Secretary Han Zheng (appointed in March 2018 as first vice-premier) to the same body: Both men are seen as accomplices of the former president Jiang Zemin, whose clique – according to some China experts – was (as we shall shortly see) the real target of Xi Jinping's merciless anti-corruption campaign.

Does the president then have less power than it appears? Is his omnipotence restricted by invisible opposing forces? We (and that also includes the vast majority of the Chinese people) don't really know, but perhaps we should not read too much into the backgrounds and rankings of those surrounding Xi Jinping. Wherever their personal and factional loyalties exactly lie, Li Keqiang, Li Zhanshu, Wang Yang, Wang Huning, Zhao Leji, and Han Zheng (named in the order of their hierarchical positions within the Politburo Standing Committee) have since 2012 worked together with the president intensively (Li Zhanshu since the 1980s), and have apparently subjugated themselves to the new emperor. By appointing them to the highest body, Xi Jinping is also making a gesture to his predecessors (and clique leaders) Jiang Zemin and Hu Jintao, without diminishing his own formidable powers. By doing so he shows respect for their age and highest level of service to the country (both men are former presidents). But most of all he gives them something without which human relations cannot flourish in China: He gives them face.

Two other results of the 19th Congress make it crystal clear that Xi Jinping has become the uncrowned emperor of China. The paranoid Mao Zedong tolerated no competition, and purged his designated successors before they had a chance to succeed him. After assuming power in 1978, Deng Xiaoping decided that the new Party Secretary should be groomed while the incumbent was still in office. Presidents Jiang Zemin and Hu Jintao thus appointed, at the beginning of their second term in office, the heir apparent to the Standing Committee – although Hu Jintao's preferred candidate, Li Keqiang, lost out to Xi Jinping and had to settle for the number 2 ranking in the Party hierarchy. Xi breaks with this tradition. All six men seated together with Xi on the new Standing Committee will according to the principle of *Qishang Baxia* be too old in 2022 (the year when the 20th Party Congress will be held) to take over the helm for another ten years. Li Zhanshu, the president's only ally on the Standing Committee, will be as old as 72. Hence the Beijing rumour mill was getting fired up that Xi Jinping wants to continue to rule for an indefinite period. He would then be breaking that same age-limit principle (he will be 69 in 2022), but would also be disregarding Deng Xiaoping's inspired amendment to the constitution that the president cannot remain in office for more than two five-year periods. Just before finalizing this book (April 2018), the

National People's Congress indeed agreed to abolish that constitutional limitation to presidential rule.* Xi Jinping can now be president, party secretary and commander in chief as long as he wants – a 'Holy Trinity' of positions that will give his rule an imperial, even divine status. The divinity of his rule was even further cemented by that other outcome of the 19th Party Congress: His 'Thought' has been elevated to the law of the land.

Xi Jinping's 'Thought'

Right after taking office at the end of 2012, Xi launched the slogan of the 'Chinese Dream'. In doing so he followed in the footsteps of his predecessors, who all added their 'thinking' or 'theory' to the canon of Marxist/Maoist philosophy. Jiang Zemin, the paramount leader from 1989 to 2002, introduced the theory of the 'Three Represents' (*Sange daibiao*), a doctrine so vague that most Chinese do not understand it. It comes down to the right of the Party to rule, because the Party represents 'China's advanced productive forces, the orientation of China's advanced culture and the fundamental interests of the overwhelming majority of the Chinese people'.[12] If we unwrap this wording from its Communist load, something interesting is revealed: The Party is legitimate not because of its role as 'Vanguard of the Proletariat' (with its goal of establishing the classless society), but because it represents the majority of the people. It even represents 'advanced productive forces'; in everyday language these people are called entrepreneurs. In other words: The Party is allowed to rule China *because* it represents capitalists. This sort of ideological virtuosity explains why the Chinese regime did not perish after the fall of the Berlin Wall in 1989, but managed to survive. A less generous explanation is that the Party has shown itself to be a master of political opportunism.

Jiang Zemin's successor Hu Jintao (2002–2012) came up with the idea of 'putting people first', but this humanistic slogan was compensated for by his second article of faith: A 'scientific outlook on development' – a catchphrase that indicates that Marxist thinking is still strong in the People's Republic, for the notion that a country can develop in a 'scientific' manner is no longer espoused in the West. That is why Xi Jinping's catchphrase of the 'Chinese Dream' is all the more remarkable, for dreams cannot be easily measured or scientifically proven.

---

* At the National People's Congress held in March 2018, Xi's trusted ally Wang Qishan was appointed as vice-president. He will focus on foreign affairs, especially the complex relationship with the United States. As with the presidency, there is no longer a term limit to the vice-presidency. Wang's return to power through the 'backdoor' of the NPC shows that having a position in the Standing Committee of the Politburo is no longer a benchmark for wielding real power.

What does Xi dream about? Given the tendency of Chinese leaders to speak in bombastic, frequently empty slogans, Xi's description of the dream is remarkably to the point: 'national rejuvenation, improvement of people's livelihoods, prosperity, construction of a better society and military strengthening'[13] – usually summed up as 'the Great Rejuvenation of the Chinese Nation'. During the 19th Party Congress, Xi unfortunately reverted to Partyspeak when he presented his thinking as 'Xi Jinping Thought on Socialism with Chinese Characteristics for a New Era'. With the typical predilection of Chinese leaders for outlining splendid, long-term visions, Xi outlined a three-part roadmap towards socialist utopia. First, by 2020, a 'moderately prosperous society' will be realized. The next phase will take another fifteen years, and be devoted to the completion of the 'Socialist Modernisation'. Finally, by 2050, China will be a country that in terms of national strength and international influence knows no peers. China will then 'be prosperous, strong, democratic, culturally advanced, harmonious, and beautiful'.[14]

How will this ideal Socialist state become reality? By committing to innovation, cultural excellence, a new harmonious relationship with nature, a peaceful international environment, and (last, but certainly not least) a strong military that will be among the best in the world. Naturally 'with Chinese characteristics', because no 'thought' of the president is complete without adding these three words. The same goes for the 'democratic China' that will have emerged in 2050, for – as Sun Yatsen already posited a century ago – the Party needs to 'guide' the people in exercising their democratic rights. As Xi Jinping himself puts it: 'We will improve the way the Party exercises leadership and governance to ensure that it leads the people in effectively governing the country. We will expand the orderly political participation to see that in accordance with the law they engage in democratic election, consultations, decision-making, management and oversight'.[15] In the same speech the president makes clear – in a refreshing break with Partyspeak – what he actually means: 'Government, the military, society and schools, north, south, east and west – the party leads them all.'[16]

The 'Thought on Socialism with Chinese Characteristics for a New Era' may sound cutting-edge, but actually it is a case of old wine in new bottles: Every ruler that comes to power proclaims his rule to be the beginning of a new age in which everything would be better and purer. Xi does not deviate from the Marxist-Maoist tradition of the People's Republic, yet he is made from a different mould than his predecessors: He has amassed vast powers, centralized the government and waged a moral campaign against corruption and decadence. In doing so, he shows a striking resemblance with Zhu Yuanzhang of the Ming Dynasty. This ruthless warlord fought many battles before he founded the Ming Dynasty in 1368 and took the dynastic name of Hong Wu ('Vastly Martial'). After coming to power, he reorganised the government by abolishing the office of prime minister. In his own words: 'Although there were some virtuous prime ministers, many of them were evil men who monopolized power and confused administration.'[17] The prime minister Hu Weiyong was duly executed for plotting against the throne. It did not stop there. Hong Wu waged a moral crusade to (in the words of one academic) 'not just reunify China politically, but also to carry out the ethical remaking of its people'.[18] To this purpose he wrote the 'Ancestral Instruction', a book containing moral exhortations and observations on politics and society – quite similar to Xi Jinping's sayings collected in the book 'The governance of China'. Hong Wu relentlessly hunted down corrupt officials by making use of the Censorate, a supra-legal body that flayed and executed a large number of officials – in some cases their family members as well. Xi Jinping's methods are different, but just like the present day 'Central Commission for Discipline Inspection' (recently renamed as the 'National Supervisory Commission') Hong Wu's Censorate was not an independent institution, but according to a group of academics of Beijing Normal University a 'tool for the emperor to rule his courtiers and plebeians'.[19]

A final difference between Xi Jinping and his communist predecessors is the nature of his 'Thought'. Firstly, because it is connected to his name – an honour not accorded to the musings of Jiang Zemin (the theory of the 'Three Represents') or Hu Jintao (the 'Scientific Outlook on Development'). Secondly, Xi Jinping *Thinks* – a mental activity that in the hierarchy of the Communist scriptures ranks much higher than formulating 'theories' or having an 'outlook'. By connecting his name to this 'Thought' during his lifetime, Xi has elevated himself to the same heights as Mao.

Chinese Dream

The well-known *New York Times* journalist Thomas Friedman has been called the *auctor intellectualis* of this catchphrase. In his column 'China needs its own dream' from 3 October 2012, Friedman argued for 'a new Chinese Dream that marries people's expectations of prosperity with a more sustainable China'. After his appointment as Party Secretary in November 2012, Xi Jinping launched the 'Chinese Dream' that the whole nation should aspire to realize. In particular, he called upon the youth 'to dare to dream, work assiduously to fulfil the dreams and contribute to the revitalization of the nation'. Since then, many have taken this notion of the Chinese Dream and run with it. Some dream of a better environment and sustainable development, others of a wealthier and better existence. The liberal newspaper *Southern Weekly* tried to post the article 'China Dream: a dream of constitutionalism', but because it advocated for a separation of political powers it did not make it past the censors. For the Party, some dreams are a nightmare.[20]

The End of Leadership by Consensus

The idea of an omnipresent Party ('north, south, east and west...') does not come out of thin air. Since the beginning of his first term in office Xi Jinping started emphasizing it, for instance at the commemoration of Mao Zedong's hundred-twentieth birthday on 26 December 2013, 'Persistent effort will enable the CPC to always be at the core of leadership for the cause of socialism with Chinese characteristics.'[21] The Party has since 1949 always been at the centre of Chinese politics, but in his relentless pursuit of autocracy Xi distinguishes himself from his predecessors. Having experienced first-hand to which disasters Mao's megalomaniacal decisions had led, Deng Xiaoping saw collective leadership as the solution for neutralising the whims of future 'great leaders'. Xi breaks with this tradition. During the third plenum of the 18th Party Congress held in November 2013, two powerful commissions were set up that supersede the Party's bureaucracy: The Commission of National Security, and the Central Leading Group for Comprehensively Deepening Economic Reforms. Both are presided over by Xi. The latter chairmanship constitutes a second break with tradition, for ultimate responsibility for the economic dossier was previously left to the premier.

Now, in 2018, Xi is the chair of just about everything. In addition to the presidency and the chairmanship of the Party, he heads commissions or 'leading groups' in the areas of defence, national security, internet security, deepening reforms, financial and economic affairs. The question is whether this accumulation of power benefits the country: Decisions must be not only formulated but also carried out, and China's colossal bureaucratic apparatus is still responsible for that. This may lead to a stalemate. The execution of the decision to partially privatise state-owned companies – a sensitive issue in a country that still calls itself Communist – is left to the Ministry of Finance, the State Council (China's cabinet), and the Organisation Department of the Party. Because of the conflicting interests of these three organisations, little has been achieved so far.[22]

A New Mao?

Straight after his appointment as Party Secretary in 2012, Xi Jinping visited Shenzhen – one of the four Special Economic Zones that Deng Xiaoping had established in 1979, and which symbolised the opening of China to the outside world. In a speech on the occasion of Deng's hundred-tenth birthday (in August 2014), Xi continued in that vein by praising the courage of the Little Helmsman for 'breaking the old rules and making new ones'.[23] The Party's propaganda apparatus quickly jumped on the bandwagon: 'To reignite a nation, Xi carries Deng's torch!'[24] trumpeted the New China News Agency. To show his human side, Xi is portrayed as a man of the people, a

Xi Jinping with his father and Peng Liyuan (on the left, in traditional Chinese dress)

loving family man and spouse – just like Deng in his time. The photo of the loving son pushing his old father in a wheelchair is famous all over China. *Xi Dada* ('Uncle Xi') has become the nickname often used for the president. Referring to the many corrupt officials Xi is taking down, the first lines of a popular song go, 'If you want to marry, marry someone like Xi Dada, who is decisive in his acts and serious in his work; no matter whether it's flies or tigers, monsters and freaks, he will all get them down and never let go.'[25]

His flamboyant wife, Peng Liyuan, a former singer and major-general in the People's Liberation Army, adds even more colour to the personification of Chinese politics. In contrast to the dreary, unremarkable first ladies before her, Peng makes a striking impression with her refined taste and fashionable dresses. In 2013, she made the list of best-dressed women in *Vanity Fair*. Her looks have not gone unnoticed outside China too. 'I think she is terrific,' said President Trump during the visit of Xi Jinping and Peng Liyuan to the United States in April 2017.[26]

In the first eighteen months of his presidency, Xi's name was mentioned more often in the *People's Daily* than any other leader since Mao. And just like in the Mao era, the face of the Party Chairman is everywhere to be seen, not only on propaganda posters but also on amulets that protect those wearing them from evil.[27] A little book with sayings from the paramount leader has even been published, with subjects ranging from the mundane to the more profound. Expressions like 'Nepotism will irritate the public' or 'Some officials only think of flattering their superiors' will not leave many Chinese spellbound, but others are more arresting because they give a hint of what the Leader is thinking: 'In some cases one's conscience is enough to make a judgement'.[28]

Deng was cast from an entirely different mould than Xi. He thoroughly disliked any form of personality cult, but also had a different view on how to rule the country. The only way, in his view, that the country could recover from Mao's disastrous economic policies was to create a greater space between the Party and the government, and the Party and the private sector. Xi is doing the exact opposite. Deng, moreover, wanted to free the debate from its ideological load. Only results counted: 'It doesn't matter whether a cat is white or black, as long as it catches mice' is probably his best-known expression. Xi, on the other hand, has started a campaign to combat Western values and restore the Maoist body of thought. What does connect the two, though, is a profound inner strength and a certain looseness of language which is rarely found among communist officials – drilled as they have been by Party discipline.

During Xi's state visit to the Netherlands, in March 2014, I had the opportunity to speak with him briefly. His physical appearance is impressive: The Chinese leader is six feet tall (important, in a country obsessed with height), sturdily built, and with his thick, dyed-black hair swept backwards. His presence corresponded to the description I had read of him – 'this face that doesn't move, never smiling'[29] – but the twinkle in his eyes made him more likeable than other, colder-looking Chinese apparatchiks I have met over the years. I pointed out to the president that we were born in the same year, down to almost the same day. *Ayah, tai you yuanfen le!* ('Oh, what a shared destiny!') he mumbled amiably.

Blind Loyalty

Not long after Mao Zedong's death in September 1976, his successor Hua Guofeng came up with the 'Two Whatevers' Policy: 'We will resolutely uphold whatever policy decisions Chairman Mao made, and unswervingly follow whatever instructions Chairman Mao made.'[30] It would be missing the mark to compare the current political climate with that of the 1970s, yet since Xi's elevation to 'core leader', countless Party and military chiefs have declared their 'absolute loyalty' to the new Mao. At the 2017 People's Congress, Xi's former rival for the highest office, premier Li Keqiang, referred seven times to his boss as 'core leader'.[31] For some officials such a simple show of support does not go far enough. The State Councillor Yang Jiechi – the country's cool and collected highest diplomat – extolled the Leader's thinking about diplomacy as his 'most precious spiritual resources'.[32]

Sun Chunlan, the only woman in the 25-member Politburo that was 'elected' in October 2017, was equally euphoric: 'With Secretary General Xi Jinping as the *lingxiu* and core leader to take the helm, our party and country will certainly brave all winds and waves and be invincible in our cause.'[33] *Lingxiu* means leader, but has a more spiritual content than *lingdao*, the more commonly-used word. It refers to people with superhuman qualities. Mao Zedong was a *Da Lingxiu* (a great *lingxiu*), yet after his death the term has no longer been in use.

Actually, the current regime is setting the clock even further back than before the era of Mao. Communism in China supposedly meant the kiss of death for the 'feudal society' that existed before the revolution of 1949. In practice, however, Party politics look remarkably similar to the feudal practices in Medieval Europe, when the vassal pledged absolute loyalty to his seigneur in exchange for that lord's protection. In 1955, Mao himself had warned against the glorification that had been accorded to Stalin, calling it a 'poisonous ideological survival of the old society'.[34] Ten years later Mao launched one of the greatest campaigns of self-glorification in the history of humanity. Many older people, not only in China, still remember clearly how millions of people were waving his Little Red Book in ecstasy. The Party has seemingly drawn wise lessons from this period, by stipulating in Article 10.6 of the Party's Charter that 'The Party forbids all forms of personality cult' – but in the present political climate that stipulation is not referred to in the Chinese media.[35]

It seems out of the question that Xi Jinping will unleash a second Cultural Revolution – he and his family were after all themselves victims of it. However, if the present policies continue – the repositioning of the Party at the heart of society, Xi's grab for absolute power and the personality cult surrounding him – then the possibility of that madness returning seems less unlikely.

Flies and Tigers

'The Party and corruption are like water and fire', declared the *People's Daily* at the end of 2014 – which caused *The Economist* to comment drily that the relationship between these two rather recalls that of tinder and matches.[36] What we do know for certain is that the water of the many campaigns waged has never been able to douse the fire of corruption. When Mao Zedong launched the first campaign at the beginning of the 1950s, he promised not only to catch 'flies, but also tigers' in its net.[37] Though many of those predators were trapped, a corrupt tiger has the uncanny ability to rear his head time after time.

Now, many campaigns later, Xi Jinping has gone hunting again. At the launch of his anti-corruption drive in April 2013, he appealed to the eighty million Party members to 'look into a mirror, neaten their dress, take a bath and have the illnesses treated'.[38]

The illnesses include 'the yearning for fame and gain, faking achievements and behaving irresponsibly; even the abuse of power and becoming morally degenerate'.[39] There is therefore, the president indirectly says, nothing wrong with the *system* itself. Corruption is not caused by a lack of checks and balances but by human weakness, which can be cured with the right approach: 'All the diseases that damage the Party's advanced nature and purity should be seriously treated, and all the tumours that breed on the healthy skin of the Party should be resolutely removed.'[40] It became clear rather quickly how Xi envisioned his role as surgeon: He personally chaired meetings in which high-ranking Party members confessed their crimes while shedding tears and wringing their hands. These images, which evoke uneasy memories of the self-criticism sessions held during the Cultural Revolution, can be seen on television with increasing frequency. More modern tools to combat corruption (and convince the people of the Party's fortitude) are also used. In October 2016, the widely watched TV series 'In the Name of the People' was launched – a kind of soap opera that features stern, strait-laced agents arresting one corrupt official after the other. One they find with millions of cash hidden in the refrigerator, another they catch in bed with his blonde mistress.[41]

By the end of 2016, Wang Qishan – the dreaded head of China's Central Commission for Discipline Inspection (CCDI) – had locked up one hundred eighty-two Party bosses at the level of vice-minister and higher.[42] In Shanxi province, known for its deeply entrenched corruption, the complete Party leadership has been swept away. Party officials are not the only target. Generals and the heads of large state businesses are also on Wang Qishan's list. To extract confessions and force people to name accomplices, torture is commonly used.[43] As a result, seventy people have committed suicide. Or rather – that is what the statistics say, for rumours are flying around that some 'suicides' succumbed under torture by their interrogators. The 44-year-old billionaire Xu Ming was the founder of the major industrial concern Dalian Shide and the accomplice of Bo Xilai, son of the 'immortal' Bo Yibo. When Bo fell from power on suspicion of corruption in 2013 (a remarkable story that will be told in the next chapter), he took Xu along with him. Not long before Xu's prison sentence of four years was up, he supposedly died in his cell of a heart attack. The cause of death was not independently determined, however, and Xu's body cremated within a few days of his demise. Shortly before he died, Xu was still telling friends that he felt great.[44]

In accordance with ancient Chinese custom, suicide is the ultimate solution to escape public shame; but it also has a practical side because, according to Chinese criminal law, family members are only liable if the accused is still living. It stands to reason that Xi Jinping's often violent anti-corruption campaign leads to resentment and opposition among the accused and their family members, but this is very difficult to assess: We only read about the 'big successes' achieved, not about people fighting back. Yet, in a rare candid commentary in the *People's Daily* from August 2015, it was noted that 'the scale of the resistance is beyond what could have been imagined'.[45]

Self-criticism

Self-criticism is as ancient as Chinese criminal law itself. By subjugating oneself to the moral superiority of the prosecutor, the suspect (even if his guilt has not been established) insures himself against severe punishment. Under Communism, this behaviour has become a psychological weapon, used by the prosecutor to yell at the victim and putting him under heavy pressure to confess his 'crimes'. During the Cultural Revolution, self-criticism was used on a large scale to unmask class enemies. Many victims committed suicide after this kind of treatment. From its inception in 2013, the anti-corruption campaign saw the re-emergence of this questionable tool. At the beginning of 2017, the Party announced that self-criticism must be seen as 'teaching material' that serves as a warning to those who violate Party discipline.[46]

A Sacred Fervour

When trying to make sense of Xi Jinping's merciless anti-corruption campaign there are, roughly speaking, two schools of thought. The first takes the president's authenticity for granted. It is convinced that Xi, like Mao Zedong and Deng Xiaoping before him, wants to put his stamp on Chinese history by transforming society. For the true leader, so the theory goes, holding on to power is not enough: He must also *act* to legitimize that power. In that respect, Xi is reaching back to the ancient Chinese notion of the *junzi* ('noble person') who is obliged to bring the world to a higher, virtuous level by reversing the nation's moral decline. The president is (supposedly) especially committed to restoring the spirit of purity, simplicity and sacrifice from Communism's early years: The period in Yan'an (1935–1945) when the Communists were united in comradery, close to the people, and saw the realization of the revolution as their sole mission in life – or so the myth goes.

It is undoubtedly true that Yan'an holds a special place in Xi's heart: He was sent there when still a teenager (in 1969), as a result of Mao's campaign to let city students 'learn from the peasants'. This period was in his own words a 'defining experience' and a 'turning point' in his life. Xi Jinping has ever since then called himself a *Yan'an ren* ('Yan'an native') whose 'roots and soul are attached to the yellow earth of Shaanxi province'.[47]

Xi's puritanical fervour is also demonstrated in his campaign against the 'three vices' (gambling, prostitution, and drugs), which in the southern China city of Dongguan alone has already led to 3,000 arrests and the firing of the chief of police.[48] These vices make up such an integral part of Chinese culture that leaders like Hu Jintao and Jiang Zemin did not even try to tackle them. Nor did these leaders do what

Xi Jinping did on 28 December 2013. To the astonishment of the guests, on that day the president walked into Beijing's Qingfeng restaurant and ordered a plate of steamed buns, vegetables and a bowl of liver soup (a standard meal for many Chinese). When the president himself paid the 21 *renminbi* for his dinner, the amazement boiled over. Of course, plenty of cameras were rolling to record this 'contact with the people', but the symbolism of the president as a populist had also come across. The *Ta Kung Pau*, a paper in Hong Kong, even called the visit a *weifu sifang* ('making a plain-clothes visit') – an incognito excursion by the emperor to find out what goes on amongst the people.[49]

Xi Jinping's own statements make clear that he too sees the battle against corruption as a crusade against Evil: 'The two armies of corruption and anti-corruption stand in a stalemate opposite each other', the president ponderously declared in the summer of 2014.[50] Because the existence of the Party is at stake, the president is even prepared to make the supreme sacrifice: 'To fight corruption, I have left life, death and reputation behind me.'[51]

The School of Cynics

The second school of thought, that of the cynics, is not impressed by this verbal grandstanding: It sees the anti-corruption campaign as an excuse for the president to get rid of his political opponents and rebellious factions. Isn't, after all, every Party member corrupt? Chen Yun, the Party's second-in-command in the days of Deng Xiaoping, had implied as much with his immortal one-liner: 'Fight corruption too little and destroy the country; fight it too much and destroy the Party.'[52] Lee Wei Lin – the daughter of Singapore's highly regarded (also in China) leader Lee Kuan Yew, who died in 2015 – is convinced that 'Xi is playing a game where he appears to weed out "corrupts" while replacing them with "his own people."'[53]

A good example of this is the fate that befell Zhou Yongkang, the all-powerful chief of domestic security from 2007 to 2012. He was accused of a 'series of serious violations of party and organisational discipline' – Party jargon for corruption. His crimes were described as ranging from 'taking bribes to leaking party and state secrets and exchanging power and money for sex'.[54] Not since the Gang of Four trial in 1976 has such a highly placed official been convicted. This may point to an unprecedented level of resolve by Xi Jinping, but it is more likely that Zhou was opposed to the appointment of the president. A March 2015 annual report from the Supreme People's Court supports this interpretation, by accusing Zhou of having 'undermined the party's solidarity and engaged in political activities not approved by the authorities'.[55] A similar accusation was made during the recent 19th Party Congress, when the chair of the China Securities Regulatory Commission, Liu Shiyu, remarked that Zhou Yongkang and his accomplices had 'high positions and great

Zhou Yongkang

power in the party, but they were hugely corrupt and plotted to usurp the party's leadership and seize state power'. Fortunately, according to Liu, 'Xi Jinping, with the historical responsibility as a proletarian revolutionist... cleared up huge risks for the party and the country.'[56]

In a closed trial held on 22 May 2015, Zhou was sentenced to life imprisonment – a sign that the Party was anxious that Zhou would throw dirt on his Party comrades in public. This fear was groundless, for Zhou confessed to all his crimes and the damage they had caused to the Party and society.[57] The ruling of the court was no surprise. Political offences are always first investigated by the Party itself and then handed over to the judge, but the court will never take another decision. The suspect is guilty in advance. The Party-controlled media spun the fall of Zhou Yongkang as proof of the self-cleansing capability of the Party. The military newspaper PLA-*Daily*, for instance, crowed in December 2014 that 'The anti-corruption campaign has already touched senior 'tigers' like Zhou Yongkang and Xu Caihou. Who is still untouchable?'[58] Many Chinese will say 'most of them', for the belief runs very deep that every official is by definition corrupt and stands above the law. As the saying goes: 'Hang a hundred officials, and one of them is innocent.'

Red Aristocrats

It is a typically Western trait to wonder whether Xi Jinping is an authentic anti-corruption crusader or a cynic purging his rivals. Our minds, moulded by ancient Greek philosophy, thinks in terms of exclusion: If A is B, it cannot also be C. Chinese thinking is fundamentally different: Influenced by Taoism, most people don't have a 'fixed' view on reality; but, rather, a fluid one. It is perfectly possible for A to be *both* B and C. This basic characteristic helps to explain Xi Jinping's seemingly conflicting motivations. On the one hand he wants to do 'big things', while on the other he is part of a political system in which the seizing and retaining of power is not determined (or restrained) by transparent institutions. The forging of conspiracies to overpower the opponent is then inevitable. How these power struggles are fought out is shrouded in secrecy – and remains so, because the narrative of the contest is always written by the winner. As the proverb cited earlier says, 'The winner becomes king, the loser a bandit.' But what we do know for certain is that Xi is determined to secure power for his class, the heirs of the Chinese revolution.

As a Chinese friend told me, this plan was already set in motion more than thirty years ago, when the patriarchs of the major revolutionary families came together to ensure the future power of their clans. They did not, however, propose a North Korean approach: The sons and daughters first had to earn their stripes in low-ranking positions, such as the Party Secretaryship of a district (of which China has more than

2,800). This shows that, even amongst the elite, meritocratic instincts in China have deep roots. Xi Jinping, for instance, was appointed Party Secretary of Zhending, a poor region in the south-west of Hebei province.

In the second decade of the twenty-first century, however, the time of the *Hongerdai* (Second Generation of Reds) has come. Xi Jinping is the best-known example of his class, but through the veins of some Communists runs even redder blood. These are the descendants of Mao Zedong's and Deng Xiaoping's inner circle, who for dozens of years dominated the government and the military. Because this clique never retired, they are known as the 'Eight Immortals'. The careers of one hundred three of their descendants are tracked in the Bloomberg report *Heirs of Mao's Comrades Rise as New Capitalist Nobility*. Most went into business. Three alone – Wang Jun (son of the former hard-line vice-president Wang Zhen), Chen Yuan (son of Chen Yun, the most powerful man in China after Deng Xiaoping), and He Ping (son-in-law of Deng Xiaoping) – managed in 2011 businesses with assets amounting to more than 1.6 trillion US dollars.* That was the equivalent of 20 percent of China's national product in that year.[59] The Second Generation of Reds is active in politics and the military as well: Bo Xilai – the former Party Secretary of Chongqing – was the son of Bo Yibo (also an 'immortal'), while the former Political Commissar of the PLA, Liu Yuan, is the son of President Liu Shaoqi, who died during the Cultural Revolution.

Some of the 'immortals' – whose lives were characterised by simplicity, deprivation and egalitarian ideals – found it difficult to swallow the way their children fell for capitalism. Right before his death, the former vice-president Wang Zhen supposedly no longer acknowledged Wang Jun – also known as the Chinese 'godfather of golf' – as his son. He allegedly even called him and his brothers 'turtle eggs' (bastards).[60] Wang Zhen remained faithful to his Communist ideals: His last words before he died on 12 March 1993 were: 'I will visit Marx, and then report to Chairman Mao.'[61]

In February 2016, the who's who of the Red Aristocracy met in Beijing to celebrate Chinese New Year. In her speech, Hu Muying, the daughter of Mao Zedong's hard line secretary Hu Qiaomu, called upon the eight hundred attendees 'to actively respond to policies strengthening Party self-discipline'. Zhuang Dehui of the Research Center for Government Integrity-Building at Peking University supported Hu's call for action: 'Many descendants have rich experience in politics. They are sensitive to political issues and have a profound understanding of policies due to their family background.'[62]

---

* The Bloomberg report was duly censored in China, as were the Panama Papers in which several Chinese top leaders were mentioned. The 'Richest People in China', published yearly by Hurun Inc. ('a leading luxury publishing group', according to their website), is allowed in China, but the only people mentioned on these lists are business people.

The Eight Immortals

The term 'Eight Immortals' refers to a group of legendary Taoist saints who live on the islands of the blessed in the East China Sea. In the 1980s it mockingly referred to the eight Party elders who had joined Mao in 1934 on his Long March, and who at a very advanced age were still holding onto power behind the scenes. They were Deng Xiaoping, Chen Yun, Yang Shangkun, Wang Zhen, Bo Yibo, Li Xiannian, Peng Zhen, and Song Renqiong. In 2007, Bo Yibo – the father of Bo Xilai, who was purged in 2013 – was the last 'immortal' to die. The sons and grandsons of this clique constitute the core of China's so-called 'Red Aristocracy'.

The Barrel of the Gun

China has a peculiar two-fold structure of governance. The Party and the government each maintain their own organisations, but in order to be considered for a high-ranking government position one must be a Party member as well. For example, the Party's deputy leader, Li Keqiang, is also the premier; and its number three, Li Zhanshu, is chair of the National People's Congress. In this way, the Party keeps the government in check, but control of the military is the key task of a Party that wants to stay in power indefinitely. Mao once observed that 'political power grows out of the barrel of a gun',[63] and his successors have never deviated from this principle. On the contrary: As chair of the Party's powerful Central Military Commission, Xi Jinping is continually hammering at the subordination of the armed forces to the Party. At a conference in November 2014, the entire leadership of the People's Liberation Army (PLA) pledged its loyalty to Xi Jinping. This happened in Gutian in Fujian province, the town where in 1929 Mao Zedong proclaimed for the first time the principle of the primacy of the Party over the military. The symbolism of this location was clear to every soldier present.[64]

In most countries the military answers to the state, not the ruling party, so the PLA's subordination to the Party is a special Chinese construct. This seems to have contributed to political stability, because as far as we know only one military coup d'état has occurred in the history of the People's Republic. In 1971, Mao's confidant Marshal Lin Biao tried to seize power, but when his coup attempt was discovered, he fled to the Soviet Union – only for his aeroplane to crash over Mongolia. It is difficult to say if this was the genuine course of events: The truth of this extraordinary story has never come to light.* With the Party now so firmly in control, it is hard to imagine another coup d'état taking place, but one can never be sure. In the summer of 2014, the PLA's political watchdog – the General Political Department – warned the military cadre that 'the party's leadership over the army must be absolutely upheld' and to guard against 'liberalism in politics'. The warning came straight after the arrest of the retired general and former vice-chairman of the Party's Central Military Commission, Xu Caihou. Xu, who has since died (he was suffering from prostate cancer), was accused of the widespread military practice of selling promotions.[66]

Even more spectacular was the fall that same year of the lieutenant general Gu Junshan, the Chinese 'Goldfinger'. The paramilitary police arresting him needed two lorries to transport the spoils he had collected over the years, including many cases of *Maotai* (Chinese 120-proof grain alcohol), a golden wash basin, a golden model boat and even a life-size golden statue of Mao Zedong.[67] The purge of the military was completed in July 2015, when General Guo Boxiong was thrown out of the Party. He was supposedly guilty of a 'serious violation of Party discipline' and of having 'left a vile impact'.[68] Both Guo Boxiong and Xu Caihou were members of the all-powerful Central Military Commission until 2012 (Guo from 2002 and Xu from 2004). The two generals were also vice-chairmen of the CMC, making them the most powerful officers in the country, since the chairman is also Party Secretary, and not involved in daily military matters.

Some Chinese think that the fight to control the military is in fact an extension of the political struggle. The key target here is supposedly the faction of the former president Jiang Zemin. In broad strokes, this theory goes as follows: The former president secretly preferred Bo, and not Xi, to be the country's paramount leader – which Xi Jinping only found out after Bo's fall in 2013. To nullify the threat posed by the Jiang clique, Xi immediately launched a counterattack to decapitate the Jiang faction by taking down his key accomplices: Chief of domestic security Zhou Yongkang and the generals Guo Boxiong and Xu Caihou, who had been appointed by Jiang as members of the Central Military Commission.[69] Given his advanced age (he turned 91 in 2017) and status as former president, Jiang himself is untouchable, but Xi has reduced Jiang to a tragic figure: An emperor without subjects, a general without soldiers. This might be acceptable for someone close to death, but not to Chinese leaders who aim to write and transform history. The notion that their regime will be regarded as corrupt and vile is intolerable.

---

* *The Conspiracy and Death of Lin Biao* (1983), a book by Yao Mingle (a pseudonym), presents another version. Mao found out about Lin's attempted plot to kill him and planned a counterplot: The Marshal was lured to a dinner in an exclusive villa in the West of Beijing. After leaving the villa in their limousine, Lin Biao, his wife and two associates were assassinated in a hail of rocket fire.[65]

All of this is speculation, for in October 2017 the Party ideologue, Wang Huning, and the former Party Secretary of Shanghai, Han Zheng were appointed to the Politburo Standing Committee. Both supposedly maintain close connections with Jiang Zemin. Interpreting the shady manoeuvres of the Chinese establishment elite is like looking into a crystal ball. As one China expert puts it: 'China is like a magic mirror showing us what isn't there, while keeping hidden what is really happening.'[70]

Commander-in-Chief

Dressed in military camouflages, Xi Jinping visited the 'Joint Command Centre' of the People's Liberation Army in April 2016. Normally, the Party leader appears in civilian clothing – a dreary, greenish blue 'Mao suit'. As the public appearances of Chinese leaders are highly-scripted affairs where no word is spoken spontaneously, and no action left to chance, it was clear that a statement was being made. But what? The state-run China Central Television provided an explanation that same evening: Xi had been appointed as 'Commander-in-Chief', a title that was last held by the legendary marshal Zhu De during the 1950s.[71] The symbolism of the camouflage suit had thus been made clear: Xi is now the boss of the military – not through his chairmanship of the Central Military (a Party organ), but because of his newly-acquired military title. 'He has become one of them.' For that same reason, none of his comrades from the Politburo Standing Committee were present at the ceremony. The military is subordinate to the Party, but by Xi's elevation to Commander-in-Chief, the military is in the first instance subordinate to Xi himself.

The presidential visit to the 'Joint Command Centre' followed a large-scale re-organisation of the People's Liberation Army, announced in February 2016. The seven military regions created in 1949 (immediately after the founding of the People's Republic) were replaced by five 'battle zone commands (BZCs)' which will defend the country against all kinds of threats, but should also 'take the initiative to win future wars'. Depending on the nature of the threat, these BZCs direct the ground forces, air force, navy, and a 'strategic rocket force'.[72]

Xi Jinping's reorganisation kills two birds with one stone. The unwieldy and bloated People's Liberation Army (300,000 soldiers have been made redundant) is being transformed into a modern fighting force that can not only face twenty-first-century threats like terrorism, but will be better equipped to win the inevitable confrontation with the United States. A no less important result of this re-organisation is that some one hundred twenty generals have been purged: Military men who belong to the clique of Guo Boxiong and Xu Caihou, or who have committed the darker offence of succumbing to 'liberalism': They have advocated a division between the Party and the military. The military expert Song Zhongping thus sees the reorganisation of the army as an opportunity to 'prevent the formation of cliques within the armed forces'.[73]

By re-organising the military, Xi Jinping hopes to achieve the same result as with his anti-corruption campaign: Eliminating competing cliques, specifically that of Jiang Zemin, and appointing his own people to crucial posts. That goal has already been partly reached: The two top positions in the armed forces are held by comrades with strong connections with Xi's favoured province. Fang Fenghui,* the PLA's General Chief of Staff, comes from Shaanxi, while Chang Wanquan, the minister of Defence, served in the Lanzhou Military Region (to which Shaanxi belonged) under various military roles from 1974 to 2002.[75] In addition, the 'Red Aristocrat' Liu Yuan – son of President Liu Shaoqi, who died during the Cultural Revolution – ensured, as Political Commissar of the PLA, that the 'liberal instincts' of the armed forces were kept in check. He was also instrumental in bringing down the above-mentioned Gu Junshan, the 'Goldfinger' of China. Liu retired in December 2015, but remains influential, and is seen as a confidant of Xi Jinping.[76]

By flushing out his opponents in the army and the Party on a scale not seen since the days of Mao Zedong, Xi has shown himself to be an all-powerful, even transformative leader. On a more grounded level, however, old wine is still poured into new bottles: Cliques are persecuted, and opponents crushed, only to be replaced by new cliques. This custom is as old as China itself: The new emperor not only disposes of those who threaten his rule; he also makes his own omnipotence manifest, giving himself an aura of invincibility, and even immortality. Nearly every Chinese god – from the third-century general Guan Yu to the twentieth-century dictator Mao Zedong – was once a human being of flesh and blood who accomplished superhuman achievements. There is nothing new under the Chinese sun: History keeps repeating itself.

---

* Fang Fenghui's shared provincial background with Xi Jinping did not save him from being purged in August 2017 for reasons of bribery. Apparently, his loyalty to the disgraced general Guo Boxiong was still strong. One source even suspects that Fang was preparing a coup against Xi Jinping with some fellow generals. Adding weight to this theory is that five members of the Central Military Commission were removed in quick succession just before the 19th Party Congress of October 2017.[74]

CHAPTER 5

The Eternal Party

> *Various systems were tried out, including constitutional monarchy, imperial restoration, parliamentarism, multi-party system and presidential government, yet nothing really worked out. It was [not] till the birth of the CPC in 1921 who adapted the basic tenets of Marxism to the reality of China that the Chinese finally found a correct path for the nation.*
>
> Liu Yunshan

With eighty million members and four billion dollars in foreign currency, the Party (i.e. the Communist Party of China) is the largest and richest political party on the face of the earth. Having founded the People's Republic of China in 1949, the CPC has already been in power for nearly seventy years, yet shows absolutely no signs of tiring of government. Quite the contrary. In his farewell speech as Party Secretary in October 2012, Hu Jintao said that the Party will never take 'the wrong path of changing its banner'.[1] For those who failed to understand this metaphor, Hu made his meaning crystal clear: 'We will never copy a western political system.'[2] Xi Jinping is equally explicit in his aversion towards Western democracy, and asserts that 'Chinese democracy' means improving its 'consultative democracy', not abolishing the one-party state.[3] Aside from these ideological nuances, the core question is whether the political system is capable of solving the country's gigantic social and economic problems. Driven by state investment and exports, China has since the beginning of the 1990s realized average growth figures of 10 percent per annum: But the expiration date for that model is in sight. China is one of the most polluted countries in the world: According to a recent report from the World Health Organisation, air pollution alone is killing nearly three million people each year[4] – and that is just one form of pollution claiming countless victims.[5] The second, very visible effect of the economic boom is the growing gap between rich and poor. After the United States, China has the largest number of billionaires in the world, flying in private jets and buying *châteaux* in France. Its *Wirtschaftswunder* has a flip side, though. According to statistics from the Chinese government, in 2017 around thirty million people still lived below the poverty level of 1.9 USD per day[6] – a huge decrease from the 99 million dreadfully poor in 2012, but the income gap between poor farmers and wealthy urbanites is still larger than in most other countries.[7] As the saying goes: *guofu minqiong* – the country is rich, but the people are poor.

This picture of rich and poor is too simplistic however: China also has a large urban middle class that – depending on which criteria are used to measure prosperity – numbers between three and four hundred million people.[8] This achievement has been good for the world – not only for the wallets of Western businesses, but also for international peace and stability. When Deng Xiaoping visited the United States in 1979, the US Congress had just passed the Jackson-Vanik Amendment, which appealed to Communist countries to allow freedom of emigration. Countries that kept their borders closed would not be able to enjoy normal trade relations with the United States. After meeting with President Carter, Deng visited Congress, where senators asked him whether China would allow emigration. Without any hesitation Deng replied: 'Oh, that's easy! How many do you want? Ten million? Fifteen million?' Congress did not pursue the matter any further.[9]

Large-Scale Urbanisation

When Deng Xiaoping launched his reforms at the end of the 1970s, the overwhelming portion of the population still lived in the countryside. As a result of the large-scale urbanisation of the past twenty years, only half of the 1.3 billion Chinese remain rural residents, including virtually every individual living beneath the poverty level. The policy of President Hu Jintao (2002–2012) for 'putting people first' led to measures for improving the lot of the poor, notably eliminating the land tax and providing free elementary education. In spite of this policy the rural population continues to fall behind that of city dwellers. In 2013, the average difference in income between an urban and a rural resident was 3 to 1.[10] The difference in wealth is even greater because many city-dwellers have profited from the strong rise in urban housing prices over recent years.[11] To close this gap the Party wants to intensify its urbanisation campaign even further: In 2020, 60 % of the Chinese population will live in the cities. In his report to the 2014 National People's Congress, Premier Li Keqiang underpinned that goal with the directive that another hundred million people will be relocated to the cities, and that the hundred million peasants already living in cities will soon acquire the same social rights as their fellow-citizens.[12] Although this top-down policy of mass migration has been rightly criticized, it is beyond dispute that urbanisation contributes to economic development. City dwellers consume more than rural inhabitants and that is why urbanisation fits seamlessly into the master plan of replacing exports with local spending as *the* engine for economic growth. At the annual World Economic Forum in

Davos in 2015, Premier Li Keqiang proved himself optimistic about the chances for success with such re-orientation: 'China has much room for urban, suburban and regional development and domestic demand has huge potential.'[13]

In terms of numbers of people leaving hearth and home, China's urbanisation leaves all previous migrations in the dust. The government stimulates (some will say 'forces') this process by building metropolises throughout the country. These cities come complete with eight-lane boulevards, shopping malls, exhibition halls for the arts, and sports venues that could easily contain London's Wembley Stadium. Living in flats sprouting up like concrete bamboo shoots out of barren, uncultivated terrain, the people themselves live far away from these utopian centres. Investments that improve the quality of life – such as parks, playgrounds or athletics fields – are seldom made. China's cities are drafted on the drawing tables of bureaucrats – people who measure 'modernisation' by the width of the streets, the size of the airport, and the height of the buildings – not by the viability of those cities for citizens. Seen economically, building even more cities seems highly irrational. In a 2014 report, the National Development and Reform Commission calculated that in China's 3,500 'new districts', living space has been created for 3.4 billion people – almost two and a half times the estimated size of today's population in China of 1.4 billion.[14] Yet Xi Jinping does not seem to take this reality to heart. In April 2017, he announced 'the construction of a perfect city, one to last a thousand years, embedded in innovation and a clean environment'. The fact that this model city (in the impoverished district of Xiongan, not far from Beijing) has to be built from the ground up is seen by the paramount leader as advantageous: 'The location is a blank piece of paper on which the most beautiful painting can be painted.'[15] For the hundreds of millions of Chinese who in recent decades have been turned from peasants into city-dwellers, the urban experience seems more like a bad movie: Small-scale social bonds have been irrevocably severed, and the spiritual ties to their forefathers buried in the ancestral land have been broken for good. The fate of the two million or so Tibetan nomads is even harsher: They are being forced to give up their centuries-old wandering existence and are lodged in gloomy, hastily-erected concrete housing blocks. China's most famous architect, the 93-year-old Wu Liangyong, argues for a return to the old tradition of urban planning that take the human dimension into account.[16] Yet in present day 'modernist thinking' there is little room for this kind of urbanism, even if the premier promised in his 2014 report to the National People's Congress that urbanisation will be 'people centered'.[17]

Lack of quality is another feature of Chinese urbanisation. Project developers do not underwrite the financing and thus feel no pressure to repay the loan with interest. As a result, a depressing quantity of *guicheng* ('ghost towns') smack anyone who travels through the country in the face. The typical Chinese way of doing business aggravates the problem. To acquire the business, the project developer must 'take into

Tibetan 'nomad village'

account' the local authorities that issue the contract. This means that he squeezes subcontractors such as the architect and the builder to make any profit at all; in return these neglected parties deliver inferior services and materials.

The mega-earthquake in Sichuan province in 2008 showed what kind of horrific consequences these practices can lead to: Countless buildings, including many schools, collapsed like houses of cards. The number of victims – nearly ninety thousand, with many children amongst them – could have been much lower, if the construction sector in China operated differently.[18] The disregard for the individual in major building projects is by the way as old as China itself. In the third century BCE, it is said that the First Emperor mobilised a million men to build the Great Wall. The majority of them died of starvation and cold; they became victims of the first of many megalomaniacal construction projects that characterise the country's history.

What Separates State and Subject

It should come as no big surprise that such a large and rapidly-developing country runs into problems like environmental pollution, income disparity, and corruption. In similar developing giants like India and Brazil, the situation is no different. The fundamental difference with these two countries is that China is governed by a party that places the nature and speed of economic and social development in the service of political expediency: The will of the Party to remain in power forever. A Party, moreover, that consciously creates the myth that without it China's development into a 'modern' nation is impossible. Straight after Tiananmen Square was cleared in June 1989, the same slogan chalked in red, appeared on walls all over the country: 'Without the Communist Party, there would be no new China. Only the party can save China.'[19] The last twenty-five years have shown no deviation from these one-liners. On the contrary: The Party has become even more boastful of its indispensable role.

Yet is this really true? Would a solution to China's massive social and economic woes not in fact come closer if the Party cedes power? Only the Chinese people can answer these questions, but in the absence of independent surveys – let alone general elections – it is difficult to say where they stand. It is clear though that the social climate is bleaker than twenty or even ten years ago – as manifested by demonstrations against the construction of chemical plants, resistance to land expropriation, self-immolations in Tibet and terrorist attacks in Xinjiang. According to some intellectuals, many, if not all, of the country's socio-political problems can be traced to the Party's monopoly on power. As Liu Xiaobo, the 2010 recipient of the Nobel Peace Prize, wonders: 'Where is China heading in the twenty-first century? Will it continue with "modernization" under authoritarian rule, or will it embrace universal human values, join the mainstream of civilized nations and build a democratic system?' For Liu, one thing is clear: 'The decline of the current system has reached the point where change is no longer optional.'[20] Most intellectuals in China reject Liu's liberal ideology, but nearly all agree with him that changing the system is unavoidable. These thinkers will be presented in the next chapter; here I focus on the thinking of the Party itself. The most striking conclusion is that it, too, perceives the need for change – albeit under the non-negotiable condition that the Party's vice-like grip on power monopoly remains intact.

'The State Is Not the Problem, But the Solution'

In his first inaugural address the 40th president of the United States, Ronald Reagan, said: 'Government is not the solution to our problem; government *is* the problem.'[21] The mirror image of this statement can be adapted to Chinese thinking. Every leader of the People's Republic of China – with the exception of the liberals Hu Yaobang and Zhao Ziyang during the 1980s – views the state as the solution to the country's problems. Economic growth? The market (as Deng Xiaoping proclaimed) must be its engine, but with the state controlling core sectors like telecommunications, electricity, and media. Corruption? The state itself can best fight this abuse through moral admonition and harsh punitive measures. The notion that a butcher cannot certify his own products, and that only a separation of powers can fight corruption (the first step being to do away with censorship and judicial subservience to the Party), is viewed as an undermining, Western concept. Happiness? The state can supply even that. In 2011 Guangdong province decided to deliver not only economic growth, but also more happiness in the coming five years. This local initiative had a national impact: At the National People's Congress in 2011, it was decided that in 2016 all China should bubble over with bliss.[22] What (according to the Party) causes happiness is the level of income, education, occupation, and possession of a municipal *hukou* (the registration permit that provides the right to live in cities). What causes happiness in more liberal, Western societies – freedom of expression and freedom of choice, for example – is not measured. That is unfortunate, because according to another survey a free internet would make a lot of Chinese happy.[23] Belief in an almighty government is closely linked to the Socialist idea of the state as the distributor of national income and the guardian of social solidarity. But it also goes back further in history: To the days when the emperor as the intermediary between heaven and earth protected the country from bad harvests, disastrous floods, and barbarian invasions – when the government existed *for* the people, but was not established *by* the people.

Does the Party Determine China's Future... ?

In his book *When China Rules the World*, Martin Jacques contends that China's increasing power is going to result in a new world order.[24] It is still too early to unmask Jacques as a false prophet, but regarding the power of the state his assumptions are deeply flawed. In his own words, 'In the Chinese tradition, government is regarded as an extension of the family; indeed, government was modelled on the family. Far from being perceived as a somewhat remote agency, the state is regarded as the head of the Chinese family.'[25] That is true to a certain extent; for good reason the word for 'state' is *guojia* ('land of family'). It does not mean, however, that the state can permanently bend the people to its will. The concept of the Mandate of Heaven ensures that the enduring legitimacy of the prince depends on his ability to provide virtuous governance. The regimes of tyrannical despots have never been long-lived. Qin Shi Huangdi – the First Emperor who in the third century BCE built the Great Wall, standardised the system of measures, and forced the people into a straitjacket of cruel laws – is a good example. His dynasty fell three years after his death. The aspirations of Mao Zedong, a twentieth-century Qin Shi Huangdi, did not reach less high: The Chinese people were to be morphed into pure Communist beings, breaking with the innate culture of humanism, moderation, and common sense – with *The Doctrine of the Mean*, as one of the four holy books of Confucianism is called. After his death, the 'Thinking' of the

Great Helmsman was for the most part thrown overboard. The cultural philosopher Lin Yutang had already in 1935 explained why Communism in China must fail in the long run: 'Even if a cataclysmic upheaval like a communistic régime should come, the old tradition of individuality, toleration, moderation and common sense will break Communism and change it beyond recognition, rather than Communism with its socialistic, impersonal and rigoristic outlook breaks the old tradition. It must be so.'[26]

> ### The Doctrine of the Mean
>
> *The Doctrine of the Mean* is the title of one of the *Four Books* of Confucianism. The book was supposedly written by Zi Si, the grandson of Confucius. Zhu Xi (1130–1200), a prominent scholar and philosopher from the Song dynasty provided the text with commentary and put it at the heart of the Confucianist curriculum. During the Ming (1368–1644) and the Qing (1644–1911) dynasties, the *Four Books* constituted the set curricular material for the state examinations that selected the country's mandarin elite. According to the cultural philosopher Lin Yutang, *The Doctrine of the Mean* forms the central teaching of Confucianism. The person who follows this path is characterised, according to Lin, by 'his love of moderation and restraint, and his hatred of abstract theories and logical extremes'.[27]

Or Do the People?

Deng Xiaoping was keenly aware how the absolutist governing style of his predecessor Mao had conflicted with the core values of Chinese culture. The Little Helmsman never openly conducted a policy of 'de-Maoification' (comparable with Khrushchev's de-Stalinisation policy in the Soviet Union during the 1950s). Yet by extricating the state and its regulations from daily life, Deng enabled his people to do what they are naturally good at: Starting a business, trading, wheeling and dealing, taking care of the family and having a good time – a policy that has resulted in the economic explosion of the last thirty years.

The statement of the Scottish philosopher David Hume – 'All plans of government, which suppose great reformation in the manners of mankind, are plainly imaginary' – can also be applied to the aspirations of the Chinese government.[28] It cannot change the Chinese at their core, even though history has seen various potentates who have tried to do so. Mao Zedong is the most recent, but certainly not the only example. Since his death, history has taken revenge on his attempts at creating a 'new man', for 'feudal' customs like veneration of the ancestors, soothsaying, corruption, and prostitution are abundantly in vogue again. During the Cultural Revolution 'bourgeois customs' like wearing a nice suit or playing the piano resulted in persecution; now the Party could not care less. Just as in the millennia-long imperial period citizens can do as they please, provided they do not challenge authority. China has, to quote the British philosopher Isaiah Berlin, a high degree of 'negative liberty'.[29] But 'positive liberty' – the capability to shape that freedom without restraint by expressing a political opinion, for example – is not tolerated. The Party has no patience for power-sharing.

In his book *One Billion Customers*, James McGregor compares the Chinese state with a water-skier behind a speedboat: Pulling the rope to the boat, he desperately tries to steer the mechanised, primitive force of the Chinese people. Sometimes it seems to be effective, but the speedboat actually determines its own course.[30] This captivating metaphor suffers from the (American?) tendency to simplify things, but is does contains a kernel of truth: In the long term, the state cannot make the people go in a direction that it does not want. Still, the state sees itself as the guardian of the national legacy and Chinese culture – not as a representative of the Chinese people. In this time of the internet, the mobility of capital, and intense cultural exchange this ages-old vision of governing is coming under increasing pressure, but this does not mean that the battle is over. The key elements of what is being called the 'Beijing Consensus' – an authoritarian one-party state, growth driven by exports and state control over strategic sectors of the economy – are popular in many emerging economies – certainly after 2008, when the fall of Lehman Brothers seriously shook the confidence in the ideological supremacy of the free market.[31]

No Tradition of Democracy

Hu Jintao's 2012 statement about changing the colour of the flag reflects a mindset that is as old as China itself. At times the Party shares power with political movements of a different shade – as in the 1930s, when an anti-Japan alliance was made with the Kuomintang. But these kinds of union are temporary and tactical in nature and always have the same goal: Securing absolute power. Political plurality is seen as unnatural and not tolerated. From an historical perspective this is understandable: Ever since the Shang dynasty, which ruled from around 1600 to 1100 BCE, the Chinese state has been absolutist. When Athens, under the leadership of Pericles, brought the democratic experiment to fruition in the middle of the fifth century BCE, China had already experienced a thousand years of imperial autocracy – a humbling perspective that is not always recognised in the West. The history of Chinese absolutism knows few fault lines. At the beginning of the twentieth century, specifically after the May 4th Movement in 1919, the door stood wide open to Western ideas about personal freedom and democracy, but also to Socialism. Just like other Western philosophies, the doctrine of Marx was essentially alien to Chinese thinking, yet the notion that an enlightened elite is indispensable for realising the ideal state struck a chord with Mao, Chiang Kai-shek, and even Sun Yatsen – after all, this fitted perfectly in Confucianist political thought.

The People's Republic continued this line of thinking. Deng Xiaoping saw the Party's absolute power as the unshakable pillar supporting his economic reforms. During the 1980s the liberal leaders Zhao Ziyang and Hu Yaobang launched proposals for a more independent press, democracy within the Party and even a separation of Party and state. This turned out, however, to be a fleeting, interim moment. The bold experiment of weakening the Party's grip on society was one of the victims of the Tiananmen crackdown on 4 June 1989. Under the administrations of Jiang Zemin (1989–2002) and Hu Jintao (2002–2012) fear reigned supreme. The crisis of 4 June 1989 could never be allowed to recur, so political reform and the introduction of democracy were shelved indefinitely. As the premier Wen Jiabao posited in 2007, 'Democracy can only emerge once the socialist system has been perfected, but that may take another 100 years.'[32]

Imperial Authority

Of the Five Relationships holding society together – as mentioned by the philosopher Mencius (372–289 BCE) – those between father and son and between emperor and subject are the two most important. The state is the extension of the family, a collection of countless families organised according to the same principle of absolute obedience to the 'supreme father'. *Guojia* ('country' or 'state') literally means 'land of family'. The emperor always remains the father of 'his family', even after his abdication. His authority then even increases. It was said of Deng Xiaoping that, after giving up his official positions, he 'ruled behind the scenes'. He filled the role of the *Taishang Huang* (the abdicated emperor), a figure who appears frequently in Chinese history.

Being a much stronger leader than the impotent Hu Jintao or the vain Jiang Zemin, Xi Jinping should be confident about his ability to carry out essential political reforms. Even so, this scion of the Red Aristocracy is not going to uproot his own privileged class. No leader wants to be compared with Gorbachev, who ushered in the disintegration of the Soviet Union with his policy of glasnost and perestroika. That label is fatal for the career of any politician; after all, the Party has coupled its *raison d'être* to the *restoration* of the Chinese empire, not its collapse. The second 'crime' of the Russian leader was the downfall of Communism in his country – a nightmare scenario for the Chinese leadership, because it would also mean the fall from power of the major families. That makes the regime extremely thin-skinned regarding signs of any political challenge. 'Paranoia,' writes Susan Shirk, the deputy assistant Secretary of State under President

Bill Clinton, 'is the occupational disease of all authoritarian leaders, no matter how serious the internal threats they actually face. The Chinese suffer from a particularly acute form of the disease because of their Tiananmen trauma [Shirk alludes here to the clearing of Tiananmen Square on 4 June 1989], the other regimes they have watched collapse, and the dramatic changes in Chinese society that surround them. [...] Paradoxically, the fears of Communist autocrats make them hypersensitive to public attitudes.'[33]

What Binds the Nation?

The Party holds an iron grip on China's political process, but it knows that lasting power cannot only be based on oppression. The leaders must also formulate a concept that is enticing, for people feel connected with one another not only from face-to-face contact, but also from a shared sense of enterprise and purpose. In order to be successful, states need an idea that appeals to what they stand for.[34] The articulation of this 'attractive idea' (the wording comes from the anthropologist Benedict Anderson), is left in democratic countries to the people themselves: In dictatorships, however, leaders do not take such risks – it might just happen that another political system is perceived to be as 'attractive'. This is why authoritarian leaders create myths that connect the identity and destiny of the country to their own person. In his book China's Destiny, Chiang Kai-shek portrayed himself as a Confucianist saint saving China from foreign pestilence.[35] Mao Zedong raised the art of myth-making to new heights: By freeing the country from imperialism and feudalism, he was the source of light and meaning for the new nation. To quote the first lines of a popular song from the 1960s: 'The East is red, the sun rises. China has brought forth a Mao Zedong.'[36] Even today Mao is still venerated like a god by countless Chinese. Deng Xiaoping lifted hundreds of millions of people out of poverty, created a prosperous middle class and restored China's place under the sun. His immortal place in history is secured as well.

In which myth does Xi Jinping play a leading role? Mao's murderous administration cannot be repeated, no matter how greatly some people still admire him. Deng is still praised for the *Wirtschaftswunder* he set off, but the horrific side-effects of environmental damage, corruption and social tensions mean that his course cannot be pursued either. How can Xi keep the masses together at the beginning of the twenty-first century? How can the sense of ideological rootlessness be reversed? By dreaming of the 'Great Rejuvenation of the Chinese Nation' – as unenticing and vague this slogan might sound to Western ears. This 'Dream' has a domestic and a foreign dimension: In China itself by creating a new connection between the Party and the people; abroad, the Dream is more about confrontation: By emphasizing in what way the old empire differs from other nations, it creates a new identity.

Marx in the People's Republic

How would a Karl Marx, miraculously come to life, react during a visit to the People's Republic of China? Shocked, confused, or approving? Would he have seen his utopian projections come true? Probably not. The size and the wealth of the country would certainly please him: Marx had predicted, after all, that the Communist state would be incredibly rich through the optimal development of productive forces. Yet negative impressions would likely prevail: The distressing inequality between rich and poor (greater than in the United States); the capitalistic bosses who do not care about the welfare of their workers and the decadent lifestyle of the hundred fabulously wealthy families. The Party's monopoly of power would have pleased him, but Marx would have disapproved of its aspiration to always remain there; in his thinking, the Party was a temporary phenomenon meant to break the resistance of the old order; it was not a goal in itself. Once the classless society has been achieved, the Party has fulfilled its historical function and had to disappear.[37] Finally, a meeting with Xi Jinping would turn out to be the proverbial blind leading the blind. Marx would certainly not be in favour of the 'Great Rejuvenation of the Chinese Nation', because states are institutions that keep the 'workers of the world' from uniting.

George Orwell, on the other hand, would have understood modern China instantly. In his subtle political fable *Animal Farm*, he describes how the pigs, as leaders of the animals' rebellion, rise up against the oppressive humans. After they have seized power, the pigs determine that 'all animals are equal, but some animals are more equal than others' and start behaving like their former oppressors. The pigs even start walking on two legs.[38] In the People's Republic we see a similar development. Business people (formerly called 'capitalists') are invited to join the Party, the market (as stated in 2013 by the third plenum of the 18th Party Congress) is 'decisive in allocating resources'[39] and any talk of class struggle has disappeared. It is now all about permanent power, and to that end the Leninist organisation of the Party – that is to say its finely enmeshed presence in every strand of society – is an extremely useful tool. The end goal of Communism – a society where everyone works according to his capability and is provided for according to his needs – has been directed to Leon Trotsky's 'dung heap of history'.[40]

Away with Marx and Mao?

Nevertheless Marxism-Leninism, supplemented with the mental musings of a few Chinese leaders, is still the official ideology of the land. Its ultimate affirmation lies in the constitutional stipulation that the country is 'under the leadership of the Communist Party of China and the guidance of Marxism-Leninism, Mao Zedong

Thought, Deng Xiaoping Theory and the important thought of "Three Represents." '⁴¹ The latest amendments to the constitution of March 2018, strengthened China's commitment to socialism even further: It added 'Xi Jinping Thought on Socialism with Chinese Characteristics for a New Era' to the preamble, and article 1 now states explicitly that 'the leadership of the Communist Party of China (CPC) is the defining feature of socialism with Chinese characteristics'. Because this kind of Partyspeak is as easy to digest for the average Chinese as a bowl of salad mixed with sand, every new leader formulates a popular maxim to make clear what his administration stands for. According to Mao, it was 'better to be red than expert', by which he meant that ideological purity is more important than mastering any subject. Deng Xiaoping's most well-known maxim was directly at odds with this: 'It doesn't matter whether a cat is white or black, as long as it catches mice'. With his slogan of 'putting people first', rigid Hu Jintao called attention to the plight of millions of people who became the victims of economic reforms that resulted in the dismantling of state pensions, free healthcare and free housing. Xi Jinping in his turn dreams of the 'Great Rejuvenation of the Chinese Nation'. What these one-liners show is that every new autocrat gives his own twist to Marxism. As Chen Yuan, son of one of the 'Eight Immortals', aptly formulated it: 'We are the Communist Party and we will decide what communism means.'⁴²

In academic and ideological circles, the legacy of Marx gets less frivolous treatment. In May 2013, I attended a conference on Chinese philosophy, organised by Utrecht University. The professors of the *Renmin Daxue* ('People's University'), who attended the conference, explained that in China the subject of philosophy is being taught on the basis of three intellectual schools: *Zhong-Xi-Ma* ('Chinese philosophy – Western philosophy – Marxism'). The philosopher Zhao Tingyang, interviewed later in this book, thinks this is nonsense: 'Marxism is just part of Western philosophy!' For the time being though Karl Marx retains his unique position in the state's ideological pantheon as the intellectual father of the People's Republic.

At the political level the love for Marx goes hand in hand with an increasing aversion for 'Western values': Lacking the critical faculties of the intellectual establishment, these politicians do not seem to be aware that Marxism also makes up part of Western thought. In February 2015, Education Minister Yuan Guiren condemned textbooks that 'promote Western values' and especially singled out those that 'attack or defame the nation's leaders and undermine socialism'.⁴³ Evidently there are still many Party members who succumb to these corrupting influences, for a year later the Central Party School issued a decree that prohibited 'attacking Party theories and glorifying Western values'. Cao Jianming, the country's Supreme People's Procurator, joined the chorus of attacks with an appeal 'to firmly crack down on attempts by hostile forces to infiltrate and damage the country'.⁴⁴ These similar-sounding statements do not mean that all political expressions in China are orchestrated at the top; they are rather a manifestation of the psychological effect that ideological campaigns have on the second-tier leadership. To prove that their political loyalty is beyond dispute, these officials strive to outdo their peers in making statements that articulate the thinking of the paramount leader.

What does Xi Jinping himself say of the relevance of Marxism for today's China? Not much in detail, though he has made it clear that the thinking of the German philosopher will remain the main foundation of the Party, and thus the Chinese state.* Before a plenary meeting of the Politburo in early 2015, the president said that dialectical materialism is the world view of the Party which should be used to unite and lead the people. Inspired by this statement Peking University, the country's most prestigious institute of learning, began building up the Ma Zang (the 'Treasure of Marxism') – a grand collection of Marxist documents, including the translation and compilation of literature from around the world about the great German philosopher and his thought. The project is supposed to be completed in twenty years. As with all prestigious projects in China, the goal is ultimately political. Translator Wang Xuedong, who is closely involved in this project, doesn't beat around the bush: 'Marxism is the foundation of the CPC's legitimacy. Enhancing Marxism is to enhance the legitimacy of the Party's rule.'[45]

As has been noted several times, Xi Jinping is also a major proponent of the 'Great Rejuvenation of the Chinese Nation', and Confucianism (as we shall see later) plays a vital role in this rejuvenation. His embrace of Marxism (certainly for a Western observer) can thus come across as conflicting and confusing. But that is not how the Chinese experience it: Taoism teaches that there is not one underlying 'truth' defining the world, but an infinite, ever-changing river of life. That which is 'true' today, is less true, or even false tomorrow. Dialectical materialism fits nicely with this notion: It is the ever-changing and constantly-recreated reality that defines our thinking, not the other way around. Adapting our thought to a situation that is always new, characterises the true Marxist. As Deng Xiaoping formulated it: shishi qiushi – 'Seek truth from facts.' Xi Jinping follows this school of thought. At the 19th Party Congress, held in October 2017, he stated that a new 'contradiction' (a favourite word in Marxist philosophy) had occurred, namely between the 'unbalanced and unequal development (of China) and the people's ever-growing needs of a better life'. According to the theory

* On May 5, 2018 a 5.5 meter high statue was revealed on the town square of Trier to commemorate the 200th anniversary of Karl Marx birth. It was donated by the People's Republic of China to the city where the German philosopher was born. The statue was meant to be even higher (6.3 meters), but this was rejected. German officials also shot down the proposal to have a meeting in Trier between Angela Merkel and Xi Jinping. In their revolutionary fever Chinese officials had probably forgotten that the German leader – having lived in Communist East Germany until 1990 – is anything but a supporter of Marxism.

of dialectical materialism this is an unavoidable phenomenon. At the same time it legitimizes Party rule *in perpetuum*, because as long as societal contradictions occur (which is basically forever) the Party is needed to 'harmonize' them.

What is valid for the position of Marx is even more true for the man who Sinicised the thought of the German philosopher: Mao Zedong. The position of the founder of the People's Republic of China, whose 'Thought' is embedded in the constitution, is therefore undisputed. In the words of the sinologist Roderick MacFarquhar, Mao constitutes the 'legitimacy factor'.[46] Right after taking office, Xi Jinping said in a speech before the Party's top leaders: 'Just imagine that we would abandon the spirit of Comrade Mao Zedong. Our socialistic system... the whole country would fall into chaos!'[47]

The Five 'Dimensions' of Liu Yunshan

The tree of Marxism may be standing unshakeably on Chinese ground, there are still shoots growing from its trunk that can overgrow or even replace it in the long run. Taking the lead in this ideological re-orientation is Liu Yunshan, a man who in October 2012 unexpectedly managed to acquire a position in the Politburo Standing Committee (PSC), the highest-ranking body of the Party. As – until his retirement in October 2017 – president of the Central Party School, chair of the Central Guidance Commission for Building Spiritual Civilization and chair of the Central Leading Group for Propaganda and Ideological Work, Liu was the central spider in the dense web of the Party's propaganda apparatus. A crucial role, because the Party's power rests on four pillars: The domestic security agencies, the military, the Party organisation and propaganda. The first two shield the state against domestic and foreign threats. The Organisation Department is responsible for the 'quality' (from the Chinese *suzhi*, a word which also implies the quality of someone's character) of the eighty million Party members. As the fourth pillar of power, the propaganda division sets the ideologically desirable course, and monitors whether the (social) media, textbooks, books and movies coincide with the political priorities of the Party – or at least do not conflict with them. Liu, a politician completely unknown to most Westerners, was therefore one of China's most powerful individuals.*

---

* During the 19th Congress of October 2017, Liu's position as supreme ideologist was taken over by Wang Huning – the man responsible for articulating the thinking of three presidents: 'The Three Represents' of Jiang Zemin, Hu Jintao's 'Scientific Outlook on Development' and 'Xi Jinping Thought'. In his book 'America against America', Wang prophesizes the downfall of the United States, because 'self-defeating' notions of liberty and democracy will lead to the disintegration of its society. It is highly unlikely that Wang will deviate from the ideological direction set out by Liu Yunshan.[48]

Liu Yunshan

In China, he is also one of the most hated. The famous dissident Dai Qing greeted his appointment with despair: 'If that is the case, if it is he who will oversee ideology, there will no longer be any hope. China will enter a period of darkness.'[49] She even compared Liu Yunshan with Kang Sheng, Mao's infamous security chief. The well-known writer Tie Liu has attacked Liu Yunshan as the evil genius behind the decline of Chinese media: 'There are no good books, nor good movies or a good TV drama. News media have completely lost their credibility, and have become more and more left-wing.' In the same article, Tie also made an intense personal attack on Liu Yunshan: '[The man] is incompetent, and has no virtue, talent and ethics. He has no morality other than his obedience to the evil and hypocritical Jiang Zemin.'[50] In December 2014, the eighty-one-year-old writer – who already spoke out against Mao at the end of the 1950s, and disappeared for twenty-three years in prison for doing so – was arrested for 'picking quarrels and provoking trouble'.[51]

In a speech held before an audience of Western sinologists in Copenhagen in June 2014, Liu Yunshan explained why the Party still has the right to govern today. He distinguished five 'dimensions' of legitimacy:[52]

1. *The Party is an historical necessity* – after failed experiments with constitutional monarchy, imperial restoration, parliamentarism, multi-party system, and presidential government, the Party adapted the basic tenets of Marxism to the reality of China and the Chinese finally found a correct path for the nation. The Party is not self-appointed but chosen by history.

2. *The support of the people* – The Party represents the fundamental interests of the overwhelming majority of the Chinese people rather than special interests of certain vested groups. That is why the Party enjoys the support of the vast majority of the people: As shown in a global public opinion poll by the Pew Research Center in 2013, 85% Chinese expressed satisfaction with the direction the country is heading for.

3. *Party policy is embedded in Chinese culture* – the nourishment of the fine traditional Chinese culture has enabled the Party to take root, to grow and to govern in the country. Classic Chinese values like benevolence, integrity and justice are consistent with the socialist core values advocated by the Party; the idea of putting people first in traditional Chinese culture is, in essence, the same as the Party's purpose of serving the people; the aspiration of peace and harmony in traditional Chinese culture can also be found in the governing philosophy of the Party.

4. *The economic success of China* – Practice is the sole criterion for testing truth. In thirty years, the Party has changed a poor and backward country into a prosperous and dynamic country with continuous improvement in people's livelihood. China's GDP per person has risen from 300 USD over 30 years ago to 6,000 USD nowadays.

5. *The Party is willing to learn from the world* – The Party maintains friendly contacts with over 600 political parties and organizations from over 180 countries and regions. It is willing to learn from their experiences and practices. In the same vein, political structures are so plural that there's no unified standard to judge all political parties. This context of diversity must also be adapted to acquire a correct, comprehensive and balanced understanding of the Party.

Liu's 'dimensions' follow from the ideas expressed by earlier leaders. One of Jiang Zemin's 'Three Represents' was the role of the Party as the representative of Chinese culture, and Deng Xiaoping based the legitimacy of the Party on its capability for achieving economic growth. The dimension of 'historical necessity' even reaches back to the imperial era, when every new dynasty received the Mandate of Heaven because the previous dynasty was depraved beyond hope. Yet what really fascinates is that these 'dimensions' imply a de facto departure from Marxism. Its teachings are still mentioned in obligatory fashion, but they no longer legitimatize the Party's policy. As the sinologist Frank Pieke notes: 'The Leninist casing around the Party's organisation is still standing, but it has been provided with an entirely new content.'[53]

During this phase of ideological re-orientation, it is difficult to tell how widely Liu Yunshan's analysis is backed, or will be translated into actual policy: The political process in China is characterised by experiments, flexibility and a circuitous route towards a final goal which is adjusted continuously. Yet I believe the trend is irreversible: Marxism-Maoism is undermined step-by-step by the increasing amounts of 'Chinese characteristics' added to it. Looking at the rich Chinese heritage of philosophical thought, Confucianism is the most likely candidate to purvey these 'characteristics' – wasn't it Liu Yunshan, the Party's supreme ideologist, himself who said that the Party is committed to classic Chinese values such as 'benevolence, integrity and justice'?

Confucianism as the New Connection?

In principle, Marxism-Maoism still offers the beckoning prospect of a classless society – though in nowadays China no one believes this anymore. Some older Party members still have a romantic yearning for Yan'an, the place where Mao in the late 1930's supposedly established an egalitarian utopia. Xi Jinping often fondly calls himself a 'man from Yan'an' who will forever be connected to the 'yellow earth of Shaanxi'. Apart from this sentimental delving in the past, Socialism offers a future perspective that strongly resembles that of Confucianism: One day, the borders between states will disappear and everyone will share in the horn of plenty that will then be produced. In *The Book of Rites*, this utopia is called the *Datong Shijie* ('World of the Great Harmony'), a society where All-Under-Heaven is divided equally. In wording that strongly resembles this vision of the future, Xi Jinping positioned in his speech before the 19th Party Congress that by 2050 'common prosperity for everyone will be basically achieved'. A synthesis between Socialism and Confucianism seems perfectly possible, but in spite of the re-appraisal of Confucianist values it is too early to talk about a merger between these two great traditions. The Party's approach is more eclectic: In its search for a new ideology it cherry picks from various value systems. In line with the imperial tradition of providing the people with moral instruction, the Party has since 2012 put great emphasis on three categories of values that every citizen is to adopt:[54]

1. Core Values at the national level: *Fuqiang, Wenming, Minzhu, Hexie* (Prosperity, Civility, Democracy and Harmony)
2. Core Values at societal level: *Ziyou, Pingdeng, Gongzheng, Fazhi* (Freedom, Equality, Justice and Rule of Law)
3. Core Values at the individual level: *Aiguo, Jingye, Chengxin, Youshan* (Patriotism, Dedication, Integrity and Friendship)

Statue of Confucius on Tiananmen Square

These values are so all-encompassing that they do not imply any preference for Socialism, Liberalism, or Confucianism. But it is telling that 'typically native' values like dedication, integrity and harmony take a prominent position.

To many Chinese (intellectuals) Confucius is still seen as a symbol of the feudal abuses of the old order: Superstition, exploitation and conservatism. Moreover, by its victory over these sinister forces (as can be read in the constitution) the Party has acquired the right to govern China. The drift away from Marx, therefore, does not mean that he will be replaced by the ancient philosopher any time soon – even if it appeared that way in 2011. In January of that year a bronze statue of Confucius was placed in front of the Museum of the Chinese Revolution in Beijing. The location was highly symbolic, because Mao, whose portrait hangs at the South Gate of the Forbidden City, was virtually looking the ancient master right in the eye. Many saw this to be an official re-appraisal of a philosopher who, during the 1970s campaign of *Pi Lin Pi Kong* ('criticise Lin Biao and Confucius') was still regarded as a 'reactionary who wanted to restore the rites'.[55] Another salient detail was the height of the statue: At 9.5 metres it was significantly higher than that of the founder of the People's Republic. Three months later, the fusion of feudal and forward-looking came suddenly to an end, when in the middle of the night the statue was mysteriously removed. Since then the Square of Heavenly Peace again serves only one master. No official explanation was given for this spectacular departure, but China's netizens were considerably more outspoken: 'The witch doctor who has been poisoning our people for thousands of years with his slave-master spiritual narcotic has finally been kicked out of Tiananmen Square!' crowed the Maoist website Maoflag.net. Professor Guo Qijia of Beijing Normal University – who is involved in establishing the so-called 'Confucius Institutes' abroad – probably represented a sentiment more widely felt: 'Students come home from school and tell their parents, "One of my classmates got run over by a car today – now I have one less person to compete against." We have lost our humanity, our kindness and our spirit. Confucianism is our only hope for becoming a great nation.'[56]

The New Technocrats

Confucianism not only offers inspiration through its system of ethical values; it also has the proven capability for selecting the best and the brightest in the country. In that regard, the Party has been unconditionally converted to Confucianism. The numerous ministers or heads of business whom I have met over the years stood out with their precise knowledge of their fields of expertise, which they managed to couple with a sense of politesse and humour – often in stark contrast to their foreign counterparts. That competence is no coincidence, but the result of a conscious policy of taking the administrative and executive qualities of the Party cadre to a higher level, not least through educational programmes abroad. The Harvard University's John F. Kennedy School of Government has had, for instance, a public administration programme for high-ranking Chinese officials for many years; the most well-known alumnus of this school is Liu He, a vice premier and Xi Jinping's top economic advisor. Interestingly, the Kennedy School calls itself a 'graduate school preparing leaders for democratic societies and contributing to the solution of public problems'.[57] The foreign training programmes are organised by China's Organisation Department, the powerful, invisible body that deals with personnel matters. The fact that the Party trains its best people in the den of the 'hegemon' gives evidence of a profoundly embedded meritocratic tradition – one that for thirteen centuries, by means of state examinations, groomed the country's smartest minds for public service. A system that was so successful that the old order did not meet its downfall until 1911. Drawing from that tradition, the Party is building an executive class of technocrats that further strengthens the ideological foundation of the 'five dimensions' – thus providing it with an even stronger claim to govern.

Approval Abroad

Daniel Bell wholeheartedly agrees with such an approach. As a professor of political philosophy at Tsinghua University in Beijing, Bell argues that the regime draws from three sources for legitimacy. It *performs well* as a result of its proven capability to feed and clothe the people, and even make them rich. It has the capability to supply *above-average* leaders who can take morally grounded political decisions, and it has succeeded in establishing a *relatively safe state* since 1949.[58] Bell contends that this 'non-democratic legitimacy' gives the lie to the Western notion that only leaders appointed by the people have the right to govern.[59]

Bell's views are of interest: He is the first foreigner to teach at the prestigious Tsinghua University after the Cultural Revolution, as well as the author of two widely discussed (and disputed) books: *China's New Confucianism* and *The China Model: Political Meritocracy and the Limits of Democracy*.[60] In November 2014, I went to visit him in Beijing. Bell is the mild-mannered, professorial type, only showing signs of emotion when the criticism that he is justifying the dictatorship of the Party comes up for discussion. Why is he a proponent of meritocracy? 'The people are not rational, only intelligent individuals of a high moral calibre possess the capability to govern. Still, the question is: How do you keep them in check, how do you prevent the abuse of power?' Bell's answer to his own question is typically Confucianist 'As long as the elite is taught to be virtuous, that problem can be solved. Human nature can be improved.' While that may sound a bit naïve, Bell puts forth a surprising argument why an authoritarian regime must conduct itself properly. 'If it does not, the people in power run the risk of being swept away by a revolution. Even their very survival is at stake. In a democracy, the old guard is just replaced by a new one in the next elections.' He feels that the Party is on the right road. Corruption has supposedly decreased, and the Party's popularity has grown: 'Studies show that the Chinese care more about the quality of their politicians than the procedures for electing their leaders.'

I admire Bell's idealism – stemming from the typical Chinese notion that public servants can morally be reformed – but I have my doubts about his observation that the Chinese people accept the Party and that corruption has supposedly decreased. Virtually no one in China gives their true opinion when polled on the legitimacy of the Communist Party – after all, every Chinese person is raised with the guideline of *motan guoshi* ('don't talk about matters of state') and no one can guarantee that those interviewed will remain anonymous. Moreover, the Pew Research Center survey mentioned also by Liu Yunshan above does not indicate any satisfaction with the Party, but with the state of the economy. Over half of those interviewed are unhappy about inflation, corruption, and inequality. 43 percent say that the government is responsible for the gap between rich and poor and 38 percent say that giving bribes is necessary to get ahead in life. These last two percentages are higher than in most of the other countries studied.[61]And as to the decrease in corruption: This conclusion is not subscribed to by Transparency International, a watchdog that keeps track of public corruption in more than one hundred eighty countries. In 2016, China had a score of 40 points (where 0 is the most corrupt, and 100 as clean as a whistle). This is somewhat better than in 2014 and 2015, but with that score it is still down on its 2013 ranking. In 2016, India was just as corrupt as China, countries like South Africa and Cuba scored better, while Mexico and Russia scored worse. Of the 175 countries measured, the 2016 score put China in 79th place.[62]

The Two-Faced Party

The leadership that was in power from 2012 to 2017 continued the two-track policy of the Hu Jintao era – albeit the execution has been much harsher. The first of these approaches is to squash every challenge to power, repressing people and groupings that until a short while ago were left untouched. The most well-known targets are civil society organisations, the creative sector and the internet. The image of repression only, however, is too one-sided; the Janus-faced nature of the Party shows another side too. The Chinese citizen still enjoys – to use the image from Isaiah Berlin once again – a high degree of 'negative liberty'. He can go wherever he wants on vacation, ride around in shiny cars and choose work that pleases him. Even so, there have been unmistakeable signs that the Party is tightening the reins of social control. In the 12th Five-Year Plan (2011–2015), *shehui guanli* ('social management') was the central strategy of the Party to deal with the rapidly changing Chinese society: 'The party leads, government takes responsibility, society coordinates, and the public participates.' In the 13th Five-Year Plan (2016–2020), the leadership has opted for a more paternalistic attitude: 'We (i.e. the Party)... guide people in exercising their rights, expressing their demands, and resolving their disputes in accordance with the law.'[63] The appeal from the Politburo Standing Committee in January 2016 to back Xi Jinping 'in thought and action' does away with these bureaucratic niceties and comes straight to the point: 'Government, the military, society and schools, north, south, east and west – the party leads them all.'[64] A quote from Mao Zedong that, as we have seen in the previous chapter, was also used by Xi Jinping in his speech to the 19th Party congress of October 2017.

'Seven Things That Should Not Be Discussed'

In May 2013 the secret document 'Communiqué on the Current State of the Ideological Sphere' was published.[65] Its all-out attack on the civil society forms a chilling departure from the more liberal days of the Hu Jintao era (2002–2012). Media and universities are henceforward forbidden to talk about seven subjects:

1. *Universal values* ('they obscure the essential differences between the West's value system and the value system we advocate')
2. *Freedom of speech and freedom of the press* ('the Western idea of journalism undermines our country's principle that the media should be infused with the spirit of the Party')
3. *Civil society* ('advocates of civil society want to end the Party's leadership of the masses, even incite the masses against the Party')
4. *Neoliberalism* ('aims to change our country's basic economic infrastructure and weaken the government's control of the national economy')
5. *Civil rights* ('undermine the strength of the Party')
6. *Historical errors of the CCP* ('promotes historical nihilism')
7. *Judicial independence*

The instruction by the Party not to talk about these subjects (rather quickly called the *Qi Bujiang* – the 'Seven Don't Speaks' – in the social media) is part of a large-scale project to take back control of the public discourse. In doing so, the Party embraces the timeless Chinese tradition of reining in the written word. The first emperor of China burnt all the philosophical works that he did not like and, as mentioned in Chapter 2, the eighteenth-century emperor Qian Long justified his literary inquisition with the words: 'None may remain to after generations, in order to cleanse our speech and make straight the hearts of men'.[66] Even so, our Western capacity to comprehend is put to the test when in this digital age a government imposes collective censorship on its 1.3 billion citizens; all the more so since Article 35 of the Chinese constitution guarantees the freedom of speech, press, assembly, association, procession and demonstration, while Article 36 establishes the freedom of religious belief. Touching on the bizarre is the persecution of individuals who actually assist the Party in fighting corruption: Investigative journalists are arrested if they put their findings on the internet.[67] In January 2014, for instance, Xu Zhiyong, leader of the New Citizens' Movement, was sentenced to four years in prison for 'disruption of the public order'.[68] The 'disruption' consisted of an appeal to the government to carry out the law that obliges officials to disclose their personal assets.[69]

Xu's arrest indicates how Xi Jinping and Liu Yunshan think: Corruption is a cancer that seriously threatens the continued existence of the Party, but in enlisting society to fight this evil lurks the greater danger that citizens will start behaving like autonomous individuals who speak out freely – even against the Party, should their consciences so dictate. When finalising this book (spring 2018), the oppression of dissidents continues unabated. Yet if history is any measure, even this repression is temporary. The future will tell, but one thing is certain: The initial optimism in liberal circles about Xi Jinping being a 'closet reformer' proves to be fully ungrounded.

Art behind Bars

Control over academic discourse is second nature to the Party: Even non-China experts have heard of the infamous 1957 campaign to 'Let a hundred flowers bloom', when Mao invited the country's intellectuals to criticise the Party, only to persecute them mercilessly later. In 2018, threats to the power of the Party are more diverse. The art sector and the internet in particular are increasingly being forced into submission. What connects these media is their capability to reach and inspire 'the masses' – also with ideas which are 'wrong' or politically objectionable. The motivations for censorship are not always clear. Foreign publications are by definition suspect. With its razor-sharp critique of the totalitarian state, George Orwell's classic 1984 remains prohibited, because it holds up an uncomfortable mirror to the regime. A 'decadent' book like D.H. Lawrence's *Lady Chatterley's Lover* is likewise forbidden, whereas the censorship of the movie *Noah* is more difficult to explain. It stands to reason why some Islamic countries have prohibited this retelling of the Biblical story of the flood – but China?

The repression of homegrown art is also on the rise. In October 2014 Xi Jinping advocated making artworks that 'are not only artistically excellent but also politically inspiring'. Many immediately recalled Mao's infamous 1942 speech in Yan'an, which instructed that art must reflect the life of the worker and promote Socialism. Mao's appeal caused the propaganda poster to flourish, but also led to the dissipation of 'feudal' art forms like the Chinese opera: During the Cultural Revolution, only four works were still allowed to be performed. In December 2014, the media watchdog known as the State General Administration of Press, Publication, Radio, Film and Television commanded artists, filmmakers and TV creators to live for a while in the countryside and to 'experience the life' of the farmers. Only then would they be able to acquire a 'correct view of art' and 'create more masterpieces'.[70] This measure calls forth uneasy memories of the Cultural Revolution, when millions of young people were summoned to *Shangshan Xiaxiang* ('up to the mountains and down to the villages') with the same goal: To learn from the peasants.

And the Internet in Chains

By the end of 2016, there were 731 million internet users in China, 43 million more than at the beginning of that year – a number equal to the total population of

Ukraine. The ceiling still has not been reached, even though this 6.2% increase was significantly less than the double-digit growth of a few years ago.[71] This development is indispensable for modernising the country, but those in power tremble at the speed, broad reach and mobilising force of the internet. In 1998, US President Clinton proclaimed triumphantly that 'trying to control the internet would be like trying to "nail Jell-O to the wall,"'[72] but the Party is determined to emerge as the winner in the fight between freedom and censorship. Thanks to a sophisticated software system – 'The Great Firewall' in the vernacular – Western social networks and websites are blocked. In China, typing in queries like 'Dalai Lama' and '4 June' produces nothing other than the message 'according to laws, regulations and policy, a portion of your search results cannot be shown'. Facebook, Twitter, and WhatsApp are forbidden in China; occupying their place are Renren, Weibo, and WeChat, respectively. As head of the 'Central Leading Group for Internet Security and Informatization', President Xi Jinping personally supervises 'internet security': '[T]here is no national security without internet security, and there is no modernisation without wide adoption of information technology'[73] – was how Xi Jinping summed up the Party's twin-track policy.

In striking a balance between society's benefits and state security, the scales continue to tip further and further towards the latter. Since September 2013, spreading 'false rumours' can lead to three years in prison, if the rumour is read more than five thousand times or re-posted more than five hundred times.[74] The popular blogger and fabulously rich businessman Pan Shiyi had to pay for his temerity in slashing Beijing's abominable air pollution with self-criticism: Wringing his hands, he confessed his 'wrongs' on TV and promised thenceforth to serve the country and the Party better.[75] China's increasing need for security was embedded in the National Security Act, which was unanimously adopted with 155 votes in favour in July 2015. The law names the many threats China must arm itself against (including 'harmful cultural influences'), yet internet security is picked out as a special concern: Information and infrastructure systems must be 'secure and controllable'. Foreign technology businesses are afraid that the new law may be a pretext for violating intellectual property, because it gives security inspectors access to these companies' 'source codes'.[76] Unmoved by such concerns, Beijing resolutely sets its own course. It basically sees internet freedom as a possible tool of 'foreign hostile forces' to undermine China's 'internet sovereignty'. As China's new propaganda tsar Wang Huning puts it: 'China stands ready to develop new rules and systems of internet governance to serve all parties and counteract current imbalances.'[77] Freedom House, a US-based organisation researching global internet freedom, ranked China bottom of the 65 countries it investigated in 2015.[78]

But it would be too simple to reduce the Party's view on the internet as a conflict between state security and economic modernisation: It has also come to realise that it is the perfect medium for manipulating the public and influencing them in favour of the

Party. The so-called 'Social Credit System' aspires to build an e-database of *every* Chinese person. It keeps track of whether someone has been involved with the police or has paid his debts, but also whether he has fulfilled his obligations as a good Confucian citizen – for example by visiting his sick, ageing parents. The goal – as formulated by the State Council in 2014 – is 'carrying forward sincerity and traditional virtues' and 'stimulating the progress of civilisation'. In fact, the 'Social Credit System' is a continuation of the *Dang-an* (file) system during the pre-digital era, when crucial information from every citizen's CV was monitored, in addition to his social and political behaviour.[79] Viewed positively, this system aids the government in understanding what is going on among the people, identifying abuses and formulating better policy. But more worrying (certainly from a Western perspective) is that it also gives the Party unlimited access to private information that can stigmatise the individual concerned. To want to know what is going on among the people, and intervene in their lives whenever 'the security of the state' so requires, has been a trait of both emperors and communist Party bosses. The people, for example, who participated in the mass demonstrations in the spring of 1989 were tracked down via the *Dang-an* system and labelled as 'suspicious or even bad elements'. This had a huge impact on their career. In the digital age the possibilities for control are infinitely greater – especially because world famous internet companies like Alibaba and Tencent share their 'Big Data' with the government.

Internet expert Michael Anti is for these reasons very pessimistic: 'We were convinced that thanks to the new technology we might make a difference. But in the meantime, the internet has shown its other face, that of a monster. Not only the American NSA (National Security Agency) has discovered the possibilities for keeping an eye on citizens via the internet; China is also making use of "Big Data" to prevent "crime". And that includes tracking down dissident voices.'[80] No wonder George Orwell's *1984* is blacklisted in China.

A Market Economy?

The economic policy of the Party also tries to reconcile different objectives. Ever since Deng Xiaoping in the early 1980s introduced the 'Socialist market economy' (a contradiction in terms that can only be conceived in China), the blessings of the market have not been fundamentally questioned. An economic model has emerged that we can best characterise as the 'invisible hand with Chinese characteristics': Inasmuch as the Party's power is not endangered, the market is given free rein. In that respect, the Party has in recent years become more paranoid: One of the 'seven subjects that should not be discussed' is 'neoliberalism' (the privatisation of the economy) because it would weaken the government's economic grip. The Chinese stock markets are a good example of this unwanted liberalism. Until early 2015, Premier

Li Keqiang had encouraged companies to issue shares; otherwise their bank debts would run too high. Henceforward the banks should not be left with irrecoverable debt in case of corporate failure; this should be the risk of the investor. In July 2015, though, the Chinese stock markets crashed, and the Party immediately took a series of (unsuccessful) measures to arrest falling stock prices. The fear that the rage of (mostly small) investors would translate into political unrest was greater than the confidence in the cyclical functioning of the market.

Still, only a few people in China are in favour of a restoration of the Maoist state economy. From personal experience I can understand why. As a businessman I visited many state-owned companies in the 1980s and 1990s, and they all looked the same: Driving through the gates of these gigantic complexes, you entered a self-contained world of factories with their own schools, hospitals and gymnasiums. Slogans like *gaogaoxingxing shangbanlai, pingpinganan huijiailai* ('go to work cheerfully and return home safely') gave the impression of bliss and regularity. The worker was cared for by the state from the cradle to the grave, and did not have to worry about dismissal, sickness, or lack of money. The image of indolence still lingers in my mind: Tea drinking went on endlessly, and in every corner of any room there was someone sleeping.

This idyllic world of the 'iron rice bowl' was untenable; the absence of competition turned most state-owned businesses into loss-making concerns and workers into listless human beings. In the middle of the 1990s, Premier Zhu Rongji took the broom to this Maoist edifice. He privatised nearly half of the state-owned businesses, putting around fifty million people onto the street.[81] In nearly any other country such a mass firing would have led to social unrest, but in China it stimulated the entrepreneurial spirit: Many state-owned businesses made a new start as private companies, and the redundant workers were employed by the urban construction and export industries in the coastal regions. During that time world-renowned firms today like Huawei (telecoms) and Haier (household appliances) were either founded or resurrected. Zhu Rongji's neoliberal shock therapy did not disrupt the economy; it led in fact to greater productivity and higher growth. Premier Zhu's fearlessness finds few followers amongst today's technocrats. The third plenum of the 18th Party Congress (November 2013) stated that 'markets should play a decisive role in the allocation of resources' and adopted a package of economic reforms. In practice, however, little came of it. The US-China Business Council concluded that by 2015, not even 10% of the announced measures had been carried out.[82] The failure may have already been built-in, for the 2013 plenum also decided that the measures were intended to strengthen the 'Socialist market economy'.

The 'Rule of Law'

Attempts to reform the judiciary bring forth a similar contradiction between the urge to maintain control and true independence. The special Party Congress of October 2014 dedicated to the 'rule of law', decided that every Party member had to swear loyalty to the constitution. From then on, the 4th December was even declared to be 'Constitution Day'. Xi Jinping sees the law as an important tool for combating the arbitrary use of power by the Party cadre – especially at the local level where Article 13 of the constitution ('lawful private property is inviolable') is violated on a daily basis by the unlawful expropriation of farmland. To counteract these abuses, local justices are no longer administered by the local government, but are henceforth 'vertically' answerable to higher judicial institutions. This measure is supposed to make the justices immune to unwanted influences. It was additionally decided that justices will remain accountable their entire lives for the verdicts they render – the intention being to counteract bribery of the court.[83]

For a country that not even sixty years ago abolished all laws as feudal remnants of the bourgeoisie, these are steps in the right direction. Yet it does not mean that China is on the way to separating judicial and executive power. The Party remains both the supervisor as well as the embodiment of the law. After the congress concluded in October 2014, Xi Jinping shed light on this role: 'The Party's leadership is the essential feature of socialism with Chinese characteristics, and the fundamental guarantee of socialist rule of law.'[84] The Chinese term for the rule of law (*yifa zhiguo* – 'rule the country with the law') makes the Party's intention crystal clear: The law is an *instrument* of governance, not a set of social agreements which everyone – including the Party itself – should adhere to and which may only be interpreted by independent justices.

In 2015, any doubt regarding the Party's view of the law was removed by the large-scale arrest of more than three hundred lawyers who had shown the audacity to defend human rights activists. One of them, Tang Jinglin, received a prison sentence of five years for undermining the state. Tang declined to appeal, explaining that he 'would continue to appeal for justice and freedom, but only to the people and to God'.[85] Xia Lin, who had defended well-known dissidents like Ai Weiwei and Tan Zuoren for their role in conducting an independent investigation into the victims of the massive earthquake in Sichuan province in 2008, even received a 12-year sentence.[86]

The most depressing display of the Party's attitude towards the law was the call from chief justice Zhou Qiang: 'Bare your swords towards false Western ideals like judicial independence!' Only two months before he had said that the Party should not intervene in the judicial process.[87] During the Cultural Revolution Mao had stated (as noted earlier) that it 'is better to be red than expert' – by which he meant to say that ideological purity (and obedience to him) was better than mastery of any subject.

Pronouncements from people like Zhou, who trade their professional dignity for a declaration of loyalty to the great leader, bring the spirit of those dark days back to life again.

Consultative Democracy

The story line repeats itself. The Party's view on 'democracy' bears resemblance to its view on the legal sector: Reforms are being carried out, but the result does not reflect what is meant by 'democracy' in the West. In a speech held in September 2014 before China's highest advisory body – the Chinese People's Political Consultative Conference – Xi Jinping called for the gradual introduction of democracy. The president was alluding, however, to the so-called 'consultative democracy'.[88] In an interview with the *Financial Times*, Minister Wang Yi of Foreign Affairs explained that this system, combined with the system for selecting officials, is by far superior to Western 'street democracy': 'The Communist Party of China (CPC) has 86 million members, including many outstanding people. China's system of selecting and appointing officials is very effective. First, our election system is not about street campaigns and one-off voting but multiple voting by different groups of people. Besides, our democratic consultation system requires comprehensive consultation with people from various sectors. A fusion of these two systems has ensured that Chinese officials are rich in experience and capable in governance. With the synergy of over 80 million party members, I don't see any difficulty that cannot be surmounted.'[89] For the positively-disposed observer this explanation is credible. The best and the brightest govern and a broad popular referendum takes place. The more sceptical mind reads these remarks as a modern variation of Mao's 'Democratic Centralism': Everyone can have their say, but in the end a small group of Party members take the major decisions.

Democratic Centralism

Democratic Centralism is the principle whereby all members of a party have the right to express their opinion regarding a specific proposal ('democratic'), but should subsequently fall in line with its execution ('centralism'). As Lenin formulated it: 'freedom of discussion, unity of action'. In China, Democratic Centralism is applied to the operations of the National People's Congress (the 'parliament') and its local divisions: 'The State organs of the People's Republic of China apply the principle of democratic centralism. The National People's Congress and the local people's congresses at various levels are constituted through democratic elections' (Article 3 of the constitution). In practice, the members of the people's congresses are 'chosen' from candidates who have been approved by the Party. The job of these congresses is supervising the state's administrative, legal, and procurative bodies, though here too reality differs from theory: All state organs in China are under the supervision of the Party. The same article of the constitution uses more torturous language to express the same principle: 'The division of functions and powers between the central and local State organs is guided by the principle of giving full scope to the initiative and enthusiasm of the local authorities under the unified leadership of the central authorities.'

As is usually the case in China, reality is tinted grey. On matters seen as sensitive to national security the people are not consulted, nor are the media allowed to write about them before the Party has taken a decision. In the conviction of high-ranking politicians like Bo Xilai and Zhou Yongkang, the legislative and judiciary branches are not involved – let alone that ordinary people have a say. However, if a road is built or a chemicals factory constructed, the people affected by these decisions are in principle consulted – even though this public participation procedure is frequently ignored as a result of the *kongsi* between Party bosses and big enterprises. Millions of farmers in China have been impotent victims of large-scale expropriation of land, yet they are hardly ever consulted. In the domain of foreign affairs – previously the realm of a small, select group of apparatchiks – the situation seems to be different, if we are to believe Cui Tiankai, the former Vice-Minister minister of Foreign Affairs. In an interview with David Shambaugh, a widely published China expert, Cui lamented that 'diplomacy is no longer the business of a few elite people. It is increasingly embedded in the public opinion. Even within the government, there are so many voices – the PLA, companies, ministries, scholars. This makes the process of decision-making extremely complicated.'[90]

That other non-institutionalised, though much older form of Chinese democracy – the intellectual debate – has also been strongly on the rise in recent years. This phenomenon goes back to the imperial era, when the righteous mandarin felt it as a moral imperative to tell the truth to his superior (sometimes the emperor himself) – even if he had to pay for his impertinence with his life. Today's intellectuals are no less outspoken, even if in the permanent fight between censorship and free speech the pendulum has in recent years swung back towards repression. A true intellectual, however, will never be silenced. In academic and literary circles lively discussions are being held about China's identity and its place in the world – by professors, intellectuals, researchers, generals, journalists, religious leaders, philosophers, entrepreneurs, and self-made analysts. The same is happening on social media, where the so-called 'netizens' are an unruly crowd with often outspoken opinions. They are talking about the 'Seven Don't Speaks' – and much more.

CHAPTER 6

An Alternative to the Party?

The difference between Western and Chinese governing systems is the difference between humane versus inhumane, there's no middle ground. [...] Westernization is not a choice of a nation, but a choice for the human race.

Liu Xiaobo

There are many conceivable models for shaping China's future political landscape. Western circles often speculate about a 'third way', one that will occupy the middle ground between today's autocratic system – Communist in name only – and Western parliamentary democracy. Opinions amongst Chinese thinkers are more pluralistic, and often more radical as well. Especially since the 19th Party Congress held in October 2017, many openly preach a 'Chinese Model' that opposes the West. It is hard to parse this wide-ranging discourse into neat trends. In his book *China Goes Global*, David Shambaugh distinguishes at least seven schools[1] – a lot fewer than the hundred that existed, it is said, during China's Golden Age of philosophy (fifth century BCE), yet their existence does show the liveliness of the ongoing intellectual debate.

The most glaring difference is that between nationalists and internationalists. What connects the former group is the sense that China is a great, ancient, and unique country whose time has come to resume its legitimate role as a major superpower. According to this school, Western technologies and processes can contribute to the achievement of that goal, but cannot be allowed to change the *essence* of China. While the internationalists do not argue for a slavish imitation of Western liberalism per se, they do resist the chauvinist noises proclaiming Chinese culture to be of a unique and higher order. They are in favour of a convergence of East and West, and believe in the *Doctrine of the Mean* which was already advocated by Confucius. In the realm of economics, the nationalists argue for a large-scale nationalisation, viewing the privatisation of state businesses as the cause of the great income disparity and acute corruption that plagues present-day China. These excesses, according to the internationalists, cannot be fought by returning to the days of Mao's 'iron rice bowl' but by expanding Deng Xiaoping's economic reforms with political reforms, such as the separation of Party and state.[2]

Liberalism Oppressed

The philosopher Tu Weiming – first mentioned in this book's introduction – sees China as the battlefield of three ideologies: Socialism, Confucianism, and Liberalism.[3] In the second decade of the twenty-first century, this last school seems to be on the losing end, especially *political* liberalism. *Economic* liberalism seems to be more sustainable, but as a result of Xi Jinping's policy to restore the Party's central role in society, the major state-owned businesses are regaining the power that they had to give up at the end of the 1990s. And yet no one – with the exception of a lone recalcitrant Maoist – would dispute the causal connection between the introduction of the market economy and the prosperity created in the last thirty years. That does not mean that Milton Friedman – the great proponent of free market thinking – is embraced as a prophet: In core sectors like steel, banking, energy, telecommunications and especially in the media (in which Party control is seen as essential to maintain power), the state calls the shots. The ambivalence between freedom and control came clearly to the fore during the third plenum of the 18th Party Congress, held in November 2013. The closing resolution pledged that the market will play 'a decisive role in allocating resources', but also that China will adhere to the 'Socialist market economy'.*[4] This disappointed many, for Yu Zhengsheng (the Party's number 4 at that time) had announced 'unprecedented reforms': It was even expected that this third plenum would be as trailblazing as the 1978 congress that set Deng Xiaoping's reforms in motion. That expectation was unrealistic, for no Party congress (not even the one in 1978) uses clear language to summarise its conclusions – vagueness and concealment are the norm. The wooden jargon of Marxism is to blame for that murkiness, but even more important is the culturally deep-rooted principle of *liu yudi* ('preserving leeway'), which avoids taking explicit positions. Politically opportune adjustments must always remain an option.

Vis-à-vis *political* liberalism, the established order takes a much less ambiguous stand; it is expressly negative. In the Chinese constitution a few liberal values have been adopted, such as the right to assemble and to demonstrate, as well as freedom of religion. However, activists who try to force the Party to comply with these values are regularly denounced as participating in a 'Western conspiracy' to undermine Socialism.[5] That is not to say that venting politically an undesirable opinion is forbidden under any circumstance. Many Chinese talk openly about their leaders,

* The 19th Party Congress held in October 2017 showed even less enthusiasm for a free market economy: in his marathon speech at the opening of that congress, Xi promised reforms that would make the State Owned Enterprises 'stronger, better and larger' in the coming five years.

even make jokes about them, but the opinion or joke may never degenerate into a *movement* that competes with the Party for power.* That is why China's most famous dissident Liu Xiaobo was only detained after more than three hundred people had signed his pamphlet *Charter 08*: Not because of his earlier writing. Any political movement, however small in number, is quickly suspected of infringing Article 1 of the constitution: 'Disruption of the socialist system by any organization or individual is prohibited.'[7] In China you may still say (mostly) anything you want, as long as you say it *on your own*.

Is Democracy Alien to the Chinese?

The frequently-heard opinion that the Chinese lack a democratic gene is contentious – to put it mildly. The island of Taiwan, where the vast majority are of Chinese descent, is the best proof of that. Like the People's Republic now, this country of more than twenty million people was once ruled by a party that had zero tolerance for anything that competed with its power; yet Chiang Ching-kuo, the son of Chiang Kai-shek, lifted the state of emergency in 1987 and cleared the way for parliamentary democracy. The Kuomintang managed to do what the Communist regime on the mainland has been unable to do so far: It reformed itself from the inside. I lived in Taiwan from 1990–1992, and can still well remember television broadcasts of massive brawls in the parliament, where the Kuomintang and the opposition savagely bashed each other with chairs, shoes and other objects. Yet the island made it through this 'primitive phase of democracy' – to paraphrase Marx – successfully, and now possesses a well-functioning democracy with fair elections and respect for the minority. While the Party in China rejects democracy time and again as a Western system that is supposedly not suited for the nation, it has strangely enough adopted a few liberal values in its constitution: For example, Article 35 states that 'Citizens of the People's Republic of China enjoy freedom of speech, of the press, of assembly, of association, of procession and of demonstration'. In 2004, two more liberal amendments were added to the constitution: 'Citizens' lawful private property is inviolable' (Article 13), and 'The State respects and preserves human rights' (Article 33).[8] Both rights, specifically the last, are

* Lately, tolerance for joking about Xi Jinping is wearing thin. When 47 year old Wang Jiangfeng called the president ' 習包子' ('steamed bun Xi' – a common nickname for Xi on social media following his visit to the Qingfeng restaurant, mentioned in chapter 4) he was jailed for two years. In its judgement the court said that Wang had 'insulted, humiliated and disrespected national leaders', thereby producing 'negative thoughts about the Chinese Communist Party, which caused public disorder of a serious nature'.[6]

violated on a large scale, yet what is striking is the enormous ideological leap forward in relation to the 1954 constitution, which was still stuffed with Communist ideals like class struggle and the complete state ownership of all means of production.

Democracy as the Benchmark

The yearning for constitutionality and democracy is not alien to China; it is already more than a hundred years old. Kang Youwei – the man who held power for a hundred days in 1898 to reform the terminally sick Qing dynasty – was the first to argue for the introduction of a constitutional monarchy; but he failed miserably. The activists of the May 4th Movement of 1919 called on China to embrace 'Mr Science and Mr Democracy'. This slogan was thought up by Chen Duxiu, the revolutionary who, together with Mao Zedong, was present at the founding of the Party in 1921.[9] Still, that dream of intellectual and political freedom has never been realised. There was a momentary ray of hope when Mao, just before the Communists seized power in 1949, made a remarkable pronouncement: 'We have found a new path. We can break free of the cycle. The path is called democracy. As long as the people have oversight of the government then the government will not slacken in its efforts.'[10] Once in power, Mao's liberal impulses went up in smoke: The word 'democracy' only appears in the constitution to precede the noun 'centralism' – and 'Democratic Centralism' is, as every Chinese knows, a euphemism for dictatorship. Song Meiling, the wife of Chiang Kai-shek, had already predicted this change of direction. George Marshall – the American general faced with the impossible task of making peace between Mao and Chiang – once reminded her that the Communists stood for a new form of democracy. As the story is told, she answered quick-wittedly that the Communists had not yet felt the spell of power. Once they did, they would behave just like the autocratic Kuomintang. Soong Meiling's prediction turned out to be fully correct. Amazingly, every leader of the People's Republic still feels a deep urge to call his rule 'democratic'. From Mao's 'Democratic Centralism' to Xi Jinping's 'consultative democracy' – the ideal formulated by the Athenians in the fifth century BCE is used time and again as the benchmark for legislation and governance.

Liu Xiaobo

Liu Xiaobo, China's most well-known dissident, had no patience whatsoever with any Chinese tainting of democracy. In 2008, sixty years after the acceptance of the Universal Declaration of Human Rights he signed with three hundred other intellectuals the *Charter 08* manifesto – a name inspired by the Czech Václav Havel's *Charter 77*. With

Speaker Nancy Pelosi with a portrait of Liu Xiaobo at the Nobel Peace Center

a doctorate in literature, Liu was not unknown to the Chinese security apparatus. In the run-up to 4 June 1989, he went on hunger strike with three of his fellow-intellectuals to express solidarity with the students (an act quickly dubbed the 'hunger strike of the four *junzi*' – i.e. 'noble persons'). On the night of 3 to 4 June, Liu negotiated with the military to give hundreds of students safe passage.[11] In spite of his conviction for 'counter-revolutionary activities', he therefore received the relatively mild prison sentence of nineteen months. This did not frighten Liu off. After his release, he continued to publish books and articles criticising the Party's autocratic regime. In his writings, Liu shows himself to be a full-blooded 'universalist', who rejects any exceptionalism of the Chinese people or the Chinese development model: 'Modernization means whole-sale westernization, choosing a human life is choosing a Western way of life. The difference between Western and Chinese governing systems is the difference between humane versus inhumane, there's no middle ground. [...] Westernization is not a choice of a nation, but a choice for the human race.'[12]

Charter 08

The combination of clear analysis, catchy language, and an energising vision for the future makes Liu's *Charter 08* an unusual piece of writing that, strangely enough, recalls the *Communist Manifesto* by Karl Marx.[13] But perhaps this is not so odd – just like Marx in his day, Liu is also going against the flow and is hated by the incumbent class. The foreword to Liu's manifesto analyses China's political history of the past hundred years, from the moment the first constitution was adopted in 1912. Liu notes that the Party's project of modernisation has led to a laundry list of abuses: 'The stultifying results are endemic official corruption, an undermining of the rule of law, weak human rights, decay in public ethics, crony capitalism, growing inequality between the wealthy and the poor, pillage of the natural environment as well as of the human and historical environments, and the exacerbation of a long list of social conflicts, especially, in recent times, a sharpening animosity between officials and ordinary people.'

Liu's analysis is not wholly one-sided, though: He praises the Party for ending the 'totalitarianism of the Mao Zedong era' and for 'relief from the pervasive poverty'. He is also positive about the human rights conventions China has signed and the constitutional amendment of 2004 obligating the state to 'respect and protect human rights'. Unfortunately, says Liu, because it is not being implemented, this amendment is worth less 'than the paper on which it is written'. 'Without freedom', Liu writes, 'China will always remain far from civilized ideals.' Freedom and human rights are innate and not granted by the state. Only a democratically-elected, constitutional government can protect these rights. A government that, in the words of Abraham Lincoln's famous Gettysburg Address, is "of the people, by the people, and for the people."'

After this historical/philosophical introduction, Liu has a few 'recommendations' for the government. In essence, he calls on the Party to contribute to the creation of a pluralistic and free society: Make the judges independent, separate the military from the Party, permit freedom of religion and treat ethnic minorities equally. In particular, Liu makes a case for establishing a *federal* state – only then is a harmonious coexistence with Tibetans and other minorities possible, and can Taiwan be peacefully reunited with the mainland. A Truth Commission needs to be set up to investigate proceedings against political prisoners; those who have been wrongly stigmatised as 'criminals' must immediately be rehabilitated. Liu closes the manifesto with an *I have a dream*-like message of hope: 'Together we can work for major changes in Chinese society and for the rapid establishment of a free, democratic, and constitutional country. We can bring to reality the goals and ideals that our people have incessantly been seeking for more than a hundred years, and can bring a brilliant new chapter to Chinese civilization.'[14]

Liu Xiaobo's Arrest

Charter 08 does not call for free elections, or a changing of the guard, yet the damning enumeration of the country's social and political abuses conveyed a message that the historically-sensitive regime could not ignore: The Party has forfeited the Mandate of Heaven. On 8 December 2008, Liu was arrested and in June 2009 imprisoned for eleven years for 'incitement of subversion of state power' – a punishment that was much longer than his earlier three stays in prison combined. This harsh treatment had everything to do with Beijing's change of policy resulting from the events surrounding the 2008 Olympic Games in Beijing. In the run-up to the Games, demonstrators disrupted the relay of the Olympic torch through various European countries (detailed in Chapter 9). Beijing's initial anger over the protests soon changed into contempt when, following the outbreak of the global financial crisis in September 2008, the governments of those same countries implored China with outstretched begging-bowls to buy their government bonds. These differing faces of the West confirmed to the Chinese elite that power and national strength are the only things that count: If Western economies suffer, 'universal' values are suddenly forgotten. That analysis was actually not quite correct, because the same West still had the audacity to award Liu Xiaobo the Nobel Peace Prize in October 2010. This turned the dissident into a cause celebre, a conscientious individual conducting a single-handed struggle against a tyrannical regime. In the Chinese analysis, however, the Nobel Prize Committee was clearly a tool of hostile Western forces, for Tenzin Gyatso, better known as the fourteenth Dalai Lama, had received the same Peace Prize in 1989. The Ministry of Foreign Affairs said the decision to give Liu the award 'profaned' the principles of the Nobel Prize: Liu was nothing more than a simple 'criminal'.[15]

It did not end with mere words: As a sign of Beijing's growing power, Russia, Kazakhstan, Tunisia, Saudi Arabia, Pakistan, Iraq, Iran, Vietnam, Venezuela, Egypt, Sudan, Cuba, and Morocco were successfully pressurised into boycotting the awards ceremony in Oslo. Of course, Liu Xiaobo was not there himself either, but the actress Liv Ullmann read from Liu's declaration '*I have no enemies*' – a text that the dissident had wanted to deliver himself during his trial in Beijing in December 2008, but which he was banned from doing.[16] In his declaration, Liu shows himself to be a true *junzi*, subordinating his personal fate to the higher ideal of improving society. Personalising his enemies, his words acquire a Mandela-like quality: 'I have no enemies and no hatred. None of the police who monitored, arrested, and interrogated me, none of the prosecutors who indicted me, and none of the judges who judged me are my enemies. Although there is no way I can accept your monitoring, arrests, indictments, and verdicts, I respect your professions and your integrity, including those of the two prosecutors, Zhang Rongye and Pan Xueqing, who are now bringing charges against me on behalf of the prosecution. During interrogation on December 3, I could sense your respect and your good faith. Hatred can rot away at a person's intelligence and conscience. Enemy mentality will poison the spirit of a nation, incite cruel mortal struggles, destroy a society's tolerance and humanity, and hinder a nation's progress toward freedom and democracy. That is why I hope to be able to transcend my personal experiences as I look upon our nation's development and social change, to counter the regime's hostility with utmost goodwill, and to dispel hatred with love. ...'

When countries shed their dictatorial skin, a leader frequently stands up who appears spiritually cleansed by the persecution the old regime has caused him. Only he or she can heal the country's wounds by building a bridge to the earlier oppressors. Václav Havel, Nelson Mandela... Liu Xiaobo can no longer play this role. In the spring of 2017, he was diagnosed with liver cancer – though some sources contend that early symptoms of the disease had been evident since 2010. In July 2017, Liu's health deteriorated rapidly. Beijing refused him treatment abroad, and at 5:35 p.m. on 13 July Liu breathed his last. 'Live well' were his last words to his wife Liu Xia.[17]

After Liu's death, the political jousting continued for some time. The late announcement of his illness, and the fact that Liu Xia virtually disappeared from the face of the earth after her husband's death, led to condemnations from the Nobel Prize Committee, US Secretary of State Rex Tillerson, and many others. Wang Dan, one of the student leaders of 1989, called Liu's death 'naked political murder',[18] but the Chinese Ministry of Foreign Affairs repeated the mantra that Liu had been sentenced in accordance with Chinese law, and appealed to everyone to respect Liu Xia's wish to deal with her grief in silence.[19] The most impressive epitaph came from Liu himself: 'What is really scary is submission, silence, and even praise for tyranny. As soon as people decide to oppose it to the bitter end, even the most vicious tyranny will be short-lived.'[20] Those words, however, are written on the waves: To prevent the creation of a place of worship, Liu Xiaobo's ashes were immediately after his death scattered at sea. Censorship in China knows no end. In life and in death.

Other Liberals

Without a doubt, Liu Xiaobo was an exceptional thinker and an exceptional individual, but he is certainly not the only one to represent the liberal voice. When writing the first, Dutch edition of this book (2014–2015), I wrote that 'most of them (i.e. the liberals) were still able to make their opinions known relatively undisturbed'. Now, in early 2018, this assertion is difficult to uphold: Liberal intellectuals, lawyers, as well as activists for the rights of ethnic minorities are being persecuted and silenced on a scale not seen since the days of Mao. Since the elevation of Xi Jinping to 'core leader' in 2016, any form of meaningful debate has been squelched within the Party itself as well. It is difficult therefore to interpret what is really going on, and whether there is any slumbering resistance behind the monotonous stream of declarations of loyalty to the Great Leader. If history offers any guide (which is usually the case in China), a counter-reaction will sooner or later come about, a movement that opposes Xi's neo-Maoism and seeks out the *Doctrine of the Mean*. As the ancient proverb goes, *Wu ji bi fan*: When matters are extreme, a reversal will surely follow. A reversal which will try to give political shape to the feelings of discontent that these liberal thinkers were formulating before they were silenced. It comprises four main themes.

1. *Reforming the political system is unavoidable*
The 1980s were a unique period in the history of the People's Republic – comparable, in a certain sense, with the years preceding the May 4th Movement in 1919. After the Special Economic Zones were created and trade and investment legislation adopted, foreigners streamed into the country for the first time since the 1930s. A promise of change hung in the air. The leaders of the time – Party secretary Hu Yaobang and premier Zhao Ziyang – sensed that the mood in the land was changing, and launched proposals for internal Party elections, transparency in government and accountability for officials. The Tiananmen Square killings meant the end of this liberal experiment, even though the later premier Wen Jiabao (2002–2012) voiced the striking appraisal that 'the people's wishes for and needs for democracy and freedom are irresistible'.[21] This statement was made to CNN, however, and not mentioned by the Chinese media.

The best-known proponent for political reforms is Hu Deping. As the son of Hu Yaobang, he can speak more candidly than his fellow liberals, although that privilege also restricts him: He cannot allow to be seen as someone who fouls the nest of his own class. In an interview in November 2014, he shows himself to be cautiously optimistic about Xi Jinping's anti-corruption campaign and his elevating of the constitution. In the Marxist jargon peculiar to his generation, Hu argues for putting a good 'superstructure' (legislation and the political system) on a solid 'substructure' (the economy). The Party congress on the rule of law held in October 2014 is, according to Hu, an important step, but must be followed up with political reforms. Only then can the stalemate of the political process be broken.[22]

Some (former) leaders go even further. Zhao Ziyang argued for the introduction of parliamentary democracy because only that system can tackle China's chronic problems of the abuse of power, corruption, and income inequality. The former premier and Party Leader wrote his plea during his sixteen years under house arrest (from 1989 until his death in 2005). It had no effect at all in China, but it did gain notoriety abroad – the manuscript was smuggled out of the country and published as *Prisoner of the State: The Secret Journal of Premier Zhao Ziyang*.[23]

2. Plurality in society must be promoted

One of propaganda tsar Liu Yunshan's 'seven things that should not be discussed' is the 'historical errors of the Party'. Still, on rare occasions that same Party does have the capability to search its own heart. The document *Resolution on certain questions in the history of our party since the founding of the People's Republic of China*, adopted in 1981, admits that Mao Zedong had made 'serious mistakes', and was thus 'chiefly responsible' for the excesses of the Cultural Revolution[24] – a movement described in that document as a 'catastrophe'. At a major congress held in 2011 to commemorate the thirtieth anniversary of this historic document, the participants seized the opportunity to pillory the evils of the one-party state. A former editor-in-chief of the *People's Daily*, Zhou Ruijin, said that the Party's exclusive hold on power contributed to the 'rampant official and judicial corruption and given rise to irrational decisions and the blind pursuit of growth at the expense of people and the environment'.[25] Other abuses, said Zhou, like the growing gap between rich and poor, and the nationalisation of farmland, are caused by the same abuse of power – as are the tens of thousands of 'mass incidents' (disturbances that frequently turn violent), bombings of local Party offices and massive brawls between migrant workers and the infamous *chengguan*, the law enforcement authorities in the cities. At that same congress Zhang Weiying, the former dean of the School of Management at Peking University, cynically summed up the importance of the constitution: 'There is only one provision in the constitution that has been truly implemented: the party's absolute leadership.'[26]

In 2018, congresses such as these can no longer be organised in China. The 2013 announcement of the 'seven things that should not be discussed' was the first shot fired to stifle the free debate. Since then things have gone from bad to worse. This also applies to discussions regarding the great trauma of modern Chinese history: The Cultural Revolution. 2016 commemorated the launching of the Cultural Revolution fifty years earlier, but the official media did everything to keep the lid closed on the Pandora's Box of 'subjective opinions': There was no reason to doubt the 'profoundness' of the official judgement that the movement was 'a complete mistake' that the Party 'will never allow to happen again'. (The word 'catastrophe', used in the 1981 judgement, was not mentioned any more).[27] In 2016, the renowned historian Yang Jisheng published *The World Turned Upside Down* – an account of Mao's mass movement. Yang – who made a name for himself in 2008 with *Tombstone*, his book on the disastrous Great Leap Forward of 1958 – said that he wrote the book 'to expose lies and restore the truth'. The nationalist newspaper *Global Times* saw it differently: 'Yang leaves the impression that he's not interested in history, and virtually all his later works display strong political tendencies.'[28] *The World Turned Upside Down* is banned in most of China, and is only available in Hong Kong.

In 2018, there is even less toleration in China for criticism of *contemporary* Party policies. In February 2016, Xi Jinping visited the headquarters of China Central

Television (CCTV). 'The media must embody the party's will, and safeguard the party's authority', the Great Leader announced. This obviously applies to Party-controlled media, but commercial channels must follow 'the right direction' too. To eliminate any doubts regarding the slavish obedience of China largest broadcasting station to Party politics, a sign was hung in the room where the president was received: 'CCTV's surname is "The Party". We are absolutely loyal. Ready for your inspection.'[29]

3. The rise of the New Left is life-threatening

In 2008, a group of Maoists created a new party: The Chinese Communist Party of Maoists. The leaders of this splinter group were soon detained and given ten-year sentences. Organised challenges to the ruling party are never tolerated, not even from orthodox Maoist corners. Still, ultraleft-wing resistance continued to smoulder, for one evening in September 2012, eighty Maoists secretly gathered. Most of them were older men and women, wearing buttons on their grey and blue uniforms from the 1960s depicting the Great Helmsman. Suddenly shouts of confusion and fear: 'The dogs are at the door!' But before the police could make any arrests, the Maoists had already dispersed.[30] What unites groups like these is a yearning for the egalitarian days of Mao, and an aversion towards the excesses of Deng Xiaoping's state capitalism: The growing gap between rich and poor, the loss of social safety nets and the rise of a new class of exploitative entrepreneurs. In the words of Zhou, a retired labourer, China's nominally Socialist system in effect 'combines the worst of all worlds: hyper-capitalism, corruption and fascism'.[31]

The discontent of these individuals has been intellectually translated into a movement called the 'New Left'. Renowned academics and military figures are adherents of this school, but its most well-known exponent is surely Bo Xilai. As the Party Secretary of the megalopolis Chongqing, this son of the 'immortal' Bo Yibo started a campaign that attacked organised crime, carried out major welfare projects and turned culture 'red' by singing Maoist battle songs. Just like in the Cultural Revolution, students were sent to the countryside 'to learn from peasants'. Leftist intellectuals praised the 'Chongqing model' as a humane alternative to predatory capitalism, but the sinister side of Bo's methods soon surfaced. The 'organised crime' that he was fighting was mainly made up of legitimate businesses blackmailed at knifepoint into contributing to Bo's megalomaniacal programmes. Critics were intimidated and lawyer Li Zhuang, who defended one of the 'criminals, was confronted with fabricated claims'.[32] He Weifang, a law professor at Peking University, became the mouthpiece for many who opposed Bo's methods. He even compared the Chongqing model with that of North Korea.[33]

Bo Xilai's downfall in early 2012 was as unexpected as it was spectacular. He fell out with his chief of police, Wang Lijun, and the dispute became so inflamed that the latter feared for his life and fled to the American consulate-general in Chengdu, the capital of Sichuan province three hundred kilometres away. Like a warlord of ancient China, Bo took the law into his own hands and surrounded the US legation – only one day before then-Vice President Xi Jinping left on a state visit to America. This was a step too far – even for the son of an immortal. The central authorities intervened by extricating Wang Lijun from the embassy and taking him to Beijing for interrogation. His revelations provided Bo's many opponents, including Premier Wen Jiabao, with sufficient ammunition to detain the demigod (his father after all was an 'immortal'). In September 2013, Bo Xilai was sentenced to life in prison for 'bribery, embezzlement and abuse of power'.[34] Many even suspected him of the much more serious crime of complicity in the murder of Englishman Neil Heywood, for which Bo's wife Gu Kailai had been convicted. As a confidant of the Bo family, Heywood had funnelled money out of the country and had arranged for their son, Bo Guagua, to be placed in a good English school. When the Englishman demanded too much money for his services, and threatened to blow the whistle, Gu Kailai got him drunk and poured arsenic down his throat. Heywood's body was subsequently taken away and burnt by her lover – the chief of police, Wang Lijun.[35] The precise circumstances of this bizarre story – which, given its high concentration of intrigue, sex, and violence, reads like a chapter from the *Romance of the Three Kingdoms* – will likely never be known. Bo Xilai's most serious 'crime' was probably that he competed with Xi Jinping for supreme power. Bo's blood is after all even redder than Xi's, and in terms of intelligence and cold-blooded pursuit of power, Bo is certainly a match for the president. Bo had supposedly, with help from head of state security Zhou Yongkang, plotted a coup against Xi Jinping – a story line that was confirmed during the 19th Party congress of October 2017, when it was revealed that Bo Xilai, Zhou Yongkang and others had 'plotted to usurp the party's leadership and seize state power'.[36]

If this really happened and how, is impossible to tell: The machinations at the highest level are too opaque. It is striking, though, that some elements of the Chongqing model – the intimidation and persecution of opponents, the glorification of the egalitarian Maoist ideology and the political interference in the judiciary – can also be found again in Xi's anti-corruption campaign.

4. Stultifying 'stability'

Bao wen ('maintain stability') is one of the most frequently occurring Party catch-phrases, read on thousands of propaganda posters across the country, especially in the troubled West that is home to Tibetans and Uighurs. This penchant for maintaining the status quo constitutes a radical break with the ideology of Mao Zedong, who viewed stability as the mortal enemy of necessary change. Moving heaven and earth was needed to ignite the revolution. Already in 1927 the Great Helmsman had written: 'Revolution is not a dinner party, nor an essay, nor a painting, nor a piece of embroidery; it cannot be so refined, so leisurely and gentle, so temperate, kind, courteous, restrained and magnanimous. A revolution is an insurrection, an act of violence by which one class overthrows another.'[37] Once in power, Mao did not abandon his iconoclast instincts: By holding the established order's feet to the fire, power's plush trappings would never start feeling comfortable. The 'campaign to suppress counter-revolutionaries' began almost immediately after the Communists seized power in 1949 and, according to estimates, cost two million people their lives.[38] And that was just the beginning. The only thing stable about the Mao regime was the regularity of its political campaigns: They never stopped. Its best known and most gruesome, the Great Proletarian Cultural Revolution, was still under way when Mao died in 1976.

Today's leaders, who vividly remember the chaos that the Cultural Revolution brought about, reject Mao's philosophy of a 'permanent revolution' whole heartedly. Step-by-step and cautious development is the present regime's credo for proper governance. How a 'temporary regulation' might work in practice is first tested on the local level; should this trial balloon rise successfully, the measure is then rolled out nationally and enacted as law. These are usually applied in the economic and social domain; on the political level fear reigns supreme: The few experiments that do take place (such as consultative democracy) resemble a dancing procession from the Middle Ages – three steps forwards, two steps back. The political scientist Fang Ning, director of the Institute of Political Science at the prestigious Chinese Academy of Social Sciences, dismisses this fear, saying that there is 'no need for a guideline, no need for a timetable, a roadmap or a designed plan by the top leadership. ... This is what we in China call "crossing the river by feeling the stones."'[39] The liberals are not in favour of a return to the days of Mao's capriciousness, but they fiercely oppose the use of 'stability' as an excuse for postponing reforms. Jiang Ping, former president of the China University of Political Science and Law, notes that the use of stability as an excuse to violate human rights is 'totally against the rule of law'.[40] For the time being, though, the Party does not seem impressed by these concerns. *Bao wen* has been elevated to one of the Party's most important principles.

The Oxford Consensus

In the summer of 2013, in the undulating, hilly countryside of central England, a group of Chinese intellectuals met to talk about 'Christian Faith and Ideological Trends in Contemporary China'. As an association of those who 'love the holy land of China and are faithful to our people', the twenty-eight participants – embodying a colourful mix of Neo-Liberal, New Left, Neo-Confucianist and Christian traditions – tried to find the words to produce a statement of principles. The result was the 'Oxford Consensus', which makes four essential points:[41]

1. *Political power comes from the consent of the people.* The goal of the state is to protect the rights of the people, as well as the pursuit of happiness for the people.
2. *Fairness and justice must be guaranteed.* This principle applies to all domains of society: Politics, economics, culture, education, justice, housing, and work. Only then can all people enjoy material security and spiritual dignity.
3. *There has to be a reasonable balance between individuality and collectivity.* The various activities of ethnic groups, communities, religions, vocational groups, and regions must be protected. Freedom of speech applies to everyone, but especially to artists, academics, and people with religious beliefs. At the same time the excellence of Chinese culture must be retained.
4. *The 'great peace under heaven for all' must be established on earth.* That can only succeed on the basis of peaceful coexistence and harmonious development.

The document is much more cautious in tone than *Charter 08*. It does not pillory abuses in society, makes no recommendations to the government, and each of the four points begins with the introductory phrase 'we hope that'. One of the initiators, Yang Fenggang, director of the Center on Religion and Chinese Society at Purdue University in Indiana, thinks the dialogue between people who normally do not talk with one another is a significant step forward. According to Yang, declarations like the Oxford Consensus are subtly influential even beyond the academic world, because they give individuals the opportunity 'to express their concerns, and for their voices to be heard'.[42] The question is to what extent the opinions expressed in Oxford reach the general public. The well-known paper *Renwu Zhoukan* ('People's Weekly') devoted an article to it, but it did not generate much more attention than that in China. Despite the document's gentle choice of words, these points (and the first one above all) are still a bridge too far for the Party.

The four points constitute an interesting mixture of Western concepts like plurality and the 'consent of the governed' with typically Chinese ideas about the state, which is supposed to provide for happiness and 'great peace under heaven'. Any suggestion that the Oxford Consensus is a political movement in disguise is carefully avoided. As a result, the document lacks the vigour or enticing allure of a *Charter 08* by Liu Xiaobo or a *Communist Manifesto* by Karl Marx. Still, the synthesis it seeks could possibly be the prelude for a new doctrine, the cautious manifestation of the 'third way' that China will seek to take after the demise of Communism. The fact, moreover, that the Oxford Consensus has been drafted by people with a Christian background improves the chances of its realisation: With the current growth of Christianity in China, the number of faithful will amount to around 250 million in 2030. At that rate, China will become the largest Christian nation on earth.[43]

Modern Day *Analects*

The *Tao Te Ching* (*The Book of the Way and of Virtue*) by Lao Zi says: 'Those who know do not speak. Those who speak do not know.' (Chapter 56) The wise mandarin preferred to write rather than talk, but such trepidation no longer exists in modern China: Nearly all the individuals I approached for an interview were willing to talk with me. In terms of academic backgrounds as well as political convictions, I tried to cover a wide range of people. The result is eight interviews: With a diplomat, a legal expert, a philosopher, a mathematician, a writer, a Buddhist, an economist and an anthropologist. The people interviewed can be roughly subdivided into 'nationalists' and 'internationalists', though those labels do not do justice to the full weight of their thinking. Aside from their areas of expertise, each had his own unique perspective on the state of the country. What did connect them, however, was their status as 'public intellectuals' and their deep affection for 'the holy land of China'. I posed a number of fixed questions – Do you consider yourself a public intellectual? Is the country heading in the right direction? Where is it going? – but they all deviated from this programmed approach. This made the conversations fun, but drawing conclusions hard – let alone formulating a general conclusion as to what connected their opinions. Nevertheless, at the end of these interviews, I will attempt to do just that. My most important and positive conclusion is that despite the repression, these intellectuals do not shrink from making their opinions known – just like in the fifth century BCE, the golden era of Chinese philosophy, when reportedly 'a hundred schools competed'.

1. Qin Yaqing, the diplomat

Qin Yaqing corresponds seamlessly to the image that you expect from a diplomat: He is courteous, speaks softly, and is elegantly dressed in a (Western) suit. We meet at China Foreign Affairs University in Beijing, the school where the country's diplomats are trained. Professor Qin has a doctorate in international studies, and is also the Party Secretary of the university, which since its founding – as the brochure mentions – has been 'blessed with kind attention from the country's top leaders'. The first minister of Foreign Affairs of the People's Republic of China, Zhou Enlai, left behind instructions for the work of diplomats in a succinct code of conduct: 'unshakeable loyalty, mastery of policy, professional competency, and obedience as well as discipline'.

I am led into a classically decorated room with wide, comfortable armchairs; paintings of cranes and Chinese poems hang on the wall. As is customary, I have to wait for a moment until the host himself enters: In this way the foreign guest is subtly made aware that the meeting is not among equals. After five minutes, Qin enters and invites me to take a seat in one of the armchairs. I am especially curious about his views on China's disputes in the South China Sea, but the conversation first takes a philosophical turn. How does an ideal society come to be? Qin acknowledges

Qin Yaqing

the importance of rules, yet gently adds that 'rules only acquire meaning through culture'. Relations and the dynamics between individuals constitute a core component of Chinese culture, and that is why Chinese society can never be based on rules only. The human factor must be taken into account, and this is inherently prone to change. 'The ancient Chinese principle of the "the doctrine of the mean" can serve as the guideline for building a society that is based on law but humane as well.'

After this reflection, the conversation smoothly turns to the South China Sea and ASEAN (Association of South East Asian Nations), for 'just like China, ASEAN is not driven by rules alone and (unlike the European Union) decisions are not taken by voting'. But how then, I ask Qin, can conflicts with Vietnam and the Philippines – ASEAN countries with whom China is embroiled in a bitter dispute about the demarcation of maritime territory – be resolved? Qin explains that while China dismisses international arbitration, it is always ready for bilateral talks, and is open to acting constructively. 'China is willing to make concessions, but will never concede if its "core interests" are endangered.' What are those? The response is highly interesting: 'Our leaders value three things more than anything else: Security, sovereignty, and development. The first core interest is the highest.' What Professor Qin meant (as became clear as the conversation continued) is that guarding the country's borders and developing the economy – important as these goals may be – are subordinate to the all-encompassing principle that the power of the Party and the country's Socialist system must be preserved. This, in Chinese communist thinking, is the true meaning of the word 'security'.[44]

Do the 'core interests', I wanted to know, explain the rise of Chinese nationalism? Qin acknowledges that nationalism can be a useful tool for guaranteeing security and sovereignty, but also sees it as a two-headed beast. 'Before you know it, the nationalists are running towards the Square of Heavenly Peace.' The diplomat concludes the conversation with a reassuring message: 'China will never return to the old days (of extreme isolation) but will continue on the path of international integration' – words that recall the inscription that President Jiang Zemin wrote on the university's fortieth anniversary in 1995: 'Serve the needs of the nation, open yourself to the changing world, look towards the future and train generations of valuable talent.' As we are driving away, Professor Qin waves to us amiably. I know for certain that this intelligent and circumspect man is putting the instructions of those top leaders to good use.

2. Wang Zhenmin, the legal expert

I am happy that Professor Wang Zhenmin has time for me: When I was due to meet him, he was very busy dealing with the aftermath of the October 2014 Party congress on the rule of law – as an adviser and drafter of documents he was closely involved in that ground-breaking assembly. The dean of the School of Law at Tsinghua University (one of the country's elite schools) expresses himself with the thoroughness you might expect from a legal expert, but his views are more those of a visionary than that of a lawyer: Wang believes he has discovered a magical formula that will safeguard the Party from the decline that strikes every ruling house: Constitutionalism. The title of his controversial essay already reveals the direction of his thinking: *Constitutional Politics. The Road to Permanent Peace and Stability on How the Communist Party of China Can Escape from the Historical Cycle*.[45] In this remarkable paper Wang proclaims that if the Party succeeds in building a firm legal foundation, it can remain in power forever – a kind of 'end of history' theory, but with Chinese characteristics.

In my meeting with him, Wang gives a concise summary of his essay: Every imperial dynasty had to go under because they were led by individuals, not by laws. That is why every change of power was as violent as it was inevitable. In Europe, the pattern was similar for many centuries, but the English broke with that natural law of history by installing a constitutional monarchy after the Glorious Revolution in 1688. Since that time, all changes of power in England have proceeded peacefully, which formed the foundation for Britain's unprecedented expansion. In his essay Wang writes that though England 'is a small country with a territory of only 240,000 square kilometres, it eventually controlled one quarter of the world's entire population, occupied one quarter of the earth's land, or 33.5 million square kilometres, and nearly all ocean passages'. Wang also lauds the constitutional achievements of America's founding fathers: Within four months in 1787, they succeeded in drafting a constitution that is still in force. China undertook a similar attempt at the end of the nineteenth century, but that project failed through a combination of foreign aggression and domestic weakness. 'The first priority of our country was to survive.' Even Mao was a covert 'constitutionalist', according to Wang, yet with a career in revolutionary activism, he had no idea how to introduce the rule of law. Now, finally, China has become mature. In 2012, for the very first time in Chinese history, a change of power took place that was both non-violent and in accordance with the constitution. Hence Xi Jinping's initiative declaring 4 December as National Constitution Day, and having every Party Member swear allegiance to the constitution, comes at the right moment.

After this historical analysis, the conversation turns to democracy. In his essay, Wang cites Mao's surprising, initial stand on democracy, as already mentioned in this book: 'We have found a new path. We can break free of the cycle. The path is called democracy. As long as the people have oversight of the government then the government will not slacken in its efforts.' I ask Wang how he views the chances that this unfulfilled promise will still be kept? His first answer to that question is hard for the Western mind to follow: Mao was actually a democrat 'because the overwhelming majority of the people supported him'. Subsequently, however, Wang pronounces several views which are commonly heard in the Party's resistance to western-style democracy. First, the relativist position: Democracy does not have any absolute value, because the historical situation and cultural environment differs for each country.

Wang Zhenmin

'American democracy emerged by accident; at that moment, there were simply a lot of good legal experts in one place.' The second line of defence is temporal: Democracy can only be introduced when a constitutional system of government has been firmly established. The great strength of constitutionality is that – in contrast to democracy – it is scientifically established, and thus has universal value: 'Constitutional scholarship studies whether worldly power is granted by God, the king, or the people, but its most important mission is to study the methods of supervisory powers, the scientific configuration of those powers and the protection of human rights.' This telling statement represents a view frequently heard amongst Chinese intellectuals: Just like the pure sciences, the social sciences are founded on an objectively measurable truth.

In this 'scientific' system of constitutionalism, however, one power is elevated above all the others with an infallible authority: The Party. This logic, which is hard to follow rationally, goes roughly as follows: The constitution is the embodiment of the principles and the policy of the Party, and *therefore*, following the constitution is equal to unconditional obedience to the Party. A further logical consequence is that the 'complete embrace of Western constitutionalism' must be avoided, also for reasons of pragmatism always present in the Chinese mind: 'The most important yardstick for judging whether a system is good or bad is its capability to resolve the specific problems of a specific country.' In view of China's countless, virtually irresolvable problems one would deduce, therefore, that its political system is not suitable; but this is not how Wang sees it. To him, the weakness does not inhere in the system per se, but in human nature. If members of the Party are taken to a higher, virtuous level, then law and self-interest will coincide and the 'permanent government' can be established. One day it will happen, just give us time... . Walking back to my car, my realistic and romantic nature enter into a heated debate. Are Wang's thoughts a cynical attempt to abuse the law as a tool for power? The rule *by* law and not *of* law? Or does his thinking constitute an authentic attempt at the political experiment that began with Confucius and has enchanted the Chinese intelligentsia to this very day: The establishment of an ideal state?

3. *Zhao Tingyang, the philosopher*
Zhao Tingyang is waiting for me by the door of the Chinese Academy of Social Sciences. The 53-year-old professor of philosophy is small in stature, but that is normal for someone from the southern province of Guangdong. When he makes a joke or says something witty, his eyes twinkle with delight. He comes across as open and relaxed – an image that is intensified by his short grey goatee and casual Mao jacket. Zhao insists that we eat Cantonese, and after having ordered copious amounts of food, settles down to talk about the book that brought him national and international renown: *The Under-Heaven System: An Introduction to the Philosophy of a World Institution.*[46] According to Zhao, Under-Heaven (*Tianxia*) has three dimensions: A physical one, a psychological

Zhao Tingyang

one (the feeling that humanity belongs to one family) and an institutional one. *Tianxia* was also the name for ancient China, when the country as the highest civilisation on earth considered itself sovereign over the entire world. Zhao still finds the idea of a superior civilisation leading the world relevant for our times, but emphasizes that the new order can never arise under coercion. Just like in Confucianism, 'people have to be enticed, not conquered'. Which philosophy should take the lead in the new world order? Zhao first examines Western philosophy, jumping with remarkable ease from one great thinker to the other. He compares the Englishman Thomas Hobbes with the Chinese legalist Han Feizi (third century BCE), because both philosophers believed that humanity's evil nature could only be held in check through severe punishments and laws – otherwise a war would break out 'of all against all'. Because of its practical and experimental approach to truth, Zhao is especially charmed by English philosophy – it is more in line with the Chinese tradition than German thinking, which loses itself in metaphysics and abstraction. Facts (*shi*) are more important than things (*wu*), because facts call upon us to *do* something, which is more important than *understanding* things. 'Do you know what the longest line between two points is?' Zhao suddenly asks me, his eyes beaming with delight. 'The line between German and Chinese philosophy!'

Zhao closes his excursion into Western thinking by concluding that no one in the West ever created a permanent order: 'Neither the Romans, nor Christianity, nor

Immanuel Kant with his Perpetual Peace.' In this regard, Chinese philosophy can make an important contribution: It does not see the individual as the 'only reality' but rather as defined in his dependence upon others. 'The individual is humanised by making the other happy.' Moreover, when it comes to establishing a new world order Chinese philosophy is more down-to-earth. Beginning with Plato's *Republic* (in which the ideal society is described), Westerners have pursued the absolute and the perfect. 'We Chinese think differently,' says Zhao. 'Perfection does not exist, everything reaches maturity and then declines – just like nature.' The highest thing attainable is a *better* world in which the individual tempers his baser instincts through li (rules of propriety). How will this world look in practice? Zhao finds that impossible to say, but one thing is certain: It cannot be a confederation of states like the United Nations; it must be something of a different and higher order. In certain respects, this new order is already being shaped: Through ever-closer cooperation between businesses and the spread of the internet, connections are occurring outside state structures. Then, suddenly, Zhao is engulfed by mystic fever: 'The peace of Tianxia will be achieved by uniting all the gods; it is not a monotheistic peace under the leadership of one god.'

While Zhao asks for the check, I manage to squeeze in a final question. 'Who is going to lead the world?' 'I don't know,' he says, 'Europe has more soft power than capitalist America and Marxist China.' There is still hope for the old continent yet, I think with a certain relief. ... I thank the professor for the fascinating conversation and warmly shake his hand. Sunk in thought, the dreamer of a better world walks up the street and then disappears from view.

4. *Wang Xiaodong, the nationalist*

The man who as co-author shocked the world of China-watchers with his 2009 book *Zhongguo Bu Gaoxing (Unhappy China)* walks into the hotel lobby with a timid smile.[47] With his sloppy clothes and unkempt hair, he rather resembles an absent-minded professor than a fervent nationalist. That image, though, is immediately corrected when Wang Xiaodong begins to talk, and with a fierce look vents his anger about the things that are wrong in present day China: Many things, according to the 58-year-old mathematician – his own life for starters. At the beginning of the 1990s he wrote an article in the *People's Daily*, in which he argued that China should follow the development model of Japan and South Korea, not that of the West. As a result, he was fired by his employer, Jingmao Daxue (University of Economics and Business). Now he is a researcher with the Communist Youth League, a prestigious training institute whose students sometimes rise to great heights. The former president Hu Jintao was once First Secretary of the League. Before I even have the chance to start my interview, Wang begins a tirade over Chinese policy in Xinjiang, the far western province racked by attacks from its indigenous inhabitants, the Uighurs, upon the

Han-Chinese immigrants. 'Our policy is much too soft, and for this Hu Yaobang (the liberal leader of the 1980s) is to blame. Before his time, the economy was almost fully controlled by the Xinjiang Production and Construction Brigade, but Hu started a policy of decentralization. Now, with the help of the Wahabi sect from Saudi Arabia, mosques are being built and terrorism fuelled. We are doing nothing about it. During the 2009 riots in Urumqi (the capital of Xinjiang), the police just stood there and watched as the Uighurs slaughtered the Han Chinese.' Stunned, I wonder what has unleashed this outburst – then I realise that the hotel where we are meeting is owned by the Xinjiang Production and Construction Brigade. This semi-military, state-owned business was set up by Mao in 1954 to develop the Xinjiang economy, but was rather quickly viewed by the local population as a tool of oppression by the Chinese occupier.

I manage to turn the conversation towards *Unhappy China*. Is he any happier with the Party leadership since the time of publication? His answer is cautiously positive. He sees Xi Jinping as a hawk, a stronger leader than his weak predecessor, but 'nobody is saying what direction the country must take, which system we are choosing, and which theory supports our system. We know only what we are against.' I suggest, somewhat provocatively, that China is still a Socialist country – or is it not? Wang smirks disparagingly: 'Anything but. Our country is an oligarchy – which is a good thing, because if you give the people too many rights, they work less, and our economic problems cannot be resolved.' Wang does think, however, that the oligarchy needs to be refined by choosing officials from three groups: Technocrats selected through examinations, individuals who make a substantial contribution to the economy and bearers of Chinese culture. This last group, according to Wang, should resemble the Senate in Ancient Rome.

The conversation moves to foreign policy. Why did he write *Unhappy China*? 'I was angry about the weak foreign policy that did not correspond to our national strength.' Is it better now? 'Yes, but we still have much further to go. Just like America, our foreign policy has to be directed towards the protection of our economic interests and we must not be afraid of intervening if those are threatened. Like in the past, we should once more become an imperialist power.' For a moment I am blown away. Imperialism is associated with everything that is wrong with the United States: Intervention in other countries, economic aggression and the foregone assumption that American values are superior. 'Wasn't China a peaceable power since times immemorial?' I ask Wang. Again, that suppressed, disparaging smirk: 'When the king of Sri Lanka refused to obey, Zheng He [the Chinese admiral who made seven major voyages of discovery in the early fifteenth century] just took him prisoner.' In Wang's world, 'comprehensive national strength' is much more important than soft power. The latter can strengthen a country's influence, but is otherwise of limited value: 'Soft power is like an individual's beauty, hard power is his size.'

Regarding the future, the fiery nationalist is optimistic: In ten years, China will be the largest economy in the world; in fifty years, it will be number one in the areas of defence and technology. Is China going to be democratic then, too? 'The West should not wish for that. The people are much more nationalistic than the Party. If they come to power, there will immediately be war.'

5. Ding Li, the liberal

The contrast between Ding Li and Wang Xiaodong is like day and night. The liberal journalist is not an academic, but became involved in the public debate through his book *Grand Geostrategy* (*Diyuan Dazhanlüe* [2010]). He is now working on a book that will be called *Freedom and the Chinese tradition: A history of Ideas* (*Ziyou yu zhongguo chuantong: yibu guannianshi*). It is about the great liberal thinkers of the twentieth century; the question that especially captivates him is to which philosophical influences these individuals were exposed to.

Unfortunately, our conversation starts off on the wrong foot. Because of Wang Xiaodong's wordiness and the heavily congested Beijing traffic, I am an hour late for our lunch date. 'It doesn't matter,' says Ding, as I excuse myself profusely, 'I have plenty of time.' It becomes clear rather quickly what he means by that. Ding works for *The Economic Observer*, a kind of *Financial Times* of China, but because of their liberal nature his articles are no longer being published. He puts a positive spin on it: 'They have constrained my freedom, but that has a good side too: Now I can write my book.' Ding feels quite glum about the current situation. 'China is one of the most unequal countries on earth. It is not Socialist at all, but fascist rather. Society is about to explode, there is threat of a total collapse in the areas of politics, education, justice and the environment.' Ding compares the situation of China today with the empire's death throes: 'It is like 1910, when just like now, no essential constitutional reforms took place, the local governors detached from the centre and the country's intelligentsia lost its hope in reforms.' Actually the situation is even more dramatic than then, for 'at the end of the Qing dynasty there were still great leaders like Li Hongzhang and Zeng Guofan – men like these we don't have any longer'.

The disarray of the current system is also evident from the growth of nationalism. Marxist doctrine is about the brotherhood among (suppressed) peoples, not about being opposed to one another. Even so, Ding is not afraid that nationalism will get out of hand, because it does not enjoy wide support from the people. 'Do you really think that a Chinese family will sacrifice their only son to a foreign battlefield?' On top of that, the solidarity required to fight for a higher cause is missing. He quotes a well-known saying of Sun Yatsen: 'The Chinese people are like sand.'

Despite his gloomy analysis, Ding Li is hopeful that in the end things will still turn out all right for his country, since the need to be free is ancient and universal – even in China where, according to Ding, a kind of proto-democracy once was the system of

Ding Li

government – comparable to that of the Celtic and Germanic peoples who elected their leaders at general assemblies. Does the liberal journalist have more concrete dreams about the future of China? Certainly. He sees a republican future ahead, in which autonomous citizens elect their own leaders and minorities like the Tibetans are on an equal footing with the Chinese. 'It will take a long time, for the burden of feudal culture weighs heavy, but free elections will be held in the end.' Because I have less time than Ding Li, I have to run after finishing my lunch. While saying goodbye, I notice how sad his eyes are.

6. Zhu Caifang, the Buddhist

With his large head and sharp nose, the professor from the International Center for Buddhist Studies at the Renmin University has an un-Chinese appearance. In 2010, the 50-year-old Zhu Caifang published *The Ordinary Mind in Chan/Zen Buddhism and Its Psychological Significance* – a work that also made him well-known in the American market.[48] Zhu, however, is more than an ivory-tower academic. As a *jushi* (lay monk), he leads a meditation group that seeks for peace of mind and meaning in the midst of the capitalist chaos of modern China. He estimates that there are a hundred-eighty million Buddhists in China, nearly 15 percent of the population. 'Buddhism is popular across broad strata of the population, even amongst businessmen. The CEO of China Southern Airlines, Chen Feng, also calls himself a Buddhist, even though he is a member of the Communist Party. Some companies even use the Mindfulness-Based Stress Reduction programme developed by John Kabat-Zinn at the University of Massachusetts, and set up special rooms for it.' Zhu sees a connection between the return of Buddhism and the 'Great Rejuvenation of the Chinese Nation' for, along with Confucianism and Taoism, the Party views Buddhism as one of the three pillars of traditional Chinese culture. That does not mean that freedom of religion prevails in China: 'There are limits on the number of monasteries and temples that can be built, and public ceremonies can only take place at permitted locations.' Zhu observes with a laugh that people work around these restrictions creatively: 'Under the guise of attracting tourists, local authorities together with Buddhist temples organise major religious festivals – the actual purpose is to promote Buddhism. I participated not long ago in the Maitreya Cultural Festival in Fenghua in Zhejiang province. A tremendously large event!'

According to Zhu, President Xi Jinping favours Confucianism more than other schools of thought, but is tolerant towards Buddhism as well – even Tibetan Buddhism, although the Party looks at that 'somewhat differently' than Chinese Buddhism.*

---

* Xi Jinping also has (according to Zhu) a weak spot for Buddhism. He has met several times with Xing Yun – a renowned Buddhist Master and founder of the order of the Foguang Shan ('Mountain of the Light of the Buddha') – and told the old master that he had read all his books.

Zhu Caifang

As dean of the Institute for Advanced Humanistic Studies at Peking University, the Confucianist Tu Weiming (who also teaches at Harvard) is making an important contribution to the renewed attention for Chinese culture. 'Tu Weiming is deeply respected by our leaders; he can allow himself things that do not fit into official policy. In 2003, I attended a conference organised by him at Harvard, where the Dalai Lama openly exchanged ideas with Chinese scholars.'

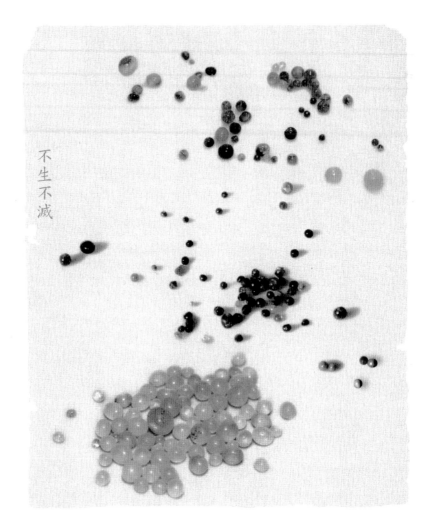

不生
不滅

The sparkling jewels remaining after the 'rainbow death' of Jing Hui

Does Zhu expect that Confucianism will soon be declared the country's official ideology? 'I don't think so. Our leaders think eclectically. There is intensive research taking place into Western and Chinese values with the goal of arriving at something new. I am trying to make my own modest contribution. At the moment, I can live with the twelve words expressing the core values of Chinese Socialism.' As already mentioned in this book, Zhu here refers to values directed at the national level (Prosperity, Civility,

Democracy, and Harmony), social level (Freedom, Equality, Justice, and Rule of Law) and individual level (Patriotism, Dedication, Integrity, and Friendship).

Is the future hopeful then? 'Broadly speaking, yes, but only if the rise of radical political or social movements can be avoided.' When saying goodbye, a small shock awaits me. Zhu is a disciple of Master Jing Hui, the patriarch of Chinese Zen Buddhism, whom I met at his monastery in 2011 (as is detailed in the next chapter). I ask him how things are with the Zen master. 'Jing Hui passed away in April 2013, but his death was exceptional. He died a "rainbow death"; he was so enlightened that his body evaporated into pure ether. The only thing that remained were a few sparkling jewels.' The professor of Buddhist philosophy tells me this without any trace of irony or doubt, nor does he feel called to give any scientific explanation. The rebirth of Chinese culture manifests itself in multiple and surprising forms.

7. Hu Angang, the Maoist

Hu Angang, the 60-year-old professor at the School of Public Policy and Management at Tsinghua University, does not hold back in sketching grand visions: 'In 2030, China will be a superpower – not only economically, but also in the areas of culture, technology, and the environment.' His book *China in 2020: A New Type of Superpower* speaks of a similarly grandiose future: 'China's twenty-first-century renaissance will manifest itself through its contribution to human development, science and technology, the green movement and culture.'[49]

Hu, a short man with spiky hair that stands straight up, receives me in his office. In the middle of a room brimming with books, the professor sits at a desk with two young female assistants quietly taking down every word of our conversation. He does not rise when I enter, 'shows me my place' with a brief hand gesture, and then begins his hour-and-a-half oration. His torrential flood of words is unstoppable; I can only ask him the questions I have prepared by interrupting him. Every now and then he jumps up, grabs one of his many publications from the bookcase and yells loudly: 'What I just said can also be found in this book!'

Many thinkers in China call themselves 'public intellectuals', but Hu certainly lives up to that label. He has had a demonstrable influence on policy. Commonly-used terms like 'Comprehensive National Strength' and a 'green GNP' (in which the costs of environmental damage are offset against the increase in GNP) have sprung from his restless brain. According to John Thornton, the former president of Goldman Sachs, 'no Chinese thinker is better at predicting the pace and direction of China's development'.[50] Cheng Li, a well-known senior fellow from the Brookings Institute, even says that 'no scholar in the PRC has been more visionary in forecasting China's ascent to superpower status'.[51] In China, Hu is the poster child of the New Left, one who defends the Party's policy through thick and thin. As Hu writes in an essay that can be read like a Communist mantra: 'China's collective leadership with Chinese

Hu Angang

characteristics is highly suitable for China's basic national conditions and cultural background, highly suitable for its stage of development and social conditions, highly suitable for facing all kinds of tests and challenges at home and abroad and is also conducive to creating China's miracles of development and governance.'[52]

In our conversation, Hu presents himself as a great admirer of Mao, especially of the Great Helmsman's capacity to direct and propel China's development. He admits that the Great Leap Forward was a failure, but the will expressed in that campaign to surpass the United States laid the basis for the country's economic explosion. 'Mao's failure was the mother of Deng's success,' Hu posits, by which he means that Mao built the industrial foundation for Deng's economic revolution. The China that one day inevitably will push America off its throne needs not be feared by the world, because of the fundamental difference between the two superpowers: 'The United States follow the *Badao* ("Way of the Hegemon"), but China follows the *Wangdao* ("Way of the Prince")' – Hu here refers to the distinction in classical Chinese philosophy between power based on might and power founded on moral authority. In the end, might is no match for ethics. Just as Confucius said in the quotation earlier in this book, 'When a prince's personal conduct is correct, his government is effective without the issuing of orders.'

According to Hu, Chinese development aid is a good example of the princely way. In 2030, 1 percent of the country's GNP will go to Africa. On that continent China's reputation, so the professor claims, is already good. 'The West criticises our policy, but nobody asks the Africans what they themselves think of it. At our school [i.e. the School of Public Policy and Management at Tsinghua University] there are many African students who return home satisfied.' In 2030, China will also be prevailing through its science and technology. 'America registered its first patent in 1874, China only in 1984, but now we are already number one in the world.' Hu anticipates that China's technological excellence will also contribute to a solution to the territorial problems in the South China Sea, for 'without help from China, the countries in the region will not be able to develop their marine resources'. The implication is clear: Through their technological dependence on China, countries like Vietnam and the Philippines will have to change their tune. Besides, Hu contends, this so-called dispute does not exist: 'From the sea charts drawn up after the Second World War it is clear that the South China Sea belongs to China.' At the end of the conversation, I succeed in asking the question that I wanted to ask from the start of the professor's oration: 'You are an economist, sir, so you look at the measurable facts. How do you reconcile that with the prophetic prediction that in fifteen years China will be the greatest nation on earth in all the domains you mention?' Hu looks at me with a glance that hovers somewhere between pity and rhapsody: 'Ever since 1989, the West has consistently been making the same mistake of underestimating China. Thanks to China, the World of the Great Harmony will in 2030 become a reality.'

8. *Xuan Zang, the 'Tibetan'*

Though approximately 90 percent of the country's gigantic population is Han Chinese, Xuan Zang makes clear that this figure is based on the whims of the Party's policy on minorities. 'In south-western China's Yunnan province alone, there were more than a hundred groups that requested 'minority' status after 1949, but only a quarter of them were granted it.' Why? 'I think because that option made the work of the minorities commission easier... but there's another reason, too. Take, for instance, the Hakkas [a minority from the south of China]: Sun Yatsen, Ye Jianying [a well-known marshal] and Deng Xiaoping were all Hakkas, but it was politically unacceptable not to consider them Chinese.'

The still young anthropologist is a specialist in the field of minorities. Xuan Zang is not his real name (he was the only one of those interviewed who wanted to remain anonymous) and he is also not Tibetan. Still, as a result of years of field research in western China, he has a greater capability to empathise with the feelings of minorities than most in his race. He sees Beijing's current policy as 'obtuse'. 'The local Chinese administrators cannot make any distinction between cultural customs and separatist acts. Take, for example, the custom amongst men in Xinjiang of wearing knives. They have always done so, but in recent years that has turned them into terrorists.' Xuan also criticises the policy of buying off the minorities' need for autonomy with money and investments. 'That doesn't work. That only solves the problem on the surface, not at its core. That's not only the case in China. Catalonia is the richest province in Spain, and yet they still want to be independent.' My assistant immediately echoes him: 'Recently I was in Tibet where the local authorities had decided to build a hydroelectric plant. The response of one Tibetan summed up the feeling of the entire community: We don't want more electricity, we want our freedom!'

Approximately half of the lower administrative cadre in the 'autonomous' regions consists of the local population group, but the Party Secretary and the head of the Public Security Bureau are always Chinese. There, says Xuan, lies the heart of the problem. 'The only solution is to grant genuine autonomy, not autonomy on paper. The earlier leaders of the People's Republic promised to make China a federal state, but after seizing power that promise was soon forgotten. The fear that the country will fall apart is too great.' And yet Xuan expects that China will go down the federal path one day, because only the local elite knows which policy works best on the spot. Until then three measures must be taken, if tensions are not to explode:

1. The adoption of a law that forbids discrimination towards ethnic minorities and the appointment of a commission to monitor its enforcement.
2. Freedom of expression without fear of repression.
3. Guarantees that socio-economic research in minority regions can be done independently and unhindered. Only then will policymakers in Beijing receive reliable information.

How does the anthropologist view Chinese nationalism that – specifically in Xinjiang – is now also turning against peoples from its own soil? In that regard, Xuan is less pessimistic: 'Social media are contributing to better understanding. Tibetans and other peoples will see that the Chinese people are struggling with the same daily problems as themselves: Livelihood, housing and medical care.' The anthropologist sees nationalism as a briefly-burning passion, not a deeply embedded emotion. 'What people really care about is their day-to-day livelihood and a better environment. Any solution to those problems would provide the regime with legitimacy, not the raising of nationalist passions.' Because of his age I am especially interested in Xuan's answer to the questions I ask in every interview: 'How do you see the future?' 'Are you optimistic?' He sighs deeply and pauses for a moment. 'In China, it is not easy to preserve your idealism; the price you pay for it can be very high. But I am not giving up, and stay optimistic. It is not important whether things change in my lifetime – over the long term, China will become a democracy of one type or another. Resistance from tyrants towards it is meaningless.' The words of the 30-year-old make me think of a well-known saying of Confucius: 'A man who does not think and plan long ahead will find trouble right at his door.'[53]

To the Left or the Right?

When the National Assembly came together for the first time in France in 1789, the royalists sat to the right of the president and the proponents of revolution to his left. On account of that historical coincidence, we now still associate 'left' with progressive, socially-inclined and believing in a strong state, and 'right' with conservative, favouring tradition and freedom of the individual. These major common denominators often cause confusion because – by way of example – the 'right of centre' VVD in the Netherlands is in many areas more 'left of centre' than the Democratic Party in the United States. China has adopted this left/right terminology from the West, but here the confusion is even greater: The *zuopai* ('the left faction') stands for a romantic yearning for the 'good old days' of Maoism, whereas the *youpai* ('the right faction') stands for the desire for fundamental change in the economic, political, and cultural structure of society. If we employ this broad definition – the will for change – as a characteristic of *youpai*, then all the intellectuals I interviewed are 'right of centre'. The only exceptions are the Maoist Hu Angang and the diplomat Qin Yaqing. In the case of the latter that is not strange, for a 'revolutionary diplomat' is almost a contradiction in terms.

A less disputed label uniting all eight interviewees is their love for 'the holy land of China'. Even freethinkers like the journalist Ding Li and the utopian philosopher Zhao Tingyang gauge their views by concepts like the Great Harmony and the 'True Liberty' that supposedly prevailed during the early days of the Zhou dynasty (around 1000 BCE). For every thinker, China is the measure of all things, and that is of course completely true for the nationalist Wang Xiaodong, the economist Hu Angang and the legal expert Wang Zhenmin – with his system for keeping the Party in power forever. Not one of them goes along with Liu Xiaobo's statement that the 'The difference between Western and Chinese governing systems is the difference between humane versus inhumane, there's no middle ground.' Deeply rooted in the holy land of China, each intellectual is attempting to contribute to the quest that, according to the Buddhist Zhu Caifang, will lead to 'a fusion of various Western and Chinese values'. This quest has yet to reach its end. What the new state will look like is – to paraphrase the title of the famous book by the sinologist Simon Leys – still veiled in Chinese shadows.

CHAPTER 7

The Perception of History:
From Supremacy to Shame

He who controls the past controls the future.
He who controls the present controls the past.

George Orwell

Only a small portion of what people do and think, some psychologists contend, is prompted by the conscious mind. A much larger part is driven invisibly by the unconscious, which contains 'the memory of every event we've ever experienced, and is the source and storehouse of our emotions'.[1] This so-called iceberg metaphor can also apply to a country like China, whose history is – allegedly – at least five thousand years old. That means that the last two centuries of foreign humiliation, the fall of the empire, the Republican period, the war with Japan, the civil war, the founding of the People's Republic of China, the mass campaigns of Mao and the reforms of Deng Xiaoping only make up a small percentage of the conscious, collective memory. The remainder of China's historical recollections are vague and amorphous, but as the unconscious portion of the collective memory they are at least as important. Marxism/Maoism writes off China's pre-modern history (that is, before the founding of the People's Republic) as 'feudal', yet this label does not even come close to embracing the present-day perception of the country's deeper past. The pride felt for the period of Chinese imperial supremacy is deeply rooted and widely shared. At present, these historical recollections are still like 'the unconscious mind that regulates all the systems of the body and keeps them in harmony with each other'.[2] However, what was once below the surface is now becoming increasingly visible. As to the restoration of the old order, it is only a matter of time before those in power start translating the ideas of nationalistically-minded intellectuals into official policy. In part, they are already doing that.

Three Circles of Civilisation

Until well into the nineteenth century, China considered itself to be so superior that it felt no need to compare itself with other countries. It did not see the world through the lenses of 'domestic' and 'foreign'. All-Under-Heaven was roughly divided into three domains, three concentric circles of decreasing civilisation. In the centre was 'China' (though it was not called that yet), where the emperors ruled and where Chinese norms and laws applied. In the second circle lived the 'inner barbarians': Peoples like the Koreans, Tibetans, Uighurs, Mongols, and Vietnamese, who fell outside Chinese jurisdiction, but acknowledged the emperor as the highest sovereign on earth and, in recognition, regularly sent tribute missions to the Chinese court. The outer circle was populated by the most ignorant barbarians – nations like the Portuguese, Dutch, and English, with whom China only came into contact from the sixteenth century. The letter Qian Long wrote to the VOC merchant Van Braam Houckgeest in 1795 makes it crystal clear that the barbarians from the outer circle were also seen as ritual vassals of the Chinese emperor. Van Braam is lauded for his effort 'to acquire the proper etiquette', while the 'king of Holland' (the Netherlands had a stadtholder at that time, but for the Chinese that distinction was neither understandable nor relevant) is addressed like a child: 'Mayest thou, o King, respectfully receiving these gifts, be strengthened in thy loyalty and integrity and, preserving good government in thy country, for ever remain worthy of Our affection. Respect this!'[3]

The closed world in which Qian Long lived was characterised by a number of foregone assumptions, which in the current foreign policy of the People's Republic are one again becoming visible.

1. *China is the highest civilisation on earth*

China's perceived supremacy results from its writing, art and architecture, but especially its organisation of the state. The ancient sages bequeathed a system in which the emperor, as the pivotal figure between heaven and earth, can create a harmonious society – provided he rules virtuously. Then, justice reigns and the people willingly follow. Just as Confucius said in the aforementioned quotation: 'The virtue of the ruler is like the wind, and that of the people is like grass. Let the wind sweep over the grass and the grass is sure to bend.' The norms of civilisation, and the ways of proper governance, are described in the sacrosanct *Five Classics* and the *Four Books*, which every mandarin had to memorise to be admitted to the country's elite. This turned China into a literary society through and through. Being able to read and write made the individual 'civilised': The word *wenhua* means both 'civilised' and 'literate'. The illiterate, uncivilised common people were there to be directed and advised, not to become autonomous citizens. This paternalistic attitude continues to have a strong impact in today's China, even though the Marxists in power now call the people 'the masses'.

2. *Foreign countries and China are not equal*

As a result of this superior sense of civilisation, the view of 'abroad' hovered somewhere between unadulterated arrogance and amiable complacency. Already in ancient times, the barbarians are described as filthy and oafish simpletons who had not yet been civilised. 'The *Xiongnu* are the people who are abandoned by Heaven for being good-for-nothing. They have no houses to shelter themselves, and make no distinction between men and women. They take the entire wilderness as their villages and the tents as their homes. They wear animal skins, eat raw meat and drink blood. They wander in order to exchange goods and stay for a while in order to herd cattle.'[4] Upon those barbarians who did embrace China's civilisation, however, blessings were showered like rain. A good example is the fifteenth century letter, cited in Chapter 2, to the emperor from the king of Cochin (a state in today's India), about his kingdom's prosperity after 'the teachings of the sages of China have benefitted us'. The classical order was founded on the literary ideal of *wen*, the gentle persuasion of barbarians by holding before them a mirror of civilisation – but if they refused to comply, *wu* (force, weapons) was also not spurned. In today's policy, *wu* seems to be getting the upper hand. With regard to the disputes in the South China Sea, Yang Jiechi, the former Minister of Foreign Affairs, said in 2010: 'China is a big country and other countries are small countries, and that's just a fact.'[5] The explanation that the nationalistic tabloid *Global Times* in 2011 gave to Yang's words embarrassed even the polished diplomats of the Foreign Affairs department: 'If these countries [with whom Beijing has territorial disputes] don't want to change their ways with China, they will need to prepare for the sounds of cannons. We need to be ready for that, as it may be the only way for the disputes in the sea to be resolved.'[6] This kind of sabre-rattling strongly resembles the 'hegemonistic' behaviour that China attributes to America; though China's standard response to such a charge is that a strong defence is indispensable for guarding its territorial integrity, and that China will never follow the Way of the Hegemon.

3. *Being virtuous is more important than the law*

The school of Legalism, which flourished in the third century BCE, took man's innate evil as its point of departure: A society was only able to function by applying severe punishments, otherwise chaos would arise. As the first, albeit short-lived, dynasty of China, the Qin embraced Legalism as the state doctrine, while the Han dynasty that followed assumed man's innate goodness and exchanged cruel punishments for clemency and the power of persuasion. This synopsis presents matters too simply, for the Confucianist dynasties used legal codes and cruel penal measures too. Their philosophical substructure, though, was fundamentally different: In the end, the organizing principle of society was not the rule of law but the virtue of the official.

The influence of these two competing, but at the same time complementary sources of thinking can still be seen in modern China. Xi Jinping's anti-corruption campaign constitutes a heroic attempt to restore the incorruptibility of the official – only then can the Party's legitimacy be restored. At the same time, Han Feizi, a philosopher who lived in the third century BCE, is also making a comeback. At the fourth Party congress dedicated to the rule of law, in October 2014, Xi Jinping quoted this founding father of Legalism: 'When those who uphold the law are strong, the state is strong. When they are weak, the state is weak.'[7] That congress, though, also closed with an appeal to govern the country with 'virtue'. Virtuous behaviour is supposedly second nature to the Party and its members, but if the Party deviates from the path of virtue, it cannot be called to account. The wording of the original communiqué for the fourth plenum makes this point clear: The 'leadership of the Party is the most essential characteristic of Socialism with Chinese characteristics and the most fundamental guarantee for Socialist rule of law.'[8] In the thinking of Xi and his soul mates, there is actually no contradiction between Legalism and Confucianism: The art of proper governance is to raise the virtue of the officials to such a level that they will abide by the laws that they themselves have made. Still, the state – by which of course is meant the Party leadership – remains the final arbiter of the 'rule of law'.

4. Unity is better than plurality

In the West, the penchant for plurality is deeply interwoven with our history. In medieval Europe there were already three estates (clergy, nobility and commoners), and with the rise of the urban bourgeoisie during the late Middle Ages, power fragmented even further. After the French Revolution, the process of democratisation took plurality to its logical conclusion: General suffrage. This kind of development never took place in China; any organised movement was seen as a threat to the autocracy of the emperor and his corps of officials. Naturally, in such a large and densely-populated country, there were social organisations that eluded imperial supervision – village communities, religious sects and secret societies. As soon as these threatened to evolve into major, national movements, however, they were quickly declared 'rebel' groups who had to be subjugated. This explains today's suspicion towards independent labour unions and NGOs; in fact, any association that shapes civil society. Religious groups are considered exceptionally suspect – they are seen as competition for the core duty of the emperor: The proper mediation between heaven and earth that ensures the harvests are bountiful and the barbarians kept outside the gate. In other words, the emergence of a *harmonious* society that reflects the cosmic order. This essential function of imperial governance cannot be shared without compromising the authority of the emperor himself.

5. One's fellow man cannot be trusted

The everyday reality of classical China seldom corresponded to the Confucianist construction of a world of virtue, harmony and non-violence, just as daily life in the West seldom corresponded to the Christian ideal. Life for most Chinese was – to quote the seventeenth-century philosopher Thomas Hobbes – 'nasty, brutish and short'. In order to survive, the qualities of deception, concealment and manipulation celebrated by Master Sun were vitally important. Aside from religious communities, there was no *social co-existence* in the Western sense of the word 'society': The only nucleus one trusted was one's family; beyond this reigned suspicion and mistrust of one's fellow man. The absence of objective rules that could be enforced by an independent judge reinforced this basic attitude. As the saying goes, *Zhongguo bushi fa, danshi renzhi de yige guojia* ('China is a country ruled not by laws but by people'). This is where the great importance of *guanxi* (relationships) comes from, shaping relations between individuals according to the principle of doing and returning favours.

Foreign policy today reflects to a large degree this domestic cultural phenomenon: What the other party or the other country says is seldom taken at face value; there is bound to be a snake hiding in the grass. In such a Hobbesian universe, there is no belief in a better world, nor the conviction that the nation-state should work for the public good – such as by fighting global poverty or giving development aid. As a result, conducting foreign policy is reduced to maximising self-interest and making deals based on 'mutual benefit' – not on ideals shared with the international community. That is why Beijing feels more at ease with President Trump than with the do-gooder Obama. 'Make America great again' is Trump's variation on 'The Great Rejuvenation of the Chinese Nation', Xi Jinping's favourite battle cry. Neither president is driven by cross-border ideologies. Aside from their current leaders determining the countries' direction, though, the isolation of China has much deeper roots than that of the United States. Uncle Sam maintains intimate political, cultural, military, and economic relations with countless – not just Western – countries. China has no substantial allies (that is to say, countries connected by the same culture), and has no leading role in international organisations like UNICEF and UNESCO that promote non-material ideals. China is a lonely power.

A Traumatised View of the World

In 494 BCE, Gou Jian – the young, reckless king of the state of Yue – attacked the much larger kingdom of Wu. He was surrounded by the enemy and had to choose between an honourable death on the battlefield or surrender. His councillors advised him to swallow his pride and surrender – otherwise the state of Yue would itself be annihilated. Swallowing his pride, Gou Jian agreed, whereupon he was transported to Wu to clean out the stables as a servant for three years. Gou Jian carefully hid his rancour and behaved so submissively that he gradually gained the favour of the king, Fu Chai. And when Gou Jian managed to cure the king of a serious illness, Fu Chai was so elated that he allowed his prisoner to return to the land of his birth. Back in Yue, Gou Jian set about strengthening his country by taking good care of the people, honouring Heaven and bringing capable military advisors into his service. Fu Chai, meanwhile, neglected precisely these tasks commensurate with being a good king, and surrounded himself with beautiful women (sent by Gou Jian). For years, Gou Jian behaved like a subjugated vassal of the king of Wu – but in order not to forget the bitter humiliations he once underwent, he would lick a gall bladder each night before sleeping.

After twenty years, the time for revenge had finally come. In a series of battles, the armies of Yue achieved a decisive victory and surrounded Fu Chai, who had gathered on a mountain with the last of his troops. The fate of the now aged king lay in Gou Jian's hands. The moment of triumph had dawned, but because Fu Chai had once spared his life, Gou Jian showed himself to be magnanimous and promised the king free passage to enjoy his old age. Fu Chai resolutely declined: 'When I sat on the throne, Heaven scattered this misfortune across Wu. The temples of my ancestors are annihilated, and the people of Wu are incorporated into the state of Yue. I am an old man and cannot become your servant.' He then grabbed a sword and put an end to his life.[9]

The four narratives from the Century of Humiliation – the two Opium Wars, the Boxer Rebellion, and the Japanese aggression – are the gall bladder that the Party has the people lick. Or does the resemblance with the ancient story go even further? Is the Party (Gou Jian) going to give the West and Japan (Fu Chai) a taste of their own medicine? This does not seem likely. With its enormous export sector, China is profiting like no other in the globalised world: To take revenge would lead to isolation and economic disruption. The Party cannot afford that; economic growth is still one of the most important sources of its legitimacy. On the other hand, the feeling of victimhood strengthens its hold on power, for only the Party can undo the historical injustices suffered by restoring the 'territorial integrity' of the country. That is why a subtle course must be charted between inciting hatred and preventing military collisions with the West and Japan. Striking the proper balance is becoming increasingly difficult, for in order to preserve the 'security of the state' (meaning the preservation of the Socialist system), the Party resorts more frequently to inciting foreign conflicts.

As a result of that policy, China has since the 2008 Olympic Games become unmistakeably more nationalistic. I will explore the most significant expression of that nationalism – specifically, the disputes in the South China Sea – in more detail in Chapter 9. Here, I focus on the psychological aspects of nationalism, for this overblown 'love for the motherland' does not come out of the blue. It starts with education and indoctrination – with the propaganda division of the Party that ensures that textbooks in schools, movies on TV, and university curricula show a 'correct' version of history. In general, one can say that from the Four Narratives of the Century of Humiliation (as described in Chapter 2) there are Four Lessons learnt. Lessons with which every Chinese, young and old alike, is indoctrinated.

Lesson 1: Preserve the 'essence' of China

Every child learns that China is the oldest and most important civilisation on earth. Even the constitution, stuffed with Marxist jargon, makes reference to it: 'China is a country with one of the longest histories in the world. The people of all of China's nationalities have jointly created a culture of grandeur and have a glorious revolutionary tradition.' The sense of being part of a unique civilisation is deeply embedded in the DNA of every Chinese. Emigrants never lose their Chinese identity, and feel an emotional attachment to the soil where their ancestors are buried – even after many generations have passed. That sense of belonging is cultural; China as a political entity does not evoke strong emotions. The core of this feeling cannot be easily described – even by Chinese themselves. It has to do with the mystical beauty of the script, the richness of the language, Confucianist values and holidays like the Spring Festival and the Moon Festival – in short, demonstrations of a 5,000-year-old culture to which the foreigner is admitted, but will never be truly be part of.

From the middle of the nineteenth century, the attacks from the West, and later Japan, confronted the elite with a dilemma they are still wrestling with: How to modernise (which was only possible through contact with the outside world) without losing the essence of China's superior civilisation? The response from the leaders of the Self-Strengthening Movement of the 1860s lay in the motto already mentioned in Chapter 2: *Zhong Ti Xi Yong* ('Chinese core, Western application'). The Chinese had to learn to produce arms themselves, and to develop in each harbour town industrial districts where they would work alongside 'barbarian' metalworkers and other artisans. However, as the reformer Zeng Guofan wrote, 'We should carefully watch and learn their superior techniques and also observe their shortcomings. We should not boast of, nor neglect our ceremonies.'[10] More than a century later Deng Xiaoping was concerned about the loss of the 'essence' of Marxism, hence his justifying opening up to the West with the following metaphor: 'If you open the window for fresh air, you have to expect some flies to blow in as well.'[11]

At the beginning of the twenty-first century, this concern about 'preserving the essence' is even greater than before. Fukuyama's proclamation that 'the triumph of the West, of the Western idea, is evident first of all in the total exhaustion of viable systematic alternatives to Western liberalism' irritates the Party because he is indirectly saying that the 'Socialist' system of the People's Republic is inferior. But the resistance to the West goes deeper than the aversion towards the universal pretence of democracy. In the West, the state is derived from the people; the legitimacy of the government is – to borrow a phrase from John Locke – based on 'the consent of the governed'. In China, the state has, in accordance with the instruction of the philosopher Mencius (fourth century BCE), an obligation to care for the people, but is not accountable to them: The mandate is given from above, not granted from below. The state is moreover the protector of China, of its refined civilisation and its cultural essence. This gives it the right to discipline those who contest that stewardship. It is this fundamentally different relationship between the citizen and the state that is the root problem of all political differences between China and the West.

There is, however, another school of thought – one that runs from Yan Fu (1854–1921) and Liang Qichao (1873–1929) to Liu Xiaobo (1955–2017), and which contends that it is impossible to separate the wheat from the chaff. One cannot 'adapt' something without adopting its core. This school believes, by way of an example, that the invention of an advanced product is only possible in an independent research environment. This view is contestable: In China, countless patents are registered by businesses closely connected to the state, like Huawei (telecommunications) and Lenovo (laptops). Though their quality is debatable, the automatic assumption that the Western application (making a high-quality product) cannot take place without the fundamental Western 'core' (an independent research environment) is factually incorrect.

Over the last century and a half, China has become quite proficient in 'applying the West'. High-speed rail lines, supercomputers and rockets to the moon testify to that skill, but did that success occur while also guarding the 'Chinese core'? The underlying question – certainly for a Chinese liberal – is why that core *should* be guarded. According to the analyst Yun Tang, preserving it is only an excuse for prolonging tyranny: 'Now more than ever, party propagandists are drumming up the spectre of a "Westernisation conspiracy" as an excuse for not enacting political reform. But in the cyber age, this noise can no longer silence the overwhelming call for social justice, which can only be guaranteed by a system of political checks and balances.'[12]

The country's leaders see things differently. As is evident from, amongst other examples, the propaganda tsar Liu Yunshan's 'five dimensions', the Party derives its right to govern from its role as the guardian of China's cultural and historical exceptionalism. That stance is strengthened by the barely-concealed paranoia that the West is out to overthrow the 'Socialist' system. That is why, as has been pointed out, 'security' means foremost keeping the Party in power. Yet, the Chinese word for security, *anquan*, also has a premodern connotation. Literally meaning 'total peace', it refers to a society in which peace and harmony are guaranteed by a wise prince. This is the ideal world of the Great Harmony, as described in *The Book of Rites* – a world without barbarian interference. That is the 'core' of the Chinese world, a world where there is no place for Western ideas about individual freedom or the state's accountability to the people.

Lesson 2: Keep geographic unity
China is the fourth largest country in the world, and it has fourteen neighbours – not including its maritime neighbours such as Japan and the Philippines. The third largest nation, the United States, has only two neighbours, with whom it maintains (generally

speaking) friendly relations. Beijing's relations with most of its neighbouring states, on the other hand, are tense. Partly this is unavoidable, because tensions always accompany the rise of a new major power; but it also stems from the fear that China wants to restore 'tributary' relationships with its neighbours. For the first time in two hundred years, Beijing not only has the power to do this but also the motivation: From the start of the First Opium War in 1839, its sovereignty was violated, and its influence in the region dismantled in a humiliating way.

The 1842 Treaty of Nanking was the first step in a long process of colonisation. The country was much too large to subjugate entirely, but Western influence grew relentlessly. In Shanghai and four other 'treaty ports' (Xiamen, Shantou, Fuzhou, and Guangzhou), Westerners were exempted from Chinese jurisdiction.

After the 1860 Convention of Peking, which concluded the Second Opium War, the number of such ports expanded, and enormous patches of land (more than 1 million square kilometres) ceded to Russia. At the end of the nineteenth century, any semblance of China's independence was cast overboard: In the so-called 'Mad Scramble for Concessions', the country was carved up 'like a melon' into territories where the imperialists acquired special rights such as the control of railways and the exploitation of natural resources. The English took control in the Yangtze River watershed; France in the southern province of Guangxi, which bordered on the French colonies in Indochina; Russia in Manchuria and Germany in the eastern province of Shandong. Japan, a latecomer on the colonial stage, went even one step further: After the Sino-Japanese War of 1894, it annexed Taiwan and the Pescadores Islands. That is why the young Communist Cai Hesen spoke in 1922 of China as being 'half-colonial' and 'half-feudal', terms that would also be adopted by Mao.[13]

The loss of sovereignty in 'China Proper' (i.e. the Chinese heartland) reduced Beijing's influence in the former tributary states to almost zero – certainly in the countries that fell into the hands of the colonial powers, like Indochina (France), Burma (England), and Korea (Japan). The situation in Tibet, Xinjiang and Mongolia was different: The campaigns of the eighteenth century meant that these territories were more firmly under Chinese authority and were not disputed by other states. (Although Russia did occupy the Ili region in northern Xinjiang from 1871 to 1880.)[14] Given the weakness of the Celestial Empire, however, Tibet, Xinjiang and Mongolia also became increasingly detached from Peking. At the beginning of the twentieth century, the Tibetan government in Lhasa operated like the government of a sovereign country, issuing passports, concluding treaties and maintaining its own armed forces.[15]

The demise of the ancient imperial order led to a thorough internal examination to bring the gravely ill patient back to life. The West became the purveyor of all kinds of medicine to the ailing imperial court: From parliamentary democracy to Marxism, utopianism to Darwinism. In those tumultuous days at the beginning of the twentieth century, all parties agreed on the usefulness of one such 'ism': Nationalism. As a

'Mad Scramble for Concessions', 1898

'normal' nation, China needed its own identity, its own flag and its own fixed territory to survive – and that is why Sun Yatsen named nationalism, *Minzu*, as the first of his 'Three Principles of the People'. Since its elevation to the country's highest principle, the term 'nationalism' has taken on various forms. For Sun, this 'ism' stood in the first place for driving out the Manchus, who were still in power when he was developing his ideas around 1900. Despite their centuries-old assimilation with Chinese culture, Sun saw the Manchus as foreign overlords: 'To restore our national independence, we must first restore the Chinese nation. To restore the Chinese nation, we must drive the barbarian Manchus back to the Changbai Mountains.'[16]

For Sun's successor Chiang Kai-shek, nationalism meant first the restoration of the country's territorial unity. In his political manifesto *China's Destiny*, he blamed the Western powers for China's failure to become an independent nation. To survive, though, the Kuomintang could not do without the support of those very powers[17] – first in the fight against the warlords, and later in the war against Japan. Once national unity was finally realised in 1945, Chiang soon had to surrender the Mandate of Heaven to the Communists. His impotence to turn those historical developments around illustrates the tragedy of his life to its core.

In 1949, for the first time since the Ming dynasty (1368–1644), China was free of foreign rulers, and – with the exception of Taiwan – national unity was restored. However, as noted in Chapter 3, this achievement did not extinguish the Party's nationalistic fire. On the contrary: Since the 2008 Olympic Games, it has more than ever before been hammering away at the restoration of the country's 'territorial integrity'. On his visit to Washington in June 2014 Fang Fenghui, the highest military chief, said that the territory passed down by previous Chinese generations will not be forgotten or sacrificed.[18] Not a single leader has exactly indicated where the borders of a restored China should lie, but it is clear that the perceptions on what once constituted 'China' are changing: On a new, 'vertical' map published in 2014, the entire surface area of the South China Sea is shown as an integral component of Chinese territory,[19] and India-occupied Arunachal Pradesh is called 'South Tibet'.

It looks as if the project for the 'restoration of territorial integrity' will never be completed as long as the Party is in power – the logic of its nationalistic agenda prescribes as much, after all. This constitutes a serious threat to peace and stability in the world, but in the short term, Beijing's threefold territorial ambitions are more of a regional nature: Fuller incorporation of Xinjiang and Tibet into the Chinese empire; reunification with Taiwan, and the transformation of the South China Sea into a Chinese lake. If that mission is successfully completed, the size of China's territory will approach the size of the empire in the eighteenth century.

Do Beijing's aspirations reach even further? Is the complete restoration of Qian Long's empire the next step? As mentioned before, China made large territorial concessions in the middle of the nineteenth century to Russia; at the beginning of the twentieth century came the further loss of Mongolia – a country three times as large as France. In 1924, after the demise of the Qing dynasty, the descendants of Genghis Khan founded – with help from Moscow – the world's second Communist country. After 1949 Mao attempted to re-incorporate the steppes; but Mongolia had by then become a close ally of the Soviet Union, militarily and economically, and Stalin

中华人民共和国地图

Vertical map of China

gave the Chinese leader a decisive *nyet*. That is why, officially at least, the People's Republic has recognised Mongolia as an independent state to which it no longer has any historical claim. For the *Republic of China*, based in Taiwan, the situation is different however. In exchange for Stalin's promise not to support the Communists in the Chinese civil war, Chiang Kai-shek gave up his claims on Mongolia. But when the Russian leader broke his promise, Chiang also rescinded his recognition of Mongolia's independence. That is why Taiwan had a Mongolian and Tibetan Affairs Commission until its abolition in September 2017.[20] As Chinese nationalism becomes ever more intense, it cannot be ruled out that Beijing will follow Taiwan's recently abolished policy towards Mongolia, and will try to reassert the ancient, imperial claim on 'the land of only heaven and earth'. In military circles the notion is certainly still alive – on some maps of China, like the one published on the military's largest website, Tiexue.net (*Tiexue* = 'Blood from Iron'), Mongolia is not listed as an independent state, but as the 'Mongolia Area'. This could be seen as a signal that, sooner or later, Beijing will demand back the enormous swathes of land that the tsars expropriated from China during the nineteenth century. As Russia is – in terms of economic and military power – falling further and further behind its southern neighbour, this is not imaginary. The article 'Revealing the Six Wars China Must Fight in the Coming 50 Years'[21] published in July 2013, outlines a concrete, step-by-step approach:

- The war to unify Taiwan (2020–2025)
- The war to recover the various islands of the South China Sea (2025–2030)
- The war to recover South Tibet (2035–2040)
- The war to recover Diaoyutai and the Ryukyus (2040–2045)
- The war to unify Outer Mongolia (2045–2050)
- The war to recover the territory seized by Russia (2055–2060)

Enacting these plans would lead to wars with Taiwan, India, Japan, Mongolia, Russia, and most likely the United States[22] – a prospect of apocalyptic proportions. These plans do not constitute government policy, but in China, these kinds of proposals cannot be made without approval from the highest level – certainly not when the official Chinese News Service (*Zhongguo Xinwenshe*) is responsible for its publication.

The occupation of Taiwan, by force if necessary, already constitutes official policy. One could even say official religion, because the constitution of the People's Republic elevates the reunification of Taiwan to a sacred mission: 'Taiwan is part of the sacred territory of the People's Republic of China. It is the inviolable duty of all Chinese people, including our compatriots in Taiwan, to accomplish the great task of reunifying the motherland.'

At the beginning of the 1950s, reunification with the small island seemed only a matter of time. President Truman, who had no patience for the corruption of the

Kuomintang, was willing to recognise the People's Republic as the sole legitimate government of all China, but the Korean War put relations between Beijing and Washington on high alert. As a result, the Americans could not possibly consent to the occupation of Taiwan by 'Red China', certainly not during the bleak ideological climate of the 1950s and 1960s. The detente employed by President Nixon and Henry Kissinger, his security advisor and subsequent Secretary of State, led to the Carter administration's recognition in 1979 of Beijing as the sole legitimate government of all China – though that decision was accompanied by the legal obligation to safeguard the island's democratic status. The Taiwan Relations Act, adopted in 1979, thus promises that 'the United States will make available to Taiwan such defence articles and defence services in such quantity as may be necessary to enable Taiwan to maintain a sufficient self-defence capability'.[23] This security guarantee is not watertight, though, for in the event of a Chinese attack, Congress and the president jointly determine to what degree and with what means the United States will rush to Taiwan's aid. In this way Beijing receives notice that the price of an attack on the island is potentially very high, while Taipei is warned that support from the Americans is not unconditional. Should Taiwan needlessly provoke China – for example, by unilaterally declaring the island's independence – the United States would not rush to its assistance. This policy of 'strategic ambiguity' has proven to be successful: More than thirty-five years after the adoption of the Taiwan Relations Act, the two adversaries have still not come to blows. That does not mean that Beijing accepts the status quo: 'Taiwan' constitutes the biggest historical shame of all (and there are quite a few), and one that must be erased if China is to restore its original grandeur. In 2005, an anti-secession law was even adopted, forbidding the island from declaring itself independent on punishment of invasion.[24]

Despite that legislative salvo, relations between 'Big' and 'Little' China – as some see the People's Republic and the Republic of China – have strongly improved since then. The Kuomintang won the Taiwanese elections in 2008, and the former mayor of Taipei, Ma Yingjiu, became the country's president. This relieved some of the pressure, for in contrast to the Democratic Progressive Party (who had been in power prior to 2008), the Kuomintang does not pursue the island's independence but, rather, its reunification with China.* How that 'one China' will take shape, however, has purposely been left in limbo to provide room for the development of economic relations. In 2008,

---

* Since the election of Cai Yingwen as president of Taiwan, in May 2017, relations have deteriorated once again. As member of the Democratic Progressive Party, Cai refuses to acknowledge the 1992 'consensus' (there is no signed document) with Beijing that there is only one China. However, as Cai does not actively promote Taiwanese independence (as did the first DPP president Chen Shuibian, who ruled from 2000 to 2008) relations have not (yet) reached the low level of the early 2000's.

the establishment of 'three connections' – direct flights, direct trade, and direct mail traffic – gave an enormous boost to economic exchanges: Prior to that, all these services flowed via Hong Kong, incurring lost time and money. Between 2008 and 2013, the volume of trade doubled.

Given their history of bitter struggle, the rapprochement between the Kuomintang and the Party is of enormous historical significance: Between 1927 (the year they broke with each other) and 1949, countless dead fell on both sides. After 1949, when Chiang Kai-shek fled to Taiwan, the fight was primarily continued verbally. The Party called the Kuomintang '"running dogs" of the Americans', while the KMT continued to label the Party 'Communist bandits'.

The Party's stance that Taiwan and China form an unbreakable entity is shared by nearly all mainland Chinese. While there are no independent surveys to establish how large this support really is, most foreigners living in China know from personal experience how deeply embedded these feelings for unity are. I once conducted a performance review with one of my employees. It was somewhat sensitive, as he had been falling short, and I had to tell him he would be dismissed if his performance did not improve. He was aware of my thoughts and entered the room fidgeting nervously with his hands. I asked him to have a seat, and he plopped down into the chair across from me. All of a sudden, he straightened his back and looked past me towards a map on the wall depicting the oil, coal, and natural gas reserves of China. Taiwan, indicated on all Chinese maps as part of the motherland, was depicted in another colour than mainland China. His eyes narrowed, and he took on a resolute and fierce expression. 'That map is wrong! China and Taiwan have been inextricably connected to each other for ages!'

The Party skilfully plays off these feelings by coupling reunification of the country to the grandeur of China. As is customary, history is brought in to underscore this point. Wang Zaixi, the former vice-minister of the Taiwan Affairs Office of the PRC's State Council, put that feeling into words precisely when he noted that the eight-year War of Resistance (against Japan, from 1937–1945) taught the Chinese people the valuable lesson that 'only a rich and powerful China can avoid being bullied by others. ... Only a reunited China can really become a powerful country in the world'.[25]

'Special' Minorities

The desire for geographical unity is driven by more than zealous patriotism alone. As noted in the interview with Xuan Zang in Chapter 6, the country's ethnic minorities have no genuine autonomy. The only exception to this is Hong Kong, which as a 'Special Administrative Region' (along with Macau) has a much greater degree of self-governance than the 'autonomous regions' in other parts of the country. With the exception of Foreign Affairs and Defence, the former British colony is allowed to manage its own affairs in accordance with the model of 'one country, two systems'.

In late 2014, the world witnessed the limits imposed on this system, when Beijing prohibited the free election of the 'Chief Executive' in 2017; yet it was still a unique spectacle to see tens of thousands demonstrating for months on Chinese territory. This showed that Hong Kong enjoys much more freedom than the rest of China, let alone Tibet and Xinjiang.

Though not stated openly, the difference in self-determination has everything to do with ethnicity: Hong Kong is inhabited by Chinese – not Tibetans, Uighurs, or other ethnic groups whose culture is light years away from the 'Civilised Centre'. That is why the people of Taiwan and Hong Kong are consistently identified as *tongbao* (literally: individuals from the 'same womb'), a designation never given to Tibetans or Mongols. And that is also why Beijing is optimistic about eventually reunifying with Taiwan. When Zhang Zhijun, the minister of the Taiwan Affairs Office, was asked whether a meeting on Taiwan between President Xi Jinping and his then-counterpart Ma Yingjiu would be possible, he answered: 'Why not? Amongst family members everything is possible.'[26] In November 2015, the family reunion actually took place when the two leaders met in Singapore. Taiwan's sensitivity about being treated like a little brother was circumvented by having both leaders walk into the same room through different entrances – a message of equality that was enforced by the fact that both men addressed each other as 'Mr Xi' and 'Mr Ma'. What happened after the meeting ended was even more symbolic: As the leader of a democratic country, Ma Yingjiu spoke jovially with the press, while Zhang Zhijun wanted to take only three questions on Xi's behalf, and only from friendly media.[27]

The difference in ethnicity also explains why Beijing can never agree with the Dalai Lama's demand for Tibet's 'genuine autonomy': Given the enormous cultural gap (not to mention the repression that has now lasted almost seventy years), such a status would unleash forces that, in the Party's view, can only lead to one result: The breakaway of Tibet from the Chinese empire. For that same reason, Taiwan can acquire the same status as Hong Kong, but may never declare itself independent. The centrifugal effect of such a move would completely unravel the country, for if one part of the empire detached itself other parts can hardly be told not to do the same – certainly not people from a 'different womb'.

Sadly, from Beijing's point of view, the feeling of being Chinese is rapidly decreasing both in Hong Kong and Taiwan. A survey held in Hong Kong in October 2014 indicated that only 8.9 percent of those questioned considered themselves to be Chinese; in 1997, it was still 32.1 percent. Nearly two thirds considered themselves Chinese *and* 'Hong Kongers'. The Taiwanese figures are even more alarming: In 2014, at least 60.4 percent of those questioned felt they were Taiwanese, and only 32.7 percent Chinese *and* Taiwanese.[28]

Beijing is very worried that 'the people from the same womb' are drifting farther and farther away. Wang Zhenmin – head of the legal division of Beijing's Liaison Office in Hong Kong (interviewed in the previous chapter) – is even threatening to abandon the model of 'one country, two systems' (which Beijing has promised to be in place until 2047) if the people who are struggling to give this concept real meaning will not yield to Beijing's interpretation of Hong Kong's 'autonomy'. Ironically enough, as the architect of 'one country, two systems', Deng Xiaoping was in fact a great proponent of genuine autonomy: As the great leader said in 1984, 'We should have faith in the Chinese of Hong Kong, who are quite capable of administering their own affairs. The notion that Chinese cannot manage Hong Kong affairs satisfactorily is a leftover from the old colonial mentality.'[29] In 2018 there is not much left of this relaxed attitude, let alone trust. Inhabitants of Hong Kong arguing for the autonomy promised them are suspected of wanting to separate from the motherland. The neo-colonial attitude of people like Wang Zhenmin actually brings closer what Beijing fears most: Hong Kong's independence. Identity cannot be intimidated by power; it defines itself, in fact, through its very resistance towards it.

Lesson 3: Spiritual division is bad for the country
The day that I was to meet the great man himself had finally dawned. I had been staying in the Temple of the Fourth Ancestor for five days already. The original thousand-year-old monastery did not survive Mao Zedong's call 'to obliterate the old', but was rebuilt in gleaming condition from the ground up. In the sixth century the Indian monk Bodhidharma settled down in this hilly eastern area of Hubei province to teach a new and exotic variety of Buddhism: *Chan*, better known in the West under its Japanese name Zen. One of his disciples read so much compassion in the Buddha's final smile that he saw the wordless revelation of all wisdom in it. Zen – the unwritten doctrine of sudden enlightenment – was born. Bodhidharma brought the doctrine to China, and later became known as the First Patriarch of Chinese Zen Buddhism. In the hall that led to the room of the current patriarch, a stele with four life-size characters engraved on it made clear that in China religion is subordinated to the state: *Ai Guo, Ai Jiao* ('love the country, love the faith'). Jing Hui received us with a warm smile. He was dressed like a simple monk and his bald head shone in the autumn sun. Just like the Dalai Lama, he was constantly making little jokes and chuckled without any obvious reason. Next to him sat a poorly-dressed younger man, who could not have been more than half of Jing Hui's seventy-eight years. The patriarch casually introduced him to our group: 'This is Mr Sun from the Party's Bureau of Religious Affairs. His job is to report on whatever I say to you' (more chuckling). His gentleness hardened, however, when he suddenly provided an analysis of the Communist economic policy that had once laid his monastery to waste: 'The policy of the Party is dumb and short-sighted, the elimination of private property has only made the desire for it grow. And that is not all. Everything that is managed by the state has the same characteristic: Lack of quality.'

Jing Hui

The unstoppable return of religion to China intrudes upon all strata of society. Buddhism, Taoism, Islam, Protestantism and Catholicism – the five officially recognised religions – have hundreds of millions of followers, but no one knows exactly how many there are. Two typically Chinese phenomena are causing this uncertainty. In the West, we are used to saying what we 'are' – you *are* a Christian, Buddhist or a Freemason. In China, such declarations lead to confusion, because all phenomena (including the individual self and his knowing subject) are part of an eternal coming into being, the *tao* that is the flow of the universe. Immutable truths, or revelations of them, are therefore an illusion. That is why in China – certainly among the elite – it is very common to adhere to multiple beliefs. Counting the faithful is made even more difficult by the fact that the oldest religion in the country is not included in the calculations – the religion that venerates local gods or spirit forces, like mountains or rivers. A religion that has no name. Sometimes it is called Daojiao (the 'Religion of Tao', in contrast to Daojia, the 'Philosophy of Tao'), sometimes Shenism – Shen meaning god or spirit, the same shen (though pronounced differently) as in Shinto, the official religion of Japan. The similarity between the Chinese and Japanese teachings is striking: Both religions view the world as being animated – not by the One, but by countless spirits and forces.

The success of the many peasant uprisings in Chinese history was often determined by a charismatic leader who promised his peasant followers, driven to despair by imperial oppression, heaven on earth. The best-known example of such a leader is Hong Xiuquan, a farmer's son who around 1840 embraced Christianity after encountering Western missionaries. He soon experienced a vision that called on him, as the younger brother of Jesus, to establish a 'Unified World of Light and Great Peace'. Hong's charismatic personality and egalitarian agenda caused millions of peasants to rally under his banner. The weakened Qing dynasty was initially no match for Hong's fanatical armies, inspired by religious zeal. By 1860, his troops had occupied most of south and central China, and even threatened the capital Peking. In that hour of need, the Qing managed to mobilise their last remaining forces. With aid from the 'Ever Victorious Army' of the English adventurer Charles Gordon, nicknamed 'Chinese Gordon', the capable generals Zeng Guofan and Li Hongzhang launched a successful counterattack. In 1864, the capital of the Taiping Tianguo (the 'Heavenly Kingdom of Great Peace'), Nanjing, was conquered, and its leaders executed by the 'death by a thousand cuts'. Hong himself was spared that gruesome fate; he allegedly died in the conflagration of his torched palace, though other sources mention that he had taken poison.

Less than a century later, another peasant leader succeeded where Hong Xiuquan had failed: Mao Zedong overthrew the corrupt Kuomintang regime that, just like the Qing, had lost the Mandate of Heaven. The Great Helmsman, a great admirer of Hong, had a museum built in the village of his birth. God or Jesus did not belong in Mao's classless kingdom, but his ideal of an egalitarian and puritanical society strongly resembled that of Hong Xiuquan. Mao's utopian dreams were (just like those of Hong) never realised – a fact that makes the historically-aware Communists even more sensitive to contemporary religious challenges. They know that a regime that strays too far from its own founding ideals is doomed to perish.[30]

Christianity and Islam are regarded by the Party with particular suspicion. Both are well-organised, have countless lay followers and offer an enticing alternative to a secular government: A caliphate or a 'New Jerusalem'. This is perceived as a threat, because Church and State have never been separated in China – at least not to the same degree as in the West. Though the end of Mao's atheistic excesses caused a religious revival, it also restored the ages-old feeling that the state is responsible for the spiritual welfare of the people. That is a second reason why the Century of Humiliation was such a painful experience: The emperors had completely lost their role as spiritual guardians. During the Taiping Rebellion, the rebels occupied half the country and proclaimed heretical ideas about the equality of men and women; at the same time, Western missionaries were converting millions of Chinese, fighting epidemics and saving orphans from starvation. In doing so, they undermined the religious role of the emperor – a point that up to this day is a delicate subject. On 1 October 2000, for instance, the Vatican beatified one hundred twenty martyrs – all Chinese Christians who had been executed by the authorities between 1648 and 1930. The timing of their canonisation was significant, for 1 October is the national holiday of the People's Republic. According to some sources, the Taiwanese had deliberately suggested that date in order to provoke Beijing – a mission in which they gloriously succeeded, for the Chinese newspapers were filled with enraged reactions. Professor Dai Yi of Renmin University wrote that the activities of the missionaries and those of the foreign aggressors had been cut from the same cloth, because 'the missionaries came to China in the wake of warships.'[31]

As always, this sensitivity towards the past is defined by the present. Because Catholicism is once again blossoming, the Party has established a church of its own – just as the English king Henry VIII did with the Church of England in the early sixteenth century. Because the Vatican does not recognise this Patriotic Church of China, a dispute has risen that resembles the 'Investiture Controversy' of the Middle Ages: Who has the right to appoint bishops? The pope or the emperor? Another consequence of the founding of the Patriotic Church is that we do not know the number of Catholics in China, because the faithful remaining true to Rome do not appear in the official statistics. What we do know, though, is that the number of evangelical Protestants is much larger. In 2010, according to the Pew Research Center, there were fifty-eight million Protestants and nine million Catholics in China. Yang Fenggang, one of the initiators of the Oxford Consensus mentioned in Chapter 6, expects that at the current growth rate of 10 percent per year, the Christian population will number around two hundred fifty million in 2030.[32] It is difficult to imagine how the largest Communist party and the largest Christian community in the world will then be able to live together peaceably. But by that time, perhaps, the Party will consider Christianity to be part of the 'essence' of Chinese culture. In view of its unlimited ideological flexibility, nothing is impossible.

Supervision of religion is in the hands of the Bureau of Religious Affairs. This intertwined, multibranched body, which is headed by an official ranked at the level of minister, must guard against religious organisations mutating into political organisations. Christianity and Islam are therefore its chief suspects, but it also keeps an eye on Buddhism (specifically Tibetan Buddhism) by dint of its enormous number of followers and the allure of leaders like Jing Hui. According to the aforementioned estimates of Professor Zhu Caifang, one hundred eighty million Chinese believe in Buddhism, which makes it the largest religion in the country. But the growth of Christianity is of greater concern to the Party, because Siddhartha does not call upon his followers to establish a kingdom on earth. The path to salvation is individual.

'The light of Asia' originally ignited in India, but at the beginning of our calendar era came via the Silk Road to China – long enough ago to be considered an indigenous religion. Through their charitable work, Buddhists are viewed even as allies by the Party, which cannot possibly realise the 'harmonious society' on its own. Nevertheless, the inherent tension between the spiritual world and earthly power cannot be resolved. Religion offers something that the Party is no longer able to provide: A sense of purpose. Meditation, mindfulness and prayer are benchmarks for more and more individuals in a society where Marx is as dead as a doornail, and mammon is worshipped as the highest god. Buddhist masters like Xin Yun – the patriarch of the *Foguang Shan* ('Mountain of Light from the Buddha') – reminds his millions of followers that it is important 'to purify the spirit, control the passions and heal the heart'.[33] China's development, according to him, cannot rely on material things alone. The Party has no answer to that.

Lesson 4: Japan is the arch-enemy
The fourth story from the Century of Humiliation has given Beijing something every form of nationalism thrives on and cannot do without: An arch-enemy. Just like Germany's existence at the end of the nineteenth century defined the identity of French nationalism, Japan's existence constitutes a magnet for Chinese nationalism. The parallel can be extended even further: Between 1871 and 1918, the Germans occupied Alsace-Lorraine, an area that before then had been in French hands for centuries. The Japanese are now doing the same with the Diaoyu Islands in the East China Sea. Other than to Chinese historians, though, this parallel is not convincing: The islands were never actually under Chinese sovereignty, and only after seventy-five years of Japanese occupation were they reclaimed by Beijing.

Deng: No Anti-Japanese Sentiment

Initially, Sino-Japanese relations were on a good track. When Deng Xiaoping in 1978 opened the country's doors to foreign capital, seducing Japan first was the obvious path. With its lightning-fast economic development after the Second World War, the Land of the Rising Sun had greatly prospered. Additionally, given the cultural connections, Japan had a much better understanding of the Chinese way of doing business than the average Westerner did. In 1972, diplomatic relations were restored between the two countries. Full recovery of the diplomatic relations followed in 1978 with the signing of the Sino-Japanese Treaty of Peace and Friendship. This took another six years because, just like the United States, Japan recognised not Beijing but the Kuomintang administration as the only legitimate government of China during the post-war years. Sovereignty over the Senkaku Islands (Diaoyu in Chinese) formed the only obstacle for the signing of the treaty, but Deng found a typically Taoist solution: He noted that the dispute was too complicated for the present generation of leaders to solve, so it was best to leave it for their successors.[34] The Party's 2012 white paper regarding the Senkaku Islands contends that Deng's statement shows that a dispute regarding the sovereignty of the islands did exist, but neither the 1972 communiqué restoring relations, nor the 1978 Friendship Treaty, mentions the islands at all.[35] When Deng met Emperor Hirohito and Prime Minister Fukuda during his visit to Japan in 1978, he was actually full of praise for the agreement: 'The Sino-Japanese Peace and Friendship Treaty... realizes a long cherished dream by the two peoples. ... Despite different social systems in China and Japan, the two countries should and can coexist in peace and friendship.'[36] Cultural and economic relations followed on the heels of these political overtures: Countless Japanese tourists visited the source of their cultural legacy, tens of thousands of students were exchanged, and businesses like Mitsubishi and Sony opened offices and factories in China.

Unwelcome History Books

4 June 1989 constituted the turning point. After the Square of Heavenly Peace was cleared, the Patriotic Education Campaign got underway, and especially aimed its arrows at Japan. After the textbook *Modern and Contemporary Chinese History* was amended in 1994, nine of its twenty-three chapters were devoted to the Japanese occupation of China. Japan's post-war reparations to China, amounting to more than sixty billion dollars, were completely ignored by the textbook.[37] In the new edition published in 2004, the Nanjing Massacre, together with other milestones in the 1937–1945 war against Japan, are described and depicted in graphic detail. It seems that fanning the nationalist fire is more important than attaining historical objectivity.

The following question, for example, is put to Chinese students: 'Japanese right-wing forces vigorously deny that the Japanese military committed the Nanjing Massacre – the ultimate act of human cruelty – during its invasion of China. They consider it a type of wartime behaviour. What do you think of the issue?'[38] The war against Japan is no longer presented as part of the Second World War, but instead features in the chapter 'World Powers' Military Aggression and Chinese Peoples'

Resistance (1839–1945)'. According to the new textbook, the Chinese people have since the Opium War carried out one 'democratic revolution' after the other, achieving complete victory domestically and the elevation of the 'international status of China'.[39]

Ironically enough, it is the wording of the *Japanese* history books that arouses deep resentment in China: Tokyo is reproached for not placing history in an objective light. But who is twisting the facts? A recent investigation from Stanford University, *Textbooks and Patriotic Education: Wartime Memory Formation in China and Japan*, comes to the remarkable conclusion that 'Japanese textbooks are relatively devoid of overt attempts to promote patriotism and contain more information about controversial wartime issues such as the Nanjing Massacre than is widely believed.' In addition, according to the Stanford study, they do not make excuses: 'They do not celebrate war, they do not stress the importance of the military, and they tell no tales of battlefield heroism.'[40] In Chinese history books, the very opposite occurs: 'In contrast, Chinese textbooks, particularly after their revision a decade ago, are consciously aimed at promoting a nationalist view of the past as part of the country's 'Patriotic Education' campaign.'[41] The media also make a significant contribution to the negative image of Japan. Numerous TV stations broadcast movies about the 'War of Resistance against Japan', in which the Japanese are presented as sadistic occupiers and the Chinese as heroic resistance fighters. Nuance is not valued in the process. The film *Devils on the Doorstep*, in which a Japanese officer is presented as someone with human qualities, won a prize at Cannes but was promptly banned in China.[42]

A like-minded editorial in *China Daily* argued that Japan's 'selective amnesia' regarding dark periods of its history is preventing it from becoming a normal member of the international community.[43] This is a bold assertion from a Party for which twisting historical facts is deeply embedded in its DNA. Because 'historical errors' cannot be talked about, the millions of victims of the Great Leap Forward and the Cultural Revolution risk disappearing into the black hole of time. Not everyone is resigned to such forgetfulness. The 'Tiananmen Mothers' (of the students who died on 4 June 1989) resist this 'forced amnesia'. On 4 June 2015, after Premier Li Keqiang had appealed to the Japanese leaders to take responsibility for the crimes of their predecessors, they wrote an open letter: 'By the same logic, shouldn't today's Chinese leaders bear responsibility for the series of crimes, manmade famine and slaughter, perpetrated in their own country by China's leaders at the time: Mao Zedong and Deng Xiaoping?'*[44]

---

* The American general Joe Stilwell, who served as Chiang Kai-shek's military advisor during the Second World War, makes an astute observation in this respect: 'The Chinese can contemplate with equanimity the most terrible injustice and cruelty inflicted by Chinese on Chinese, but as soon as there is trouble with a foreigner, a patriotic orator is found on every street corner ranting and roaring about foreign oppression and the rights of the native.'[45]

The party's inclination to twist or deny the historical facts also affects academic research. In December 2012, the Japanese news service Jiji secured a Chinese Ministry of Foreign Affairs document, dating from 1950, in which the Senkaku Islands were designated by that Japanese name – a revelation that did not correspond with the official claim that the islands have been Chinese territory 'for centuries'. Since then, access to the national archives for foreign researchers has been made very difficult. Hans van der Ven, professor of modern Chinese history at the University of Cambridge, supposes that 'the changed climate' has to do with the new leadership.[46]

The Yasukuni Shrine

Yet Beijing's indignation is not only about Japanese history books. Conservative governments – like those of Koizumi (2001–2006) and Abe (2006–2007, and since 2012 prime minister once again) – think that Japan was not the only guilty party in the Second World War in Asia, and that it is time to behave more self-confidently. That is why stains on its historical record, like the Korean comfort women, are hushed up or played down. Korean and Chinese feelings are most deeply hurt by the visits of Japanese government leaders to the Yasukuni Shrine – the holy shrine where more than two million fallen soldiers are commemorated, but also fourteen high-ranking military sentenced to death as war criminals by the 1945 Tokyo Tribunal. Abe and others see nothing wrong in these visits: It is an homage to the victims, even a religious act, because in the shrine a 'meeting' takes place with the ancestors, who now advise the leaders on how to act.[47]

The website for the Yasukuni Shrine underscores this religious experience by calling the victims 'venerable divinities' who died when performing their public duty to protect the motherland: 'This difference [between Yasukuni Shrine and other foreign memorial institutions] might be causing misunderstanding. However... it is not an abnormal institution.' The website even contains lyrical musings on the last thoughts of the deceased: 'Now then, older and younger brother, I want to thank you from my heart for the friendliness you have given me during the many years of my life. With peace in my heart I am going – a step earlier than you – on the journey to the eternal garden. Do not be sad and take good care of yourselves. Farewell.' An earlier version of the website still honoured the 'martyrs who were cruelly and unjustly condemned as war criminals by the sham tribunal of the Allies [i.e., the 1945 Tokyo Tribunal]', but that version has been taken down.[48]

That revision does not put Beijing in any kinder mood. On the contrary. During Abe's visit to the Yasukuni Shrine in December 2013, the declaration from the Chinese ministry of Foreign Affairs was, if that were possible, even fiercer than before. The Japanese prime minister was accused of 'paying homage to devils' and of 'not understanding the evils of the fascist war'.[49] It did not end with declarations: In 2005, when Tokyo switched to revised versions of the history books unacceptable in Chinese eyes, Japanese restaurants in Shanghai and more than twenty other towns were attacked.

The Senkaku Islands

In addition to textbooks and visits to the Yasukuni Shrine, Beijing has in recent years found a new *casus belli*: The dispute over the Senkaku Islands. As laid out in Chapter 3, their territorial status is contested, and in the foreseeable future there is no solution in sight: Beijing rejects any international arbitration and refuses to conduct bilateral talks. The islands' nationalisation in 2012 escalated the dispute still further. The Japanese government took that step to head off Shintaro Ishihara, the ultra-nationalist governor of Tokyo, who wanted to buy the islands to 'protect' them against the Chinese threat. 'If we leave them as they are, we know what will happen to the islands,' he told a press conference in Washington in April of that year.[50] If Tokyo had expected this measure to be well-received in China, it had calculated wrongly, for Beijing interpreted the nationalisation as an act to anchor Japanese sovereignty. To put pressure on Tokyo, anti-Japanese demonstrations were organised in many towns – as in 2005. The crowds carried banners calling to 'Never forget the national humiliation!' and 'Kill all Japanese!' Japanese flags were also burned and the marches quickly became violent.[51] An innocent man was dragged out of his newly-bought Japanese car and struck so hard with an iron bar that he was hospitalised with a skull fracture. Nissan and Honda showrooms were turned into heaps of scrap metal and shattered glass.

Demonstrations in China can only take place with the Party's approval, but there is always the risk that public anger will be directed towards other issues. This is exactly what happened at an anti-Japan protest in 2012, when some demonstrators carried banners saying, 'Long live Chairman Mao!'[52] The Great Helmsman is widely admired as a man who dared to stand up to foreigners – even to the powerful Americans in the Korean War of 1950–1953. The implication was clear: Today's leaders are a bunch of weaklings, who only dare to lash out at the Japanese verbally. The demonstrations were thus quickly forbidden, though to show its resolve Beijing now regularly sends 'research ships' escorted by frigates to the territorial waters of the Senkaku Islands. Hazardous situations may occur as a result: In January 2013, a Chinese naval vessel put so-called 'radar-locks' on Japanese helicopters and ships.[53] This tactic is deployed before firing at enemy ships and aeroplanes, and is seen in military circles as a provocative act.

As was to be expected, Tokyo devised a series of counter-measures. In 2013, the military budget was increased for the first time in eleven years, and that year's defence report reproaches Beijing for wanting to change the status quo by force.[54] Washington's position in this cat and mouse game is crucial: Article 5 of the Treaty of Mutual Cooperation and Security between the United States and Japan obliges Washington to come to Tokyo's aid in the event of an attack on Japanese territory. Ever since the US intervention in Iraq, Washington has been reluctant to rush into foreign adventures; though during his visit to Tokyo in April 2014, President Obama made it clear that any unilateral change of the status quo in East Asia through force is unacceptable.[55] China was not named, but the implication of his words was loud and clear. The Trump administration continues this policy, despite that candidate's noisy rhetoric in the presidential election that America can no longer be the world's policeman. During his visit to Tokyo in February 2017, US Secretary of Defence Jim Mattis affirmed that the Senkaku Islands fall within the scope of the Japanese-American security treaty.

The steadfastness of America and Japan to defend their interests in the East China Sea means that China has less wiggle room for changing the status quo there. Nevertheless, provocative pinpricks continue. According to Japanese sources, in 2017 alone the Chinese coast guard violated Japanese territorial waters thirteen times.[56] In addition, the Chinese air force and navy have in recent years regularly held exercises in the Miyako Strait, not far from the USA's large military base at Okinawa. According to the nationalistic paper *Global Times*, it is normal for relations to change: 'Japan must accept the reality that China is increasing its military activities in the Western Pacific.'[57]

The Past as a Stick to Beat the Present

For Beijing, Japan's wartime past remains an irresistible stick with which to beat Tokyo. Uncertainty about the Party's domestic position plays an important role here; it is no coincidence that the anti-Japan campaigns only got under way after 4 June 1989. Susan Shirk, deputy assistant Secretary of State under President Bill Clinton, says that Chinese politicians are using Japan-related issues to cast themselves as strong leaders, or to take attention away from difficult domestic problems.[58] Demonising Japan is also caused by the relatively weak standing of recent Chinese leaders. Mao Zedong (ruler from 1949–1976) and Deng Xiaoping (1978–1992) enjoyed an untouchable domestic authority; they did not need any foreign enemy to unite the people, and looked at the world with a cool, geopolitical vision. Japan was seen as a useful regional ally that offered a counterweight to US – and from the 1970s Soviet – dominance. This is why diplomatic relations with Japan were established as early as 1972, seven years before those with the United States. Furthermore, in that same year Tokyo expressed guilt for its wartime past in the accompanying communiqué: 'The Japanese side is keenly conscious of the responsibility for the serious damage that Japan caused in the past to the Chinese people through war, and deeply reproaches itself.'[59] For Mao and his premier Zhou Enlai, that was the end of it. In the opinion of someone with knowledge of these bilateral relations, they did not think it was 'necessary for Japan to apologize all the time'.[60]

The capricious president Jiang Zemin, the conservative Party Secretary of Shanghai who was pushed forward after 4 June 1989 to become the supreme leader, decided on a different course. During his state visit to Japan in 1998, he offended his hosts by constantly bringing up the wartime past – even during the emperor's state dinner. As a result, Jiang did not get what he wanted: A written apology for Japanese conduct during the Second World War. Not long before Jiang's state visit, the South Korean president Kim Dae-jung had received just such a declaration.[61] This made the rejection even more painful.

Yet the iceberg metaphor with which I began this chapter still offers the best explanation. From the seventh to the ninth centuries, Japan sent at least nineteen missions to the Chinese court, bringing back not only merchandise such as porcelain, but also books about Buddhism, architecture, law, administration, and medicine. The Chinese regarded the envoys as vassals humbly submitting to a superior civilisation, but the Japanese saw it as a relationship between equals: As the empress Suiko wrote in 607, in the letter she sent with her envoy to the court of China: The ruler of Wa (Japan's name at that time) is 'the Son of Heaven in the land of the rising sun', while the ruler of the Sui (the dynasty that ruled China at the time) is 'the Son of Heaven in the land of the setting sun'.[62]

In the centuries that followed, overseas contact decreased, and Japan managed its own affairs in 'splendid isolation'. After the Meiji Restoration of 1868, the Land of the Rising Sun came out of its shell: It modernised dramatically and initiated an aggressive foreign policy that led to the annexation of the Ryukyu Islands (1879) and Korea (1910) – countries that had paid tribute to China for centuries. The 'Land of the Dwarves' unabashedly pursued domination in a region where China had reigned supreme since the beginning of our calendar era. However, now that the Celestial Empire has reclaimed its natural position as a major power, Japan must once again know its place. Only if Tokyo abases itself and bangs its head on the ground nine times (modern translation: Offers its apologies again and again), can the modern-day Chinese emperor approach Japan benevolently. That is why Beijing insists upon ever more strongly-worded apologies for Japan's wartime past: Apologies that would also express Japan's inherent acknowledgement that China is again the dominant power in the region. In the words of a Chinese expert on these bilateral relations: 'Right now there is close competition between China and Japan for leadership in Asia. When China is clearly number one, then Japan will accept the situation and relations will be better.'[63]

Anti-Japanese protesters demonstrating at the gate of Bell Tower Hotel in Xi'an on Sept 15, 2012

Ironically enough, the Party has, by and large, to thank Japan for its seizure of power. The sixty years of aggression from the Land of the Rising Sun were instrumental in creating China as a modern nation. The May 4th Movement of 1919, the start of China's national awakening, flared up as a result of Japanese manoeuvres to take over German interests in Shandong province. Japan's influence on the national consciousness became even greater after the annexation of Manchuria in 1931. The cultural philosopher Lin Yutang wrote in the 1930s: 'It was the armed invasion by Japan that brought the nationhood of China into being and unified China as a modern nation ought to be unified. For the first time in modern history, the whole nation moves as one man, and China hates and fights like a modern nation. Thus, a modern China is being born under the baptism of fire.'[64] On top of that, it was due to the Japanese attack that the Party was able to survive and grow. In 1934, it barely managed to escape being overpowered by Chiang Kai-shek, but the total annihilation of the Communists was simply a matter of time: The difference in weapons and troops was just too great. But the increasing Japanese threat prevented Mao's downfall: In 1936, Chiang Kai-shek's generals forced their leader at knifepoint to form an anti-Japanese alliance with the Communists.

During the subsequent eight years of the War of Resistance against Japan, the Kuomintang and its large standing armies had to bear the brunt of the beating. According to one estimate alone, the number of KMT victims was ten times greater than those of Mao's Red Army.[65] The Communists' way of fighting also contributed to that difference: They disappeared invisibly into the massive peasant population. To quote a favourite saying of the Communist leaders from those years: 'Between the people and the troops... the former may be likened to water, the latter to the fish who inhabit it'.[66] When the Japanese were forced in 1945 to withdraw, the People's Liberation Army had more than a million men, and ruled over the countryside.[67] Though the Kuomintang still constituted the legitimate government, it inherited a country in which industry and infrastructure had been laid to waste by the Japanese war machine. The KMT accelerated its own downfall through economic mismanagement and acute corruption, and lost the Mandate of Heaven after a bitter civil war that lasted four years. Decades later, in the 1972 visit of Japanese prime minister Kakuei Tanaka to Beijing, Mao told Tanaka that he need not apologise for the Japanese invasion of China. Indeed, he said, 'I have to thank you, because without Japan the Communist Party could not have defeated the Nationalists.'[68]

CHAPTER 8

Foreign Policy under Mao and Deng:
From Rebellion to Harmony

We will only become a big political power if we hide brightness, cherish obscurity and work hard in the years to come; we will then have more weight in international affairs.

Deng Xiaoping

History, as written by the Party, sees 1949 as a dividing line between the Old and the New China. That is nothing exceptional: Every new dynasty presents itself as the founder of a new order that casts aside its old and depraved predecessor. Since the first days of its nearly seventy-year-old existence, this New China has gone through unprecedented changes: Not only as a result of Mao's ambition to change China into a Communist utopia, but also because of Deng Xiaoping's 1978 decision to liberate both the peasants and businesses – with the result that China is well on the way to becoming the largest economy in the world. The core of this new state cannot be easily interpreted. A hybrid creature has emerged, one that venerates its founder like a demigod, while discarding the bulk of his policies; one that clings to Marxism-Leninism as its state ideology, while behaving like a Confucianist emperor; and one (perhaps the biggest 'contradiction') that allows its people to enter the modern world, while telling them that the West and China can 'in essence' not be reconciled. In short, a schizophrenic country that does not know what it is, what it stands for or where it is going. Its foreign policy has a similarly split personality: Beijing talks incessantly about the 'peaceful development of China' and 'a harmonious world order', but in practice its behaviour has become ever more assertive and nationalistic. To understand these two constituent elements – aggression and cooperation – in China's foreign policy better, we must take a closer look at its two creators: Mao Zedong and Deng Xiaoping. Despite their difference in policies, both these leaders adhered to the sacrosanct principle that no single leader of the People's Republic tampers with: The sovereignty of China.

The Ideological Basis

The founding of the People's Republic of China on 1 October 1949 was accompanied by great optimism. For the first time since the Ming dynasty (1368–1644), China was free of foreign domination, and in the eyes of many Chinese this exceptional achievement gave the Communist Party the mandate to rule. In the preamble to the new constitution, the link between driving out the foreigners and the legitimacy of the Party is clearly indicated: 'The Revolution of 1911, led by Dr. Sun Yat-sen, abolished the feudal monarchy and gave birth to the Republic of China. But the historic mission of the Chinese people to overthrow imperialism and feudalism remained unaccomplished. After waging protracted and arduous struggles, armed and otherwise, along a zigzag course, the Chinese people of all nationalities led by the Communist Party of China with Chairman Mao Zedong as its leader ultimately, in 1949, overthrew the rule of imperialism, feudalism and bureaucrat-capitalism, won a great victory in the New-Democratic Revolution and founded the People's Republic of China. Since then the Chinese people have taken control of state power and become masters of the country.'

Without Marx, Lenin, and Mao, this achievement would not have been possible: 'The victory in China's New-Democratic Revolution and the successes in its socialist cause have been achieved by the Chinese people of all nationalities, under the leadership of the Communist Party of China and the guidance of Marxism-Leninism and Mao Zedong Thought. ...'[1]

The words of the constitution convey a double message. The Party has the right to rule over China, *because* it united the country and drove out the ancient, morally depraved regime. In this regard, the Communists align themselves with the ages-old dynastic tradition. Breaking with the earlier imperial houses, however, this new elite took their inspiration from a radical ideology alien to China. What is more, the constitution posits that it was *thanks to* this ideology that victory was attained. Internationally, the revolution in China produced shockwaves as well, for Mao viewed the victories of Communism in Russia and China as a prelude to world revolution. That brought the country into conflict with the United States, but later on also with the Soviet Union, because the initial cooperation between these two 'brother states' rather quickly succumbed to mutual suspicion and ideological squabbling over which was more closely adhering to pure Marxism.

Foreign Affairs Serve Domestic Interests Only

In China's political system, the Minister of Foreign Affairs has a relatively weak position. He does not belong to either of the two highest Party organs – the Politburo with its twenty-five members, and the Standing Committee, which has seven. The situation was different in the early years of the People's Republic. The first Minister of Foreign Affairs was the renowned Zhou Enlai, also the country's premier. Since that time the power of the Minister of Foreign Affairs has only decreased – given China's growing international power, a rather strange development. In part this has to do with the complexity of our globalised world, where businesses, the military, local authorities and NGOs have become foreign policy players in their own right. That fact has made it a lot harder for the Ministry of Foreign Affairs to conduct any uniform policy – as the former vice-minister Cui Tiankai, cited earlier in this book, has already observed. This is not unique to China: It occurs in all countries. A second reason for the weakness of the ministry lies in China's changing international position. In the 1950s and 1960s, the People's Republic was at war, first with America and later with the Soviet Union – countries which Beijing suspected of plotting a regime change in China. To avert that existential threat, the brightest minds of the nation were being deployed to forge 'anti-imperialist coalitions' with friendly countries. Zhou Enlai, as friends and foes agreed, was well-equipped for that task. He was intelligent, shrewd, worked relentlessly and had lived abroad as a young man – an experience that few leaders of the People's Republic shared. At the beginning of the twenty-first century, China feels less threatened internationally, and the nation's talent is being deployed to face domestic threats – protesting peasants, rebellious Uighurs and religious extremists. For an ambitious apparatchik, the way to the top lies in the successful handling of those problems, not in concluding trade agreements or reining in climate change.

The Goal of Mao's Foreign Policy

During the first thirty years of the People's Republic, no country in the world waged more border wars than China.[2] The most important of these were with South Korea, the USA, Russia, and India. Mao's aggression was driven by two forces: As the self-appointed leader of the international Communist movement, he supported – both morally and materially – rebels from Angola to Burma. But the more fundamental instinct driving him was the restoration of China's greatest territorial reach – in which he almost succeeded. Russia gave back Manchuria (which it had conquered from Japan) while Tibet and Xinjiang were occupied by the People's Liberation Army – though the word 'occupation' never appears in Chinese history books, for these maintain the fiction that both territories were 'liberated' from their feudal rulers. But as mentioned in the previous chapter, two important regions remained beyond Mao's reach. Stalin was unwilling to surrender Mongolia (under Soviet influence since 1924) and Taiwan was, since the outbreak of the Korean War in 1950, protected by the US Navy's seventh fleet. Nearly seventy years later, this situation remains essentially unchanged: Mongolia is an independent country; and so is Taiwan de facto, even though the vast majority of the world's nations will not openly acknowledge that. Beijing considers Taiwan to be an inseparable part of the 'sacred territory' of China, and imposes sanctions on countries establishing official relations with the island state.

Wars in Korea and India

Korea was the first theatre of war. Mao felt threatened by the US military, which had come close to the Chinese border when intervening in the Korean War in 1950. Attacking in human waves, the People's Volunteer Army (thus called to disguise Chinese intervention) drove the Americans back to the south. The tide of war ebbed and flowed, but in 1953 it was agreed to divide the country along the thirty-eighth parallel, which more than sixty years later still forms the border between North and South Korea. While the Korean War can still be seen through the prism of the Cold War, the 1962 conflict with India is more difficult to explain. Relations between the two Asian giants were excellent during the 1950s: As chief ministers, Nehru and Zhou Enlai jointly played a leading role at the Conference of Non-Aligned Countries in Bandung in 1955, where the famous 'Five Principles of Peaceful Coexistence' were formulated. By the end of the 1950s, though, their love story ended. After the Tibetan uprising against the Chinese occupation was defeated in 1959, the Dalai Lama fled to India and established his government in exile in Dharamsala. This stirred up bad blood with the Chinese, whose suspicion grew even further when, under New Delhi's so-called 'Forward' policy, Indian troops were stationed in the Himalayan regions disputed by both countries. Mao decided to teach India a lesson, but did not act impulsively. Henry Kissinger, a great admirer of China's strategic acumen, praises Mao's approach for its 'thorough analysis, careful preparation, attention to psychological and political factors, quest for surprise and rapid conclusion'.[3] Beijing left the Indians under the delusion that it accepted the new situation – but then broke through the Indian lines with vastly superior numbers of troops and materiel, pressing on to the borders that Beijing regarded as legitimate. The Chinese subsequently withdrew to the territory they had already occupied before the war – for Mao this was not about permanent occupation, but delivering a psychological blow. The result is that Arunachal Pradesh (called South Tibet by Beijing) is still in Indian hands, while Aksai Chin in the western Himalayas is controlled by China. Even for mega-states like India and China these are considerable territories: The first region is as large as Portugal; the latter, the size of Switzerland.

The Bandung Conference

The Asian-African Conference took place from 18 to 24 April 1955, in Bandung, Indonesia, and is therefore also called the Bandung Conference. Twenty-nine, for the most part newly independent, countries took part in it. The goals of the conference were to stimulate economic and cultural cooperation between African and Asian countries and to oppose colonialism 'in all of its manifestations' – which implicitly included criticism of the occupation of Eastern European countries by the Soviet Union. The influence of India's Prime Minister Nehru and China's Premier Zhou Enlai at the conference is evident from the adoption of the ten-point 'Declaration on promotion of world peace and cooperation', for these include the five principles of peaceful coexistence that the Indian and Chinese leaders had already agreed to on a bilateral basis in 1954. The Bandung Conference is seen as a precursor to the 'Movement of Non-Aligned Countries'.[4]

Indian Resentment

The 1962 war left behind a bitter taste in both countries – particularly in India, which believed that it stood on an equal footing with China (Nehru frequently spoke about the *Hindi-Chini bhai-bhai* relationship – the brotherhood between India and China) but was brutally reminded of its military inferiority. That kind of wound does not heal easily, all the more so because fifty years later, China's lead over its southern neighbour had widened even more – both economically and militarily. 'The Chinese-Indian relationship is strange and difficult,' said Li Xiangyang, director of the National Institute of International Chinese Academy of Social Sciences, in 2014. 'India has a deep-seated lack of self-confidence as it compares itself with China all the time – almost like China used to measure itself against the US and the UK in the 1950s and 1960s.'[5]

India is rightly proud of its religious and political freedom, but many Indians complain that those advantages do not guarantee good infrastructure or a higher standard of living. Prime Minister Modi says that India can learn from China's economic vitality, but cannot pursue the same development model 'because India is a democracy'. When Modi took power in May 2014, Beijing responded with cautious enthusiasm; one commentator even expected the new Prime Minister to become a second Richard Nixon, who normalised relations with China in 1972.[6] This seems to be a serious case of wishful thinking, for Modi's first trip abroad led him to Japan, a country with which India maintains close economic relations and which is an important supplier of technology. During that visit, the Prime Minister remarked that 'Everywhere around us, we see an eighteenth century expansionist mindset: encroaching on another country, intruding in others' waters, invading other countries and capturing territory.'[7] Which country Modi specifically had in mind was not difficult to guess. The Japanese Prime Minister Shinzo Abe, with whom Modi maintains a warm personal relationship, even proposed a military alliance between India, Japan, Australia, and the United States with the (unspoken) goal of checking China's aggression in the region.[8]

This alliance, which Chinese analysts soon called a 'mini-NATO', has yet to materialise, although the four countries do conduct yearly joint naval exercises. The nationalistic paper *Global Times* subtly pointed out that the Chinese economy is five times as large as India's, and that instead of emotions, national interests must guide any major power in its foreign policy.[9] On top of that, the military relationship is unequal: China's military budget is four times that of India. 'China actually has many ways to hurt India,' says Professor Shen Dingli of Fudan University. 'It could send an aircraft carrier to the Gwadar port in Pakistan. China had turned down the Pakistan offer to have military stationed in the country. If India forces China to do that, of course we can put a navy at your doorstep.'[10] During his visit to New Delhi in September 2014, President Xi Jinping promised to invest twenty billion dollars (US) in India over the next five years, and to contribute to the construction of high-speed rail lines; while on Prime Minister Modi's reciprocal visit to Beijing, twenty-four agreements were signed, ranging from space research to tourism. Yet despite a lot of talk about the twenty-first century being the 'Asian century', the resolution of the border dispute did not get any closer.[11] If anything, the stand-off in the summer of 2017 between the two military forces in the disputed area of Doklam (near the Bhutanese border) shows that the mistrust and suspicion between the two Asian powers has grown even worse. A major conflict was prevented by diplomatic exchanges at the highest levels, but only after both sides had hurled jingoistic and racist attacks at each other in the press and social media. The lowest attack was probably launched by the official news Agency Xinhua, who broadcasted a mock video portraying a caricature of an Indian who in 'funny Indian English' clumsily defends his country's 'untenable' position.[12] Also impeding the normalising of relations are Beijing's close bonds with New Delhi's arch-enemy Pakistan. More than 40 percent of Chinese arms exports are sent to Islamabad, and with the help of Chinese technology, that unstable country now has its own nuclear arsenal.[13] The spirit of goodwill that permeated the Bandung Conference seems to have been extinguished for good.

The Break with the Soviet Union

The third war Mao conducted was with the Soviet Union. At first glance, this was an even stranger affair than the conflict with India, for the Russians had traditionally

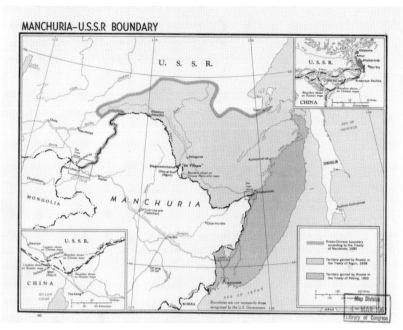

Map of the areas that China ceded to Russia in 1858 and 1860

supported the Party – financially, materially and ideologically. As far back as the 1920s, Mao clashed with the Soviet dogmatists by preaching a peasant revolution (instead of an urban upheaval), yet after the rift with Kuomintang in 1927 Stalin supported the Communists. The Soviet leader's decision to hand Manchuria over to the Party at the end of the Second World War, moreover, was of crucial importance for the outcome of the Chinese civil war. After the People's Republic was founded in 1949, the role of the Russians became even more important: They supplied thousands of experts and technicians to help rebuild the badly battered Chinese industry. But this seemingly close friendship proved to be fragile, and was quickly overshadowed by ideological disputes.

In 1956, Stalin's successor Khrushchev announced a new course: In a secret speech, he criticised the cult of personality surrounding Stalin, and called for détente in relations with the West. In Mao's eyes, this turned the Russians into 'revisionists', a term of abuse for Communists willing to cooperate with non-Communist parties. Relations completely fell apart with Khrushchev's decision in 1960 to withdraw 1,400 Russian technology experts working in China and to put an abrupt halt to two hundred joint projects. As a reaction to the twenty-first congress of the Russian Communist Party in 1961, the Party launched a venomous counter-attack. The jargon employed is bizarre, but highly indicative of their ruined relationship: 'At the 22nd Congress of the CPSU, the revisionist Khrushchev clique developed their revisionism into a complete system not only by rounding off their anti-revolutionary theories of "peaceful coexistence" and "peaceful transition" but also by declaring that the dictatorship of the proletariat is no longer necessary in the Soviet Union, and advancing the absurd theories of the "state of the whole people" and the "party of the entire people".[14]

In 1962, diplomatic relations between the two countries were in fact completely ruptured, with the Soviet Union taking India's side in the border conflict with China, and Mao accusing Khrushchev of 'capitulationism' in the Cuban crisis with the Americans.

War on the Amur

Just as with India, a border dispute constituted the proverbial last straw. The more than 4,000-kilometre-long border between China and the Soviet Union had been for the most part demarcated, but the small islands lying in the Amur and Ussuri rivers were not included in that settlement: These were occupied by the Soviet Union, though they were closer to the Chinese shore than the Russian side. In March 1969, the People's Liberation Army took over the river island of Zhenbao, killing dozens of Russians; but only a few weeks later the Chinese were driven off themselves, suffering great losses. The Soviets then considered destroying the Lop Nor nuclear test facility in a first strike, but the Americans deterred them from taking this inflammatory action.[15] The visit to Beijing on 11 September 1969 of the Russian premier Kosygin took the worst chill out of the air: Diplomatic channels were re-opened, and talks begun, in order to settle the border disputes. These were ultimately resolved by the 1991 Sino-Soviet Border Agreement.[16]

At first glance, it is a mystery why, during the hottest moment of the Cold War with America, Beijing triggered a confrontation with the other superpower of the period. The causes are diverse, but the complex psychological relationship between Stalin and Mao played a major role. The Russian leader did not think highly of Mao; he saw him as a pretentious country bumpkin who had been refusing to comply with Moscow's instructions since the 1920s. Stalin therefore took every opportunity to put the Chinese leader in his place. When Mao visited Stalin in December 1949, shortly after his victory in the Chinese civil war, he was compelled to wait for days in a dacha outside Moscow.[17] This is also why Stalin's death in 1953, as the sinologist Frank Dikötter writes, 'Was Mao's liberation' – his moment to take the helm as Communism's world leader had finally dawned.[18] Mao read the 1956 attack by Khrushchev on Stalin as an indirect attack on himself, and on his new position as the paramount leader. This explains his ferocious lashing out at Khrushchev: He treated the Russian leader just as Stalin had once treated him.

Apart from these clashes of personalities, history provides a more profound explanation for the conflict between the titans. For centuries, Russia was a vassal state of the Golden Horde, the westernmost portion of the Mongol Empire that had been divided into four parts after the death of Genghis Khan in 1227. The subjugation by the Mongols impeded the flourishing of Russian trade and science – precisely at the moment when Western Europe was on the rise. This profoundly influenced not only the economy, but also the Russian soul, turning them into semi-Mongols. As the proverb goes: 'Scratch a Russian, and you will find a Tartar.'[19] In the seventeenth century the roles were reversed: Moscow began its colonial expansion to the east and brought Siberia and large portions of Central Asia under Russian control. This process led to the annexation of more than 1 million square kilometres of Chinese territory in the middle of the nineteenth century. Though Beijing has never formally challenged this land grab, it is well known that Mao viewed the treaties of Aigun (1858) and Peking (1860), which confirmed that annexation, as inequitable.[20] The fact that the Russians controlled the railways in Manchuria and the naval port of Port Arthur (Dalian) for six years after the founding of the People's Republic in 1949 intensified China's sense that Moscow's colonial instincts were still alive and kicking. On top of that, Beijing viewed Russia's close military cooperation with neighbours like Mongolia, India, and Vietnam as an attempt to encircle China. For its part, Moscow saw relations through the same, historically-loaded filter. It regarded Mao as an emperor who called himself a Communist, but who looked down on other peoples and was guilty of 'Great Han Chauvinism'. In 1958, five years after Stalin's death, Mao said to the Russian ambassador Pavel Yudin: 'The Russians never had faith in the Chinese people, and Stalin was among the worst.'[21]

Relations Today: a Little Bear and a Big Panda

Contemporary relations between both countries have been strongly improved by the convergence of two common interests: Energy, and opposition to the West. Moreover, Putin and Xi Jinping recognise in one another strong-willed leaders who through tough, nationalistic policies attempt to increase their domestic popularity. On 9 May 2015, the Chinese president attended the Red Square parade (eschewed by the West) commemorating the end of the Second World War. For both countries, the significance of the Allied victory lies in its protection of the international order that has emerged since that time – and for that reason the return of 'fascist' forces in countries like Ukraine and Japan must be combatted. This rather imaginative analysis serves to justify Russia's own adventures in Crimea and Ukraine, as well as those of China in the East and South China Seas. In May 2015, the two countries held joint naval exercises in the Mediterranean Sea. The symbolism was clear: China and Russia are major military powers with a global reach, who conduct their military exercises wherever they want – even in the backyard of Putin's despised NATO.[22]

The West also influences both countries' close cooperation on energy. On 21 May 2014, both presidents attended the signing of an agreement between Gazprom and the China National Petroleum Corporation, which ensures the supply of Russian natural gas for thirty years, and is estimated to be worth four hundred billion US dollars.[23] At first glance this deal seems to be a victory for Putin: It creates an alternative to the Western Europe market, which – given Russia's annexation of Crimea – is doing everything it can to lessen its dependence on Russian natural gas. Putin is thus showing his immunity to Western sanctions, because there are still countries willing to trade with Moscow – even a major nation like China. In fact, Putin's position is weak: With falling energy prices and competition from countries like Turkmenistan, this 2014 natural gas deal has not yet been implemented, despite the hype when it was announced.

In the long term, things look even less favourable for Moscow. China has a much stronger and more diversified industrial capacity, a broader technology base, gigantic financial reserves and more than five times as many inhabitants. Since its former days as a global industrial power, Russia has slumped to become a Third World exporter of raw materials; only in the field of military technology can it still compete globally. Just like China, Russia has a clique of extremely rich entrepreneurs connected to the regime – but in China, the kleptocratic tendencies of the elite are compensated for by a deeply-felt pride in the country. This ensures that national income is also spent on better roads, and new universities and museums.

The biggest difference, though, lies in China's prosperous middle class: Hundreds of millions of people showing confidence in the future, setting up businesses and consuming ever more and more. Mao once bragged to Khrushchev that 'The east wind prevails over the west wind' and, sixty years later, he seems to be right.[24] The signing of the major natural gas contract in 2014 in Shanghai was accompanied by euphoric statements about a new era of bilateral relations, but the Russian political analyst Andrey Piontkovsky coolly observed that the relationship reminded him above all of that between a rabbit and a boa constrictor: There is a semblance of equality, but through Chinese economic superiority the Russian rabbit is getting slowly strangled.[25] On the part of the Chinese, a sense of disdain dominates. Russia is important as a supplier of energy and a strategic partner against the United States, but that is as far as it goes. Wang Yiwei, director of the Institute of International Affairs of Renmin University, provides an apt synopsis: 'The West, and not Russia, is the major partner for China in the process of opening up and economic reforms. The West, not Russia, represents the future for most Chinese.'[26] Setting up a formal alliance with the Russians is therefore out of the question. Referring to the painful memories of the failed collaboration of the 1950s, Tian Chunsheng, an analyst for the Russian Development Research Centre, said that both parties know 'not to repeat any historical tragedies by forming any alliance'.[27] On the Russian side, too, people are starting to realise that Moscow's 'pivot to China' is undesirable. As Dmitri Trenin of the Carnegie Moscow Center wrote in 2016, 'A country that refused to be a junior partner of the United States can't find it in its interest to become a tributary of a Chinese great power.'[28]

A United Front with the Hegemon

In July 1971, National Security Advisor to US president Richard Nixon, Henry Kissinger, visited Beijing in utmost secrecy – so secret that even the American Secretary of State William Rogers was unaware of it. This mission was a *volte face* of monumental proportions, a move on the geopolitical chessboard that, by its spectacular, totally unexpected nature, rivalled the monstrous 1939 German-Russian alliance that led to the partition of Poland. Over the previous twenty years, the Chinese state-owned media had been spitting out endless streams of anti-American propaganda. 'American imperialism is the most fiendish enemy of world peace!' was one of the friendlier-sounding catchphrases.[29] The Americans, from their side, were equally one-sided in their anti-Communist paranoia. In the 1950s, the arch-conservative senator Joe McCarthy had unleashed a witch-hunt in which many respected scholars were unmasked as 'Communist spies' and their careers broken. At the beginning of the 1970s, though, ideological emotions were subordinated to the shift in geopolitical relations that Kissinger and Chinese premier Zhou Enlai recognised as no others did at the time. Economically and militarily weakened, China needed an ally against the Russian bear; and the Americans were only too glad to drive a wedge between the two Communist giants – all the more so as President Nixon sank deeper and deeper into the quagmire of the Vietnam War, while China supported North Vietnam as its Communist brother state. Yet apart from these strategic considerations, Nixon believed that the time had come to integrate China into the world again, with that unique form of idealism that is peculiar to Americans: 'We simply cannot afford to leave China forever outside the family of nations, there to nurture its fantasies, cherish its hates, and threaten its neighbours. There is no place on this small planet for a billion of its potentially most able people to live in bitter isolation.'[30]

Nixon in Beijing

The secret meeting between Kissinger and Zhou Enlai led in February 1972 to a ground-breaking visit by Nixon to Beijing. Despite his brittle health (he suffered from Parkinson's disease), the 78-year-old Mao was closely involved in the negotiations.

Mao Zedong and Richard Nixon, 1972

Both countries agreed that after twenty years of bitter confrontation, it was time for rapprochement. In the words of Nixon: 'There is no reason for us to be enemies. Neither of us seeks the territory of the other; neither of us seeks domination over the other. ...'[31] The visit was concluded with the famous Shanghai Communiqué, in which the Americans recognised the principle that there is only one China – a logical consequence of the world view that *Realpolitiker* like Nixon and Kissinger adhered to. The Communist regime effectively exercised authority over Chinese territory, whether that was desirable from an ideological perspective or not. Nevertheless, the American recognition created domestic problems, for dropping the Republic of China (which in 1972 was still recognised as the legitimate government of all China) like a stone was hard for Nixon's conservative base to swallow. The way in which the Shanghai Communiqué circumvents this delicate issue is textbook material for any school of foreign service: 'The United States acknowledges that all Chinese on either side of the Taiwan Strait maintain there is but one China and that Taiwan is a part of China. The United States Government does not challenge that position. It reaffirms its interest in a peaceful settlement of the Taiwan question by the Chinese themselves.'[32]

Chinese-American Relations Today

Forty-five years later, the relationship between China and America is the most important, but also the most complex in the world. Economic interests constitute its foundation: Bilateral trade amounted to 636 billion dollars in 2017, and every major American business has invested in China or opened offices there. Walmart, the largest retailer in the world, imports goods worth more than 30 billion dollars from China annually – that is more than most countries in the world import from China *in total*. But the exchange is anything but one-way: Beijing has put a large share of its enormous trade surplus into American treasury bonds (at the end of 2016, their value amounted to 1,058 trillion dollars),[33] making China Washington's biggest foreign creditor after Japan. The Chinese business community is right on the heels of the Chinese state: In May 2013, the Shuanghui corporation bought Smithfield Foods, headquartered in Virginia, for 4.7 billion dollars, the largest acquisition that a Chinese business had ever made in America.[34]

Acquisitions like this show a new balance in relations, but the entanglements are not just economic. In domains like climate change, combating terrorism, cross-border pollution, cybercrime, and security in East Asia, the world's largest and second-largest economies are trying to devise joint approaches. This makes Chinese-American relations not only more important but also more complex than Chinese-European relations, which are primarily defined in economic terms.

At the time of this book's revision (the spring of 2018), the Party is grappling with how to interpret the Twitter phenomenon of President Trump. Initial optimism about his 'pragmatism' (versus the 'Cold War mentality' of Obama) soon dissipated when the newly-elected president accepted a phone call from Taiwanese president Mme Cai Yingwen, congratulating Trump on his election win. This broke with the tradition that American administrations – let alone the president himself – maintain no official contact with the 'renegade province'. Chinese anger turned into total confusion when Trump publicly announced that he felt no longer bound to uphold the One China policy, if Beijing did not reduce the American trade deficit or halt the threat of a North Korean missile attack on the United States.[35] The bottom seemed to have fallen out of Chinese-American relations, as the Chinese Ministry of Foreign Affairs was quick to assert that the One China principle is not negotiable. As always, the nationalistic *Global Times* phrased government policy more bluntly: 'Listen up, Trump: The One China Policy Cannot be Bought or Sold'.[36] Soon, however, the more experienced staff in the new administration intervened and in a telephone conversation with Xi Jinping on 10 February 2017, Trump said that he recognised the One China policy after all.[37]

The initial chill in the air disappeared entirely during the first summit between the two leaders in April 2017 at Trump's Mar-a-Lago estate in Florida. Walking and talking, the men spent much more time together than the agenda had foreseen, with Trump praising 'the great chemistry' that he had built up with Xi. In terms of substance, however, not much was achieved. Trump's hope that China would resolve the threat from North Korea flew out of the window when Xi Jinping explained to him 'in ten minutes' that Beijing's influence in the hermit state is limited. Discussions over trade relations led shortly afterwards to an accord that provides facilitative measures (China will, for instance, again allow the importing of American beef) but does not impose any obligation on Chinese state businesses to buy American products.*[38]

What will especially be remembered from the Trump-Xi summit was the missile attack on Syria carried out at the same moment – whereby an unintended(?) signal was given that America can take matters into its own hands in the world wherever and whenever it wants.[39]

Trump's unpredictability provides the regime in Beijing (groomed as they are in the Taoist tradition of *yin* and *yang*) both a threat and an opportunity: The Party hates instability, but it also sees a chance to be portrayed on the international stage as a steadfast power that leads the battle against climate change and safeguards free trade. 'The Paris agreement [on climate change] is a hard-won achievement, all signatories should stick to it rather than walk away', Xi Jinping said at the Davos World Economic Forum in 2017.[40] The world could hardly believe its ears: China had played a destructive role at the 2009 climate conference in Copenhagen by rejecting any international obligation – even though it had been the world's biggest emitter of CO_2 since 2007. The international applause Beijing garnered in 2017 as a climate protector satisfied its desire to be seen as a morally superior nation. Yet the highest objective remains beyond its reach: The recognition from the United States that both countries are on an equal footing. China regularly appeals for a 'new form of relations for major powers', but for the time being, the Americans are not going along with it. They feel that this 'new form' would give Beijing the right to have its own sphere of influence. In the context of Chinese history, as well as current foreign policy, it is not hard to guess where that sphere would be located: In the countries that traditionally paid tribute to Beijing, and that lie within the borders of the 'Maps of National Shame' still being published.

---

* The positive effect of this accord was short lived: In the spring of 2018 the United States and China are on the brink of a trade war, with each side threatening to raise import duties on specific exports from the other side. Washington took the first step, because it claims that Beijing's support for key domestic industries and the Chinese practice to force foreign companies to transfer their technology, are causing serious damage to the American economy.

Deep Mutual Distrust

A constructive cooperation between the United States and China is only possible when the deeply-felt sense of suspicion amongst the Chinese elite is eliminated. In that respect closely-involved advisors are not optimistic. At a seminar organised by the Netherlands Institute of International Relations-Clingendael in September 2011, Bonnie Glaser – a researcher at the Center of Strategic and International Studies (a Washington think tank) and advisor to the American government – complained about 'the fundamental and deep distrust on the Chinese side concerning every proposal that Americans launch'.[41] According to an internal Party document from 2014, Washington is pursuing five strategic objectives: Isolating, constraining, weakening, and dividing China, as well as undermining the political leadership of the Party.[42] The reasons for this paranoia are complex. The friendly relations that Washington maintains with most of China's neighbours recalls Beijing's ages-old anxiety of being surrounded – just as Moscow's relations with India and Vietnam did in the 1970s. But the Party document's fifth point represents Beijing's deepest fear: That Washington is still intent upon bringing about regime change. This suspicion reaches back to the 1950s, when the Communist-basher Joe McCarthy ranted about the 'loss of China', alluding not only to the billions of dollars Washington had thrown at the corrupt regime of Chiang Kai-shek, but also to the loss of China as a democratic and Christian country.[43]

President Nixon's visit in 1972 opened a new chapter, but some fifty years later the foundations for relations are still weak. In the United States, the belief that China intends to make a constructive contribution to today's world order is waning. The April 2015 report 'Revising US Grand Strategy Toward China' by Robert Blackwill – American ambassador to India under President George W. Bush – proposes a robust response to China's increasing power by strengthening the military, limiting Beijing's access to high-level technology, combating cybercrime and quickly completing the signing of the Trans-Pacific Partnership, the free trade accord propelled by Washington and Tokyo.[44] In a speech on national security, given in December 2017, President Trump named Russia and China as 'strategic competitors' that were seeking to challenge US power and erode its security and prosperity. This requires, according to the document, Washington to 'rethink policies based on the assumption that engagement with rivals and including them in international institutions would turn them into benign actors and trustworthy partners'. New thinking is needed, because 'For the most part, this premise turned out to be false.'[45] Trump's speech indirectly acknowledges that his assumed ability (as former businessman) to strike 'good deals' with Putin and Xi Jinping was highly imaginary. In fact, Washington's new China policy constitutes a return to the policy of former president George W. Bush, who also regarded China as a 'competitor' (albeit not a 'strategic' one). But whoever sits in the White House, there is a deeper lesson to be learned from Trump's capricious China policy: As long as China remains Communist there can be no real meeting of minds between the two sides.

As will be argued in Chapter 12: The odds for substantial rapprochement are better should China opt for a different political system. Fed by years of propaganda, the Chinese people are annoyed by Washington's China policy, but positive about America's soft power: The plurality of its institutions, its free elections and judicial independence. On top of that, Uncle Sam is like a magnet to countless young Chinese for whom studying at Harvard or Yale constitutes the realisation of their wildest dreams. And then there is the temptation of the land of unlimited opportunities. The glamorous lifestyle of its Hollywood stars, and the freedom of choice which clashes with the Chinese obedience to authority – be it parental or to the state. That is why surveys by the Pew Global Attitudes Project show that more than 50 percent of Chinese see American culture as positive.[46] Just like Washington, Beijing wants to entice through its 'soft power', and is pumping hundreds of millions of dollars into English-language TV stations and major events like the World Expo in Shanghai – yet to no avail. According to a survey from the same Pew Research Center, the number of Americans judging China favourably did indeed climb in 2017 (from 35 to 43%), but 60% have no confidence that President Xi Jinping will 'do the right thing'. In particular, cyberattacks from China targeting the American government and businesses have created a negative image.[47]

Deng's Foreign Policy

Deng Xiaoping's seizure of power in 1978 ensured that foreign policy came to serve the predominant domestic priority: Restoring the economy destroyed by Mao. In November 1978 – just before the monumental third plenum of the 11th Party Congress that launched the economic reforms – the new leader paid a visit to Singapore, the city-state whose population for the most part originates from China. With South Korea, Hong Kong and Taiwan, Singapore became famous in the 1970s as one of the 'four tigers', countries in which the export-driven economy grew at a rate of 10 percent annually. Deng could not believe his eyes. 'Singapore's social order is rather good. Its leaders exercise strict management. We should learn from their experience, and improve our own performance.'[48] Shortly after his visit, the Special Economic Zones were established in the south of China: Four enclaves detached from the rest of the country, and to which foreign businesses were lured for production and export. The choice of South China was no coincidence. From the days of the Song dynasty (960–1279), junks had sailed from the harbours of Guangzhou (Canton), Fuzhou (Foochow), Quanzhou (Chinchew) and Xiamen (Amoy) to do business with South and South-East Asia. In the thirteenth and fourteenth centuries, Quanzhou was one of the largest harbours in the world; it

Deng Xiaoping with Jimmy Carter during his visit to the United States, 1979

was here that Marco Polo embarked in 1292 to return to his Venice after his eighteen-year stay in Cathay. Beginning with the Ming dynasty (1368–1644), the Chinese fleet ruled East Asian trade; but unlike the English or Dutch, the merchants did not form companies that built factories and enforced monopolies. The Chinese method was more quiet and subtle. From Surabaya to Hanoi, the South Chinese created informal networks with people coming from the same town or region, connected as they were by one common forefather. For the members of these clans, trust is everything: No contracts are signed, and credit is extended without collateral. With his Open Door Policy, Deng Xiaoping killed two birds with one stone: He seduced Western businesses into investing in China, *and* he convinced Chinese from abroad that it was safe to start rebuilding ties with the motherland (or, rather: 'clanland'). The latter accomplishment was essential. The Chinese *Wirtschaftswunder* did not happen thanks to investments from, say Proctor & Gamble, Exxon and Shell, but rather to the enormous, invisible wave of knowledge, contacts and money that flowed back to the motherland after 1978.

A New Ideology

The second priority of Deng's foreign policy – creating a stable international environment – also served the reconstruction of the Chinese economy. Ideologically, Deng drew from the 1955 Bandung Conference where, on the initiative of premier Zhou

Enlai and India's Prime Minister Nehru, the well-known five principles of peaceful coexistence had been adopted:

1. Mutual respect for the sovereignty and territorial integrity of all nations
2. Mutual non-aggression
3. Non-intervention or non-interference in the internal affairs of another country
4. Equality and cooperation for mutual benefit
5. Peaceful coexistence[49]

Sixty years later, these five principles – with sovereignty at the core – still constitute the cornerstones of Chinese foreign policy. In the white paper on the Senkaku (Diaoyu) Islands, published by the Ministry of Foreign Affairs in 2012, the word 'sovereignty' occurs eight times,[50] and in every communiqué that China issues with other nations this principle is repeated with liturgical regularity. The message of Bandung's third principle, that of non-intervention, is two-fold. On the one hand, it contains a warning that foreign countries should not interfere in the internal matters of China. The other message, though, is that China will no longer intervene in the domestic affairs of other countries.

Under Mao, that position was fundamentally different. True to the principle of 'international proletarian solidarity', the Great Helmsman supported Communist rebels in countries like Burma, Vietnam, Thailand and Indonesia.[51] Chaos, disruption and rebellion were seen by Mao as a necessary phase for bringing the final victory of Communism closer. 'Everything under heaven is in utter chaos; the situation is excellent!' is one of his more memorable sayings.[52] Deng wanted to have nothing to do with this, for only if China presented itself as a reliable partner would foreign trade grow and international businesses invest in China. The new face of the old empire had to radiate peace, harmony and stability. 'Even if China is well-developed and has become a strong nation in the future, we will never seek to become a leader, never seek hegemony, never seek a sphere of influence, never involve ourselves with any faction in world politics and never interfere with the internal affairs of other nations.'[53]

'Hide Brightness and Cherish Obscurity'

Deng's highest priority was to rebuild the economy that Mao had torn apart. But it was not his ultimate goal. In the end, it was about completing the project that had already obsessed the nineteenth-century Self-Strengthening Movement and the early twentieth-century Kuomintang: Returning China to the highest platform on the global stage. That goal could only be attained on the foundations of a stable society and a strong economy. That is why Deng formulated in the 1980s China's long-term objectives. By the year 2000, the economy should be four times as big as in 1980: An objective that was achieved as early as 1995.[54] Because Chinese leaders like to sketch broad vistas that transcend the course of their own lives, Deng added that by the middle of the twenty-first century per capita income must be equal to that of a 'semi-developed' country. In a certain sense, even that goal has already been reached: In 2015, the annual income of a resident of Shanghai amounted to more than 15,000 dollars (US) – as much as a citizen of Turkey.[55]

As to the principles that should guide the foreign policy of this economic superstate, Deng gave at the end of his life several 'instructions' to the next generation of policymakers. The famous document 'A 28-Character Foreign Policy Guideline' contains seven aphorisms, which in their abstract, sometimes purposely vague wording unmistakably carry the imprint of Master Sun:

- Observe coolly.
- Hold our ground.
- Respond calmly and don't be impatient.
- Hide brightness and cherish obscurity.
- Keep a low profile.
- Absolutely do not take the lead.
- Take some actions.[56]

The most well-known is *Taoguang yanghui* – 'Hide brightness and cherish obscurity'. The most important characteristic of a good strategist is his invisibility – in deeds, but also in words – so the exact meaning of Deng's aphorisms has been fiercely debated. My interpretation is that the Little Helmsman did not doubt the country's destiny: The restoration of China's former glory is a matter of time, as certain as the sun's rising – the qualities (the 'brightness') of the Celestial Empire being as they are, no other outcome is possible. Flaunting those features or wanting to accelerate China's rise, however, makes no sense – it can even have the opposite effect. That is why he also says: 'Keep a low profile' and 'Respond calmly and don't be impatient'. The last aphorism – 'Take some actions' – seems to conflict with the first six, yet it can also be read as a call to action when the world has been lulled to sleep by China's peaceful intentions. We do not know. What we do know, however, is that China's *current* leadership is conducting a foreign policy that is anything but characterized by patience and modesty. The time to 'take some actions' seems to have arrived.

War with Vietnam

Deng, for that matter, also 'took some actions' when he saw fit. The most famous example was his attack on Vietnam in 1979. After President Nixon's visit to Beijing in 1972, relations between China and Vietnam, the closeness of which was once described as 'wind rain, same boat' (i.e. able to withstand any change), came under increasing pressure; even more so as Hanoi was growing closer to Moscow, and in 1979 gave the Russian navy access to the harbour of Cam Ranh Bay. When Vietnam invaded Cambodia in 1978 to overthrow the Maoist-inspired regime of the murderous Pol Pot, Beijing had had enough. Deng decided to 'teach a lesson' to Vietnam and invaded North Vietnam with great military force.*

The Chinese campaign ended in a disaster: The untrained soldiers of the People's Liberation Army, mobilised from the country's seven military regions to gain combat experience, were no match for the hardened Vietnamese who had been waging war incessantly since the start of the 1950s – first with the French, and then the Americans. Just as in the Korean War in 1950, the People's Liberation Army tried to overwhelm the enemy lines with human waves: Four thousand Chinese soldiers died on the first day alone. Eventually, 75,000 Chinese soldiers lost their lives. Vietnam's losses were also considerable, though not as great as those of its northern neighbour. After twenty-seven days of battle, the Chinese military withdrew. Vietnam was clearly the moral winner of this senseless war, which almost forty years later is still concealed by the Chinese media and thus, it seems, erased from the collective memory of the Chinese people.[58]

Crisis in the Taiwan Strait

China has not waged any war since 1979, but that is not to say that it has stopped preparing for it. On the contrary: In the period 1990–2016 the annual defence budget has grown at more than 10 percent annually. The disastrous result of the war with Vietnam taught the PLA generals that, in order to win battles, the quality of the armed forces is more important than its size. A milestone in this learning process was the crisis in the Taiwan Strait in 1996. In June of the previous year, Taiwan's President Lee Tenghui had secured a visa to give a speech at his alma mater, Cornell University – thus breaking the American policy of not inviting any Taiwanese leaders into the

---

* In his book *Everything under the heavens* Howard French posits that Vietnam's invasion of Cambodia in 1979 constituted a challenge to China's traditional position as overlord of the Indo-China region. A challenge that could not go unanswered.[57]

country (even in an unofficial capacity). By arguing in his speech for the island's independence, Lee rubbed extra salt into the Chinese wound. President Jiang Zemin – who before Lee's US visit had unfolded an initiative for reunifying with the island (the so-called Eight Point plan) – felt personally offended, and gave the military a free hand to hold naval exercises off Taiwan's coast. Purposely, this intimidation took place right before the Taiwanese presidential elections in March 1996. Jiang Zemin, however, had overplayed his hand: President Clinton sent two aircraft carriers to the region to bring the Chinese back into line, and the people of Taiwan re-elected Lee as president by a vast majority. To prevent total embarrassment, the Chinese also held an exercise off their own coast; but it was clear to the entire world who the moral victor was in this pseudo-conflict.

A better grasp of American politics might have prevented China's loss of face. The Democrat Bill Clinton was less hawkish than his Republican predecessors Reagan and Bush Sr., but even he had to take into account the Taiwan lobby, which felt strongly that America had a duty to protect a democratic Taiwan against Communist aggression. Such an obligation was not only moral: The aforementioned Taiwan Relations Act stipulates that the United States shall come to the aid of the island in case it is attacked by China. Though not clear in its effect, this obligation contains a veiled threat: 'The United States consider any effort to determine the future of Taiwan by other than peaceful means, including by boycotts or embargoes, a threat to the peace and security of the Western Pacific area and of grave concern to the United States.'[59] The act was adopted in 1979 – in that same year President Jimmy Carter recognised the People's Republic as the only legitimate government of all China. To accommodate conservative forces in the US Congress, a gesture had to be made to Taiwan as well.

New Strategic Thinking

On his visit to Moscow in 1957, Mao Zedong stunned his host Khrushchev with a statement that was extreme even by Mao's standards: 'I'm not afraid of nuclear war. There are 2.7 billion people in the world; it doesn't matter if some are killed. China has a population of 600 million; even if half of them are killed, there are still 300 million people left. I'm not afraid of anyone.'[60] In Mao's way of thinking, the actual impossibility of deploying nuclear weapons reduced the United States to a 'paper tiger'. But the Taiwan crisis of 1996 showed clearly that the predator still had teeth, for not since the Korean War had the American war machine come so close to Chinese territory. The first wake-up call happened six years earlier, when during the Gulf War of 1990 the Americans rapidly drove Saddam Hussein out of Kuwait. The Chinese generals came to realise that communication, the integration of various combat

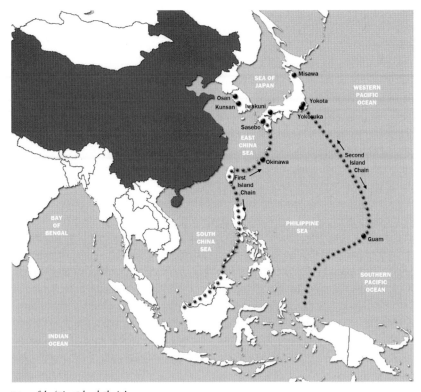

Map of the 'First Island Chain'

elements, long-distance missiles, silent submarines and jet fighters are determining factors in winning modern wars – not the number of soldiers.

American military superiority also constituted a political threat, because re-unification with Taiwan has since its founding been the most important foreign policy objective of the People's Republic of China. A thorough revision of China's military strategy was therefore required. An arms race with the United States was seen as unrealistic, but the capability to occupy Taiwan could still be developed. The large-scale installation of ballistic missiles in Fujian province, across from Taiwan, constitutes an important component of this strategy. In 2013, over sixteen hundred such projectiles had been mounted there[61] – a form of intimidation that the military strategist Sun Zi had also advocated: 'Hold the bow taut without shooting, and increase pressure without fighting.' Yet China's provocation did not end with ballistic missiles; large-scale investments were made in landing vehicles, silent submarines and minesweepers, the strategic goal being to keep the Americans behind the 'First Island Chain' – a line that runs from the Ryukyu Islands via Taiwan and the northern Philippines to Borneo. This so-called 'Anti-Access, Area-Denial' strategy also explains

Beijing's aggressive behaviour in the South China Sea (as is detailed in the next chapter) and signals the beginning of a new phase in geopolitical relations in East Asia. During a meeting with then Secretary of State John Kelly in May 2015, Xi Jinping declared that 'The broad Pacific Ocean is vast enough to embrace both China and the United States', but in reality, this immense ocean forms the new theatre of war for the existing and the up-and-coming world power.[62]

Revanchist Reaction

The crisis in the Taiwan Strait did not only bring about the modernisation of the military. It also saw the start of a movement that can best be characterised as revanchist militarism. Song Qiang's book *China Can Say No* (1996) articulates this new thinking accurately. In it, the colonel criticises what he believes to be the cowardly policy of President Jiang Zemin, which is only directed at avoiding conflicts with the Americans. According to Song, all means are allowed when it comes to undermining the hegemony of Uncle Sam: Cyberattacks, guerrilla campaigns, even the disruption of the financial system.[63] This method of fighting – which by its indirect and invisible nature carries the unmistakable imprint of Sun Zi – is known as 'asymmetrical warfare', and has become standard thinking in military circles today.

The policy of the government, however, continues to take a very different tone. The white papers from the Ministry of Foreign Affairs constantly contend that the country has traditionally only focussed on peace,[64] a mantra regularly recited by President Xi Jinping: 'In Chinese blood, there is no DNA for aggression or hegemony. ... Chinese people do not accept the logic that a strong country must also be hegemonic. History has told us that wars are like devils and nightmares.'[65] The president's historical account is based on a fiction: In its long history, China has waged countless wars with its neighbours (not to mention the domestic wars between rebels and imperial troops); yet for the time being, words like 'peace' and 'harmony' dominate its statements on foreign policy. At the same time a polyphonic chorus of think tanks, military staff and bloggers are arguing for a more aggressive foreign policy to protect China's interests abroad. China expert David Shambaugh even calls Wang Xiaodong, an outspoken nationalist whom I interviewed earlier in this book, a 'nationalistic demagogue'.[66] This growing tide of nationalism, together with Xi Jinping's comments at the 19th Party Congress that 'The Chinese nation now stands tall and firm in the East', confirms that Deng Xiaoping's maxim 'hide brightness and cherish obscurity' is a thing of the past.

Sovereignty as the Core Principle

The foreign policy of the People's Republic is like the ocean. The ebb of Deng's confrontation-averse foreign policy followed the flow of Mao's aggressive interventions. In recent years, China is flexing its muscles again – both rhetorically and in reality. These differences, though, gloss over the fact that, until now, not one of China's Communist power-brokers has tampered with the most important of the five principles expressed at the Bandung Conference. *Sovereignty* is the crucial article of faith upon which the other four principles rest. In nineteenth-century Europe a similar belief reigned: The balance of power between sovereign states was supposed to have stamped out war for good. Yet this order, constructed by the Austrian diplomat Klemens von Metternich at the Congress of Vienna in 1815 came, from the Crimean War of 1853–1856 onwards, under increasing pressure during the second half of the nineteenth century. With the outbreak of the First World War in 1914, it collapsed like a house of cards. The catastrophe of the twentieth century's two world wars changed Western thinking radically: Sovereignty does not eliminate war – it increases the risk of them occurring. Only by checking the power of the nation-state can such disasters be prevented. The founding of the United Nations, the European Union and countless other international organisations proves that the transfer of power from national states to supranational institutions is irreversible. The success of that process is not universal, and certainly hotly disputed, but the days of absolute sovereignty in the West are numbered.

The People's Republic of China draws the opposite conclusion from history: Not the *excess*, but rather the *shortage* of sovereignty caused the string of plagues inflicted by foreigners upon the ancient empire – the Opium Wars, the Eight-Country Invasion that suppressed the Boxer Rebellion, and the Japanese wars of aggression. That is why the 'New China' hammers continually on the importance of sovereignty – the preamble to the constitution even speaks of the 'holy territory of the People's Republic of China'. During the negotiations over the transfer of Hong Kong in 1997, Prime Minister Margaret Thatcher pushed hard to keep the island of Hong Kong for the British, while only returning 'The New Territories' to China. Legally, she had a point, because in the 1842 Treaty of Nanking the island of Hong Kong had been ceded to England 'in perpetuity', while the 'New Territories' had been leased in 1898 to Great Britain for ninety-nine years. Deng Xiaoping immediately swept that argument off the table: 'China cannot but resume the exercise of sovereignty over the whole of the Hong Kong area.'[67] In May 2014, Vietnam and China clashed after the Chinese oil corporation China National Offshore Oil Company (CNOOC) had placed a drilling platform in disputed waters. Faced with this issue, Fang Fenghui, China's highest-ranking general, pledged that 'We will not cede an inch of the territory our ancestors left behind.'[68] On the eve of the occupation of Tibet in 1951, the *People's Daily* used exactly the same wording. Much in China has changed, but ideas on sovereignty have not budged one inch in the last sixty-five years. In his intriguing book *What Does China Think?*, Mark Leonard even perceives a movement towards the strengthening of sovereignty: 'The idea of recapturing sovereignty from global economic forces, companies and groups of individuals such as terrorists, is a potentially revolutionary element of the Chinese world-view.'[69]

CHAPTER 9

The New Nationalism

*We will not cede an inch of the territory our
ancestors left behind.*

Fang Fenghui

In 1999, the American journal *Foreign Affairs* published the article 'Does China Matter?'
The answer given by its author Gerald Segal was devastating: 'Odd as it may seem, the
country that is home to a fifth of humankind is overrated as a market, a power, and a
source of ideas. At best, China is a second-rank middle power that has mastered the art
of diplomatic theatre: It has us willingly suspending our disbelief in its strength. In
fact, China is better understood as a theoretical power – a country that has promised
to deliver for much of the last 150 years but has consistently disappointed.'[1] In 2018,
this opinion is no longer tenable. China has grown into an economic superpower. Its
market for cars is bigger than that of the United States; four of the ten biggest banks
in the world are Chinese; and through its large-scale investments, the economies of
most African countries have been unrecognisably changed. And we could go on like
this for a while. Even so, Segal's position is not altogether outdated, for *mentally* China
is still not ready for global leadership. It remains – as substantiated convincingly by
David Shambaugh in his book *China Goes Global: The Partial Power* – an introverted
country that does not *want* to take the lead in world affairs. 'It is punching below its
weight,' as Americans so nicely put it.

But as with most things in modern China, this position of reticence is changing as
well. China increasingly manifests itself as a regional, even global power, fighting
pirates off the coast of Somalia, evacuating its nationals from Libya and Yemen,
and holding naval exercises with the Russians in the Mediterranean. Domestic
developments are the reason for this willingness 'to take some actions'. Since the 2008
Olympic Games, control of Chinese society has been tightened: State-owned businesses
have regained the influence they had lost under Zhu Rongji (China's premier from
1998–2003), the presence of the Party in people's everyday lives has intensified, and
enthusiasm for political reforms has evaporated. Abroad, this situation translates into
a more assertive and more nationalistic policy.

Small wonder that China's neighbours feel threatened by the traditional regional
overlord, whose defence budget on average has been growing more than 10 percent

annually since the 1990s. According to Fu Ying, the wily former vice-minister of Foreign Affairs, there is no reason to be worried. How can a country as large and prosperous as China, she wonders rhetorically, achieve 'real peace' without a strong national defence?[2] This purported pursuit of peace, however, is difficult to reconcile with the growing number of maritime conflicts with Japan (East China Sea) and Vietnam and the Philippines (South China Sea). As a result, anti-China feeling in those countries has risen to new heights. Benigno Aquino, former president of the Philippines, bade farewell to any semblance of diplomatic civility in 2015, when he condemned the tepid response of the international community to the Chinese policy of island-grabbing: 'At what point do you say: "Enough is enough"? Well, the world has to say it – remember that the Sudetenland was given in an attempt to appease Hitler to prevent World War II.'[3]

Nationalism Binds the Nation

The myths used to justify the creation of the Great Rejuvenation of the Chinese Nation (see Chapter 5) also have a foreign dimension: China should once again take the 'centre stage in the world' (as Xi Jinping put it at the 19th Party Congress) and the rest of the world had better respect this position. This narrative has triggered emotional waves of nationalism – though the Party itself prefers to speak of 'patriotism' (*aiguo zhuyi*). Still, if the difference between these two terms consists of a positive or negative expression of love for the motherland, then China is clearly nationalistic. More and more, the old empire affirms its identity in opposition to countries that have previously offended it, or continue to do so. The increasing number of disputes with its neighbours, the chauvinistic tone of newspapers like *Global Times* and the Patriotic Education Campaign are all manifestations of the search for a 'rejuvenated China'. The emotional eruptions that accompany this process are (as far as we can judge) genuine, but behind this passionate façade hides the cool calculation that nationalism is a useful tool for bonding the people behind the Party's banner. Xi Jinping himself has said that the 'China Dream' could only be realised by seeking 'China's own path, cultivating patriotism, and following the Communist Party's leadership'.[4] Nationalism and obedience to the Party are two sides of the same coin.

Nationalism flourishes under the loss of territory. French nationalism at the end of the nineteenth century was directed at regaining Alsace-Lorraine, while Hitler's Germany schemed to reunite that and other German-speaking regions with the Third Reich. At the Xiangshan Forum – a regional security meeting held in Beijing in November 2014 – the Minister of Defence, Chang Wanquan, said that the most important reason for China's rapid military modernisation lay in the 'deep reflection of the country's bitter suffering in modern history'.[5] The most important goal for

Chinese nationalism is conquering Taiwan – though to this 'core interest' has in 2010 been added another one: Complete control of the South China Sea.[6] Who knows which other 'interests' will be added to these, for as the 'Maps of National Shame' show, China has never quite reconciled itself with the idea that a modern nation-state has fixed borders. Even more crucial is the fact that completing its constitutional mission – reunification with Taiwan – takes away an important component of the Party's raison d'être. Abroad, just like at home ('only the Party can save China'), new reasons must constantly be found for the Party's indispensability. If the domestic grip on power weakens, the temptation to protect its 'core interests' abroad becomes even more irresistible. It is this direct connection between the *domestic* situation and *foreign* policy that makes the Party so prickly and unpredictable. In fact, domestic and foreign policy are two sides of the same coin: Both are tools for keeping the Party in power forever.

In part, this new nationalism constitutes a break with the foreign policy of Mao Zedong and Deng Xiaoping. For those two legendary leaders, sovereignty was an inviolable principle too, but (certainly in Mao's day) foreign policy was less directed at propping up the Party domestically. On the contrary, under the principle of 'proletarian internationalism', food and technological support was given to faraway countries like Tanzania and Albania. This even reached the point where China was exporting grain to its Socialist brother states at dumping prices – while at the same time the famine caused by the Great Leap Forward cost the lives of at least 45 million people.[7] Of this proletarian brotherhood little remains. Beijing has friends where its interests lie. In recent years, its financial support to developing countries has been recalibrated by replacing grants with loans at commercial interest rates and firm assurances for repayment. The most striking break between today's policy and that of Deng Xiaoping has been the abandoning of his principles of modesty and reticence. One could even say that since 2008, Beijing only adheres to the last of Deng's seven instructions for conducting proper foreign policy: 'Take some actions.'

The 2008 Olympic Games

In the run-up to the Olympic Games in 2008, Beijing promised to improve its human rights record and to lift restrictions on the foreign press. Journalists would no longer need to seek approval for conducting research and recording interviews in China's provinces. 'We will give the foreign media complete freedom,' Wang Wei, the vice-president of the Olympic Committee, said.[8] But then the issue of Tibet got in the way of these good intentions. In April 2008, the Chinese Olympic Committee organised a torch relay, in which the Olympic flame was carried in a triumphant procession through the towns of various countries. Beijing was expecting a procession of happy scenes, but instead witnessed fierce demonstrations protesting against Chinese policy in Tibet. In Paris, the demonstrators even tried to extinguish the flame and hung a Tibetan flag from the city hall.[9] The Chinese were dismayed; they did not understand where this 'anti-China' mood came from. Quickly, the ages-old feeling of victimhood reared its head via social media: The world is against China and wants to hold back the country's legitimate rise. 'Chinese people should all be indignant!' wrote Du Chunhua, an employee at a trading company in Beijing.[10] What the demonstrators were calling for – the freedom of Tibet – was not raised in these reactions. That is not surprising, though, because after many years of relentless propaganda, few in China doubt that Tibet has always belonged to 'the motherland'. That additional reflex of Chinese nationalism – seeing the world through the lens of conspiracy – also reasserted itself. 'Hostile foreign forces' supposedly conspired to sabotage the successful outcome of the Games, and the correctness of this theory was 'proven' by the fierce demonstrations in Lhasa in March 2008 against the Chinese occupation. Shops were destroyed, cars set on fire and at least nineteen people died. 'This riot was deliberately manipulated by the Dalai Lama clique and our government has taken legal actions to restore order in Lhasa and other places', said Qin Gang, the spokesperson for the Ministry of Foreign Affairs.[11] In spite of this turbulent run-up, the Games themselves were a great success: The host country ended number one on the gold medal table, and no disruption of public order took place – let alone any terrorist attack. Yet the feeling that the West had not allowed China the satisfaction of its 'coming out' party lingered. It was time to make clear that the new superpower was not be pushed around anymore.

No Intervention

One of the characteristics of nationalism is a dissatisfaction with the international status quo. Officially, though, Beijing adheres to the third principle of the 1955 Bandung Conference: 'non-intervention or non-interference in the internal affairs of another country'. Furthermore, as one of the five permanent members of the U.N. Security Council, China can veto any interference in states by other states, even though it seldom exercises that right. With the world looking over its shoulder, Beijing does not like taking any position that brings it in conflict with another permanent member of the Security Council – in most cases, the United States. A much more preferred strategy is to lobby so hard behind the scenes that the proposal does not proceed to a vote. Sometimes, though, a confrontation cannot be prevented. In February 2012, China and Russia voted against a resolution by the Security Council that called for an immediate end to the hostilities in Syria, protection of its population and the initiation of a peace process.[12] Behind this seemingly constructive appeal, Beijing and Moscow suspected a Western conspiracy to bring about regime change in Syria – comparable with the Security Council resolution in March 2011, which installed a no-fly zone in Libya to prevent the bombing of innocent people by Gaddafi's air forces.[13] At that time, Moscow and Beijing abstained from voting, but to their disgust it resulted in the fall of the dictator, Muammar Gaddafi, when the rebels under the protection of NATO air forces advanced unhindered towards Tripoli. The recurrence of that scenario in Syria had to be prevented at all cost.

In this issue, as is usual, Beijing's position was the same as that of Moscow. It can thus be seen as the guardian of the principle of non-intervention, shared by another permanent member of the Security Council – not as a lone obstructionist. This *kongsi* with Moscow was nevertheless severely tested by the Russian annexation of Crimea in March 2014. Putin's argument that the people of Crimea had expressed themselves via a referendum – and the annexation was therefore 'in accordance with international law' – was anathema to Beijing: As a result of that logic, minorities like the Tibetans and Uighurs would have carte blanche to secede in the same way. Jin Canrong, a widely-cited professor of international studies at Renmin University, even openly expressed his condemnation: 'China insists that Crimea's fate should be decided by all Ukrainians. We will not support a Russian occupation of Crimea.'[14] The official statement of the Ministry of Foreign Affairs tried to strike a balance between the principle of non-intervention and an aversion for the sanctions that the West had imposed on Russia. The result was a text that wanted the wolves to be sated and the sheep kept intact: 'China respects the independence, sovereignty and territorial integrity of Ukraine, but rejects any sanctions against Russia. A political solution is the only way out, sanctions do not help to solve the underlying problems in Ukraine. It may lead to new and more complicating factors.'[15]

Key Maritime Interests

While difficult to prove, Beijing's reservations about shaming Putin probably have a lot to do with its own actions in the region. In the East China Sea, Beijing is on a collision course with Japan. As described above, Beijing has in recent years been playing up the dispute surrounding the five minuscule Senkaku (Diaoyu) Islands by regularly sailing inside the exclusive twelve-mile zone with 'research vessels'. In November 2013, the pressure was ratcheted up even further: Beijing declared an Air Defense Identification Zone (ADIZ) over the East China Sea, which specifies that every flight over that region must be notified beforehand. According to Beijing, the airspace above the Senkaku Islands falls under this ADIZ as well.[16] Other countries declare these sorts of zones as well, though seldom, if ever, unilaterally. The incremental change of the status quo is a time-tested Chinese tactic, but is Beijing playing this game adroitly enough? Robert Kaplan, a writer of many books on geopolitical topics, sees in Beijing's expansion an old historical pattern: 'Greece sought to control the Aegean, Rome the Mediterranean, the us the Caribbean.'[17] From a perspective of *Realpolitik*, this observation certainly holds water, but does not suffice to explain the complex geographical and political environment of East Asia's maritime waters. In Japan, China encounters an opponent who will not bend. The nationalistic prime minister Abe has raised defence expenditures, and in 2014 interpreted the constitution in such a way that 'overseas collective self-defence' is now possible.[18] This means that Tokyo can come to the aid of friendly nations if it is attacked – even if Japanese territory is not the target of the aggressor (read: China). In September 2015, the right to collective self-defence was affirmed by the Japanese parliament.[19] Beijing depicts the Japanese prime minister as a militant nationalist, but his China policy can count on overwhelming domestic support: At least 90 percent of the people view their big neighbour as a threat.[20] Even more threatening for global peace and security, however, is the situation in the South China Sea. In a frenzy of construction, Beijing has without consultation been transforming coral reefs and small islands into military fortresses – even though most of these islands and reefs are also claimed by other states.

The South China Sea triggers the same emotional response in Beijing as the Crimea does with Putin: It has always belonged to us, and will sooner or later return to the motherland. Ever since the Song dynasty (960–1279), Chinese trading fleets have sailed these extensive waters (five times as large as France), though they were not the first and certainly not the only mariners to do so: Indians, Arabs, Malaysians, Persians and, from the sixteenth century, Europeans conducted trade there, each leaving their cultural influence. The presence of Buddhism in Thailand, Burma, Laos, and Cambodia, as well as that of Islam in Indonesia and Malaysia, is due to Indian and Arab sailors. This historical context is important, because Beijing's claim on the two most important archipelagos in the region – the Paracel and the Spratly Islands – is to a large extent based on maps of the Chinese merchants and Zheng He, the admiral whose 'treasure fleets' reached as far as Africa in the early fifteenth century to impress the barbarians with the might of the Chinese emperor. Yet being the first nation to chart a region does not grant any title on property in international law – if that were the case, the Netherlands could claim the island which was discovered by Dutchman Abel Tasman and still carries his name: Tasmania. What validates such a claim is effective and continuous occupation, and historically there has been no question of such Chinese control.

The various appellations for the region already indicate the absence of any Chinese *mare nostrum*. In Vietnam, they speak of the East Sea, in the Philippines the West Sea and in China they call this maritime region the South Sea (not the South *China* Sea). Still, that does not keep Beijing from claiming the dozens of tiny islands and reefs of the Spratly and Paracel archipelagos as well as the surrounding maritime areas.

According to the United Nations Conference on the Law of the Sea (UNCLOS), states may exploit the seas to a distance of two hundred nautical miles from their coastline. This so-called 'exclusive economic zone' can extend even further if the ocean floor is a natural continuation of the land; in that case is it called the continental shelf. The same rights apply to islands, but to be able to exercise such rights, two points must be clear: First, who is the legitimate owner? And secondly: Are these features 'islands' from an international law point of view, because 'rocks which cannot sustain human habitation or economic life of their own shall have no exclusive economic zone or continental shelf'.[21]

All the Islands Are Ours

Beijing is fending off that second condition by making uninhabitable coral reefs 'inhabitable'. By early 2017, seven reefs in the Spratly Archipelago alone had been converted into military bases with runways, aeroplane hangars, underground munitions depots and radar installations.[22] From a legal perspective, China's activities make no sense, because UNCLOS stipulates that only *natural* islands can claim an exclusive economic zone or a continental shelf. Beijing's response, as it were, to this legal hurdle is its infamous 'nine-dash' line (see following page), which designates not only the Spratly and Paracel archipelagos but the whole area within this line (90 percent of the South China Sea) as Chinese territory. *Womende Haiyang – mare nostrum –* our sea.

There has been no deviation from this map since it was first published in 1947, even though the southernmost designated line is only fifty kilometres off the coast of Borneo and more than 1,500 kilometres from the Chinese mainland. The claiming of parts of the open sea violates the traditional principle of the *Mare Liberum* ('The Free Sea'), formulated in the seventeenth century by Holland's Hugo Grotius, as well as the current UNCLOS Treaty ratified by Beijing. Legally, China does not have to be concerned about that: It has made a reservation to the UNCLOS article that provides for binding arbitration. China is open, however, to that other form of dispute settlement, negotiation, by talking with the ASEAN member states about a binding code of conduct for preventing disputes. The question is whether that makes any sense. In an earlier version – the 'Declaration on the Conduct of Parties in the South China Sea', adopted in 2002[23] – Article 5 calls for exercising 'self-restraint' and obliges parties to refrain 'from action of inhabiting of the presently uninhabited islands, reefs, shoals, cays, and other features'. But according to a 2015 Pentagon report, China reclaimed more than 2,900 acres of land in the Spratly Archipelago between 2013 and August 2015 alone – nearly twenty times as much land as Malaysia, the Philippines, Vietnam and Taiwan combined in the forty years before then.[24]

In order to be seen as cooperative, Beijing agrees to talk about a new code of conduct, but it will never accept any document that is binding – let alone be willing to hand

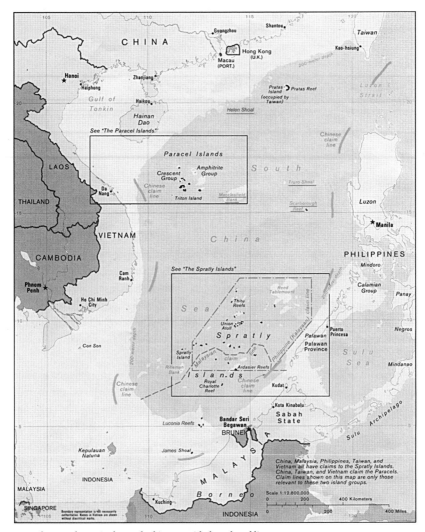

Map of contested areas in the South China Sea with the 9-dotted line

over territory that has already been 'Chinese for two thousand years'. For that matter, Beijing need not worry about an anti-Chinese front among ASEAN countries – member states like Burma and Laos are too dependent economically on their neighbour to the north. Cambodia is even an outright vassal state: The private army of its president Hu Sen, an ex-Khmer Rouge commander, has been trained by China, and the country is a major recipient of Chinese investments and soft loans. In 2012, Cambodia refused to sign a joint ASEAN declaration that condemned Beijing's behaviour in the South China Sea – the first time since the organisation's founding in 1967 that it failed to agree on a joint resolution.[25] What remains is China's preferred way of dispute settlement: Bilateral consultations. There have been talks with Vietnam and the Philippines, but they always get bogged down in grandiose declarations. No form of consultation – multilateral, regional, or bilateral – can hold Beijing to account. Because of the huge difference in power between the contestants, the *Weiqi* (Chinese chess) game to transform the South China Sea into Chinese territory can have only one outcome: The strangling of every opponent whose claims overlap with those of Beijing. The first move in that game was already made in 1974.

Conquering the Paracel Archipelago
In that year, China waged a brief war with South Vietnam (the country was then still divided) and conquered the Paracel Archipelago. One of the Vietnamese ships was heavily damaged, but Captain Ngụy Văn Thà refused to abandon ship, and died beneath the waves. At least fifty-three Vietnamese military personnel were killed in action with him.[26] North Vietnam – at that time still an ally of China – withheld comment, but in 1976 the government of a reunited Vietnam put the archipelago under the administration of its Hoang Sa district. China responded by classifying the islands as part of its Sansha prefecture. Apart from these administrative measures, though, the two countries' policies diverge on one crucial point: The possibility of using force and intimidation to back up its claims. Given its naval inferiority, there is little more that Hanoi can do than expressing impotent rage and making protests. The exploratory drilling 150 nautical miles off the Vietnamese coast by CNOOC – China's largest producer of offshore oil and gas – in May 2014 proved as much. When a Vietnamese fishing boat came too close to the drilling site, it was rammed and sunk by the Chinese navy. In response, violent demonstrations broke out in Vietnam in which more than twenty people lost their lives.[27]

Reactions in the Region
The years of Chinese bullying set a chain reaction in motion. In April 2014, the Philippines concluded a defence agreement with the United States and, for the first time since 1991, allowed the Americans to make use of the military bases of Subic Bay and Clark Air Base.[28] President Truong Tan Sang of Vietnam asked former US president Bill Clinton, on his visit to Hanoi in 2014, to help lift the restrictions on American arms exports to his country.[29] During an emergency meeting of the Central Committee of the Vietnamese Communist Party in May of that year, it was even considered to abandon the so-called 'Three-Nos Policy': No foreign military bases in the country, no military alliances, no associating with one nation against another.[30]

When politicians in China's neighbouring countries stand up to the regional hegemon, they can count on broad domestic support. In the first century BCE the *Hai Ba Trong*, or Trong sisters, had already resisted occupation from *Trung Quoc* – the 'Central

Anti-Chinese protests in Vietnam, 2014

Kingdom' – in the north, and many streets in Vietnam's towns are named after these and other heroes of resistance.[31] Another example is Mongolia. Though this country does not border the South China Sea, the feelings about its southern neighbour are also quite negative. I spoke to a man there who was grateful to the Russians for dominating his country for seventy years, because that had prevented Chinese occupation. 'But wasn't the Russian occupation horrible?' I asked him. 'That is true, but when the Chinese conquer a people, they also try to take over its soul. Look at Tibet. The Russians never do that.' As usual, China suspects 'ulterior' motives behind the opposition in neighbouring countries against its policies. As always, the United States is condemned for going fishing in troubled waters, or worse: Of whipping up the waves to restore their own weakened position in East Asia. At an ASEAN conference in August 2014, Wang Yi, the Chinese minister of Foreign Affairs warned that 'someone has been exaggerating or even playing up the so-called tension in the South China Sea. We do not agree with such a practice, and we call for vigilance in the motives behind them.'[32]

Beijing's feeling of disdain is at least as strong. Sooner or later, the region's countries will realise that they cannot develop economically or technologically without the support of a large and benevolent China. Vietnam is told that it can profit much more from 'mutual friendly relations' than the 'petty interests' gained by cooperating with another power.[33] In the article containing this appeal, there is a drawing of an angry little man with a straw hat (Vietnam) standing on the shoe of a giant (China), while sticking his sword in the air and making a lot of fuss. This condescending attitude strongly recalls what Professor Hu Angang said when I interviewed him: 'Vietnam ought not get too far on its high horse, for it is dependent on China's technological expertise for the exploitation of the South China Sea.' At the beginning of the twenty-first century, this traditional attitude of superiority is built on actual power. That

Cartoon describing the relationship between Vietnam and China

is why Vietnam will need to find a balance – as described by Howard French in his excellent book *Everything under the heavens* – 'between resistance and dependence, subservience and noncompliance'. After centuries of practice, Vietnam has become very skilled in this balancing act – but with the fierce Chinese nationalism of recent years, it will need to take this skill to new heights.[34]

The Monroe Doctrine in Asia?
In his 1823 State of the Union address, the fifth president of the United States, James Monroe, made a pronouncement with far-reaching consequences: 'We owe it, therefore, to candor and to the amicable relations existing between the United States and those powers to declare that we should consider any attempt on their part to extend their system to any portion of this hemisphere as dangerous to our peace and safety.'[35] With 'those powers', the president was alluding specifically to Spain, which had lost the lion's share of its colonies in South and Central America by the beginning of the nineteenth century. The United States wanted to make clear that any restoration of this colonial status would not be tolerated, but that the USA was free to expand its own influence. The Monroe Doctrine – which can crudely be summarized as 'Stay out of my backyard!' – was born, and would develop into a cornerstone of American foreign policy. Nearly two centuries later, are Beijing's actions in the South China Sea the manifestation of a 'Xi Doctrine', that means to repel the United States from the region?

This comparison fails for two reasons. First, China has been active in the South China Sea for centuries, long before the United States appeared on the scene – so China has older 'historical rights'. On top of that, Beijing claims sovereignty over virtually the entire *maritime* region, something that Uncle Sam has never pursued in the Caribbean. But perhaps there is a third, even more disquieting reason that this comparison does not hold: Beijing's ambitions extend *farther* than the South China Sea. In his book *The Influence of Sea Power Upon History, 1660–1783* – a sensation in Chinese strategic circles – the nineteenth-century American historian Alfred Thayer Mahan wrote that a strong fleet has the effect of a stone thrown into the water: It protects trade and provides military and political access to important parts of the world. As a result, trade and prosperity increase, which in their turn make the upkeep of an even larger fleet possible. Commercial prosperity and naval power, in other words, reinforce one another indefinitely.[36]

The lessons of Mahan have a wide following in Beijing, for the country's prosperity depends to a large extent on the import of raw materials for making products, which (for the most part) are then exported again. To keep these economic arteries open, China is building a navy that can carry out tasks far from its own shores – an ambition that is confirmed by a white paper from the Ministry of Defence in May 2015, redefining the strategic goal of the navy from 'off-shore defence' to 'open-seas protection'.[37] Where do the limits of this maritime projection of power lie? In principle nowhere, for China's economic tentacles encompass the entire globe. As early as 2006, Professor Zhang Wenmu of the Centre for Strategic Studies wrote that 'Wherever China's interests lead, there too must follow China's capabilities to protect those interests'.[38] The nationalist Wang Xiaodong, interviewed earlier in this book, thinks the same way: Just like the United States, China must establish itself as an 'imperialist power' that does not shy away from protecting its overseas economic interests by military means.

'Historical Rights'

In addition to the assumed right to protect its economic interests, there is also historical sentiment: The feeling that Beijing has a naturally privileged position in the countries once located along the 'Maritime Silk Road'. Beginning in the eighth century, this trade route flourished from Canton in South China to the port cities of Basra and Siraf in the Persian Gulf. The closer these cities or kingdoms were to China, the greater the level of Chinese influence. Vietnam's north was colonised for long periods by dynasties like the Han and the Ming, and Siam (Thailand), Laos and Burma (Myanmar) regularly brought tribute to the emperor in Peking. When King Kertanegara of Singhasari, located on Java, refused to do the same – and cut off the ears of the Chinese envoy – the Yuan dynasty's Kublai Khan sent a fleet of thirty thousand men in 1293 to punish the rebellious king. The expedition ended in woeful failure, but what mattered was China's willingness to use force, should the barbarian not behave according to the etiquette of the Celestial Empire. The feeling that imperial history justifies present-day actions is much more important than any consideration of international law, for – as Bill Hayton convincingly demonstrates in his book *The South China Sea: The Struggle for Power in Asia*[39] – Beijing has never effectively exercised authority in the countries surrounding the South China Sea (with the exception of northern Vietnam), or on the islands located in it. The 'inalienable 2,000-year-old rights' in the South China Sea are a product of the Chinese nationalism that reared its head at the beginning of the twentieth century – just when the country began publishing the aforementioned 'Maps of National Shame', on which all of South-East Asia (not just the maritime areas) are depicted as belonging to China. In fact, the first Chinese government official did not set foot on any of the Paracel Islands until 1909.

Hayton also demonstrates that barely any islands are shown on the old Chinese maps, and that for that reason the islands on today's maps are translations of English names. For example, Zhenmu Ansha, an island located close to Borneo, is a bastardisation of 'James Shoal'. Antonio Carpio, a justice of the supreme court of the Philippines, even calls Beijing's claims a 'gigantic historical fraud'. In the summer of 2014, Carpio presented fifteen historical Chinese maps (the oldest dating from 1136), all of which show Hainan to be the southernmost Chinese territory. Carpio has invited the Chinese authorities to look at the 'historical facts', but Beijing has yet to respond.[40] In addition, China refused to cooperate with proceedings brought by the Philippines before the Permanent Court of Arbitration in The Hague to judge the status of the eight islands occupied by China in the Spratly Archipelago.[41] Four of these islands lie underwater at high tide, while the other four are rocks unsuitable for human habitation. The Court was also asked to judge the legality of the 'nine-dash' line published in 1948, which constitutes the basis for China's appropriation of 90% of the South China Sea (even though Beijing has never made clear precisely *which* rights it enjoys within the dashes of that map).

The verdict of 12 July 2016 surprised most observers: The Court did not opt for the politically correct line of meeting the upcoming superpower halfway. With the Convention on the Law of the Sea as a basis, it used strictly legal arguments to parse the untenability of the Chinese position and reject three steps taken by Beijing. These were the expulsion of Filipino fishermen from the 200-mile Exclusive Economic Zone of that country; the construction of artificial islands in the Spratly Archipelago (the Court did not judge on the question of ownership, but made it clear these 'islands' cannot create twelve-mile territorial waters, let alone 200-mile Exclusive Economic Zones); and finally, the fishing and exploitation of oil and natural gas within the nine-dash line (the 'historical rights' claimed by Beijing to justify these actions are in breach of the Convention on the Law of the Sea).

The Chinese Response

The Chinese response to the Court's verdict was an exercise in uniformity as disheartening as it was fascinating. In March 2017, the University of Groningen organised a conference on the verdict, which I attended. The participating Chinese diplomats and academics were united in their blistering critique. One denounced the fact that the Court had not taken certain jurisprudence into consideration; another posed the fundamental question as to whether the Court had jurisdiction in the first place. With barely suppressed rage, Jiang He of the Zhongnan University of Economics and Law even argued for an 'Eastphalian development of international law' that takes into account the cultural traditions and colonial history of Asia, and which resists the 'hegemonistic internationalism' of the United States. The Court of Arbitration, he said, was nothing more than a 'puppet regime' that had no right to judge China. The sum and substance of the Chinese feelings was articulated by Professor Fu Kuen-chen of Xiamen University: What Westerners fail to understand is that from the Han dynasty onwards, the South China Sea was part of China: By that time, the authorities had already sent out expeditions to that region, fought pirates, and implemented laws for conduct at sea. The countries of South-East Asia had accepted Chinese sovereignty by complying with the tribute system: Trade with China was only possibly by submitting to the court in Peking.

Professor Fu and his fellow Chinese speakers made it abundantly clear that their legal analysis is subordinate to a perception of history that is unshakeable: China has, since the early days of its empire, exercised undisputable sovereignty over the South China Sea; and given their colonial past, Western countries have no right to pass judgement. Chinese fury did not only erupt after the verdict was rendered in July 2016: In the months before, Beijing had already unleashed a propaganda blitz, which clearly indicated that they had little confidence in a favourable outcome. The words of political heavyweight and state counsellor responsible for China's foreign policy until 2013, Dai Bingguo, probably best sums up the sense of historic injustice: 'China suffered enough from hegemonism, power politics and bullying by Western Powers since modern times. The Versailles peace conference at the end of World War I forced a sold-out [sic] of Shandong Province. The Lytton Commission, sent by the League of Nations when Japan invaded China's northeast provinces, only served to justify Japan's invasion. Even the US-led negotiations on San Francisco Peace Treaty excluded China. These episodes are still vivid in our memory. That is why China will grip its own future on issues of territorial sovereignty, and will never accept any solution imposed by a third party.'[42]

Confrontation with the United States

The increase in tensions in the South China Sea inevitably causes disputes between Beijing and its great strategic rival. In 2010, Secretary of State Hillary Clinton called free navigation in the South China Sea a matter of 'national interest', a pronouncement that resulted in the 'Pivot to Asia' policy during Obama's second term in office.[43] This strategy was based on the perception that East Asia again needed to receive the political, economic, and military attention that had been diverted as a result of American engagement with Iraq and Afghanistan. At the 2014 'Shangri-La Dialogue', an annual meeting on regional security, the US Secretary of Defence Chuck Hagel denounced Beijing's destabilising and unilateral actions in the South China Sea and promised that the United States would oppose any nation's use of intimidation or threat of force to assert territorial claims.[44]

By the beginning of 2015, tensions were running even higher. To secure freedom of navigation, the Pentagon said it was considering sending warships to the Spratly Islands – the archipelago that is the special target of China's land reclamation frenzy. The Americans had international law on their side: As the verdict of the 2016 Court of Arbitration affirmed, artificial islands do not create 12-mile territorial waters, so any other state may sail along the 'coastline' of such a construction.[45] Under the auspices of the so-called 'Freedom of Navigation Operations' that is precisely what the Americans did – even under Trump, though this president is far less interested than his predecessor in asserting America's global military presence. Beijing reacted angrily that should the US fleet approach 'Chinese territory' too closely, China would certainly defend itself.[46] Until now, Beijing has not taken any action to sustain these threats – probably based on the calculation that two developments are working to China's advantage.

Despite the big talk by President Trump that, if necessary, the United States will put an end to North Korea's nuclear threat on their own, his defence experts know that any armed resolution brings with it incalculable, potentially disastrous consequences – such as a large-scale attack on the South Korean capital Seoul. This makes Beijing's position stronger, for only the Chinese still have any leverage over the maniacal regime in Pyongyang. In return, the United States cannot get too far on their high horse in the South China Sea. At the Shangri-La forum for defence specialists in Singapore in June 2017, US Secretary of Defence James Mattis condemned Beijing's militarisation of the South China Sea as undermining regional stability – though his words were less threatening than those of his predecessor Chuck Hagel in 2015. Indirectly, Mattis admitted as much: Answering a question from the audience as to whether the world was witnessing the destruction of the international order maintained by the United States, he responded: 'Bear with us. Once we've exhausted all possible alternatives, the Americans will do the right thing.'[47]

Secondly, China is well aware that its enormous military and economic superiority limits the capacity for resistance by states like Vietnam and the Philippines. The case brought before the Permanent Court of Arbitration by the Philippines delivered a resounding legal victory, but it was rejected out of hand by the Chinese, and hardened their position even more. So, after succeeding Aquino in June 2016, the new president

Rodrigo Duterte radically changed course: Just like Dai Bingguo, he labelled the Court's ruling 'a piece of paper', and announced 'separation' between his country and the United States.[48] A startled Beijing could not believe its good fortune, and rewarded the Mindanao warlord by lifting import restrictions on tropical fruit and granting 24 billion in US dollars in financial aid in loans and investments. In exchange for Duterte's 'correct conduct', Filipino fishermen were again permitted to fish in the waters of the Scarborough Shoal – a reef that lies 900 kilometres from the Chinese island of Hainan, but only 230 kilometres from the Philippine island of Luzon. Manila's abrupt turn-around certainly reflected the criticism directed by its former colonial ruler, the United States, at Duterte's anti-drug campaign. Already well-known for his vulgar language, the president surpassed himself by calling Obama a 'son of a whore'. Yet Duterte's kowtowing to Beijing also stems from a deeply-felt sense of impotence. Questioned by journalists, Minister of Defence Delfin Lorenzana admitted to being seriously worried about China's stealthy undermining of Philippine sovereignty, but with an almost touching sense of helplessness he added: 'What can we do? Really, what can we do?'[49] And yet, just like in Vietnam, the pendulum swinging between 'dependence' and 'resistance' will once again sway towards resisting China.* In this game, the United States remains the indispensable force against creeping Chinese domination: The American and Philippine navies patrol the seas together and are fighting the rebels on Mindanao. Surveys amongst Filipinos show that Uncle Sam is much more popular than the colossal neighbour to the north – even though many Filipinos, including Duterte himself, are of Chinese descent. A survey from 2016 indicated that 76% of those interviewed like the US 'a lot'; only 22% were as positive about China.[51] The Philippine Minister of Foreign Affairs Perfecto Yasay has said that his country had turned towards China to break away from a 'mindset of dependency and subservience' vis-à-vis America.[52] But that call from above has obviously not resulted in a change of heart among the Philippine people.

* Philippine resistance is particularly focused on the Scarborough Shoal ('Huangyan' in Chinese), because of its proximity to Luzon, the main island of the Philippines. Supported by the United Sates, Manila has informed Beijing that Chinese land reclamation on this shoal would be tantamount to crossing a red line. So far, this line has not been crossed. Philippine fishermen are even once again allowed to fish there, but on the matter of sovereignty Beijing has not budged from the South China Sea policy that Deng Xiaoping formulated in the 1980's: 'sovereignty belongs to China, disputes can be shelved, and we can pursue joint development.'[50]

Pivot to Asia

The Pivot to Asia strategy was born in 2011 as a one-liner to sum up the United States' freshly-turned attention to East Asia. In November of that year, Secretary of State Hillary Clinton wrote the article 'America's Pacific Century', in which she formulated six strategic goals: Strengthening bilateral security agreements; deepening America's relations with emerging powers (i.e. China); a closer involvement in regional multilateral institutions; expansion of trade and investments; establishing a widespread military presence, and advancing democracy and human rights.[53] In the same month of that year, President Obama said in a speech before Australia's parliament that the presence of the United States in East Asia was a top priority. 'The United States is a Pacific power, and we are here to stay.' This American initiative was greeted with suspicion in China, and seen as the repackaged continuation of Washington's traditional policy to block the rise of China with the help of existing (Japan, South Korea and the Philippines) and new (Vietnam and Indonesia) regional allies.

'Wherever China's Interests Lead...'

In official declarations, Beijing's claims to the South China Sea are presented as a simple historical fact: The region has already belonged to China for two thousand years, and the country is simply exercising the sovereignty that it has *de jure* always possessed. Intellectuals who think outside the straitjacket of this official narrative view the takeover of the South China Sea as the first step in a much farther-reaching strategy. Back in 2006, the aforementioned Zhang Wenmu said that China had to develop the means to be present where its interests lie. Philip Yang, the president of the Taiwan Association of International Relations, puts it in a less roundabout way: 'In addition to upholding its territorial claims, mainland China has the ambition to eventually expand its naval reach to the world. ... To do so, China must also make the archipelagos it controls large enough to accommodate military and naval facilities.'[54] Yang's prediction from 2015 has become reality much sooner than expected: In 2017 most of the islands occupied by China in the Spratly Archipelago have been converted into military bases. Just like at the beginning of the fifteenth century, the era of the great seafarer Zheng He, China's interests stretch from South-East Asia to Africa – and even further still. The world had better be prepared.

Propaganda poster of 'The dream of China'

Domestic Nationalism: Propaganda and Patriotic Projects

Less visible than its foreign ventures are the array of *domestic* propaganda campaigns for whipping up patriotic sentiment. Billboards (unreadable for foreigners) hang everywhere in China, appealing to the people to 'focus on the party with the trust of a child',[55] while Tibetan monks are required to fly Chinese flags from their monasteries and hang portraits of Mao Zedong and Deng Xiaoping. Indoctrination begins with the youth: This is why history, as rewritten by the Campaign for Patriotic Education, is a core component of the curriculum taught every day to hundreds of millions of children. Before entering the classroom single-file, the children sing the national anthem and marching songs like 'My Chinese heart'.[56] The media, obviously, are also targets of the propaganda division. *Deng Xiaoping at History's Crossroad*, the TV series that began in 2014, glorifies the life of the Little Helmsman by presenting him as the architect of the New China.[57] The film *Lei Feng in 1959* tells the life of this model Communist, who died young and was set upon a pedestal by Mao Zedong as an exemplar of selflessness and obedience to the Party.[58]

Major events are also designed to fan the flames of the national fire. No expense or effort was spared for the 2008 Olympic Games in Beijing, and with a budget of at least sixty billion dollars, Shanghai's 2010 World Expo was by far the most expensive in history.[59] These grand spectacles show the world that China is back again on the highest level of the global stage. Even more important for its own people, though, is the message that China's power could supposedly only be regained thanks to the Party. By placing the People's Republic like a crown on China's 5,000-year-old history, the dazzling opening ceremony for the Olympic Games made that connection quite clear.

Another project is reaching higher still. In 2025 a Chinese man or woman will stand on the moon, just as American Neil Armstrong did in 1969.[60] The first, vital step was made in 2003 when the astronaut Yang Liwei orbited the Earth. After his landing, Yang received the honorary title of 'Space Hero' and went on a series of victory processions across the country[61] – images that recalled the New York City parade of March 1962, when cloudbursts of confetti rained down from the balconies onto America's first astronaut, John Glenn. Why, more than fifty years later, is China also reaching for the moon? Zhang Wei from the National Space Administration provides a poetic explanation: 'Chinese people are the same as people around the world. When looking up at the starry sky, we are full of longing and yearning for the vast universe.' He added, however, that China also expects to make technological breakthroughs in spaceflight.[62]

Economic Power Serving Political Power

For Deng Xiaoping, economic development served the higher purpose of restoring China's place under the sun. Xi Jinping follows the same policy, but has infinitely more means at his disposal. Large surpluses on the account balance have given Beijing considerable leverage in Washington and Brussels: The Western economic blocs are struggling with substantial government deficits, so China is warmly welcomed as the purchaser of their government bonds. The State Administration of Foreign Exchange (SAFE) invests the surpluses – which amounted to more than three trillion dollars (US) at the beginning of 2017[63] – primarily in treasuries, because the US government bond market is the largest and most liquid market in the world. In recent years, Beijing has diversified the investments of its foreign exchange reserves, but it will not convert its dollar investments into another currency from one day to the next. Were that to happen, the value of the dollar would fall substantially against the renminbi, which would be harmful to Chinese exports as well as the value of Chinese investments in the dollar. Beijing criticises Uncle Sam regularly for its 'addiction to debt', yet that reprimand is not convincing because China, as its most important banker, is also responsible for the Americans' habit.*[64]

---

* Moreover, one could say that China is addicted to debt as well. Its domestic, RMB-denominated state-owned debt was 265% of China's GDP at the end of 2017 – much higher than the same debt ratio of the US government, but this is caused by the fact that the debts of China's state-owned enterprises are also measured as government debt.

These short-term considerations do nothing to affect Beijing's long-term goal of undermining the dollar's status as the world's reserve currency – one day to be replaced by the renminbi. That is why Beijing is concluding so-called swap agreements with many countries: Agreements for paying for bilateral trade in renminbi, without the country involved running the foreign exchange risk for its own currency. Additionally, Chinese banks are issuing renminbi bonds more and more frequently in financial centres like London and Hong Kong. To knock the dollar off the throne, however, Beijing also has to be willing to open up its *domestic* market: By making its capital markets (trading in stocks and bonds) accessible to foreigners, making the renminbi convertible, and permitting Chinese citizens to invest their money where they want – even if that is abroad. For the time being, these steps are still a few bridges too far for a regime obsessed with stability; the risk that citizens will park their savings *en masse* abroad – and in so doing disrupt the Chinese banking system – is seen as too great. The crash of the Chinese stock markets in the summer of 2015, which the government tried in vain to halt with a series of imposed measures, only further accentuated the Party's ambiguous stance vis-à-vis the functioning of the market.

A much less risky step (from Beijing's point of view) to increase China's economic power into political influence is the establishment of investment banks. In June 2014, the BRICS group of nations (Brazil, Russia, India, China, and South Africa) set up the New Development Bank for financing infrastructure and development projects in their countries. This initiative arose from a shared sense of unease about Western domination of the international order. 42 percent of the world's population lives in the five BRICS countries, and their economies – measured in terms of purchasing power – are approximately one fourth of the global economy, the same share as the United States. And yet the BRICS countries have only 11 percent of the votes between them in the International Monetary Fund, while America has 17 percent. China is far and away the largest economy in the group, and that is why the headquarters of the New Development Bank are in Shanghai.[65]

The second banking initiative is the Asian Infrastructure and Investment Bank (AIIB), which, as its name indicates, is directed towards the Asian market. America lobbied actively to discourage its allies from investing in the bank – arguing that the AIIB will not adhere to conventional norms like transparency, care for the environment and good governance – but many countries suspected that the Americans did not want any further competition for the US-dominated World Bank. The American lobby failed spectacularly. The United Kingdom, whose economy depends upon London as an international financial centre, was the first Western country in March 2015 to accede to the AIIB. Dozens of countries followed. Geoffrey Raby, the former Australian ambassador to China, calls the AIIB a 'bold idea whose time has come'. Its establishment, according to Raby, reflects the changing power relations in the world and offers Beijing the opportunity to diversify its foreign currency reserves. Additionally, the new bank can serve as a vehicle for financing Chinese contractors building motorways, airports and power stations. This sector struggles domestically with a large overcapacity, and is therefore an increasingly active player in the international market. With the help of the China-controlled AIIB, their chances of success abroad are becoming even greater.[66]

State-Owned Businesses as Party Vehicles

The most visible expression of China's new economic nationalism is the revival of state-owned companies. Under the motto *zhuada fangxiao* ('hold on to the big ones, let the little ones go') the hands-on premier Zhu Rongji privatised most of these companies during the 1990s. As a result of a decision taken in 2006 to create 'national champions', this policy has acquired a new meaning: China needed companies that are able to compete at the global level with the likes of Samsung, Sony, and Sharp. At first glance, this corporatist approach seemed successful: In 2009, the joint profit of Sinopec (the Chinese Shell) and China Mobile (the largest telecom business) were two hundred billion dollars (US) – more than the total earnings of the five hundred largest private companies.[67] As the renowned economist Mao Yushi has demonstrated, however, these 'national champions' pay no interest on loans and no taxes – costs paid by every other company. They do not even distribute dividends to the state, though measures have been announced to eliminate that exemption. Mao Yushi calculates that after deducting this unfair advantage, the largest state-owned businesses booked an average negative return on equity of 6.3 percent in the period from 2001 to 2009.*[68]

As noted previously, *economic* liberalism is viewed less negatively than political liberalism, and that is why the Party decided in November 2013 to allow private investment in state-owned businesses. The question is what kind of effect this commitment will have in practice, as one of the 'don't speaks' of former propaganda tsar Liu Yunshan was 'neo-liberalism', an ideology that is aimed at 'weakening government control over the national economy'. Liu Zuoming – president of the Aviation Corporation of China (an industrial-military conglomerate) – was even more blunt when he formulated the Party's perennial fear of foreign hostile forces. In 2012 he warned of a conspiracy of international enemies who want to privatise the state-

---

* In 2018 China's two biggest companies are Alibaba and Tencent. Although officially not registered as state-owned companies, these two internet giants are also incorporated in Beijing's economic and security policies. Big data gathered from their customers are shared with the Party to build up the 'Social Credit System' mentioned in chapter 5, and several companies headed by members of China's 'Red Aristocracy' have invested in Alibaba. Tencent's CEO Pony Ma was a member of the 12th National People's Congress (2013–2018).

owned businesses – 'the mainstay of the Party strength'. Those same forces were supposedly out to destroy the military.[69]

The Myth of Pacifism

The wide array of domestic measures for strengthening national solidarity – the history curriculum, the anti-Japanese movies on TV, the organisation of large-scale projects, economic diplomacy and the strengthening of state-owned companies – is shaped in the context of several national myths. One of them is the inherent pacifism of the Chinese race. To reassure countries worried about the country's rise, Beijing contends over and over that aggression does not jibe with the nature of the Chinese. 'There is no gene for invasion in our [Chinese] blood,' said Xi Jinping quite categorically in May 2014,[70] and the white papers regularly issued by the Ministry of Foreign Affairs emphasise that China has never founded any overseas colonies. Admiral Zheng He's famous expeditions at the beginning of the fifteenth century are placed in the same pacifist light: 'The famous Ming Dynasty navigator Zheng He made seven voyages to the Western Seas, visiting over 30 countries and regions across Asia and Africa. He took along with him the cream of Chinese culture and technology, as well as a message of peace and friendship.'[71]

The Party is well aware that many people abroad see things differently, and that is why, in 2005 Zheng Bijian, advisor to President Hu Jintao, came up with the slogan of 'China's peaceful rise' – a phrase that was rather quickly replaced with 'China's peaceful development', because of fears that 'rise' still sounded too threatening. Does all this peacefulness accord with the nature of the Chinese, as Xi Jinping contends? The historical facts do not support this statement at all. According to the Chinese Academy of Military Science, there have been 3,756 wars waged in the nearly three thousand years of documented history (770 BCE–1912), an average of 1.4 wars per year.[72] This is probably no more than in Europe, yet the popular image first propagated by Voltaire of a Heavenly Kingdom administered by peaceful mandarins is completely misleading. Chinese history is an endless succession of peasant rebellions, civil wars, invasions by 'barbarian' tribes or, conversely, imperial expeditions to fight the enemy on their own territory.

There is even a well-known case of genocide. Because of their tenacious resistance towards the Chinese conquest of Central Asia, Qian Long commanded in the 1750s to murder all men from the Dzungar tribe (also called the 'Western Mongols') and to enslave their women and children. 'Show no mercy to these rebels. Only the old and weak should be saved. Our previous military campaigns were too lenient.' According to some sources, nearly one million Dzungars lost their lives, which meant the end of their existence as a people. Qian Long justified his mass murder with the argument that, through their resistance, the Dzungars 'had turned their backs on civilisation'.[73] To celebrate his victory the emperor built the splendid *Puning Si* ('Temple of Universal Peace') in Chengde, the Manchus' summer retreat located two hundred kilometres north of Peking.

The 'Peaceful' Expeditions of Zheng He

Were, then, the Chinese *outside* China peaceful, perhaps? Alas, this myth also does not stand up. The fifteenth-century admiral Zheng He, extolled by the Party as an apostle of peace, certainly did not only bring a 'message of peace and friendship'. His treasure fleets also carried twenty thousand soldiers, armed to the teeth, who did not hesitate to interfere in the internal affairs of other countries. On his first expedition in 1405, he annihilated Palembang on Sumatra, where the rebel Chen Zuyi had ensconced himself after fleeing China. According to the Ming dynasty archives, 5,000 men were killed in the process, and ten ships set ablaze. Chen himself was despatched to China and mercilessly decapitated. During the same voyage, Zheng He established a garrison in Malacca – already in those days a crucial location for controlling trade through the strait of the same name. On a later expedition, the admiral invaded Sri Lanka, took the king prisoner and put a Chinese puppet on the throne.

According to the Australian historian Geoff Wade, who has meticulously studied the *Ming Shilu* (the 'Veritable Records of the Ming'), Zheng He's expeditions served two strategic goals: To give China control over the international trade routes, and to 'persuade' as many nations as possible to bring tribute to the emperor Yong Le. This paranoid despot, builder of Beijing's Forbidden City, had thrown his nephew off the throne in a bloody civil war, and was seen by many as a usurper. His reception of tributes from foreign kings strengthened his image as a powerful ruler of All-Under-Heaven and propped up his domestic legitimacy.[74] To be sure, Zheng He's expeditions proved an exception to the rule that China never occupied overseas territories or founded overseas colonies, yet this had nothing to do with any inherent sense of a shared humanity. Like Russia, China was a power oriented towards its huge continental hinterland, subjugating the people living there by persuasion or brute force if they refused to adapt to 'civilisation'. The similarity with nineteenth-century Western imperialism, which also occurred under the guise of civilising savages, is striking.

The Myth of the Yellow Race

The strength of a state, as the aforementioned philosopher Yan Fu posited a hundred years ago, is determined by the health of its race.[75] Together with other thinkers of his era, he was worried whether the yellow race would survive. This sounds amazing, for even at that time there were already many more Chinese than Europeans and Americans combined. What Yan referred to, however, was that the very survival of China was at risk because of the deeply-rooted Confucianist culture, in which *wen* (being learned) ranks higher than *wu* (being martial). A new course was needed: In order to survive in the harsh modern world, the body and the will had to be tempered like steel. In his essay 'A study of physical education', the young Mao Zedong also expressed his concern about the bodily weakness of most of his fellow countrymen: 'The military spirit has not been encouraged; The physical condition of the population deteriorates daily. [...] If our bodies are not strong we will be afraid as soon as we see enemy soldiers, and then how can we attain our goals and make ourselves respected?'[76]

The notion that physical strength increases national power is still very much alive. At the Olympic Games in 2004, the athlete Liu Xiang won a gold medal in the 110-metre hurdles (the first athletics medal ever attained by a Chinese man at the Games) and dedicated his win to the yellow race: 'It is a proud moment not only for China, but for Asia and all people who share the same yellow skin.'[77] The myth that the Chinese all belong to the same race goes back to the beginning of the twentieth century, when the country's thinkers were searching for a national identity. To the founder of modern China, Sun Yatsen, the idea that shared bloodlines were a potential source of great national strength was beyond doubt: 'The greatest force is common blood. The Chinese belong to the yellow race because they come from the blood stock of the yellow race'. Sun Yatsen's thoughts in this respect were later followed and elaborated by Darwinist thinkers such as Yan Fu.[78]

Today's veneration of the Yellow Emperor gives new substance to this racial myth. This legendary patriarch, who lived in the twenty-seventh century BCE, supposedly equipped the people with tools of civilisation like agriculture, animal husbandry and the compass. In Shaanxi province, the heartland of Chinese civilisation, there is a mausoleum to commemorate him, the 'Great Hall of Man and Civilization's First Ancestor'. In this 2,000-year-old building offerings have been made to this ancient patriarch since 2004. Unfortunately for nationalists, the colour that supposedly connects the Chinese is as fictional as the 'Yellow Emperor' himself. The 'yellow race' constitutes a hodgepodge of countless people who left behind their traces and their blood in this immense country. 'China' is a cultural idea, not a racial fact. Yet, historical facts do not stop the Party's spin doctors from calling the vast majority of the people 'Children of the Yellow Emperor'. The myth even casts doubt on the generally-acknowledged theory that the roots of *homo sapiens* were in Africa – after all, it is impossible that the yellow race and the 'dark' continent could have anything to do with each other.[79] 'Racism with Chinese characteristics' is also manifest in one of Xi Jinping's favourite slogans: *'Zhonghua minzu weida fuxing'*, usually translated as the 'Great Rejuvenation of the Chinese Nation'. It actually means the 'Great Rejuvenation of the Chinese Race'. The same word, *minzu*, was already used a hundred years ago by Sun Yatsen as the first of his 'Three Principles of the People'. In that context, it is usually translated as 'nationalism', but 'one's own people first' actually renders a more precise meaning of the first principle. The strength of the nation lay, after all, in the common blood of the yellow race. On the other hand, Sun Yatsen was president of a 'multi-ethnic state'. At the beginning of the twenty-first century, this inherent contradiction about what 'China' stands for is causing increasing tensions, for minority peoples like the Tibetans and the Uighurs of course do not descend from the yellow patriarch. After the riots in Urumqi in 2009, in which hundreds of Chinese and Uighurs lost their lives, a few bloggers contended that the violence had been provoked by the 'uncivilised' and 'savage' Uighurs.[80]

The Threat of Nationalism

At the beginning of the twenty-first century, Chinese nationalism has devolved into a complex cocktail of complacent paternalism, pent-up resentment and racial superiority endangering the peace and security of the region. My pessimism derives from three developments.

1. *Nationalism = loyalty to the Party*

Is nationalism embedded in the nature of China's people, or is it an emotion whipped up by the Party, a feeling that evaporates as quickly as it arises? The individuals I interviewed differ strongly in their opinions here. The author of *Unhappy China*, Wang Xiaodong, is convinced that the Party still reins in the people's inborn nationalism, while liberal thinkers like Ding Li and Xuan Zang contend precisely the opposite: The people are only interested in solving the daily concerns of their lives and improvement of the environment. 'Do you really think,' says Ding Li, 'that a Chinese family will sacrifice their only son's life on a foreign battlefield?' A 2014 survey conducted by the University of West Australia regarding the nationalist sentiment amongst the Chinese people seems to agree with Ding Li. More than 90 percent of the 1,400 interviewees support China's claims in the East and South China Sea, but less than half are willing to wage war over them. Much more popular is the choice of supporting Beijing's claims with international PR campaigns and tactics like boycotts and diplomatic reprisals: More than 80 percent are in favour of these.[81]

This survey shows that Chinese nationalism is rational in a certain sense: The majority of the people do not want to bear witness to their love of the motherland by blindly running after the Party. This fits seamlessly into the Confucianist tradition of common sense, but the Party insists that patriotism and loyalty to itself are two sides of the same shiny coin. That is why the leaders of Hong Kong must be 'patriots.... who sincerely support China's sovereignty' – as Zhang Dejiang, the Party's former number three, put it, just before Carrie Lam was chosen in June 2017 as 'Chief Executive' of the autonomous region by an election committee comprised of Beijing loyalists.[82]

Patriotism is a quality that cannot be tested objectively, so what the requirement of love for the motherland comes down to is loyalty to the Party. The identification of love of country with loyalty to the regime in place is as old as China itself, but it is directly at odds with the global trend that citizens make their own choices where they work and live, and whom they are loyal to. The direction of the Party is not only anachronistic, but also dangerous because of the forces unleashed by it – certainly in a society where public demonstrations on issues other than one's love for the motherland are almost always prohibited. As the diplomat Qin Yaqing, interviewed in Chapter 6, rightly says: 'Nationalism is like a two-headed beast; before you know it, the nationalists are running towards the Square of Heavenly Peace.'

2.   *The vicious circle of China's aggression*

China's aggression in both the East and South China Sea has led to bitterness and opposition, specifically in Japan, Vietnam and the Philippines. That is why those countries are cozying up to the United States militarily, and why Vietnam and the Philippines are even considering forming an anti-Chinese alliance.[83] In other Asian countries, discontent is also on the rise. Since 2014, Indians who come from the disputed region of Arunachal Pradesh (South Tibet) and travel to China are only admitted on a visa that is stapled separately to their passport – thus conveying the message that the visitors' Indian passport is not recognised.[84] Indian politicians subsequently objected to the 'humiliations' that Beijing had visited on the people of Arunachal Pradesh.[85] In view of the history of (mutual, for that matter) domination, Mongolia is one of the countries most sensitive to the expansionist drives of its southern neighbour. When, for instance, the Chinese ambassador in Ulan Bator declared that the Chinese and Mongols both descended from Genghis Khan – who is worshipped as a demi-god in Mongolia – the diplomat was promptly expelled from the country as a 'most unwelcome foreigner'.[86] Connecting these incidents is the conviction that China, as an irredentist power, is seeking to reconquer lost territory, or at least restore its former position as *primus inter pares*. That goal creates outright resentment. Kim Jin Hyun, the South Korean president of the World Peace Forum, detests 'the mentality of Sinicism and the relationship between lord and vassal, which will no longer be accepted'.[87]

China is not a monolithic nationalist bloc. There are plenty of academics and journalists, as well as officials at the Ministry of Foreign Affairs, who understand the concerns of neighbouring countries, and are willing to make concessions. These voices of moderation are, however, drowned out by the ever-stronger *kongsi* of generals and conservative intellectuals with their slogans about 'inalienable historical rights', 'core interests' and 'holy territory'. The Party cannot ignore these feverish emotions: They themselves have let the genie of nationalism out of the bottle.

3. Nationalism sells

The spread of nationalistic propaganda is not only the domain of sinister and unknown Party officials – it has become a viable business in its own right. The market for chauvinistic media grows like grass. The best example is *Global Times*, a newspaper affiliated with the *People's Daily* (the mouthpiece for the Party). *Global Times* has a circulation of nearly three million, and is well-known for its extreme, if not maniacal viewpoints, such as its proposal for attacking Japan with nuclear missiles.[88] The tone of the English-language edition is softer, and also gives foreign writers a chance to voice their opinions – even if they are always 'friends of China'. *Global Times* likes to paint the contrast between China as a morally-elevated nation, and the United States, which merely acts as a 'hegemon' in pursuit of raw power. Ding Gang, the editor for International Affairs, also writes opinion pieces for the *People's Daily*, and ties like these explain why the newspaper is not troubled by censorship. Almost the opposite: As a mouthpiece for the fiery emotions present in the nationalistic constituency of the Chinese public (which surpasses the Party on the 'left' in many respects), Beijing must keep a close watch on what *Global Times* is writing. Xiang Lanxin – a well-known historian and political scientist, who certainly does not avoid criticism of the West – detests *Global Times* because the paper 'hijacks the policymaking process by turning the web-conscious leadership into psychological hostages'. He remarks wryly that *Global Times* has an infamous precursor: *Der Stürmer*, the Nazi newspaper published by Julius Streicher from 1923 to 1945. 'The paper flourished in Germany on the theme of that extreme version of ethnic-nationalism: Anti-Semitism.'[89]

For inflammatory books the market is excellent as well. Titles like *China Can Say No* and *Unhappy China* fly off the shelves by the hundreds of thousands. The best-selling book in this genre is by Liu Mingfu, a colonel teaching at the University of National Defense. More than half a million copies of his *The China Dream: Great Power Thinking and Strategic Power Posture in the Post-American Era* have been sold.[90] Henry Kissinger describes the book as an example of China's 'triumphalist vision'.[91] Liu argues for converting China's economic power into military might – not to wage war, but to ensure that America does not attack China. Win-win scenarios do not occur in Liu's thinking: Just like Yan Fu, the Darwinist who a hundred years ago envisioned states enveloped in a constant struggle for survival, the colonel thinks that China *must* become the greatest power in the twenty-first century – otherwise the country will seem like a 'plump lamb' waiting in the market to be slaughtered.[92] Liu's book is seen as a continuation of the TV series broadcast in 2006, *The Rise of Great Powers*, which tells the history of the world through the rise and fall of Western nations like Spain, the Netherlands and England.[93] Now it is China's turn, according to Liu Mingfu, to take advantage of this 'period of strategic opportunities' and take over the number one position in the world.

CHAPTER 10

The Party on a Dead-End Street

*If language be not in accordance with the truth
of things, affairs cannot be carried on to success...
What the superior man requires is just that in
his words there may be nothing incorrect.*

Confucius

I began this book with the prospect that China can take three paths: Continuing the current line of 'socialism with Chinese characteristics', following the route of Western parliamentary democracy, or going a third way. Once upon a time, in the heady days of the early twentieth century, the introduction of a Western parliamentary system seemed only a matter of time. The general elections of 1912, in which forty million men cast their votes, seemed to ring in the beginning of a new epoch. That hope went up in smoke when President Yuan Shikai refused to recognise the victory of the Kuomintang, abolished the republic and crowned himself emperor. The tone had thus been set for the coming century: Every ruler after Yuan (the warlords, Chiang Kai-shek, Mao Zedong and Mao's successors) tolerated no opposition and made clear why his regime was superior to the one before him. The KMT has constituted the only break with this triumph of tyranny, by shedding its Leninist skin in the 1980s and turning Taiwan into a democratic nation. Can the Communists follow that example? Nicholas Kristof, the well-known columnist for *The New York Times*, thinks that, thanks to the wealth that has been created and China's spectacularly-improved medical care, the Party has nothing to fear from free elections. Because of their popularity in the rural districts, he even expects them to win with a 'landslide'.[1]

And yet nothing points to a turn towards democracy in present-day China. Democracy is associated with the fall of the Soviet Union, which caused economic and political chaos and – worst of all evils – the collapse of the country. Within the foreseeable future, there will be no deviation from Deng Xiaoping's line that 'the Party's power has to be maintained for at least a hundred years'. The course set by Deng is further elaborated by Liu Yunshan's 'first dimension' (of the five, mentioned in Chapter 5) that the Party is a *necessary* historical movement because of the failed experiments with 'constitutional monarchy, imperial restoration, parliamentarism,

Xi Jinping and Putin, May 2015

multi-party system and presidential government'. Nothing points to the existence of a liberal faction inside the top ranks of the Party. On the contrary. This means that democracy can only be brought about by a violent revolution. It is questionable if that would be a preferable option: Ever since the French Revolution of 1789, experience has shown that countries without democratic institutions quickly fall into the hands of new autocrats. The Arab Spring is the latest example of this historical trend.

The most obvious scenario, then, is a continuation of the current line of repression and a constant refining of the autocratic system. The 'constitutional coup' of March 2018 to do away with the rule that restricted the presidency to two terms of five consecutive years in office, means that Xi Jinping – just like his fellow defender of the illiberal world order, Vladimir Putin – can stay in power as 'supreme leader' until his last gasp. Given that scenario, a crucial question arises: Can the Party break the dynastic cycle and stay in power permanently? Many people (not just those in China) are optimistic that it can. The series of measures described in this book – the anti-corruption campaign, the restoration of the 'simple life' among the Party cadre, the repression of political dissidents, the repositioning of the Party in the heart of the society, and the creation of the myth that the Party is indispensable – are supposedly adequate measures to keep the Party in power during the 'The New Era of Socialism with Chinese Characteristics' and beyond.

That optimism is strengthened by the Party's willingness to change its curriculum for training officials as well. Inspired by the Confucianist tradition of selecting the best and the brightest, major commitments have been made to improving the quality of officials. 'Quality' does not only mean knowledge of economics, law and public administration; ethics is also receiving more and more attention. In Qufu, the birthplace of Confucius, public schools are experimenting with a Confucianist curriculum[2] and, starting in September 2015, the Chinese Academy of Governance – the highest-ranking training school for officials – has made the so-called *Guoxue* ('National Studies') a component of the curriculum. This eleven-book course of study teaches students in which areas Chinese culture is superior to others, which administrative practices were employed by imperial China, and how officials can become persons of integrity while living harmoniously with nature. Administrative efficiency and integrity in Ancient China seem to be at odds with each other, however. Professor Qi Fanhua of Renmin University explains that the most important book for imperial administration was the *Zizhi Tongjian* (*Comprehensive Mirror in Aid of Governance*), an eleventh-century work describing the history of sixteen dynasties that ruled between 403 BCE and 959 CE. The *Zizhi Tongjian*, one of Mao Zedong's favourite books, depicts a drawn-out succession of struggles between the emperors and their foes for supreme power – frequently by means of intrigue and treachery.[3]

Democracy with Chinese Characteristics

Another package of administrative reforms can be summarised under the heading of 'democracy with Chinese characteristics'. The annually-held National People's Congress (the Chinese parliament) is becoming livelier each year: More motions are submitted, and the number of parliamentarians voting against some government proposals is growing. Even at the lowest level of administration, politics is in motion: Since 1998, smaller villages have been allowed to elect their own leaders according to the 'Organic Law of Village Committees', but in recent years this legislation seems to be getting real teeth.[4] After the provincial government sided with rebel farmers in their struggle against corrupt local Party bosses, village elections were held in 2012 in Wukan in South China under the watchful eye of the world's press. This was described as 'support from above for democracy from below'. Furthermore, there is the growing phenomenon of 'consultative democracy', in which decisions are only made after taking into account the views of the public, and hearing expert opinions.

The Party's capacity to reform itself is inspiring various thinkers to propose optimistic future scenarios. In an essay written in 2011, Zhou Ruijin, the former editor-in-chief of the *People's Daily*, distinguishes three phases. The first stage of economic reforms is already completed. The second phase of social reforms will be finished in 2021. This will involve areas like healthcare, education, pensions, and housing being properly regulated; it is on this platform that the final phase of political reforms can be built. With a typically Chinese predilection for comprehensive timetables,

Zhou's structure will be completed in 2049, a hundred years after the founding of the People's Republic. Then China will be a democratic country governed by laws.[5] This vision has a strong resemblance to the 'the prosperous, strong, democratic, culturally advanced, harmonious and beautiful China' that according to Xi Jinping will become reality by the mid-twenty-first century. The prospect of an orderly road towards law, liberty and prosperity, like those described by Zhou Ruijin and Xi Jinping, give many people confidence that China is on the right track: Over the course of time, the system is becoming more just, and the leadership representative. Was it not the previous premier of China, Wen Jiabao, who himself said that 'the people's wishes for, and needs for, democracy and freedom are irresistible'?

The School of Gradual Improvement

There are various reasons why I am not a follower of this 'school of gradual improvement'. The Party has shown a great capacity for reform, but the 'easy' reforms of the 1980s and 1990s – farmers making decisions on their own production, the privatisation of most state-owned businesses, and admission to the World Trade Organisation – have already been carried out. The Party could conduct these reforms without giving up political control. Now it faces a more fundamental choice: If China wants to become a fair, sustainably prosperous, clean and modern country, it will have to let go of its control over the internet, give farmers back their land, permit the independence of judicial and legislative powers and free the press – reforms that, in the Party's analysis, will be tantamount to preparing its own downfall.

Fear of losing power characterises the 'democratic' reforms at the central and local levels, too: They are half-hearted and insufficient. Formally, the People's Congress is authorised to 'elect' the president and a host of other government officials, yet the candidates put forward by the Party are never rejected. The record even shows that in recent years opposition to the candidate proposed by the Party for the presidency has dissipated. As mentioned in Chapter 4, Xi Jinping was elected for his first term as president (in 2013) with only one mysterious delegate in opposition. In 2018 *none* of the 2,958 delegates voted against him. The same goes for the votes on changing the constitution. In 1999, there were still 21 delegates voting against the amendments then proposed, and 24 abstaining. In 2018, these numbers had dwindled to two and three. Xi Jinping obviously provokes greater fear among the delegates than his predecessors Jiang Zemin and Hu Jintao did, but there is also the structural reason of the personal entanglement between the parliament and the Party. Nearly all members of the National People's Congress are members of the Party too; its chairman is even a member of the Standing Committee. Li Zhanshu, President Xi Jinping's trusted lieutenant since the 1980's, presently heads the NPC and also occupies

The National People's Congress, 2018

third place in the Party hierarchy. That is why the increased activity of the National People's Congress is a sign of the system's sophistication, rather than a modification of it.

The same is true for the Chinese People's Political Consultative Conference (CPPCC). This body is a product of the notion of a United Front, bringing together influential individuals who are not Party members – people like Yang Yuanqing (the head of Lenovo, a large computer company), Yao Ming (a basketball player) and Mo Yan (the recipient of the Nobel Prize for Literature). This produces a win-win situation: The members of the CPPCC end up with a network of valuable contacts, while the Party bandies this organisation about as an example of the 'harmonious society' and 'consultative democracy'. Just like the People's Congress, its top ranks consist of Party members. Wang Yang, the number 4 in the Party hierarchy, has at the annual meeting of the CPPCC in March 2018 replaced Yu Zhengsheng as chairman.

Finally, there is power-sharing at the village level, consultative democracy and judicial reforms – all of them being raised as evidence of China's gradual steps toward democracy and justice. As regards the first of these: The initial hope that local democracy would constitute a blueprint for freedom at higher levels has evaporated – only the smaller villages are allowed to choose their own leaders. That cannot be called particularly revolutionary, for already during the imperial era the mandarins delegated administrative tasks in the countryside to the local gentry. 'Consultative democracy' – which Wang Yi, the minister of Foreign Affairs, considers superior to Western 'street democracy' – leads indeed to a wider public referendum, but the ultimate decisions are always taken by the Party. The same is true for judicial reforms: The Party is the highest embodiment of the law, and therefore exempt from any judicial review by the judges. In other words, this series of half-baked reforms offers little hope for substantial changes. Its 'Chinese characteristics' interpret words such as 'democracy', 'human rights' and 'the rule of law' in such a way that all connection with their linguistic origin is lost. The simultaneous repression of dissident voices – specifically those who intend to shape civil society – makes it clear that there will be no deviating from today's autocratic line.

In his *The Old Regime and the Revolution* [1856], Alexis de Tocqueville reasons that revolution does not erupt as a reaction to cruel oppression, but rather when the old regime loosens the reins and initiates cautious reforms. Forces are then unleashed that can no longer be reined in. The fact that de Tocqueville's book is required reading for the Party's top leadership shows a deep-seated fear of a repetition of June 1989 – when what began as an insignificant protest culminated in a massive popular uprising.[6]

The Party will not go under today or tomorrow – its control over society is so deeply-embedded that any opposition is nipped in the bud. In the long term, however, its days are numbered, because its incapacity for reform intensifies a number of cultural phenomena that will inevitably lead to its downfall.

Institutional Corruption
'We have achieved unprecedented success in the last two years. 237,627 Party members were disciplined, thirty-five of whom were at the level of minister or provincial governor. All are equal before the law, no matter how high his position. Confidence in the government's determination to eradicate corruption has soared.'[7] Whoever regularly follows the news in China would swear that this quote is from Wang Qishan, the widely feared former head of the all-powerful Commission for Disciplinary Inspection. However, the statement was in fact made in 1996 by Li Yufu, at that time the Minister of Supervision. The fight against corruption is as old as the Party itself, and is repeated with ritual regularity. Just two years after the founding of the People's Republic of China, the first battle already took place. Mao Zedong was worried that Party members, now that they were in power, would not be able to resist the temptations that came with their new position: 'There may be some Communists, who were not conquered by enemies with guns and were worthy of the name of heroes for standing up to these enemies, but who cannot withstand sugar-coated bullets; they will be defeated by sugar-coated bullets.'[8] Of the 1.2 million officials who were trapped in the net of that first campaign, many were persecuted and tortured to death.[9] Because of the country's size, quotas were set to determine the minimum number of corrupt people to be caught at the local level. This led to a perverse kind of competition, because every local Party secretary did his best to make more arrests than the others. As mentioned already in Chapter 4, Xi Zhongxun, father of the current president, was himself guilty of this sort of behaviour by more than doubling his own quota of required arrests. At the same time, pressure was put on the people to report offenders – just as in the imperial era. During the Cultural Revolution in

particular, this was a customary practice. During that campaign – as I heard from a Chinese friend – employees of a certain company were instructed to hand over at least one colleague as a 'counter-revolutionary element'. They sat down together in utter despair, for they had been working together for years, and were more friends than colleagues. After much deliberation, they still could not make a decision: Nobody was willing to sacrifice himself for the greater good. At a certain moment, one of them had to go to the toilet – a fateful decision, for in his absence it was easier for the others to point him out as the scapegoat. He was reported and sentenced to ten years' heavy labour.

The anti-corruption campaign launched in 2013 has been unprecedentedly harsh, far-reaching and long-lasting. While this book is being written it is still fully under way. To avoid any unwanted attention, officials at the beginning of the campaign kept to the maxim 'Eat quietly, take gently and play secretly',[10] but this tactic does not appear to work any longer. Even so, many Chinese think that this campaign too will soon pass, because patronage and the practice of doing and returning favours are the indispensable building blocks of the political system. Once the fear recedes, these phenomena will shamelessly rear their heads again. On top of that, Xi Jinping's initiative seems to have had little impact: In the 2016 international corruption index from the watchdog group Transparency International, China came in at 79, lower (i.e. more corrupt) than countries like South Africa and Cuba.[11] By that time, the anti-corruption campaign had already entered its fourth year.

The Spell of History

Institutional corruption is as old as China itself. In the imperial era, provincial officials supplemented their meagre allowance from the capital with money acquired by granting favors or by extortion. The growth in the sheer number of officials over the course of time led to ever greater corruption. According to a study by Ren Yuling, member of the Chinese People's Political Consultative Conference, the Han dynasty (206 BCE–220 CE) had one official for every eight thousand inhabitants. At the end of the Qing dynasty (1644–1911), it was one for every nine hundred; in 2005, there was one official for every nineteen Chinese. During the same 2,000-year period, government income also increased extensively, so there was much more revenue to distribute – even per official.*[12]

Another institutional reason for corruption is the predominance of state-owned companies. The top executives are all appointed by way of politics, or are themselves political creatures. Many of these companies are listed on foreign stock exchanges;

---

* Which is undoubtedly caused by the much more sophisticated ways of extortion that present day party officials have at their disposal than their distant colleagues in the, let's say, Han-dynasty.

though always less than 50 percent of the shares are sold to the public, meaning that the Chinese state will stay in control and no real transparency is given. The best-known example of such unhealthy connection between business and politics is Zhou Yongkang. During his time as CEO of Petrochina, this 'tiger' (sentenced for corruption at the end of 2014) accumulated billions of dollars for himself and his gang of cronies.[13] Circling around the major state-owned businesses are countless agents, brokers and intermediaries who pride themselves on their good (family) relations with the top executives of these companies. Whenever another company wants to work with the state-owned business, the services of an intermediary are used as a go-between. Part of the agent's income flows back to the man in the state-owned business taking the decision. This deeply-rooted practice of 'kickbacks' already occurred during the imperial era, when officials of the 'outermost court' provided, against payment, access to the 'innermost court'. For the 'old hundred names' (the ordinary people), there is no doubt that the official's bed is made of roses: 'When a man becomes an official, even his chickens and dogs go to heaven.'

Nepotism
Nepotism is corruption's twin brother, 'as closely connected to each other as lips and teeth'. The book *Red Capitalism* calls China a 'family business' in which the big decisions are taken based on 'a carefully balanced social mechanism built around the particular interests of the revolutionary families who constitute the political elite'.[14] Four of the seven members on the Standing Committee who were in power from 2012 to 2017 come from the hundred main 'revolutionary families' – making it the most privileged and hereditary of top leaderships in the history of the People's Republic.[15] It caused the *Financial Times* to declare 2012 the year of the 'princelings'. Membership of a good family yields fortunes. *Heirs of Mao's Comrades Rise as New Capitalist Nobility*, the report mentioned in Chapter 4 of this book, shows that the descendants of the 'Eight Immortals' (the original revolutionaries who together with Mao acted as midwives at the birth to the People's Republic of China) control banks and businesses, the assets of which in 2011 represented more than 20 percent of the national product. The families of these central figures have profited immensely: According to Bloomberg, every one of the major families is worth hundreds of millions, in some cases even billions of dollars.[16] As reported in an investigation by *The New York Times* in 2012, even the family of the folksy and apparently incorruptible Wen Jiabao, premier from 2002 to 2012, scraped together the unlikely fortune of 2.7 billion dollars (US).[17]

The wealth of the super-rich is for the most part invested beyond mainland China; the most popular destinations include the Hong Kong stock exchange and London's real estate. The Bloomberg report emphasizes that there are no indications that the heads of these families have used their direct influence for getting rich. Actually, as everyone who has done business in China knows, there is no need for them to do so: The fact that the family leader's brother, cousin, son or daughter owns a company ensures that every other company wants to work with them – these relationships are seen as an insurance policy that provides coverage against political risks.

In his book *China's Crony Capitalism*, Minxin Pei – a frequently cited analyst, whom the journal *Prospect* declared one of the world's hundred most prominent intellectuals in 2008 – explains that the country's structural corruption is the logical consequence of the reforms launched by Deng Xiaoping in the 1980s. Though they modernized the economy, they also gave the Party a central role in that process. Unbothered by legal restraints, the Party can at any moment intervene in the economic process – e.g. by means of expropriations or revoking licenses. Thanks to the enormous increase in prosperity, this unlimited power has led to an entrenchment of corruption 'because elites in control of unconstrained power cannot resist using it to loot the wealth generated by economic growth'. At the local level, this situation has resulted in the emergence of mini mafia-states, where Party bosses work hand in hand with local entrepreneurs (frequently family members) to collect and distribute the spoils.[18]

Corruption is Cultural
Institutional corruption does not come out of the blue: Its breeding-ground is found in the primal Chinese phenomenon called *guanxi* – a concept so difficult to translate that it is one of the few Chinese words that has made its way into other languages. Literally it means 'relation', but it is not about love, friendship or a business relationship, even though all of these are also based on *guanxi*. It is a personal connection that is mutually beneficial to both parties, an implicit bond for doing and returning favours that is so deeply embedded in Chinese culture that it constitutes the grease that makes society turn. From childhood onwards, every Chinese person is occupied with building up a network of *guanxi* to ensure that his children will be placed at good schools, doctors will help him more quickly and he will get a promotion at work. When making a 'transaction', there is no need per se for a monetary exchange: The head of the school, for instance, can put the doctor's child in his school in exchange for quick medical treatment. In economic dealings, though, it is more customary to pay money to get something done – among companies themselves, but also between companies or individuals and corrupt officials.

When I had just arrived in Beijing in the mid-1980s, I owned a so-called *mianbaoche* (a 'bread car'), a small delivery van that only Chinese drive. During my trips through Beijing I was regularly stopped by the police, because the officers noticed too late that the driver was not Chinese, but a *laowai* ('foreigner'). 'Why are you stopping me?', I always asked. The reasons varied. Often they said that I was driving too fast or that I had driven in the wrong lane. Because there were no rules for such offences yet (let alone traffic signs) in Beijing, I knew that they were after something else. At the start of the negotiations they would usually ask for fifty renminbi, but after 'friendly consultation' I never paid more than ten in the end. Some foreigners point out that Western countries are not much different; even in our societies one does not get much done without the right connections. It is true that everyone prefers to do business with someone they know and trust, but there is one essential difference: Relations in the West *supplement* the societal activities encoded in laws and rules; in China *guanxi* *replace* the legal codes. To quote a saying used earlier: 'China is a country ruled not by laws but by people.'

Corruption in the Armed Forces

On the military base of Zurihe in Inner Mongolia, Xi Jinping barked out his instructions to an 'audience' of 12,000 soldiers standing in tightly-ordered ranks under the burning sun of the Gobi Desert. 'You shall be unswervingly loyal to the absolute leadership that the party has over the army! You shall be ready to assemble at the first call and be capable of fighting and winning any battle!'[19] This appeal for loyalty to the Party was one of many that Xi Jinping has made since he took office in 2013, though this time it was a special occasion: On that day, 30 July 2017, the People's Liberation Army celebrated the Nanchang Uprising of 1 August 1927, which is regarded as the birthdate of the PLA. When the PLA was two years old (in 1929), Mao Zedong had already made the same appeal, but even after all these years the loyalty of the 90-year-old military to the Party is obviously still very much in doubt – as is its combat readiness. These feelings of anxiety are closely connected to the cases of Xu Caihou and Guo Boxiong, for these two disgraced generals (mentioned in Chapter 4) are only the tip of the iceberg of a corrupt military. In 2015, when an investigation into sixteen generals was announced, the famous retired general Luo Yuan complained about the 'disgusting corruption' in the armed forces, which was seriously undermining the preparedness of the troops. 'Which soldier will be willing to sacrifice for a corrupt officer, or to fight a battle for a corrupt officer? That corrupt officer has his own private coffer; how will he risk his own life for the country?'[20] Luo thinks that with this kind of military, China 'would lose any war before fighting it'.[21]

Ni Lexiong, director of the Defense Policy Research Center in Shanghai, agrees with Luo's remarks. To give his analysis maximum impact, he makes reference to the sensitive war of 1894, in which Japan inflicted a heavy defeat upon China. According to Ni, human failure was to blame for that debacle, for the Chinese *Beiyang* fleet matched that of the Japanese in terms of the number of ships and firepower. 'The Chinese sailors and officers mocked their well-paid foreign instructors – in sharp contrast to the humble and serious desire to learn on the part of the Japanese navy.' The situation has since then, according to Ni, not improved: 'It is an open secret that the current problems with corruption inside the military are more serious than those of the Qing dynasty's *Beiyang* fleet.'[22]

The Party would probably not survive a battlefield defeat against Japan. So Xi Jinping must purge the military, though there is every indication that he is making powerful enemies in doing so. In March 2015, the leadership of the Central Security Bureau was replaced: The Bureau is the praetorian guard that protects the personal security of China's top leaders. A successful military coup d'état has never happened in the history of the People's Republic, and Xi Jinping is fully committed to keeping it that way.[23]

Absence of Virtue

Being virtuous entails more than leading a non-corrupt lifestyle; virtue must also be made visible. Just as the father educates his children by leading by example, so the emperor too must demonstrate *ren*, the virtue of humaneness, to his people. This quality, however, is still rarely encountered amongst the Communist Party cadre. Western media report on the arrest of dissidents like Liu Xiaobo, but they seldom notice that people are apprehended on a much larger scale for fighting for their property, a better environment, or more autonomy. Once, on a pretty spring day in 2011, 50-year-old Cai Julan was making breakfast for her grandson, when suddenly the door was kicked in and she was handcuffed by armed men. Fifty more people from Yaojiang, Cai's village, were arrested with her and taken away in cars. The raid was the climax of a drawn-out dispute. The community of Ningbo, a nearby town, wanted to build a distribution center in Yaojiang and nationalize the land; but because the villagers could not prove they owned the land, they were offered no compensation and a deadlock arose. At first the local authorities tried intimidation by hiring gangsters who dumped garbage on the fields, but when this had no effect the village was cleared by force, and Cai arrested. After her release she was allowed to go home, but her house had been razed to the ground and all her money and possessions confiscated.[24]

Cai's story is not isolated; it illustrates the clashes that occur every day in China between the authorities and citizens. In 2013, at least ninety thousand incidents of this sort took place, though that figure is probably on the low end for only so-called 'mass incidents' are mentioned. Contrary to popular opinion, the central government is well-aware of the abuses of the local authorities, but for the sake of the country's 'stability' it will seldom intervene. The local Party boss is judged by the employment opportunities he creates and the disturbances he prevents; these are accomplishment for which he gets promoted, not by listening to the often-justified complaints of the common people. In 2005, Li Qun, Party secretary for the Linyi prefecture in Shandong province, imprisoned and tortured the blind activist Chen Guangcheng. Now, as the Party secretary for the city of Qingdao and its over two million inhabitants, Li is one of the most powerful individuals in the province. The previous president Hu Jintao climbed as high as he did because during his years as Party secretary of Tibet (1988 to 1992), he repressed every form of resistance with an iron fist.[25]

Apart from rewarding the enforcement of law and order (above all, the latter), it is difficult for Beijing to assess the true situation at the local level: Stories circulated on the internet or by independent journalists are repressed by local power-brokers as much as possible, and in some cases the whistle-blower is even threatened or locked up for 'spreading rumours', 'seeking trouble' or 'disturbing public order'. The internal Party report is therefore often the most important source of information. Local authorities even have an ideological excuse for arresting troublesome journalists, because the 'freedom of speech and freedom of the press' is one of the seven topics one 'must not discuss' according to the former propaganda tsar Liu Yunshan. As long as the provincial Party boss is not corrupt (or knows how to hide it well), he can shamelessly go about doing things his own way.

The Small People

Not only *ren* (humaneness) is lacking in the behaviour of many Party officials; the virtue of *li* (etiquette or propriety) is also neglected. Proper behavior is the external proof of internal refinement, and is given shape by education and discipline. 'Yan Yuan asked about perfect virtue [i.e. *ren*]. The Master said, "To subdue one's self and return to propriety [*li*], is perfect virtue."'[26] Those who do not reach that level are dismissed by Confucius as *xiaoren* ('little people'). The extreme Maoism of the 1960s and 1970s seriously damaged the norms of etiquette, because correct behavior was associated with the old order, and could have serious consequences for one's career – or even worse. Unrefined behavior like belching, eating noisily and spitting in public became generally accepted, even (or perhaps specifically) among the elite. During negotiations with Margaret Thatcher on the future of Hong Kong (so the story goes), Deng Xiaoping regularly cleared his throat and with great precision aimed his phlegm into the spittoon next to his chair.

Public manners have since then improved, but Mao's heirs constitute an elite who only think in terms of power and, for fear of losing it, are continually fighting their opponents – both real and imaginary. The Party rails most fiercely against those individuals who hold a mirror up to its own lack of virtue. The dissident Liu Xiaobo wrote that he had no enemies, and praised the respectful behaviour of his guards. The Dalai Lama tells his young, sometimes fanatical supporters that the use of violence conflicts with Tibetan Buddhism, which teaches unconditional compassion with every living being. Morally superior people such as these drive the heirs of Sun Zi into a rage. In 2006, the Dalai Lama appealed to his people to stop wearing the skins of leopards and tigers, because of the threat this habit posed to these animals' survival. Though the Chinese authorities had imposed a similar ban a long time ago, most Tibetans ignored the occupiers' orders. The appeal from their supreme spiritual leader had an entirely different effect, however: Throughout Tibet, the skins of these big cats were burnt on a large scale. On the very same evening of the Dalai Lama's appeal, news anchors appeared on Beijing-controlled local television wearing snow leopard furs.[27]

The Gap Between Language and Reality
In one of his conversations in *The Analects*, Confucius says: 'If names be not correct, language is not in accordance with the truth of things. If language be not in accordance with the truth of things, affairs cannot be carried on to success. [...] What the superior man requires is just that in his words there may be nothing incorrect.'[28] Politicians in general are not known as champions of the truth, but the Chinese leaders belong in a special category. The People's Republic is not administered by the people, but by the Party; the autonomous regions are not allowed to administer themselves, and the harmonious society is one of tension and conflict. Propaganda, as has already been observed, is seen by the Party as one of the pillars for continuing its power, but it has a much more ancient breeding-ground in Chinese culture. Language is first of all used as a tool to embellish or obscure reality. In Europe, one does not readily encounter place-names like the City of Eternal Peace (Chang'an – today's Xi'an), the Hall of Supreme Harmony and the Square of Heavenly Peace. That other function of language – throwing up smoke screens – is also widely practiced. The answer 'in principle, I agree with it' actually means no. The need for political correctness obscures reality even more. In political campaigns, catchphrases like 'Serve the people', 'Learn from Lei Feng' and 'It is better to be red than expert' were repeated by the people like mantras. They actually had no choice, for those who remained silent were suspected of not supporting the regime. This declaration of loyalty is called *biaotai* – 'declaring where one stands' – but it says nothing about the internal acceptance of what the slogan calls for. It is difficult to tell how this endless stream of propaganda (now running for almost seventy years) has affected the Chinese soul on a deeper level. Sometimes most Chinese seem to accept the government's reading of foreign questions at face value; especially when it strikes a nationalist chord. Nearly everyone in China believes, for instance, that the Americans deliberately bombed the Chinese embassy in Belgrade in May 1999. Still, skepticism about news reported by the Party is increasing, too – certainly among the more intelligent segment of the nation that reads the news 'conversely': When the Party says that A has happened, it will most likely be B.

Politics in China has traditionally been an ethical affair. The Mandate of Heaven is bestowed upon the morally distinguished monarch, but in case of moral degeneration, it can be taken away again from him. The loss of inner strength (the Chinese word for virtue, *de*, also means 'inner strength') inevitably leads to the loss of 'outer strength', i.e. worldly power. The Party is very conscious of this dynamic – for good reason, the study of 'virtue' has been part of the curriculum for Party members-in-training in recent years. The question is whether this measure will refrain the average Party member from enriching himself at the expense of the people and in doing so restore their trust. If not, the Party is doomed – as the former vice-president Zeng Qinghong already predicted in 2004: 'A party that is not dynamic and does not change with the times will become moribund and cut off from its popular base until it ultimately dies.'[29]

CHAPTER 11

The Third Way

The Master said, 'There was Shun: – He indeed was greatly wise! Shun loved to question others, and to study their words, though they might be shallow. He concealed what was bad in them and displayed what was good. He took hold of their two extremes, determined the Mean, and employed it in his government of the people.'

from *The Doctrine of the Mean* (Ch. 6)

Karl Marx believed that capitalism would succumb under the weight of its own contradictions.[1] 'Socialism with Chinese characteristics' runs the risk of meeting the same fate, because its 'contradictions' at the beginning of the twenty-first century are as staggering as they are many: A capitalist economy led by a Leninist party; a Socialist state with greater income differences than most capitalist countries; an upcoming power whose defence budget grows at more than 10 percent annually, yet who promotes peace and harmony. Our Western mind is not equipped to make sense of these contrasts: We need a clear-cut explanation. The co-existence of different realities confuses us – all the more so when they reside in one and the same person. The Qian Long Emperor, a refined man of letters and patron of Buddhism, slaughtered nearly one million Dzungars in the middle of the eighteenth century. The no less refined poet, Mao Zedong, was responsible for the deaths of many more victims. And to give a recent example: How can Xi Jinping foster an almost blind reverence for Mao, while still wanting to modernize the country economically? As the sinologist Orville Schell has said, 'Modern China is best understood by those capable of embracing contradictions.'[2]

Classical Chinese philosophy is fascinated by duality. Taoism teaches that the existence of opposites is a natural phenomenon: *Yin* is not worse than *yang*, but by keeping nature in balance they drive it forward in an eternal rhythm. Opposition to this duality, or wanting to 'harmonise' its antipodal character, is useless. The best thing one can do is to surrender to it; that is why, for the followers of Lao Zi, living a virtuous life means the casting aside of civilisation. To the Confucianists, living a virtuous life requires exactly the opposite: The improvement of society, not the forsaking of it. They see society as a reflection of nature, with the essential difference that in the world of man opposites are not resolved by themselves (the Chinese word for nature is *da ziran*, 'the big by itself'). Human intervention is demanded through strict education in values like honesty, propriety, sense of duty and humaneness. Only then can the natural goodness of the heart be cultivated; only then can people develop into 'nobles' (*junzi*) who spread virtue and relate properly to one another. Yet the day when virtue prevails, and every person knows his place, is still far on the horizon – until that time, the *xiaoren* ('small people') under the spell of their passions and desires will populate the earth. Hence the vital importance of the *pater familias* and the wise prince: By their elevated morality they know how to reconcile the contradictions among the 'small people', be it among their family members or subjects of the state. They are the judges of their fellow humans, even if it is virtue rather than the law that directs them. If they manage to live the 'kingly way', then the World of the Great Harmony as described in the *The Book of Rites* is close at hand.

In Marx's thinking, contradictions are also crucial, but to him they are the engine for progress. Every situation, be it in nature or in human society, calls forth a counter-action that results in a new and 'higher' situation. This so-called 'dialectical materialism' determines the development and progress of society. Applied to history, this doctrine means that any given historical phase must make room for the next one, the ideal final phase being a world that is characterised by profuse material abundance and labour relations in which everyone 'works according to his ability and receives according to his need'. The world of Communism. In his famous treatise 'On contradiction' (1937), Mao Zedong shows himself to be both a gifted Marxist theoretician as well as a political opportunist. He states that the contradictions between the proletariat and the other classes cannot be 'harmoniously' resolved, but are characterised by conflict: 'The supersession of the old by the new is a general, eternal and inviolable law of the universe.'[3] What represents the 'old', and who is the enemy, is ultimately determined by the Party, or rather by Mao himself.[4] In his Marxist writings, China's supreme iconoclast deviates on two essential points from classical Chinese thinking: History does not run a circular, but a linear, course and contradictions are not reconciled through moral persuasion, but through struggle.

The Ideal State in the West

Mao's thinking on progress places him in an ancient Western intellectual tradition. Nearly twenty-five centuries ago, Plato first set things in motion: The ideal state can be realised by taking children from their parents at a young age, and training them to become 'Guardians' of the state through a fixed curriculum of physical and intellectual education. These leaders only do what is Good – an infinitely deeper source of happiness than having possessions. The elite class of Guardians ensures the excellence of this education, whereby the continuity of the state is forever guaranteed. Once, in ancient times, the ideal state had truly existed, but it had fallen into decline through the desire for personal possessions and the admission of the lower classes to the Guardians. By Plato's time (around 400 BCE), society had even degenerated into democracy – a form of government in which the people place power in the hands of a demagogue, who prevails by fooling the masses with empty promises and by satisfying their needless amusements. At a certain moment, power goes to the demagogue's head, and he morphs into a tyrant who, with a small flock of trusted retainers, represses the people who once elected him.[5]

A restoration of the blissful original society is possible, but only if the sick patient (the degenerated state) embraces Plato's curriculum. Once healed, the state must prevent the fate of its fallen predecessors by never changing again: 'Any change whatever, except the change of an evil thing, is the gravest of all the treacherous dangers that can befall a thing – whether it is now a change of season, or of wind, or of the diet of the body, or of the character of the soul.'[6] It is striking that Plato, the founder of Western philosophy, developed political ideas that have a Chinese ring to them: Confucius too supposed that an ideal early state had existed, and he too believed that an elite that was trained through virtuous education had the right (and even the duty) to lead the state.

For Christian thinkers like Augustine, the end of history does not lie in the establishment of a secular state but, rather in the founding a heavenly city (*civitas dei*) that will make its arrival on the 'Day of Judgement'. Humanity will then be liberated from its earthly existence.[7] As with the thinking of Plato and Confucius, this passage towards salvation cannot be left to the common people; they have to be led by a class that understands the will of God and can convey that to them. The role of Plato's Guardians and Confucius' wise mandarins is fulfilled in Augustinian thinking by the priests of the Catholic Church.

Georg Wilhelm Friedrich Hegel – admired by Francis Fukuyama, author of *The End of History and the Last Man* – also saw a linear movement in history, but his climax was not the world coming to an end, or change coming to a standstill. As Fukuyama notes, Hegel's end of history does not mean the end of birth, death, or human interaction, nor does it constitute the termination of human knowledge. It is rather the highest form of human freedom, as embodied by the modern constitutional state.[8] Karl Marx follows Hegel in his historical determinism, but rejects the idea that the liberal state has superseded the contradiction between bourgeoisie and proletariat. His end of history lies 'one station further', in the final victory of the proletariat and the establishment of a classless Communist society.

The Ideal State in China

The notion that history, just like nature, occurs in cycles constitutes a fundamental difference between Chinese and Western thought. The aforementioned philosopher Yan Fu (1854–1921), first president of Peking University, even regarded this as the biggest distinction between the two ancient civilisations: 'I think the greatest difference between China and the West, which can never be made up, is that the Chinese are fond of antiquity but neglect the present. The Westerners are struggling in the present in order to supersede the past. Chinese consider that a period of order and a period of disorder, and a period of prosperity and a period of decline are the natural course of heavenly conduct of human affairs; while Westerners consider that daily progress should be endless, and that what has already been prosperous will not decline, and that when things are well governed, they will not be in disorder again – all of which they take as an absolute law of academic thought and political ideas.'[9] Zhao Tingyang, the philosopher interviewed in Chapter 6, mirrors the same relativistic thinking a century later. He finds the ideal state to be a typically Western creation: 'Perfection does not exist, everything reaches maturity and then declines – just like nature. The highest thing attainable is a *better* world.'

The teachings of Marx reject this axiom of Chinese thinking. Marxism believes that the ideal state is possible, but in China its elaboration has seen many twists and turns. Once upon a time, in the early, heady days of Yan'an, Marxism in China stood for revolution and change, with the establishment of a classless society as its ultimate goal. The modern Chinese 'Marxist' racks his brain over an entirely different question: How can the Party stay in power *ad infinitum*? The two most significant answers to that question have been described in this book: By declaring that the Party is a 'necessary' historical movement and – in order to justify such a grandiose claim – by waging the relentless campaign to restore the 'virtue' of the Party officials. Xi's actions are steps on 'The path to permanent peace and stability' which enable the Party to 'escape the historical cycle' – to paraphrase the title of the essay by the lawyer Wang Zhenmin, interviewed in Chapter 6. Just like Plato, the Party wants to arrest time.

As in Europe, religious movements in China also proclaimed 'end of times' theories. The numerous peasant rebellions were frequently led by a messiah who promised his followers eternal salvation. Hong Xiuquan, the leader of the nineteenth-century mass uprising of the *Taiping Tianguo* (the 'Heavenly Kingdom of Great Peace') saw himself as the younger brother of Jesus. He prophesied that what was old had been cast off, and a new millennium was about to dawn: 'Now at last the murky mists begin to lift, / And we know that Heaven plans an age of heroes. / Those who brought low our sacred land shall not do so again; / All men should worship God, and we shall do so, too.'[10]

The Great Harmony

Older – but at the same time more current – than Socialism, or a religious 'end of times', however, is the vision of the World of Great Harmony. Just like Plato, Confucius believed that a golden age had existed in the past, an epoch in which people lived together in harmony and were guided by wise leaders. *The Book of Rites*, one of the five classic works of Confucianism, predicts that this age shall dawn again: 'When the Great Way prevails, the world will belong to all. They chose people of talent and ability whose words were sincere, and they cultivated harmony.'[11] This dream has throughout the centuries continued to inspire. It offered an enticing vision to the intellectuals who despaired of China's survival at the beginning of the twentieth century. Kang Youwei's *Datongshu* (*The Book of the Great Harmony*) names various phases mankind must go through to finally enter the era of the Great Harmony. Professor Hu Angang from Tsinghua University predicts that – through China's global contributions to science, technology, the environment, culture and the war on poverty – the Great Harmony will be realized by 2030. In that world, China will be the 'kingly' leader. The philosopher Zhao Tingyang sketches the world of *Tianxia*, a somewhat vaguer vision of the future in which virtue and harmony prevail, and which is led by a global government.

The Party is paying increasing attention to these creative purveyors of neo-Confucianist ideas. Just like Kang Youwei, the Party thinks in historical phases: In his speech before the 19th Party Congress in October 2017, Xi Jinping predicted that the *Xiao Kang* (the 'Era of Lesser Prosperity') will be realised in 2021. By 2035 China will be a 'modernised' country, a leader in innovation with a clean environment and a large middle-income group. The final target of the country being 'strong, democratic, culturally advanced, harmonious and beautiful' is set for 2049. These visions do not (yet) tally with Kang's 'Era of Complete Peace-and-Equality' and 'The Era of Great Harmony', but a further convergence of Marxist and Confucianist terminology is quite likely.* The ideological leap in that direction is not difficult to make, because the ideal of Great Harmony – the equal distribution of All-Under-Heaven – connects splendidly to the Communist ideal of the property-less society.

* For instance at the huge military parade held in Inner Mongolia on July 30, 2017, to commemorate the 90th anniversary of the People's Liberation Army, Xi Jinping said that 'All under heaven is not at peace.'

A Confucianist State?

Does this embrace of Confucianist concepts mean that the position of the old master is being restored? Not only as a function of good governance (the meritocratic selection of officials), as a way of elevating citizens morally or as a propaganda tool for the barbarians (the Confucius Institutes abroad), but also as the lawgiver for day-to-day life and the philosophy of the heart? In other words, will a genuine conversion take place, healing the country of the wounds inflicted by Marxism and reuniting it with its original soul? Some signs point to such a change. At a major conference on Confucius held in September 2014, Xi Jinping said: 'If a country or a nation does not cherish its own thinking and culture, if they lose their soul, no matter which country or which nation, it will not be able to stand.'[12] A couple of months prior to that, the president had paid a visit to Tang Yijie, a scholar heading the 'Confucian Canon', a project that aspires to compile all known Confucianist works. The four hundred academics collaborating on this monumental edifice expect to produce more than five hundred titles. Tang will not be participating in the completion of the project in 2025: At the age of eighty-seven, he died right after Xi Jinping's visit. The president praised the elderly scholar for his 'exceptional contribution of inheriting and promoting the essence of traditional Chinese culture'.[13]

Yet despite this official encouragement, the elevation of Confucianism to the religion of the land seems a bridge too far – in the first place because, as an ethical doctrine, it is not equipped for that purpose. Confucius does not make any comments about major religious questions like life after death, relief from suffering or the relationship between God and man. That is why his teaching has always remained the doctrine of the elite – the vast majority of the population were adherents of Buddhism or Taoism, or venerated local deities. The second reason is that the elite itself has drifted too far from the foundation Confucianism is built upon: Virtue. It is naïve (or at best romantic) to suppose that classical China was led by virtuous mandarins, but the pre-modern elite had not yet been afflicted by the two viruses now prevalent everywhere: The greed of capitalism and the materialistic thinking of Socialism. The anti-corruption trials of recent years have brought to light the intense, personal entanglements between the Party and the world of big business. In the imperial era, that relationship was different. The mandarins extorted the merchants, but they did not take up business themselves. It was, rather, the other way around: A merchant who had 'made it' tried to become a member of the non-productive elite of landowners and mandarins. And as far as materialistic thinking is concerned: The gulf between the ideal and reality was often gapingly large, but the mandarins nevertheless felt a part of an ethical world order that elevated virtue and looked down upon material possessions.

The loss of the social and ethical context of the imperial era has led to a rudderless elite that feels no restriction at all in making themselves rich. To the Western mind (or mine, in any case), it is as fascinating as it is incomprehensible that Xi Jinping seems to be sincere in his belief that the Party can rediscover virtue and recover its moral claim to ruling the country. Quite a few Western analysts share for that matter the president's belief, but it seems to me that these people suffer from what the philosopher Karl Popper calls 'the spell of Plato' – the belief in the ideal society. On the other hand, it is not conceivable that an ancient country with such a totally different history and culture will embrace Western parliamentary democracy. Which path, as the well-known intellectual Pan Wei wonders, is China going to follow in the next thirty years? 'Will it preserve China's rejuvenation? Or will it have superstitious faith in the Western "liberal democracy" system, and go down the road of decline and enslavement?'[14]

That is why the most likely way forward – and probably the most desirable – is the third way. Continuing in the current direction increases the chance of a violent explosion, while the sudden introduction of a parliamentary democracy will most likely lead to chaos: As we have seen in many cases, only countries with democratic institutions, and a history of living by democratic rules, can properly channel the pent-up social tensions that erupt with the demise of the old order. If not, a 'strong man' will rise – like general Yuan Shikai, who in 1914 dissolved parliament and subsequently declared himself emperor.

East-West Synthesis?

Born in 1940, Tu Weiming has had an exceptional career. As a professor of Chinese philosophy, he has been affiliated with Harvard University since 1981 and holds countless honorary professorships, both inside and outside China. In 2001 he was invited by Kofi Annan, at the time the secretary-general of the United Nations, to join the Group of Eminent Persons, which was to develop the Dialogue Among Civilisations. Despite (or perhaps because of) the fact that he built his career in the United States, he has the ear of China's leaders, and is well known as one of the most prominent Confucianists in the world.[15]

Can the values of Confucianism and those of Western political philosophy be united? Can a new synthesis emerge? In his essay 'Beyond the Enlightenment Mentality',[16] Tu argues that it can, though only if a fundamental intellectual change takes place on a global scale. The eighteenth-century movement of the Enlightenment led to individual freedom and scientific progress, yet these gains brought about the unleashing of forces that could not be controlled. Modern man, like an 'unbound Prometheus, wants to explore, to know, to conquer and to subdue' – which has led to the disastrous disintegration of communities and the devastation of the planet. To turn the tide, Tu argues that we must draw, in an eclectic way, from three spiritual

Tu Weiming

traditions. First of all, from Western thinking – as shaped by Christianity, Judaism and the philosophy of Ancient Greece – which is responsible for the rise of the modern, individualistic human being, but also for the typical Western dichotomy of mind and body, humanity and nature, sacred and profane. In this dualistic thinking (for example, in the Biblical notion that nature is subordinate to man), Tu detects the seeds of the Enlightenment individual, who subjugates nature and has lost his sense of community.

Secondly, the spiritual traditions of Asia, specifically Confucianism, can also contribute to a new synthesis, according to Tu, because values like collectivity, public governance, and meritocracy constitute a welcome supplement to the three pillars of Western modernity: The market, democracy and individualism. As a third source for a new world consciousness, the philosophy professor finds inspiration in ancient, indigenous traditions like those of the Native Americans and Maori, for whom being human consists of connecting with their ancestors and the earth. We Westerners are connected by Boeing 747s, high-speed rail lines and the internet, yet we feel increasingly alienated from our neighbours and our land. Tu does not mean to dismiss the gains of the West – the independence of the intellect, freedom, and individualism – but argues for softening them with the collectivity of the East and the sense of connection that characterises indigenous traditions. In this regard, he shows himself to be a full-blooded Confucianist: The man averse to dogmatic extremes who is always seeking 'the middle way', as elaborated in *The Doctrine of the Mean*.

What can Confucianism contribute specifically to this new synthesis? The shortest answer is humanism. For Tu Weiming, the true man is more than 'rational being, political animal, tool-user or language-manipulator'. Through an unending process of self-improvement and 'dialogue with heaven', he transforms himself, family, society, the earth and even the cosmos. That is his destiny, his highest self-realisation. Whoever reaches that goal is a *junzi* – a true human being, a noble person. Yet Tu Weiming's humanism goes even farther than the practice of *ren* (humaneness), for the golden rule of this principle – 'Do not do unto others what you would not want others to do unto you' – is too limiting. It even goes further than Confucius' 'holy man', who carries out good works for the well-being of the people.[17] The supreme humanist, according to Tu, is guided by Wang Yangming (1472–1529), the mysterious neo-Confucianist, who in his introduction to *The Great Learning* writes that 'The great man regards Heaven, Earth, and the myriad things as one body. ... Even when he sees tiles and stones shattered and crushed, he cannot help a feeling of regret. ... Such a mind is rooted in his Heaven-endowed nature, and is naturally intelligent, clear and not beclouded.'[18] If we succeed, according to Tu, 'to be in touch with that silent illumination that makes the rightness and principle in our heart-mind shine forth brilliantly' then the ideal of the unity of heaven, earth, and humanity – as mentioned in the book of the *Zhong Yong* (*The Doctrine of the Mean*) – can be realised. The attainment of this ideal would be of great benefit to Western man as well, because the equilibrium in the Enlightenment ideals of liberty, equality, and fraternity has been lost. The freedom realised in the West has come at the expense of equality and fraternity.

Tu Weiming's lofty body of thought supplies the building blocks for the philosophy of the third way, but offers no concrete advice on how to organise the new state. That gap is filled by Jiang Qing, a neo-Confucianist who lives with a few followers in the mountains of Guizhou province, and wears long, classical Chinese robes. Jiang rejects the Western idea that popular sovereignty is the only source of legitimacy. The truly sovereign state is supported by a tricameral legislature: The House of the People, the House of Eminent Persons and the House of the Nation. The first House is elected by the people through general suffrage, and is thus comparable to a Western parliament. The House of Eminent Persons (House of Ru, 儒, that is of 'Confucian Scholars') will be staffed by people who have passed Confucianist examinations similar to the ones that existed in imperial days. The House of the Nation will be led by a direct descendant of Confucius, who will select members 'from among the descendants of the great sages of the past, descendants of the rulers, descendants of famous people, of patriots, university professors of Chinese history, retired top officials, judges, and diplomats, worthy people from society, as well as representatives of Daoism, Buddhism, Islam, Tibetan Buddhism and Christianity'.[19] Legislative proposals are only adopted if one of the other chambers also agrees, but the house of Eminent Persons holds veto power. On top of this structure Jiang Qing puts two other institutions: an Academy of Confucian scholars, which supervises and examines the three chambers, and a monarch (also a descendant of Confucius) who can 'effectively uphold the stability, continuity, and eternal nature of the state'.[20]

Jiang Qing supports his institutional organisation by going back to the *Gongyang Zhuan*, a commentary on the *Chun Qiu* (*The Spring and Autumn Annals*), one of the five classic works of Confucianism. The *Gongyang Zhuan* distinguishes three forms of legitimacy: That of heaven (the conveyor of transcendental morality), of earth (the wisdom that is transmitted through history and culture) and the legitimacy of the people (the will of the masses). The House of Eminent Persons conveys the wisdom of heaven, the House of the Nation ensures that Chinese culture will be handed down, and the House of the People expresses the popular voice. The state that finds the right balance between these three sources of legitimacy follows the kingly way, and is truly sovereign.[21]

China as a Moral Paragon?

It is difficult to see how Tu Weiming's ideas on 'moral awakening' can become reality in China, for in very few other countries has the 'modernity' of the Enlightenment inflicted so much damage – both to human relationships and to the natural world. Socialism through Mao's disruptive campaigns directed by class struggle; capitalism through the plundering of the environment and the creation of huge income differentials. Tu Weiming therefore notes sadly that 'the rationality of the Enlightenment' has inflicted much more damage in China than in Japan – a country that fosters its Confucianist roots better by not allowing the gap between rich and poor run too high. Whoever has lived and worked in China knows that Tu is right. There is nothing wrong with the innate humanity of the Chinese: Countless NGOs, religious groups and individuals strive daily to improve the lot of the poor, and save the environment. These groups and people have to compete, however, with a political system that on the one hand distrusts civil society, while on the other allows the leading families to retain power and enrich themselves. As the nationalist Wang Xiaodong noted when I interviewed him (Chapter 6): 'China is not a Socialist country; it is ruled by oligarchs.'

Disillusionment with the system is best illustrated by the enormous increase in emigration. Until recently the Canadian government required immigrants to have assets of 1.6 million Canadian dollars, and to invest 800,000 Canadian dollars in non-interest-bearing government bonds. For many Chinese, this turned out to be a minuscule threshold, and tens of thousands signed up. At the beginning of 2014,

Canadian officials could no longer handle the avalanche of Chinese applications, and the programme was discontinued.[22] Though criticised by Beijing every day, the United States has the opposite problem: In spite of President Trump's anti-immigration policies, millions of immigrants keep knocking at the door. America's popularity proves that the line on the Statue of Liberty – *Give me your tired, your poor, your huddled masses yearning to breathe free* – still has not lost its appeal: Not even today, when the country is ruled by a president who wants to build walls and refuse immigrants from 'shithole' countries.

Nobody wants to emigrate to China, inasmuch as that is possible for a non-Chinese.* In the book *Day of Empire: How Hyperpowers Rise to Global Dominance – and Why They Fall*, Amy Chua, history professor at Yale University, reasons that major powers founded on ethnicity and nationalism cannot last long. Open, tolerant empires that welcome the best and the brightest from around the world are wealthier, more successful and will endure longer. In the Roman Empire, the Spaniard Trajan could become an emperor, and China's most cosmopolitan dynasty, the Tang (618–909), was led by emperors of Turkic descent. And we all know the story of the half-Kenyan who became an American president. In today's ethnocentric China, that is out of the question. Chua tells how she asked various policymakers whether a foreigner who speaks fluent Chinese could acquire Chinese citizenship. She found the answer in most cases to be negative or uncertain – with the telling addition that the foreigners *themselves* do not want it anyway.[24]

China can draw from an enormous pool of indigenous talent, but the parochial and racist features of today's policy mean that the race for global leadership cannot be sustained in the long run – all the more so, because China's median age is now approximately the same as that of the United States (37.1 versus 37.9, in 2016[25]). But with its only recently abolished one-child policy and its closed borders, the old empire is greying much faster than the hegemon on the other side of the ocean. China must re-invent itself again, this time as an open and modern country that is not only economically, but also mentally connected with the world.

A Sage King?

Even a China that casts aside its distrustful nationalism, and regains the cosmopolitan grandeur of the Tang and Song dynasties, will have difficulty embracing the Enlightenment values of freedom, individualism and democracy. Its aversion to

---

* China has favorable policies – such as long-term visa arrangements and 'The Thousand Talents Program' – to attract foreign talent to work in China, but becoming Chinese through naturalization is not considered in these policies.[23]

these ideals is not just felt (and fed) by a Party wanting to keep a bankrupt system in place: The resistance is more deep-seated. In the spring of 1919, the students of Peking University cried loudly that only 'Mr Science and Mr Democracy' could save the country. Yet the hope that emerged at that time has never been fulfilled. External reasons like the war with Japan and the dictatorship of Mao have certainly had a great influence on that development; still, it was also for 'internal' reasons that the potential for democracy was never realised. Xiang Lanxin, the influential political scientist mentioned earlier, observes that Chinese thought never engaged in the 'Cartesian obsession' for determining in an absolute sense what *is* or *is not*: ' "Where *is* the way (*dao*)" is about as far as Chinese ontological inquiry goes. In this sense, *universal values* have little intuitive appeal to the Chinese.'[26]

The same is true for the values of the Enlightenment. The proposition, for example, that God 'created all men equal' presupposes the existence of a creator who does not appear in any Chinese religion or philosophy. In addition, the core Western value of individualism is problematic, according to Xiang, because the autonomous human being is not a 'real' human being: 'In Chinese tradition only a social person, that is, a person with social relations, can qualify as a real individual.' The inclination to place the collective interest higher than the desires of the individual means that another gain from the Enlightenment – independent, critical judgement – also never really came to the fore in China. This can be seen from the widespread phenomenon of plagiarism at Chinese universities, though I have also experienced it personally: Even for my highly-educated Chinese friends it is difficult to confront objective information, for example about the number of victims of the Cultural Revolution. Their reaction of discomfort in such instances cannot be only explained by the reflex of 'my country, right or wrong'; it seems that centuries of emphasis on collective thinking have disabled their minds of seeing things in an alternative way.

For Nobel Peace Prize recipient Liu Xiaobo, China can never become a civilised country without respect for *individual* human rights, such as freedom of religion and freedom of expression. Yet this school of universal liberalism, for which Liu was the poster child, certainly does not represent the mainstream in China, and this explains on a more profound level why the country took no democratic turn in the twentieth century – and why it will probably not do so in the short term. The moral vacuum created by the Party has created a situation in which the better angels of China's nature – propriety, tolerance, modesty and humaneness – are overshadowed by the qualities of deceit, manipulation and treachery, as honed by Master Sun.

For salvation from this decline there is a typical Chinese way out: The coming of the 'Sage King', an archetypal figure who, by his moral authority, heals the empire and brings stability and prosperity – a superior man whose 'virtue is like the wind that the grass (the inferior man) must bend to'. For many people, this is more than a mythical story from a primeval time.

Han Deqiang and Henk Schulte Nordholt

On a sunny day in November 2014, I spoke with Han Deqiang, a Taoist philosopher who has set up a commune near Beijing where organic produce is grown. Han knows for certain that the Sage King will come. Is Xi Jinping that king? 'No,' said Han, as he fished sunflower seeds out of a big basket, shelled them and threw the kernels into another container. 'He is not a bad leader, but he's no Yao or Shun (kings from primeval times) who eradicated evil. One day, though, he will come.'

People like Han are not dreamers with their heads in the clouds, but the cultural context guiding their thoughts and dreams is miles away from ours. For where is this king? Is he still hiding in the mountains? Perhaps (as my Western mind is inclined to say) the people should just do away with a Sage King, a Great Helmsman or Saviour, and take matters into their own hands. A country cannot move forward without leaders, but let him or her be a Chinese version of Mandela instead, someone who through integrity, moral authority and modesty knows how to reconcile the country's deep-rooted contradictions – not by 'harmonising' them from the top down. Or, staying inside the Chinese cultural realm, someone like a Chiang Ching-kuo, the dictator of Taiwan, who let go of the authoritarian reins in the 1980s, built up democratic institutions, and ultimately relinquished power. He was certainly no Mandela, but 'holy' nonetheless, in recognising that China must break with its autocratic tradition, and that a new era had dawned.

Power to the People

A leader must point the way, but to break with the history of tyranny a 'cultural revolution' is needed. Whether through gentle persuasion (the Confucianist ideal) or through violence (the school of Legalism or Maoism), the essential feature of the Chinese political tradition is to put the resolution of societal contradictions into the hands of a higher authority. The judgement of the autonomous individual, or group of individuals, is not respected – not by Confucius, because the organisation of the state cannot be left to 'little people'; and not in Maoism, because 'the masses' cannot function without direction from the Party. Behind this disdain also hides a deep fear of the disorder that will arise if the 'power of the people' is given free rein. Without the supervision of the Sage King, the people lose their sense of decency and propriety. Chaos then follows, just as nature becomes disrupted without the quiet, regulating influence of Heaven. In modern China, the feeling that nature and society belong to the same realm has for the most part become obscure, but the association of popular power with chaos is still very much alive. For the Chinese leadership, democracy brings two unacceptable visions ever closer: The division of the motherland (a democratically-governed Taiwan will never vote for reunification with China); and the attack by the young on the established order, as happened in the Cultural Revolution (1966–1976) and in the run-up to 4 June 1989 – though the essential difference between these movements was that in the 1960s Mao manipulated the youth to eliminate his political opponents, while 4 June 1989 was a grassroots movement that arose spontaneously.

In the West the point of departure is fundamentally different: Social harmony cannot be imposed top-down; only a government that is elected (and can be overthrown) by the people is in a position to do that. Contemporary challenges to this statement are numerous: From the dysfunctional democracy in America to the indifference of citizens towards the European Parliament; from Thailand's unending military coups to the Egyptian generals ousting their legally-elected Muslim Brotherhood president. On top of that, the experience of the Arab Spring shows that democracy does not last for long without institutions that have matured through experience. Freedom House ('an independent watchdog organization dedicated to the expansion of freedom and democracy around the world') offers the bleak assessment that 'Democracy faced its most serious crisis in decades in 2017'. Yet the number of countries designated in that year as Free stood at 88 – representing 45 percent of the world's 195 polities. The Partly Free countries numbered 58. That means that of all the states in the world, 75% can still be called (Partly) Free. In terms of population 2.7 billion people (37%) are Not Free, the remaining 4.7 billion are (Partly) Free. If China were to become democratic in one way or another, the people who don't live in freedom would be reduced with 1.3 billion – roughly 50% of the present total. An even more hopeful statistic is that since the fall of the Berlin Wall in 1989, the number of countries appointing their leaders via elections has grown from 69 to 116.[27] Not all these elections pass the test of fairness, nor is the requisite respect shown for the minority; but what matters is the generally accepted *norm* that the leader must be elected by the people. The ideal of freedom cannot be eradicated. Immediately after 4 June 1989, Jiang Zemin, then the Party secretary for Shanghai, appeared before a group of students to explain the decision to suppress the 'counter-revolutionary uprising' in Beijing. One of the students stood up during his speech and shouted: 'By what right do you speak here, sir? Who has actually elected you?' The future president of China was allegedly so enraged he could not utter another word.

A New Harmony

The view that Western political thought stands for freedom and Chinese political thought for dictatorship is a generalisation that sells both traditions short. Plato already developed sophisticated ideas about the absolutist state, and these have time and again (albeit in different varieties) been put into practice – from the Roman emperors to Hitler's thousand-year Reich. In China, on the other hand, the desire for political freedom has existed since the dawn of history. Ding Li, the author interviewed in Chapter 6, even contends that in the early years of the Zhou dynasty (1046–256 BCE), the people freely elected their leaders – just as the Celts and the Germanic tribes did in Europe. According to Ding, even Confucius – the great advocate for loyalty to authority – was a covert liberal who, just like the Taoists, glorified the hermit's life in the mountains. 'Freedom is older than dictatorship,' Ding categorically contends.

More verifiable than the primal need for freedom is the liberal activism of the last century – a line that runs from the May 4th Movement in 1919 to the mass demonstrations of 1989, and from early twentieth-century reformers like Kang Youwei and Liang Qichao to Liu Xiaobo, the recipient of the Nobel Peace Prize in 2010. Even the father of the fatherland, Sun Yatsen, argued in his 'Three Principles of the People' for the right of the people to elect their leaders. After the 1912 elections were cut short, however, that experiment was never repeated on the Chinese mainland.

It is clear that Confucianism and Socialism – both of which have planted deep roots in China – are at odds with Western liberalism. That is why Tu Weiming sees China as a 'battlefield' where these three movements are fighting for supremacy – even if he (in typically Chinese fashion) does not rule out a combination of these three contenders: 'Socialism ensures a more just distribution of wealth, capitalism a better-functioning marketplace while Confucianism corresponds with the soul of our country.'[28] Taoism, that most quintessentially Chinese philosophy of all Chinese schools of thought, might be able to act as peacemaker. At first glance its candidacy is not so obvious, because the teaching of Lao Zi orders its followers to forsake worldly matters. Yet there are two salient similarities with Western liberalism: A penchant for individual freedom and the recognition that all political power is temporary in nature. For a Taoist, the Platonic vision of an ideal state that arrests time is as unreal as bringing the stars to a standstill. It is *impossible*. To this notion, Western liberal thought adds that it is also *impermissible*, because human beings are fallible, and power corrupts them sooner or later.

These two similarities may be able to supply the building blocks for a 'democracy with Chinese characteristics': A political form that respects the ancient, never-extinguished need for freedom, but which also raises liberalism to a higher plane by adding the values that Tu Weiming argues for: Meritocratic governance, fraternity and due care for the planet. The ideas of Jiang Qing and Daniel Bell offer guidelines for the institutional framework: A hybrid national government, whose leaders are partly elected by the people and partly selected for their qualities (intelligence and virtue) and their capacity to convey Chinese culture. In this way a truly harmonious society can emerge.

The shockwaves of such a philosophical and political U-turn in China would also be internationally palpable. The country would then react less defensively to theories it perceives to be offensive, such as the irreversible final victory of political liberalism; and the West would not have to fear the return of the physical *Tianxia*, with Beijing as the political centre of the world. The result might look like the world that Henry Kissinger sketches in his book *World Order*: A morally neutral order in which no nation imposes its values on another, and international issues – based on a well-proportioned balance of power – are tackled pragmatically.[29]

An order, in other words, similar to the one created by Metternich, the Austrian statesman who at the Congress of Vienna in 1815 put a structure into place that kept the major European powers in balance for a century.* Will it be sufficient for resolving the pressing problems of climate change, overpopulation, epidemics, and the overall depletion of the planet? That is highly doubtful, unfortunately. Sovereign states are always navigating between national and international interests. That is why radical thinkers like the philosopher Zhao Tingyang view the establishment of a 'world government' as the only solution. The history of the League of Nations and United Nations, however, shows that the gap between that lofty ideal and existing realities cannot – for the time being – be easily bridged.

How can this dilemma be resolved? Twentieth-century attempts to establish an ideal state have caused unspeakable suffering – Russia under Stalin and China under

---

* Kissinger's doctoral dissertation, written in the early 1950's, was titled 'Peace, Legitimacy, and the Equilibrium (A Study of the Statesmanship of Castlereagh and Metternich).'

Mao are the most glaring examples – yet that does not mean that the desire for a *better* world has to be given up, for dreams are the engine of progress – materially, but certainly also spiritually. There is never an end to this journey, for history knows no end – a notion that the Chinese have always embraced more spontaneously than we Westerners. It moves through time like the circles from a stone thrown into the water: Every circle is a continuation of, but never the same as, the one before. Thinkers like Tu Weiming also have this image in mind when they talk about the *junzi*, the noble men or women who are continually taking themselves to new heights while drawing on global sources of wisdom. The prospect that the Chinese leadership will chart such a new, inclusive course is unlikely, to put it mildly – after all, the country's inequality and social tensions are a direct result of the Party's policies, and the hundred major families presently in power have too much to lose.

Nevertheless, if there is anything that characterises the Chinese spirit it is the insight that nothing is eternal, and that humanity can play a crucial role in that process of change. The old man Yu Gong started digging up the mountain in front of his house because it hindered his view. His neighbours wondered what was wrong with him, as death was approaching. 'After my death, my sons will take over this work. When they die, then their sons will in turn take it over. And when they die ...' That is the Chinese soul to the core. A human being is nothing more than a link in an endless chain of generations. If human life is thus made 'eternal' and the harvest of each individual effort will someday be reaped, then nothing is impossible. Not even the realisation of a World of Great Harmony, where the world will belong to all, sincere people of talent and ability are chosen, and harmony cultivated. A China that goes down that path will regain its soul. The soft power of such a nation would be irresistible.

CHAPTER 12

The World of the Great Harmony

> *The people of all countries should join hands and
> strive to build a harmonious world of lasting
> peace and common prosperity.*

Hu Jintao

As China's great reformer Kang Youwei already knew, realising the Great Harmony is going to take centuries. The Party posits that the Lesser Prosperity is around the corner, but that is a domestic objective. Abroad, it is pursuing a 'harmonious world order', though what Beijing has brought about seems rather like the 'Great Disharmony' – certainly in East Asia. Would a politically-reformed China conduct its affairs differently? It probably would, for a democratically-elected government must direct its energies toward issues like housing, healthcare and employment – otherwise it will not be re-elected. Nationalism causes, in the words of the 'Tibetan' Xuan Zang (interviewed in Chapter 6), a 'briefly burning passion', but in the long term its base is too narrow to provide an elected government with any legitimacy. This general observation, though, does not do justice to the complexity characterising the foreign policy of every major power. The United States is a democratic country, but in the twentieth and twenty-first centuries it has waged many wars sanctioned by Congress. Democracy does also not necessarily lead to an openminded attitude towards the world. The short-sighted policy of 'America First' testifies to that. Trump's turning away from the world is, however, not a unique phenomenon in American history. The pitching back and forth between isolationism and involvement defines every major power.

A democratic China will still fight to defend its 'core interests', just as today's regime does not engage in power politics alone. It also conducts an active soft-power policy, provides concessional loans to developing countries on a large scale and supplies soldiers for UN peacekeeping missions. But despite these necessary nuances, an authoritarian China is more inclined to pursue military adventure than a reformed China will. The logic of nationalism as a new source of legitimacy requires it to do so. The psychological impetus for this expansion of power – the yearning for reputation and respect – weighs heavier on a regime that is unsure of its domestic legitimacy than for a democratically-elected government; and certainly, when that same regime regularly plays the humiliation card for past ills inflicted on China. I expect that with the continuation of the current political system, five foreign policy priorities will get even more attention than they are being given now.

Transforming the South China Sea into a Chinese inland sea
Since 2010, when Beijing elevated its claim on this maritime region to a core interest bearing equal weight to its claims on Taiwan and Tibet, tensions and military skirmishes have increased considerably. The July 2016 rejection by the Permanent Court of Arbitration of Beijing's maritime claims in the South China Sea has only intensified 'China's resolve to safeguard territorial sovereignty'[1] (as Premier Li Keqiang put it in November 2014). This 'stick' of the hard-line approach to the islands' reclamation and militarisation is – as is often the case with China's foreign policy – accompanied by a 'carrot': In June 2015, Beijing announced that the newly-constructed islands would be used in setting up works for the 'public good', such as the construction of lighthouses to aid international shipping.[2] The facts point to another development: At the beginning of 2017 – in spite of the personal pledge Xi Jinping made to President Obama in 2015 not to militarise the islands – seven reefs in the Spratly Archipelago alone had been converted to military bases equipped with radar installations, hangars for aeroplanes and underground munitions depots.[3] According to a July 2017 article in *Study Times* (the paper for the Party academy), Xi Jinping was personally involved in the decisions concerning 'building of islands and consolidating the reefs'.[4] Beijing's policy in this region will therefore not change as long as Xi remains in power – that is to say, indefinitely, after the term limit of his presidential rule was scrapped by the National People's Congress in March 2018.

The deeper reason for this policy of island-grabbing is strategic: Apart from the recently-established base in Djibouti, China has no military bases overseas, and only one operational aircraft carrier. By constructing landing strips and military harbours in the South China Sea, Beijing is in a better position to protect the soft underbelly of its southern shores by keeping the United States farther away from the Chinese mainland.

Waging a permanent Cold War with Japan
The island nation is the perfect target for Chinese nationalism. Three official days have been created to keep the memory of the war with Japan alive: 3 September, Victory Day in the Chinese People's War of Resistance against Japanese Aggression; 18 September, commemorating the Mukden Incident staged by Tokyo as an excuse for the Japanese occupation of Manchuria; and 13 December, in memory of the Nanjing Massacre. Then there is Martyrs' Day on 30 September. Because many of these Communist heroes were killed while fighting Japan, one could say that Tokyo is tied to the whipping-post four times every year. In his annual report to the National People's Congress in 2014, Chairman Zhang Dejiang explained that these days were created for 'pooling

the will and strength of the people of all of our ethnic groups, realizing the Chinese Dream of the great rejuvenation of the Chinese nation, and promoting the lofty cause of human peace and development'.[5] The realisation of the Chinese Dream thus goes hand in hand with inflaming negative feelings about Japan. The persistent, personal demonization of Japan's prime minister Abe is also part of this strategy. These campaigns will never end until Japan carries out a modern form of the kowtow ritual by acknowledging China as the superior nation in East Asia.

Compelling the United States to recognise that China is the dominant power in East Asia
Amongst the Chinese people, feelings for America are much more positive than those for Japan. However, the country's elite shares the firm belief that Washington is pursuing two strategic goals: Frustrating Beijing's legitimate rise as a major power, and undermining China's political system. President Obama regularly repeated that he welcomed the rise of a strong and prosperous China, yet almost no one from the Chinese intelligentsia takes him at his word. 'The United States' "pivot to Asia" strategy... has proved to be an American fantasy to maintain hegemony,' wrote Ruan Zongze, vice-president of the China Institute of International Studies, in November 2014.[6] The same writer expresses the oft-heard opinion that the Pivot is the *cause* of China's problems with countries like Japan and the Philippines: 'By hiking its defence budget to strengthen its alliance with countries such as Japan and the Philippines, which have contributed to the US-led policy to contain China, Washington has brought nothing but rivalry to the region.'[7] The conclusion that these countries are cosying up closer to Washington as a *result* of China's assertiveness is not reached.

For several years now, Chinese politicians have been insisting that Washington accepts 'a new kind of relationship between major powers' – diplomatic language for America acknowledging that both countries stand on an equal footing, and that China receives the strategic space in East Asia it has been yearning for. For now, the Trump administration has declined this request. In spite of the president's isolationist streak, the 'Freedom of Navigation Operations' in the South China Sea have continued, and US defence minister Mattis has re-affirmed the security agreement with Japan.

Creating an international order of its own
China's return to the global stage runs parallel with its entry into all kinds of organisations and treaties. In 2001, joining the World Trade Organisation anchored the country in the international economic system. Yet being anchored is not the same thing as acceptance: Despite the evident benefits these and other organisations brought China, Beijing has never converted to the idea that supranational order could, let alone *should* prevail over national order – certainly not where organisations created by the Bretton Woods Conference are involved, like the World Bank and the IMF.

In his book *China Goes Global: The Partial Power*, David Shambaugh distinguishes four historical phases that characterise Beijing's stance vis-à-vis the international order: Challenging the system; studying the system; exploiting the system, and maintaining a system of its own.[8] In the meantime, this last phase has arrived. The November 2014 meeting of APEC (the Asia-Pacific Economic Cooperation), a regional consultative body of twenty-two countries, sounded the clarion call for the Chinese world order. Beijing announced a large-scale initiative for connecting the APEC countries – an area that accounts for 44 percent of world trade, and more than half of global GNP – via a free trade zone.[9] With this initiative, Beijing killed two birds with one stone: It threw sand into the gears of the Trans-Pacific Partnership – the American initiative pursuing the same goal (albeit based on Western values like good governance, care for the environment, and less state support for business) – and it established China as a major, benevolent nation pursuing a greater good than its own self-interest.

The simultaneous launch of the Asian Infrastructure and Investment Bank (with Beijing as its biggest provider of capital) as well as the initiative for breathing new life into the old Silk Roads, both by land and sea, are the same sort of gestures of unselfish benevolence – a twenty-first-century variation on the fifteenth-century expeditions of admiral Zheng He, who made it clear to overseas barbarians that the well-being of the region depended on the blessings of the emperor.

Tump's election as president presented Beijing with a gift in two ways. The decision of the new American leader to withdraw from the Trans-Pacific Partnership put an end to the economic encirclement by the US and its allies (as Chinese geopolitical thinkers saw it). Launched by President Obama, the TPP's role was to create a free trade zone for Pacific Rim countries. But because of the plan's liberal nature, China did not want to sign up to it. For this 'victory', Beijing did not have to fire a shot: Seemingly ignorant of its geopolitical effect, the new administration incredulously shot itself in the foot.

A second consequence of Trump's 'America First' agenda is that the Chinese can pitch themselves as the champions, if not the saviours, of the international trade order. Deploying the bombastic style that he often uses, Xi Jinping said at the World Economic Forum in January 2017: 'To grow its economy, China must have the courage to swim in the vast ocean of the global market. If one is always afraid of bracing the storm and exploring the new world, he will sooner or later get drowned in the ocean. Therefore, China took a brave step to embrace the global market'. Adding even more drama, he also noted that 'Protectionism is like locking oneself in a dark room. No one would emerge a winner in a trade war.'[10] Klaus Schwab, the chair of the World Economic Forum, was euphoric in his praise for Xi's speech: 'Your commitment, Mr President, to the innovative, open and inclusive world is crucial.' Many other listeners chimed in with their support. Xi was seen as the saviour of globalisation.[11]

Unfortunately, the listeners heard what they chose to hear. Almost nowhere in his speech did the president use the word 'globalisation' without the adjective 'economic'. As Yongjin Zhang, professor of international politics at the University of Bristol, astutely observed: 'China may attempt to defend that part of globalisation that China has benefited from, free trade for example, but it is not committed to globalisation as a liberal project for constructing the future world.'[12] Globalisation with Chinese characteristics means that the free flow of goods and services is embraced, but not the flow of ideas.

Conducting an active soft-power policy

This term, coined by the American professor Joseph Nye, means that the power of a state cannot just rely on hard power; the country's culture must also be attractive. This notion appeals to policymakers in Beijing, because as far back as five hundred years before our common era, Confucius saw the seduction of foreigners as significant: 'The duke of She asked about government. The Master said, "Good government obtains, when those who are near are made happy, and those who are far off are attracted"'.[13] In 2007, the former president Hu Jintao provided a modern translation of this conversation: 'We will further publicize the fine traditions of Chinese culture and [...] also strengthen international cultural exchanges to draw on the fine achievements of foreign cultures and enhance the influence of Chinese culture worldwide.'[14]

Since that time, Beijing has invested enormous amounts in improving its image. The most telling examples are setting up CCTV-9 (modelled after America's CNN) and the Confucius Institutes abroad (in 2017, there were at least five hundred of these). The goal is to spread China's language and culture and, in doing so, promote international friendship and cooperation – this according to the website of the Hanban, the Beijing organisation directing the Confucius Institutes. The unspoken goal is promoting China as an attractive colossus that constitutes no threat to other countries.

Unfortunately for Beijing, these investments are delivering only meagre returns – at least in the United States, the country the Party sees as its major rival and thus as a special target for its soft-power weaponry. In 2017, 65 percent of Americans saw China as a 'serious problem' or even as an 'opponent'.[15] In public opinion in Japan, China has gone into a freefall: In 2016, only 11 percent still had a favourable opinion of their big neighbour (it was 34 percent in 2011), although this low point has everything to do with the dispute over the Senkaku Islands in the summer of 2012.[16] Professor Yan Xuetong, the dean of the Institute of International Relations at Tsinghua University, blames China's 'ridiculous credibility' on its friendly relations with countries like North Korea, Iran, Myanmar, Sudan, Zimbabwe and Venezuela. 'We have a big [image] problem!'[17] Shambaugh draws a sharper conclusion as to why Beijing's soft-power policy is failing: 'The question is not: What is *unique* about China, but what is *universal* about China? This is the essence of soft power: To possess national attributes that transcend one's own country and appeal to others. Here, China seems to have few answers other than "peace and harmony."'[18]

The Way of Democracy

The chances that China will embrace a parliamentary democracy based on a Western model seem small. The age-old concept of the subordination of subject to monarch has made it difficult for Western ideas about the freedom of the individual and the plurality of society to take root. Nevertheless, at the beginning of the twentieth century the establishment of democracy had a reasonable chance of succeeding – witness the third ('power to the people') of Sun Yatsen's 'Three Principles', as well as the free, national elections of 1912. But through the domestic chaos wrought by the warlords, and Japan's aggression, the totalitarian-minded Communist Party managed to seize power, and the democratic experiment was nipped in the bud. The reason, therefore, that China has not become a democratic state is not only caused by the cultural acceptance of the innate difference between humans; the historical evolution over the last hundred years has also contributed a lot to the present political system.

Even so it is meaningful, if only for the sake of an intellectual exercise, to map out the foreign policy of a democratic China: It throws light on the contrast with current policies, and offers elements of a foreign policy of the third way. A democratically-elected government would have to deliver a clean environment, sustainable growth, and a fair distribution of wealth. That is what brings re-election closer, not playing up to any nationalistic agenda. A less nationalistic policy also ensures lower defence expenditure, and reduces the risk of foreign trade and investment channels being blocked, or crucial technology no longer being transferred because of international tensions. In this case, the government would no longer have to invest in an enormous defence apparatus that is supposed to rival the United States within the foreseeable future.

This 'responsible stakeholder' (in the words of the former World Bank president Robert Zoellick) is the partner the West has dreamt about. A partner, moreover, who is no longer obsessed with reputation and a yearning for respect. As Fukuyama writes, 'Liberal democracy replaces the irrational desire to be recognized as greater than others with the rational desire to be recognized as equal. A world made up of liberal democracies, then, should have much less incentive for war, since all nations would reciprocally recognize one another's legitimacy.'[19] The chance of any armed collision with the West will then decline considerably. From a democratic China we could expect the following initiatives.

Ending territorial disputes as soon as possible
Beijing's aggression has stirred up bad blood with most of its neighbouring countries. On the other hand, economic relations with those same countries are close: China is the most important trade partner for the ASEAN countries, and invests on a large scale in the development of their infrastructure. The establishment of the Asian Infrastructure and Investment Bank, with its headquarters in Beijing, will continue to deepen their economic entanglement. Nevertheless, nobody will want to be too dependent on a country that has traditionally dominated the region, and is now regaining its power. Myanmar's opening-up to the West in 2011, for instance, is widely explained as the result of the country's semi-vassal status, which gave Chinese state-owned companies free rein in plundering its natural resources. That is why, during that same year, President Thein Sein suspended the construction of a hydroelectric power station financed by Beijing, and expected to deliver 90 percent of its electricity to China.[20] A Chinese national government not held hostage by nationalistic sentiments will be more willing to make substantial concessions to resolve the territorial disputes in the South China Sea. The dispute with Japan over the Senkaku Islands will be more difficult to resolve (even for a democratic China) for as long as Japanese dignitaries continue to pay visits to the Yasukuni Shrine. Should this custom that deeply offends China be given up, however, space for substantial rapprochement would likely emerge. The proposal launched by Deng Xiaoping decades ago for deferring this dispute by jointly developing undersea energy sources could then be taken off the shelf again. In general, a democratic China will no longer follow a '*yin* and *yang*' approach to sovereignty: Interfering *in* China is strictly forbidden, while interfering *by* China in other countries is permitted if there are 'historical claims'. The positive effect that such a policy change would have on the structural tensions between China and its neighbours would be immeasurable.

Concluding security agreements with neighbouring countries and the United States
The number of incidents between the Chinese military and that of the United States, Japan, the Philippines, India, and Vietnam has increased dramatically in recent years. In August 2014, a Chinese jet fighter flew so close to an American reconnaissance craft that a collision was only just prevented.[21] Incidents of this kind have also recently occurred with Japan in the East China Sea, and New Delhi complains that Chinese troops regularly penetrate Indian territory.[22] Should a crisis break out, Beijing has no hotline with any of these countries, and there are no clear channels of communication. In such cases, minor incidents can quickly escalate – all the more so since Beijing cannot afford to be seen as 'cowardly' in the eyes of its own people.

In November 2014, China and the United States concluded an agreement on improving military communications,[23] though the question remains as to whether the deep mistrust between the parties has not already undermined these arrangements before they can be implemented. Pete Pedrozo, former legal advisor to the American navy, argues that Beijing consistently and wilfully violated an earlier agreement in that domain – the US-PRC Military Maritime Consultative Agreement. He sees the radically-different concepts regarding the rights of states within the 200-hundred-mile Exclusive Economic Zone (EEZ) as the most important reason for that violation. Beijing views any presence of an American navy vessel within the Chinese EEZ as a threat to China's security; the Americans see the EEZ as international waters, where the coastal state has only limited, economic sovereignty.[24] Concluding these sorts of agreements with Beijing therefore makes no sense whatsoever – according to Pedrozo. Concluding agreements with a democratic China that does not foster 'the irrational desire to be recognized as greater than others' would probably have a different effect, because that vital ingredient that sustains any agreement would prevail: Good faith.

Participating constructively in the resolution of international problems
A China whose values converge with those of the West will be more willing to develop and improve today's international order. This would also be in Beijing's own interest. In the globalising world, problems like climate change, terrorism, and nuclear arms proliferation are of a cross-border nature. The environment of Tibet is a good example of this transnational condition. As a result of climate change, the glaciers of the Land of Snows are melting at an alarming speed. This means that the Yangzi and the Yellow River in China, the Indus in Pakistan, the Ganges and Brahmaputra in India, and the Mekong in Indochina are at risk of drying up, endangering the lives of more than two billion people. Activity that accelerates this process – such as the construction of hydroelectric power stations and the diversion of rivers – is currently carried out by China without consulting its neighbours. And given the sensitive situation in Tibet, Beijing rules out each and every proposal for international collaboration to rescue the situation. A democratic China will have – in accordance with the expectations of the Nobel Peace Prize recipient Liu Xiaobo – a different, more federal relationship with its minorities, and will respond less fitfully to international relations between the (now genuinely) autonomous regions and foreign countries.

A new relationship with the United States
Xi Jinping has on many occasions spoken about a 'new kind of relations between the two major powers', yet in reality, the relationship is characterised by suspicion and quickly-inflamed frustrations. Perhaps this is how it has to be – relations between an existing and a developing power are rarely harmonious – but the essential difference between the American and Chinese political systems makes a 'meeting of the minds' virtually inconceivable. A democratic China will not agree with the United States on every point, yet will also not see a conspiracy to halt China's rise behind every American initiative.

A joint approach by the two superpowers, based on trust, can solve problems too large to resolve for multilateral organisations, with their sluggishness and lack of effectiveness. A good example is fighting terrorism. There are more than ten million Uighurs living in Xinjiang province, some of whom have been radicalized by the oppression of their culture and religion, and are carrying out terrorist attacks with increasing frequency. Hundreds of deaths occurred during various attacks in 2014; the most shocking of these was at the train station in Kunming in Yunnan province, where a few Uighurs stabbed to death more than twenty Chinese.[25] A democratic China would be more willing to grant genuine self-governance to its provinces, and the free practice of Islam. Still, the question remains as to whether all terrorism would be driven out as a result: One of the essential characteristics of Muslim fundamentalism is that it does not care about the borders of sovereign states. The USA, still the dominant power in the Middle East, and China, the up-and-coming power in Central Asia, could be much more effective in fighting international terrorism if they trusted each other; at present, Beijing blames Washington for providing cover for Uighur 'terrorists' (a word defined by the Chinese as anyone pleading for substantial autonomy) who have fled abroad. This is just one example. A different kind of relationship between the two major powers would certainly diminish the chance of *Hu xiang dou, bi you yi shang* ('When tigers fight, one is wounded for sure').

The Third Way

The China of the third way will chart a course that keeps to the middle ground, somewhere between the black-and-white initiatives outlined above. The voice of the people will carry more weight – leading to more international cooperation and less agitated nationalism – though the new government will also draw inspiration from China's traditional global position, the world order of the *Tianxia*. In the twenty-first century, there will be no caravans carrying gifts along the Silk Road to Beijing, nor will barbarian princes prostrate themselves in the dust before the emperor: But China will still expect their neighbouring countries to align their policies with the core interests of the Celestial Empire. If not, appropriate economic – and, if necessary, military – measures will be taken to restore the natural order. In any scenario, the biggest challenge will be taking the right approach to relations with the United States, for, as Thucydides – the Ancient Greek historian writing about the war between Athens and Sparta in the fifth century BCE – determined long ago, the collision between an existing and an up-and-coming power is inevitable. Twenty-five centuries later, Bruce Jones of the Brookings Institute has repeated the same sentiment in so many words: 'China is simply too big to rise without causing some concern from its neighbours about its intentions. Major powers create distrust simply by being powerful.'[26]

More unsettling is the comparison with the First World War, when the major powers were sucked into a conflict that no one wanted – certainly not on such a large and annihilating scale. The major European powers were connected by the same civilisation, and the royal houses even by family, but the assassination of the Austrian archduke Franz Ferdinand unleashed an insane slaughter that sent millions of young men to their deaths. It is frightening that the largest and second-largest economies in the world, both armed to the teeth, are provoking and spying on each other in the air and at sea – without the cultural connection (let alone a common language) to understand one another's signals. And to make matters worse: Where one party is convinced that the other is out to force a regime change.

An Inevitable Collision?
Thucydides is seen as the first exponent of realism in international relations: The school that teaches that the foreign policy of states is driven purely by self-preservation and the expansion of power. In the mechanistic world view of the realists, states react like billiard balls; sooner or later, they *have* to collide. The liberals, counterweights to the realists, believe that international actors (not only states, but companies, international organisations, and individuals) are also motivated by higher values, such as eliminating poverty and spreading freedom. These instincts lead to understanding and international solidarity: Democratic states therefore rarely, if ever, wage war upon one another. In the liberal ideal, international order ultimately corresponds to domestic democracy: A system in which the majority decides, the minority is respected, and differences are never resolved by force.

Beijing talks a lot about the desirability of a 'democracy amongst states', but what this suggests is an alliance of states behaving in accordance with the core principle of the Bandung Conference: There should be no interference in one another's affairs. How will the China of the third way conduct itself? The emperor harboured the pretence of sovereignty over the Tianxia, yet did not impose his value system on the barbarians – they would be attracted to the light of civilisation of their own accord. This view differs significantly from that of Western imperialism, which imposed its values and norms actively, and frequently by force, upon the conquered peoples. In imperial China, *wen* (civilisation) usually won out over *wu* (weapons), even if Zheng He's expeditions and Qian Long's genocide in Central Asia show that classical China certainly did not shy away from violence and the expansion of power.

These conflicting instincts will also shape the foreign policy of the third way. *Realpolitik* will be tempered by a soft policy of persuasion, the search for practical solutions and the alleviation of suffering – policies which are becoming to China's status as a great and benevolent country. Still, this Confucianist compassion is founded on the foregone assumption that the country (or, rather, the centre of civilisation) is of a higher order. The French Revolution's principle of equality never took root in

China. Hierarchy is part of the human condition: the *pater familias* is superior to his family members, the emperor rules over his subjects, the Middle Kingdom is elevated above other nations on earth. The country's increasingly strong economy and military forces are tools for intensifying the power of the nation-state of China. On a deeper, cultural/philosophical level, though, they serve the restoration of the natural order of the *Tianxia*.

The United States also has a dichotomy between realism and idealism, albeit of a different nature. The American collective consciousness is firmly anchored in the values of the Enlightenment: Every individual is the same as the other ('all men are created equal') and is free to shape his own life ('the pursuit of happiness'). The reality that the country is powerful entails advancing its own interests, but American hard power is tempered by the ideal that the international order should reflect the domestic order: States are equal, and determine their destiny in sovereign freedom. The essential unfamiliarity with (or rather lack of understanding of) each other's political and cultural traditions constitutes the greatest risk for a collision between the two major powers, for despite the countless discussions Sino-American talks still recall the meeting between Qian Long and George Macartney in 1793: Words, translated through interpreters, are exchanged in the same space, but there is no understanding of one another's motives. Fortunately, there is a ray of hope. In his book *Destined for War: Can America and China Escape Thucydides' Trap?* the Harvard University professor of government Graham Allison investigates sixteen conflicts between developing and existing powers.[27] Fourteen ended in war, but the last two (the Cold War between the United States and the Soviet Union, and the reunification of Germany) were resolved peacefully. Both conflicts took place during the nuclear era. The likelihood of mass annihilation urges caution for even a country with enormous military superiority: That is why the US defence minister Mattis says that the resolution of his country's conflict with North Korea cannot be resolved by military means, because that country possesses a modest nuclear arsenal. For that same reason, the chance of war between the USA and China seems unthinkable on rational grounds – an observation that unfortunately does not preclude a minor conflict (such as a dispute in the South China Sea) escalating into a bigger one, because neither party can afford to be seen as weak. Specifically, China, which has proclaimed China's sovereignty of the South China Sea as a 'core interest' to be defended at all cost.

Core Interests
Where are the limits to Beijing's desire to re-occupy its former place in history? Where are the 'core interests' of this new China? First of all, the regions that had subjected themselves to the emperor and brought him tribute: North-East Asia, Central Asia, and South-East Asia. The areas, in other words, indicated as Chinese territory on the 'Maps of National Shame' that were first discussed in Chapter 1.

These aspirations are hardest to realise in the first region, North-East Asia. South Korea and Japan are militarily and economically strong states who work closely with the United States on defence issues. On top of this, Japan has never considered itself a vassal state of China. On the contrary: In 1879 it annexed the Ryukyu Kingdom, which had previously brought tributes to the Chinese emperor. Japan and Korea are becoming increasingly entangled with their big neighbour, but as exporters of capital goods and technology they are less dependent on Beijing than the countries in Central and South-East Asia who export natural resources. Moreover, China's aggression is accelerating Japan's quest for a new identity: It wants to be seen as a 'normal' country that can defend itself militarily without being constantly reminded of the Second World War. The chances that Tokyo will leave the direction of East Asian policy to Beijing are therefore nil; the situation with South Korea, though, is different. It is a smaller nation, and the shared wartime suffering connects it to China. Indeed, with its annexation by Tokyo in 1910, Korea has suffered Japanese aggression for much longer. On the other hand, Koreans are arguably even more nationalistic than the Japanese. In 2004, the website of the Chinese Ministry of Foreign Affairs announced that the Koguryo Kingdom – which at the beginning of our calendar era ruled Korea and parts of what are now North-East China – had actually belonged to China. Enraged protests took place in Seoul, with some Korean parliamentarians even proposing to unite with the Vietnamese, Tibetans, and Mongolians against 'Sinocentrism'.[28]

Chinese expansion in Central Asia meets less resistance than in North East Asia. The states there are weaker, and are not protected to the same extent as Japan and Korea by American armed forces. That is why they are being drawn ever closer into the Chinese orbit – especially via joint infrastructure and energy projects. With Chinese financial and technological support Kazakhstan and Turkmenistan are developing their oil and natural gas fields, with a considerable portion of these energy sources flowing in the direction of Beijing and Shanghai. Energy is also the most important reason for setting up the Shanghai Cooperation Organisation, a club of countries comprising China, Russia, Kazakhstan, Tajikistan, Uzbekistan, Kyrgyzstan, Pakistan and India (the latter two since June 2017). The name of the body already indicates who is in control: There is a very good reason that the headquarters are in Shanghai. The SCO also has another goal: Fighting the 'three evils of terrorism, extremism, and separatism' – excesses that, in the Chinese view, the minorities in Xinjiang province are particularly guilty of in their struggle for genuine autonomy. The SCO is a useful vehicle for cutting off cross-border contacts among the Uighurs, Kyrgyz, Tajiks and Kazakhs – which is why, for some observers, the acronym is better rendered as 'Suppression, China, and Oil'. The only state in Central Asia that can still offer any counterweight to Beijing is Russia: But with the ever-greater difference in economic power, and Moscow's confrontational politics with the West, Putin has few cards to play to counter China's increasing dominance.[29]

South-East Asia is even more interesting to Beijing. It is a supplier of oil and natural gas (Malaysia and Indonesia), natural resources (nearly all ASEAN countries) and capital and technology (Singapore). On top of that, the South China Sea is rich in fishery stocks – though these have been seriously depleted because of overfishing – as well as large, potentially-extractable energy reserves. However, as is evident from Beijing's reaction to the July 2016 Court of Arbitration verdict on the South China Sea, China's claims to that maritime region are primarily driven by historical entitlement and a sense of aggrievement that many foreigners should challenge that position.

China's control of the South China Sea would, in effect, be the fulfilment of a policy that the eminent statesman Wei Yuan had already advocated in the mid-nineteenth century. In his book *Haiguo Tuzhi* (*Illustrated Treatise on the Maritime Kingdoms* [1843]), Wei blames the success of Western imperialism (Britain had just won the Opium War) on the Qing dynasty's disregard for the region known as the *Nanyang* (the 'Southern Ocean'): The South China Sea, but also present-day Indo-China and the archipelago states of Indonesia and the Philippines. As a continental power, the Qing had successfully brought Central Asia under Chinese influence but, according to Wei Yuan's analysis, this had come at the expense of Beijing's position in the *Nanyang*. The glory days of the Ming dynasty at the beginning of the fifteenth century, when the treasure fleets of Zheng He ruled the South China Sea and the Indian Ocean, must be restored (said Wei Yuan) by rebuilding a powerful fleet and placating the southern barbarians with economic advantages by giving them access to the Chinese market.[30] One hundred seventy-five years later, Beijing is in a position to follow up on Wei Yuan's recommendations. The South China Sea is again in Chinese hands, and a powerful fleet is being built at a feverish pace. The *yang* of this hard power is balanced by the *yin* of an initiative designed to convince all the barbarians of Eurasia and Africa of the beneficial influence of the new emperors: To bring back to life the Silk Roads that connected China with the rest of the world since the beginning of our calendar era.

One Belt, One Road

Economic historians – including Joseph Needham, mentioned in Chapter 1 – have demonstrated convincingly that for centuries, the Middle Kingdom was far and away the largest economy in the world. Even in 1820, when the decline of the Qing (the last imperial dynasty) had already set in, the Chinese economy accounted for thirty percent of the global figure.[31] In 2016, it was fifteen percent. Today's leaders are wholly committed to surpassing the United States in financial terms, and turning China into the economic superpower it once was. Three mutually-reinforcing reasons underlie

Map of the new silk roads

that resolve. These are the yearning for the respect that the number one position brings; the legitimacy that it bestows on the Communist Party to rule China; and the capability possessed by an economic superpower for aligning other states with its foreign policy objectives. Deeply embedded in the DNA of the Chinese leaders (and certainly the current generation) is the need to do 'great things', to make enthralling gestures that fill the barbarians with awe, convincing them of the omnipotence and far-reaching vision of the Chinese emperor.

In the economic domain, this ambition is manifested through two initiatives now familiar worldwide. Established in 2015, the Asian Infrastructure Investment Bank (AIIB) – which, in attracting the engagement of many Western countries, became the triumphant symbol of a new world order dominated by Beijing – will finance harbours, airports, and railways with a start-up capital of fifty billion US dollars.

The second initiative of 'One Belt, One Road', launched in 2013, is an even more engaging symbol for the policy of the third way and the revival of the *Tianxia*. 'The Silk Road Economic Belt and the twenty-first-century Maritime Silk Road' – abbreviated as 'One Belt One Road' (OBOR) – aims for an economic revival of the ages-old Silk Road, both by land and sea. What it exactly entails, no one knows: There is no institutional framework, nor any one organisation in charge within the Chinese political system. Nevertheless, it has unleashed an enormous amount of energy in the Chinese business world: Every exporter or overseas investor wishing to realise a project calls it an 'OBOR project', thus increasing its prospects for financing from a Chinese bank or the AIIB. In principle, non-Chinese companies may also compete for OBOR projects, but given the competitive strength of Chinese construction and engineering businesses, the chances of foreign companies participating are small.*

Official declarations never tire of emphasising that the AIIB and the Silk Road initiative are only intended to promote economic integration that will benefit all countries in the region. But the statements of prominent intellectuals cast another light on the matter. Not beating about the bush, Professor Zhang Xizheng of Peking University says that this economic offensive is a move made in the geopolitical conflict with the United States. According to Zhang, deepening regional integration, with China as the centre, creates a level of interdependence that makes it easier for Beijing to push back the influence of the United States in Asia and the Pacific.[33]

The explanation of Jin Yongming from the Shanghai Academy of Social Sciences places the 'One Belt, One Road' initiative in a historical context that leaves little room for misunderstanding: 'Given that the ancient Silk Road passed into history with the gradual decline of the Chinese empire and the rise of Western countries, [...] implementation of the "road" initiative is expected to help restore the lost glory of Chinese civilization.'[34]

The clearest prospect was outlined at a conference in Brussels in April 2015, where the aforementioned Wang Yiwei, professor of International Relations at Renmin University, was the invited speaker. With an almost ecstatic intensity he reeled off the glories of the new Silk Roads in an hour-long account. First, they accelerate trade: Currently, a container ship takes thirty-five days to sail to Rotterdam from Shanghai; in the future, the time by rail from Chongqing (in western China) to Rotterdam will be just sixteen days. Eurasia will become the new centre of world trade, with the forgotten inland countries of Asia receiving an enormous boost through their role as depots between Europe and China. Yet the outer regions will also profit, for 'One Belt, One Road' is in fact many roads branching out towards Russia, South-East Asia, the Pacific and East Africa. Economic integration brings with it political benefits as well: As the core poles of the new centre of the world, Europe and China will have an ever-greater interest in working together. Europe will profit the most: Greater Eurasian interdependence will bring more 'balance' into its relationship with the United States, and Beijing can also help to reconcile Europe with Russia.

After Wang's account, the primarily Western listeners raised a few critical comments. Would these new Silk Roads, particularly the overland routes, also not serve to fight Islamic terrorism in Central Asia? Was the economic development of Western China not primarily intended to anchor the rebel province of Xinjiang more firmly in the Chinese state? Were the larger neighbouring countries like India and

---

* According to a report, published in January 2018 by the Washington based Center for Strategic and International Studies, 89% of the contractors working on OBOR infrastructure projects in 34 countries in Europe and Asia were Chinese.[32]

Russia not worried about being excluded? As is often the case after a Chinese speaker's address, no debate ensued. Packed tightly into his Mao uniform, Wang Yiwei looked at the audience complacently, ignoring the questions raised. Dialogue is a typically Western phenomenon; it is not appropriate for barbarians to doubt the truth of the 'edict'. As an encore, however, Wang cited one more ancient Chinese proverb: 'He who dreams big, always achieves something. The little dreamer achieves nothing.'

Back on the train to Amsterdam, I looked out at the quiet fields of our old continent. Suddenly, I saw the contours of the new world order sharply before me. The new 'central state' (*Zhongguo*, the name for China) will not only comprise China, Central and South-East Asia but the entire Eurasian continent, where more than 60 percent of the world's population live – a brave new world filled with high-speed railways, megacities and shipping hubs. For the United States and Japan – the two countries that have resisted the rise of China most intensely – it is a matter of adapt or die: If they do not participate in the new world order, they will be reduced to states on the periphery. Given the 'pull' of the supercontinent, Africa and South America – in their role as suppliers of natural resources already dependent on China – will become even more firmly entrenched as economic vassals. What will the position of China be within Eurasia itself? Through the softness of its persuasion, the benevolence of its behaviour but, above all, the irresistible strength of its economy, China's leading role is assured. Slowly, borders will disappear: But what remains will not be some half-baked European Union whose semi-sovereign members squabble with one another like cats and dogs but, rather, a totally new order in which Beijing, as the hegemon of civilisation, ensures peace and harmony. All peoples will be autonomous, but will also recognise that their singularity may not come at the expense of the cosmic order, of which the Chinese emperor is the representative on earth. Only he can realise the Great Harmony. Only he can rectify its disruption.

Epilogue

On 7 June 1989, three days after Tiananmen Square had been swept clean, I went to my office just outside the city centre. It was in the *Guoji Dasha* ('International Building'), a high-rise office building on the *Jianguomenwai*, the eastern portion of the wide avenue that criss-crosses Beijing from east to west. The scars from the military advance of the People's Liberation Army were still everywhere to be seen: Burnt-out busses, uprooted trees and bullet holes in the walls. The streets usually crawling with masses of people were deserted. In many places banners against the government were still hanging: 'Bloodshed must be answered with blood!' 'Death to Premier Li Peng!'

I parked my grey Jeep Cherokee a short walk away from the office, went into the abandoned lobby of the building and took the lift to the fifth floor. When I entered the small AMRO-Bank office, the crystal-clear light of Beijing streamed serenely through the windows. There were stories going around that the offices of foreign businesses had been searched by the Public Security Bureau, but there was no evidence of that. The tray with the outgoing mail on my desk was full of stacks of paper, patiently waiting for the office staff who had been sitting at home for weeks. I took a few important documents, like insurance policies, out of their folders, grabbed the money out of the safe, and sat down behind my desk. Aimlessly, I looked out across the wide deserted lanes of the *Jianguomenwai*. The window was open, the curtains rustled softly in the wind – the traumatised city was shrouded in an unreal silence.

The rumble of heavy vehicles yanked me out of my slumber. I jumped up and looked outside. In a long and threatening ribbon of potential violence, tanks and open lorries with soldiers were driving in from the west. It seemed as if they were going to drive past our office building, but suddenly the very first vehicle stopped. One soldier after the other jumped out onto the street and ran for the bushes, seeking cover. A commanding officer barked orders, and all eyes and gun barrels were aimed at my office building. Then all hell broke loose. A rainstorm of bullets burst in through the windows of the higher floors. Within a tenth of a second, I was lying under my desk – at any moment my windows would also shatter, and just like in an Al Capone movie, everything in my office would be riddled with holes, Was this my end at the tender age of thirty-six? 'AMRO-Bank director loses his life in his Beijing office'.

The intense fireworks of the gunshots just kept going. Seconds, minutes? In those final moments of my life, one thought after the other raced through my mind. Why was the People's Liberation Army using their Kalashnikovs to shoot the International Building to shreds? To intimidate foreigners? To isolate China from the world for good? And, an even more helpless thought, was my car insured or not? I knew for certain that they had shot it to pieces too.

Then an unexpected sound cut through the ra-ta-tat and whistling of bullets: A telephone was ringing on the desk I had sought cover under. In order to keep my body hidden under the desk, I grabbed the receiver from the hook in a circular arm motion. 'Wei, wei, hello, who's this?' 'Hi, Johan here, how's it going there?' Johan Nanninga worked for the shipping line Nedlloyd in Tianjin, a harbour town not far from Beijing. 'Um, what can I say, things here are. ...' Johan interrupted me: 'Everyone's saying that Beijing is very chaotic these days. Is that true? Things here are dead quiet.' I held the receiver up in the direction of the window: 'Just listen.'

Slowly the shots ebbed away. One last salvo, then it was silent. The curtains softly rustled again in the wind. For a couple of minutes, I let the silence engulf me, then stood up and stared cautiously outside. The soldiers and their vehicles were still in place and the building was surrounded. A commanding officer put a megaphone to his mouth: 'All persons who are inside the building must come out *now*. Come out *now!*'

I stuffed the papers into my bag and took the lift downstairs. Walking through the lobby, I saw two rows of heavily armed soldiers standing in position – little boys who, judging from their height and dark faces, came from the countryside somewhere far away in the south of China. They stared at me with cold indifference; these soldiers had never seen a foreigner before. I hesitated and stood still. Should I look at them, or not? Keep a straight face, or not? If you smile, you show your teeth. ... I did not know how they would react to that.

The commander barked out an order that I had to get going. Avoiding any eye contact, I slowly started to move. How did that expression go again? Oh, right, running the gauntlet... any moment now the gun butts would be pounding onto my shoulders, spittle and taunts raining down on me. I slowly walked through the hedgerow of soldiers, tensely keeping my thoughts hidden – as if these aliens had the capability to read them.

I made it, and walked straight towards my car, which had also survived the ordeal. I grabbed the Dutch flag out of the boot, stretched it across the bonnet to prove my nationality and innocence, and slowly drove back home. I looked at the streets that were once again deserted, at the plane trees that softly swayed in the breeze and at the jagged tops of the Western Hills. A picture of overwhelming peace and harmony. Time seemed to stand still.

Acknowledgements

The solitary confinement I sentenced myself to for the last couple of years was now and then lifted by helpful, knowledgeable, even wise people. My gratitude towards them is great. First of all, towards the two young ladies I hired to help with my research. The sinologist Tabitha Speelman always managed to find the source for quotes that I remembered the words to, but no longer the origin of. In addition, she referred me to a few publications that constitute an essential substructure for the story I tell. Gemila, a freelance journalist in Beijing, organised the interviews documented in this book and provided me with feedback when she felt I had missed the mark – a refreshing candour that is not uncommon amongst individuals of Mongolian ethnicity.

The eight Chinese intellectuals whom I interviewed – Qin Yaqing, Wang Zhenmin, Zhao Tingyang, Wang Xiaodong, Ding Li, Hu Angang, Zhu Caifang, and Xuan Zang – shared with me their precious time and valuable insights. The result is a richer, or in any case more authentic book, because they are involved in the public discourse on what kind of country China could be.

Three readers, each in his own unique way, contributed to improving the final outcome. The sinologist Arjen Schutten (whom I burdened with the first, still rough manuscript), by advising me to make the story more thematic; as well as the social historian Lucas van Oppen, with his vast knowledge of Chinese history at the end of the nineteenth and beginning of the twentieth centuries. Finally, Professor Paul Scheffer, who investigates the image of Europe in China, India and Brazil, employed his disciplined brain to purge the text of excessively bold assertions and structural imperfections.

Professor Frank Pieke put me on the trail of Liu Yunshan's 'five dimensions' and shared his estimable insights into the *shehui guanli* (social management) project of the Chinese Communist Party. The philosophers Jan Bor and Hein van Dongen carefully went through my philosophically-tinted assertions with a red pen, pointing out to me the essential difference between oppositions and opposites. Fokke Obbema – editorial head of the economics desk at *de Volkskrant* (the Netherlands' centre-left daily) and fellow author (also on China) also read a few chapters and alerted me to several important sources. The entrepreneur and Sinophile Albert van Lawick van Pabst read the passages on the economy, providing them with valuable commentary.

Janny Nijhof made the introductions for me at the Amsterdam publishing house Querido; without her, there would have been no book. The same is true of course for Querido itself. Hugo van Doornum did excellent work in photo selection and editorial tasks.

Anniek Meinders of Leiden University Press was convinced that this book deserves more readers than the Dutch ones only, and committed LUP to translating it in English. If only to prove that her confidence was well founded, I hope that the English version will sell well. I also want to thank editors Jonathan Earl and Romy Uijen and translator John Eyck for their professionalism and enthusiasm.

My daughters Floor and Machteld noticed that I was spending even more time in my study than usual, and encouraged me to persevere in my efforts. They even promised to read this book. Finally, my beloved Kiek sensed without fail when it was time for me to retire to my study once more. I hope that as a 'multilingual artist' (sculptor, painter, and poet) she also understands the language of this book, and that it will inspire her. Just as she inspires me, over and over again.

Chronological overview of dynasties in China

ca. 2100–1600 BCE	Xia dynasty
ca. 1600–1050 BCE	Shang dynasty ca.
1046–256 BCE	Zhou dynasty
(ca. 551–479 BCE)	Confucius
221–206 BCE	Qin dynasty
206 BCE–220 C.E.	Han dynasty
220–589 C.E.	Period of Division
(220–280 C.E.)	Three Kingdoms: Wei, Shu and Wu
(265–420 C.E.)	Jin Dynasty
(386–589 C.E.)	Northern and Southern Dynasties
581–618 C.E.	Sui dynasty
618–906 C.E.	Tang dynasty
907–960 C.E.	Period of the Five Dynasties
960–1279	Song dynasty
1279–1368	Yuan dynasty
1368–1644	Ming dynasty
1644–1912	Qing dynasty
1912–1949	Republic of China (prior to exile on Taiwan)
1949–present	People's Republic of China

Chairmen* and Party secretaries of the People's Republic of China

1949–1976	Mao Zedong
1976–1981	Hua Guofeng
1981–1987	Hu Yaobang
1987–1989	Zhao Ziyang
1989–2002	Jiang Zemin
2002–2012	Hu Jintao
2012–present	Xi Jinping

*At the 12th Party Congress (Autumn, 1982), the title 'Chairman of the Central Committee of the Communist Party' was replaced with 'General Secretary of the Central Committee of the Communist Party'. The Communist Party additionally has the position of 'Paramount Leader' – an informal title meant to indicate in whose hands the real power lies. Deng Xiaoping was the 'Paramount Leader' from 1978 until his death in 1997.

Notes

Introduction

1   F. Nietzsche, *Beyond Good and Evil*, Chapter 1 Prejudices of Philosophers, sections 6 and 10.

2   The democratic movement of 1977–1978 (when dissidents like Wei Jingsheng hang 'Great Character Posters' on the 'Wall of Democracy') was also called the 'Beijing Spring'.

3   D. Sneider, 'Textbooks and Patriotic Education: Wartime Memory Formation in China and Japan', *Asia-Pacific Review* 20:1 (2013), pp. 35–54.

4   'Own shoal', *The Economist*, January 28th, 2017.

5   'Philippine President Aquino compares China to Nazi Germany', *World Socialist Website*, February 6th, 2014.

6   F. Fukuyama, 'The End of History?', *The National Interest* 16 (1989).

7   Fukuyama, op. cit., p. 4; F. Fukuyama, *The End of History and the Last Man* (Londen, 1992), p. 60.

8   'World's Greatest City: 50 reasons why Shanghai is No. 1', CNN, October 5th 2009 (http://travel.cnn.com/shanghai/play/worlds-greatest-city-50-reasons-why-shanghai-no-1-590704).

9   The Declaration of Independence (http://www.ushistory.org/declaration/document).

10 Universal Declaration of Human Rights, Article 21 (www.un.org/en/documents/udhr/).

11 Gan Yang, 'The Grand Three Traditions in the New Era'. Quoted in M. Leonard, '*What does China think?*', New York, 2008, p. 13.

12 'Hillary Clinton: Chinese System Is Doomed, Leaders on a "Fool's Errand"', *The Atlantic*, May 11th, 2011.

13 Fukuyama, 'The End of History?', p. 1.

14 Quoted in '"We won't fall like the USSR", vows Beijing', *South China Morning Post* (SCMP), December 28th 2011.

15 Cited in M. Ignatieff, 'The New World Disorder', *The New York Review of Books*, September 24th 2014.

16 Lin Yutang, Lin Yutang, *My Country and My People* (Singapore, 2001), Part one, Bases.

17 VPRO (i.e. Vrijzinnig Protestantse Radio Omroep, or 'Liberal Protestant Radio Broadcasting Corporation'), *Tegenlicht*, March 28th 2011.

18 S.P. Huntington, *The Clash of Civilizations and the Remaking of the World Order* (Londen, 1996), pp. 169–174.

19 http://en.wikipedia.org/wiki/Hai_Rui_Dismissed_from_Office.

20 'Xi Jinping opens "New Era" for China and the world'. http://www.bbc.com/news/world-asia-china-41744675, October 25th, 2017.

21 Liang Qichao, "Travel Impressions from Europe", quoted in *Sources of Chinese Tradition, Volume Two*, Compiled by Wm. Theodore de Bary and Richard Lufrano, New York, 1999, p. 378.

22 'Xi Jinping Thought – the Communist Party's tighter grip on China in 16 characters', SCMP, October 25th, 2017.

23 Liang Qichao on 'The consciousness of rights', quoted in *Sources of Chinese Tradition, Volume Two*, Compiled by Wm. Theodore de Bary and Richard Lufrano, New York, 1999, p. 294.

Chapter 1

1 Confucius, *The Analects*, Book 13, Ch. 6, transl. James Legge, in *The Chinese Classics*, Vol. 1, 2nd rev. ed. (Oxford, 1893); reprint (New York, 1971), p. 266.

2 J.K. Fairbank, *East Asia: The Modern Transformation* (London, 1969), p. 80.

3 J.D. Spence, *The Search for Modern China* (New York, 1990), p. 101.

4 Pliny the Elder, *Natural History*, Chapter 20 ('The Ceres'), transl. and ed. John Bostock and H.T. Riley (London: Taylor and Francis, 1855); see also: http://www.perseus.tufts.edu/hopper/text?doc=Perseus:text:1999.02.0137:book=6:chapter=20&highlight=silk.

5 Cited in Ulric Killion, *A Modern Chinese Journey to the West: Economic Globalization and Dualism* (New York, 2006), p. 68.

6 *Through the Jade Gate to Rome: A Study of the Silk Routes During the Later Han Dynasty, 1st to 2nd centuries* CE, transl. and ed. John E. Hill (Charleston, SC, 2009), pp. 24–27.

7 Cited in H. Kissinger, *On China* (New York, 2012), p. 21.

8 See: http://afe.easia.columbia.edu/cosmos/irc/emperor.htm.

9 Mengzi, Jin Xin II, 60, at China Text Project (http://ctext.org/mengzi/jin-xin-ii).

10 *Shujing* (*The Book of Documents*), cited by Mencius in *Wan Zhang I*, 5, at China Text Project (http://ctext.org/mengzi/wan-zhang-ii).

11 J.D. Spence, *God's Chinese Son* (New York, 1995), p. xxi.

12 Joseph Esherick, 'How the Qing Became China', in: *Empire to Nation: Historical Perspectives on the Making of the Modern World* (Lanham, MD, 2006), pp. 232–233; B.J. ter Haar, *Het Hemels Mandaat* (Amsterdam, 2010), p. 12.

13 Li Zhisui, *The Private Life of Chairman Mao: The Memoirs of Mao's Personal Physician* (London, 1994), p. 122.

14 J. Florcruz, 'Unearthing the Army of Emperor Qin', *Time*, 27 September 1999.

15 Cited in A. Chua, *Day of Empire: How Hyperpowers Rise to Global Dominance and Why They Fall* (New York, 2007), p. 30.

16 'A language lost', SCMP, 29 August 2011.

17 H.E. Richardson, 'The Sino-Tibetan Treaty Inscription of A.D. 821/823 at Lhasa', *Journal of the Royal Asiatic Society* 2 (1978), pp. 153–154.

18   Cited in T. Shakya, *The Dragon in the Land of Snows* (New York, 1999), p. 9.

19   F. Wood, *Did Marco Polo Go to China?* (Dartmouth, 1995).

20   J. Weatherford, *Genghis Khan and the Making of the Modern World* (New York, 2012), p. 173.

21   David Morgan, *The Mongols* (New York, 1986), p. 135.

22   'De wereldreiziger Willem van Rubroek', in *Voortrekkers van den Nederlandschen Stam. Een bundel levensbeschrijvingen* [bezorgd door het Bestuur der groep "Nederland" van het Algemeen Nederlandsch Verbond] (Amsterdam, 1925), p. 21.

23   'The Provisional Constitution of the Republic of China', *The American Journal of International Law*, Vol. 6 (1 July 1912), p. 149.

24   *The Constitution of the Republic of China*, Ch. III, Art. 3 (10 October 1923); see: http:// digitalrepository.trincoll.edu/cgi/viewcontent.cgi?article=1058&context=moore; see also: http://baike.baidu.com/view/2148150.htm.

25   W.A. Callahan, 'The Cartography of China's National Humiliation and the Emergence of China's Geobody', *Public Culture* 21:1 (2009); see also: http://williamacallahan.com/wp -content/uploads/2010/11/ Callahan-Public-Culture-09.pdf?.

26   *Constitution of the People's Republic of China* (Beijing, 1982), Ch. 1, Art. 4; see also: http://en .people.cn/constitution/constitution.html.

27   'The four great inventions' (www.china.org.cn/e-gudai/8.htm); cf.: http://chineseposters .net/themes/patriotic-education-1994.php.

28   Francis Bacon, *The New Organon* [*Novum Organum Scientiarum*] (1620), Book 1, Ch. CXXIX, in *The Works* (Vol. VIII), transl. J. Spedding et al. (Boston: Taggard and Thompson, 1863).

29   'China noses ahead as top goods producer', *Financial Times*, 13 March 2011.

30   See Ter Haar, *Het Hemels Mandaat* (Amsterdam, 2010), pp. 210–221.

31   R. Latham, *The Travels of Marco Polo* (London, 1958), pp. 213–214.

32   Latham, *op. cit.*, p. 23.

33   Yingqui Lui and Chunjiang Liu, 'Diagnosing the Cause of Scientific Standstill, Unravelling the Needham Puzzle', *China Economist* 10 (2007), pp. 83–96.

34   M. Elvin, 'The high-level equilibrium trap: The causes of the decline of invention in the traditional Chinese textile industries', in W.E. Willmott, *Economic Organization in Chinese Society* (Stanford, 1972), pp. 137–172.

35   K. van der Leeuw, *Het Chinese denken* (The Hague, 1994), p. 34.

36   Confucius, *The Analects*, Book 2, Ch. 4.

37   This study uses the classic translation of James Legge, as found in his *Confucian Analects, the Great Learning, and the Doctrine of the Mean*, revised, 2nd ed. (Oxford, 1893). More recent, authoritative translations with commentary are given by D.C. Lau, *The Analects* (*New Bilingual Edition*) (Hong Kong, 2000); and by Edward Slingerland, *Confucius: Analects, with Selections from Traditional Commentaries* (Indianapolis, 2003). For an authoritative Dutch translation, see: K. Schipper, *Confucius. De gesprekken; gevolgd door het leven van Confucius door Sima Qian* (Amsterdam, 2014).

38   Confucius, *The Analects*, Book 15, Ch. 24.

39   J. Bor, *Een nieuwe geschiedenis van de filosofie* (Amsterdam, 2011), p. 77.

40   Confucius, *The Analects*, Book 12, Ch. 19.

41   Confucius, *The Great Learning* [The Text of Confucius], Ch. 5, transl. James Legge, (Oxford, 1893), p. 358 f.; cf. www.humanistictexts.org/confucius.htm.

42   Confucius, *The Analects*, Book 10, Ch. 12.

43   Confucius, *op. cit.*, Book 11, Ch. 12.

44   *The Great Learning* [The Text of Confucius], Ch. 1, transl. James Legge (Oxford, 1893), p. 356.; see also: J. Engberts, 'Immanent Transcendence in Chinese and Western Process Thinking', *Philosophy Study* 2:6 (2012), p. 379.

45   *The Sacred Books of China. The Texts of Confucianism*, Pt. III, incl. the *Lî Kî*, transl. James Legge (Oxford: Clarendon, 1879), pp. 364–366. Cf. taousa.org/classic-texts/4The-World-of-Da-Tong.pdf; and see: W. Callahan, *China Dreams: 20 Visions of the Future* (Oxford, 2013), p. 110.

46   *The Sacred Books of China. The Texts of Confucianism*, Pt. I, incl. the *Hsiâo King*, transl. James Legge (Oxford: Clarendon, 1879), p. 466 (Ch. I). See also: *Xiao Jing* ('The Classic of Xiao') at www.tsoidug.org/Papers/Xiao_Jing_Comment.pdf.

47   Confucius, *The Analects*, Book 15, Ch. 39.

48   Cf. Schipper's original Dutch translation, as found in: Lao Zi, *Het boek van de Tao en de innerlijke kracht*, vertaald door K. Schipper (Amsterdam, 2010), p. 23.

49   *The Sacred Books of China. The Texts of Tâoism*, Pt. II, incl. the *Writings of Kwang-ze* [i.e. Zhuang Zi], transl. James Legge (Oxford, 1891), p. 49 (i.e. Book XXI, Pt. II, Sec. XIV, Ch. 4). Cf. the Dutch translation by K. Schipper in *Zhuang Zi. De volledige geschriften* (Amsterdam, 2007), p. 273.

50   K. Schipper points out that nearly nothing is known about Zhuang Zi as an individual, and that the book that bears his name is in fact the work of several authors; see: Schipper, *Zhuang Zi. De volledige geschriften* (Amsterdam, 2007), p. 10.

51   *The Sacred Books of China. The Texts of Tâoism*, Pt. II, incl. the *Writings of Kwang-ze* [i.e. Zhuang Zi], transl. James Legge (Oxford, 1891), p. 37 (i.e. Introduction, Ch. IV). Cf. Schipper, *op. cit.*, p. 16.

52   'Autumn wind', in Kenneth Rexroth, *Songs of Love, Moon & Wind* (New York, 2009).

53   'Loushan Pass' (see: http://allpoetry.com/Loushan-Pass).

54   See, for example, K. Schipper, *Tao, de levende religie van China* (Amsterdam, 2014), Chapter 9.

55   Lin Yutang, *My Country and My People* (Singapore, 2001), p. 117.

56   'Away from it all', *Global Times*, 20 April 2015.

57   Fung Yu-lan, *A short history of Chinese philosophy*, ed. Derk Bodde (New York, 1948), p. 20.

58   'Even with Ping-Pong, a Formal Meeting in China', *The New York Times*, 21 March 2014.

59   Retold in J. Clavell, *The Art of War* (London, 1981), pp. 8–10.

60   Clavell, *op. cit.*, p. 7.

61   Stefan Verstappen, *The Thirty-Six Strategies of Ancient China* (San Francisco, 1999), Ch. 2, pp. 9 ff.; see also: H. von Senger, *Strategemen. Listen om te overleven* (Rotterdam, 1990), pp. 38–39.

62   S. Seagrave, *Lords of the Rim* (New York, 1995), p. 9.

63   See: http://history.huanqiu.com/people/2011-11/2177025.html.

64   Kissinger, *On China*, pp. 23–24.

65   'APT1: Exposing One of China's Cyber Espionage Units', *Mandiant*, February 2013 (see: http://intelreport.mandiant.com).

66   Clavell, *The Art of War*, p. 6.

67   Seagrave, *Lords of the Rim*, p. 33.

Chapter 2

1   J.C. Caldwell and Z. Zhao, 'China's demography in perspective', in: F. Guo and Z. Zhao, *Transition and Challenge: China's Population at the Beginning of the 21st Century* (Oxford, 2007).

2   https://en.wikipedia.org/wiki/Siku_Quanshu; Fairbank, *East Asia: The Modern Transformation*, p. 88.

3   P. Turchin, J. Adams and T.D. Hall, 'East-West Orientation of Historical Empires', *Journal of World-Systems Research* 12:2 (December 2006), pp. 219–229.

4   'Korean Music', entry in *Encyclopaedia Britannica* (see: www.britannica.com/EBchecked/topic/322408/Korean-music/283442/Court-instrumental-music).

5   L. Levathes, *When China Ruled the Seas* (Oxford, 1994), p. 146.

6   'Battle of Macao', C.R. Boxer, *Fidalgos in the Far East, 1550–1770* (The Hague, 1948), p. 83.

7   C.R. Boxer, *The Dutch Seaborne Empire* (London, 1977), p. 236.

8   Seagrave, *Lords of the Rim*, pp. 116.

9   Jane K. Leonard, *Wei Yuan and China's Rediscovery of the Maritime World* (Cambridge, MA, 1984), pp. 70–71.

10   Cited in J.D. Spence, *Chinese Roundabout: Essays in History and Culture*, rev. paperback ed. (New York, 1993), pp. 82 f.

11   Adam Smith, *The Wealth Of Nations*, Book IV, Ch. II, paras. 11–12.

12   http://acc6.its.brooklyn.cuny.edu/~phalsall/texts/qianlong.html; E. Backhouse and J.O.P. Bland, *Annals and Memoirs of the Court of Peking* (Boston, 1914), pp. 322–331.

13   https://en.wikipedia.org/wiki/The_empire_on_which_the_sun_never_sets.

14   R. Macartney, *Our First Ambassador to China: An Account of the Life of George, Earl of Macartney, with Extracts from His Letters, and the Narrative of His Experiences in China, as Told by Himself, 1737–1806* (Cambridge, 2011), p. 386.

15   J. Barrow, *Travels in China, Containing Descriptions, Observations, and Comparisons* (London, 1804), pp. 9–13.

16   For a report of Van Braam's mission, see: J.J.L. Duyvendak, 'The last Dutch Embassy to the Chinese Court (1794–1795)', *T'ong Pao* 34 (1938), here: p. 88.

17   Fairbank, *East Asia: The Great Tradition* (London, 1960), p. 392.

18   J. Gibson, *Otter Skins, Boston Ships, and China Goods: The Maritime Fur Trade of the Northwest Coast, 1785–1841* (Montreal, 1992), p. 104.

19   'Commissioner Lin: Letter to Victoria', Fordham University (see: www.fordham.edu/halsall/mod/1839lin2.asp).

20   Spence, *The Search for Modern China*, p. 154.

21   See: https://en.wikipedia.org/wiki/First_Opium_War.

22   See: http://acc6.its.brooklyn.cuny.edu/~phalsall/texts/qianlong.html.

23   As per the subtitle for: Barrow, *Travels in China*.

24   *High School textbooks modern Chinese modern history books (compulsory) teaching reference books* (Beijing, 2000).

25   M. McDonald, 'Chinese bidder says he will not pay for looted bronzes', *The New York Times*, 2 March 2009.

26   Edward Wong and Steven Erlanger, 'Frenchman Will Return to China Prized Bronze Artifacts Looted in 19th Century' *The New York Times*, 26 April 2013.

27   Scheherazade Daneshkhu, 'Pinault family offers to return bronze heads to China', *Financial Times*, 30 April 2013.

28   Fairbank, *East Asia: The Modern Transformation*, p. 317.

29   D. Shambaugh, *China Goes Global* (Oxford, 2013), pp. 63–65.

30   C.P. Fitzgerald, *Horizon History of China* (New York, 1969), p. 200.

31   Spence, *The Search for Modern China*, p. 233.

32   Spence, *op. cit.*, p. 234.

33   B.W. Tuchman, *Stilwell and the American experience in China*, New York 1971, p. 40.

34   Spence, *op. cit.*, p. 235.

35   S. Shirk, *China: Fragile Superpower* (Oxford, 2008), pp. 79 f.; see also: 'Professor hits back at critics on the internet', SCMP, 7 April 2006.

36   Fairbank, *East Asia: The Modern Transformation*, p. 383.

37   See: www.npm.gov.tw/exh100/diplomatic/page_en04.html.

38   J.W. Finney, *The New York Times*, 11 November 1971; 'Senkaku purchase bid made official', *Japan Times*, 11 September 2012, p. 2.

39   Security treaty between Japan and the US (see: www.mofa.go.jp/region/n-america/us/q&a/ref/1.html).

40   See: 'US would side with Japan in clash over Diaoyus, says Pentagon chief', SCMP, 3 February 2017; see also: http://thediplomat.com/2014/04/obama-senkakus-covered-under-us-japan-security-treaty/.

41   Spence, *The Search for Modern China*, pp. 443–447.

42   Fitzgerald, *Horizon History of China*, p. 378.

43   B.W. Tuchman, *op. cit.*, p. 212.

44   Spence, *The Search for Modern China*, p. 448.

45   Shirk, *China: Fragile Superpower*, pp. 154–155.

46   S. Pinker, *The Better Angels of Our Nature* (New York, 2011), cited in 'To history, today's violence is a speck', SCMP, 28 October 2011.

47   Fairbank, *East Asia: The Modern Transformation*, p. 634.

Chapter 3

1   Main source: 'International Covenant on Economic, Social and Cultural Rights' (ICESCR) (see: http://www.refworld.org/docid/3ae6b36c0.html).

2   H. George, *Progress and Poverty* (New York, 1879); 'Sun Yat-sen's three principles', cited in: 'Children of the revolution', SCMP, 10 October 2011; and Fairbank, *East Asia: The Modern Transformation*, pp. 636–637.

3   Fairbank, *op. cit.*, pp. 636–637.

4   Callahan, *China Dreams: 20 Visions of the Future*, p. 110.

5   Kang Youwei wrote the book in 1920, but it was not published until after his death in 1935. See Callahan, *op. cit.*, pp. 109–114.

6   For Hu Jintao's complete report to the 17th Party Congress, see: http://www.bjreview .com.cn/17thCPC/txt/2007-10/25/content_83051.htm.

7   Spence, *The Search for Modern China*, p. 301.

8   Callahan, *China Dreams: 20 Visions of the Future*, pp. 106–107.

9   Leonard, *What Does China Think?* (New York, 2008), p. 85.

10   'China's "great rejuvenation" threatens to harden racial attitudes', *Financial Times*, 31 August 2014.

11   'Chinese company offers apology over 'racist' advert, but it doesn't wash', SCMP, 29 May 2016.

12   As cited in Callahan, *China Dreams*, p. 107. See also: Xi Jinping (ed.), *Kexue yu aiguo: Yan Fu Sixiang Xintan* ('Science and Patriotism: New Investigations into the Thought of Yan Fu') (Beijing, 2001).

13   Spence, *The Search for Modern China*, p. 280.

14   For an evocative account of the election and Song's assassination see, amongst others, 'The death of a revolutionary. The song of Song', *The Economist*, 22 December 2012.

15   Main source: https://en.wikipedia.org/wiki/Feng_Yuxiang, which moreover also notes that this story is not supported by objective sources.

16   Fairbank, *East Asia: The Modern Transformation*, p. 658.

17   W.J.F. Jenner, *The Tyranny of History: The Roots of China's Crisis* (London, 1994).

18   Fairbank, *East Asia: The Modern Transformation*, p. 666.

19   For an excellent description of the May 4th Movement, see: Spence, *The Search for Modern China*, pp. 310–319.

20   Cited in 'Why China's leaders fear looking in the 1911 mirror', *Financial Times*, 19 October 2011; see also: Chang Ping, 'Rights from Wrong', SCMP, 15 October 2011.

21   E. Vogel, *Deng Xiaoping and the Transformation of China* (Harvard, 2013), p. 631.

22   Wu Zhong, 'Hu warns successors over "peaceful evolution"', *Asia Times*, 11 January 2012 (see: http://www.atimes.com/atimes/China/NA11Ad02.html).

23   Cf. Wu Zhong, *op. cit.*

24   See *Romance of the Three Kingdoms* at the Chinese Text Project (http://ctext.org/sanguo-yanyi/ch1).

25   T. Saich, 'The Chinese Communist Party during the Era of the Comintern (1919–1943)' (see: https://www.hks.harvard.edu/fs/asaich/chinese-communisty-party-during-comintern.pdf).

26   'Huang He floods', entry in *Encyclopaedia Britannica* (see: www.britannica.com/ebchecked/topic/1483621/Huang-He-floods).

27   J. Fenby, *Chiang Kai-shek* (New York, 2003), p. 148.

28   Ng Yi Ming, 'Generalissimo Chiang Kai-Shek and the Second Sino-Japanese War (1937–1945)', *Pointer: Journal of the Singapore Armed Forces* 38:1 (2012), p. 89.

29   Spence, *The Search for Modern China*, pp. 498–504; R. Mitter, *China's War with Japan, 1937–1945: The Struggle for Survival* (London, 2013), p. 386.

30   'Double Ten Day Fervor Humiliates History', *Global Times*, 10 October 2014.

31   Cong Xiaoping, *Teachers' Schools and the Making of the Modern Chinese Nation-State, 1897–1937* (Washington, 2007), p. 159.

32   For these and other socio-economic successes in the Nanking Decade, see J. Fenby, *Chiang Kai-shek*, pp. 226–233.

33   G. Chow, *China's Economic Transformation* (Malden, MA, 2007), pp. 20–21.

34   F.P. van der Putten, *Corporate Behaviour and Political Risk: Dutch Companies in China, 1903–1941* (Leiden, 2001), pp. 219–258.

35   The South China Sea was first described as a core interest in 2010, the East China Sea in 2013. See, among other sources, 'China's "Core Interests" and the East China Sea', U.S.-China Economic and Security Review Commission (10 May 2013). See also: (https://www.uscc.gov/sites/default/files/Research/China%27s%20Core%20Interests%20and%20the%20East%20China%20Sea.pdf).

36   'Diaoyu Dao, an Inherent Territory of China' (26 September 2012). See: (http://english.gov.cn/archive/white_paper/2014/08/23/content_281474983043212.htm).

37   'Children of the revolution, grown older and apart', SCMP, 10 October 2011.

38   'High price for airing Sun Yat-sen criticism', SCMP, 18 August 2011.

Chapter 4

1   'Does China's next leader have a soft spot for Tibet?', Reuters, 1 September 2012.

2   F. Dikötter, *The Tragedy of Liberation* (London, 2013), p. 161.

3   https://wikileaks.org/plusd/cables/09BEIJING3128_a.html.

4   'Xi's imperial presidency has its weaknesses', SCMP, 15 July 2015.

5   'Towards a new world order: Xi Jinping touts Asia-Pacific dream', SCMP, 17 November 2014.

6   'Party rules ban groundless comments on major policies', *Global Times*, 23 October 2015.

7   'All the president's men: Xi Jinping tells Communist Party Politburo to unite behind him in thought and action', SCMP, 9 January 2016.

8   'Chinese Communist Party expands Xi Jinping's political power, anointing him "core leader"', SCMP, 28 October 2016.

9   'China's next leader Xi Jinping "suffered heart attack"', https://www.telegraph.co.uk/news/worldnews/asia/china/9539184/Chinas-next-leader-Xi-Jinping-suffered-heart-attack.html.

10   'Chilling history lesson for 'no' voter in Xi election', SCMP, 15 March, 2013; 'Mystery over lone vote against Xi', SCMP, 16 March 2013.

11   'Xi Jinping has been good for China's Communist Party; less so for China', *The Economist*, 14 October, 2017.

12   For the theory of the 'Three Represents' see: 'Report on the Work of the Government', The 16th National People's Congress of the People's Republic of China (8 November 2002), in *Selected Works of Jiang Zemin*, Vol. III, Eng. ed. (Beijing: FLP, 2013), p. 519; see also: (http://english.cpc.people.com.cn/66739/4496615.html).

13   'Dream of the red future: will the Chinese dream become an enduring classic? *World Policy*, 18 July, 2013.

14   'Xi steering China to greater prosperity', *China Daily*, 20March, 2018, and 'Xi Jinping speech at the 19th National Congress of the Communist Party of China', *Voltairenet.org*, 18 October 2017, http://www.voltairenet.org/article198700.html.

15   'Xi Jinping speech at the 19th National Congress of the Communist Party of China', http://www.xinhuanet.com/english/special/2017-11/03/c_136725942.htm.

16   'Xi Jinping Thought – the Communist Party's tighter grip on China in 16 characters', SCMP, October 25th, 2017.

17   Cited in '*Sources of East Asian Tradition*', Volume 1: Premodern Asia, edited by Wm. Theodore de Bary, New York 2008, p. 397.

18   De Bary, *op.cit.* p. 395.

19   Cited in 'Xi Jinping's anti-corruption drive mimics a Ming obsession', *Financial Times*, 6 December 2017.

20   'Chasing the Chinese Dream', *The Economist*, 4 May 2013.

21   'Speech in remembrance of Comrade Mao Zedong's 120th Birth Anniversary', *Xinhua*, 26 December 2013; see also: (http://www.globaltimes.cn/content/834337.shtml).

22   See Barry Naughton, 'Shifting structures and processes in economic policy-making at the centre', in *China's Core executive. Leadership styles, structures and processes under Xi Jinping*, eds Sebastian Heilmann and Matthias Stepan, in *Merics. Papers on China* 1 (June 2016): 40–

45. See also: (https://www.merics.org/fileadmin/user_upload/downloads/MPOC/MPOC
_ChinasCoreExecutive.pdf).

23   'Xi upholds China's unique path as marking Deng's birth anniversary', *The Standard*,
21 August 2014.

24   'Xinhua Insight: To reignite a nation, Xi carries Deng's torch', *Xinhuanet English.news.cn*,
20 August 2014 (see also: http://www.china.org.cn/china/Off_the_Wire/2014-08/20/
content_33283585.htm).

25   'The ideal Chinese husband: Xi Dada and the cult of personality growing around China's
president', SCMP, 29 February 2016.

26   'Gushing Trump Seems to have Fallen in Love with Xi Jinping', *That's China*, 13 April 2017.

27   'The power of Xi Jinping', *The Economist*, 20 September 2014.

28   'Quotes from Xi Jinping on hot issues', *People's Daily Online* (http://english.peopledaily
.com.cn/n/2014/0930/c90785-8789845.html); see also '274 quotes from Xi Jinping: Propaganda machine publishes book to bolster his image', SCMP, 30 May 2014.

29   By an anonymous observer, quoted in 'Xi Jinping, China's new revolutionary hero',
Financial Times, 20 October 2017.

30   'Hua Guofeng', *The Guardian* (21 August 2008); see also: https://www.theguardian.com/
world/2008/aug/21/china.

31   'Chinese premier's lavish praise shows Xi power before reshuffle', *Bloomberg News*,
5 March 2017; see also: https://www.bloomberg.com/politics/articles/2017-03-05/chinese
-premier-s-lavish-praise-shows-xi-power-before-reshuffle.

32   'The man behind the Xi-Trump summit', SCMP, 1 April 2017.

33   Cited in 'James Mulvenon, 'The Cult of Xi and the Rise of the CMC Chairman Responsibility System' https://www.hoover.org/sites/default/files/research/docs/clm55-jm-final
.pdf.

34   Cited in Maurice Meisner, *Mao Zedong: A Political and Intellectual Portrait* (Cambridge,
2007), p. 133.

35   Constitution of Communist Party of China (Adopted on Nov. 14, 2012) http://www.china
.org.cn/china/18th_cpc_congress/2012-11/16/content_27138030_3.htm.

36   'Tiger in the Net', *The Economist*, 1 December 2014.

37   Dikötter, *Tragedy of Liberation*, pp. 159–161.

38   'Xi Jinping urges party to "toe mass line" to win over public', SCMP, 20 April 2013.

39   *Ibidem*.

40   'Mao Zedong was no god, says Xi Jinping, in delicate balancing act', SCMP, 27 December
2013.

41   'China's new TV show about how good it is at fighting corruption has been viewed 350 million times', *Quartz*, 30 March 2017; see: https://qz.com/945710/the-first-episode-of-chinas
-new-tv-show-about-how-good-it-is-at-fighting-corruption-has-been-viewed-350-
million-times.

42   'Can China Finally Solve Its Corruption Problem?' *The Diplomat*, 29 October 2016.

43   'The devil, or Mr. Wang', *The Economist*, 28 March 2015.

44   'Suicide "epidemic" haunts corruption crackdown as deaths of billionaire Xu Ming and scores of others reminiscent of darker times', SCMP, 20 October 2015.

45   'China's president has been going to funerals lately – it's a sign of trouble', *Yahoo Finance*, 20 September 2015.

46   'China uses confessions of officials to educate cadres', *Global Times*, 30 March 2017.

47   Cf. Cheng Li, 'Xi Jinping's Inner Circle', *China Leadership Monitor* 43 (30 January 2014); available through: https://www.brookings.edu/research/xi-jinpings-inner-circle-the -shaanxi-gang/.

48   'Crackdown on "three vices" goes national after Dongguan scandal', SCMP, 17 February 2014.

49   'Photos of Xi Jinping eating at a popular Beijing restaurant go viral', SCMP, 28 December 2013.

50   'Political and economic reforms key if Xi Jinping is to win the war on graft', SCMP, 8 July 2014.

51   Xi Jinping tells Politburo, he will fight corruption at the risk of his life, *AsiaNews.it*, 6 August, 2014.

52   E. Osnos, 'China's Fifteen-billion-dollar Purge', *The New Yorker*, 2 April 2014.

53   As cited in 'Xi Jinping's anti-corruption campaign "to weed out rivals", says Lee Kuan Yew's daughter', SCMP, 2 January 2017.

54   'Zhou Yongkang kicked out of Chinese Communist Party', SCMP, 6 December 2014.

55   'China's disgraced security tsar may face political charges: analysts', SCMP, 20 March 2015.

56   'Coup plotters foiled: Xi Jinping fended off threat to 'save Communist Party', SCMP, 19 October, 2017.

57   'Former China security chief Zhou Yongkang jailed for life', *Financial Times*, 11 June 2015.

58   Cited in: 'Ling probe receives widespread approval', *Global Times*, 24 December 2014.

59   See: 'Heirs of Mao's comrades rise as new capitalist nobility', *Bloomberg News*, 27 December 2012.

60   'Heirs of Mao's comrades.'

61   As cited in: https://en.wikipedia.org/wiki/Wang_Zhen_(general).

62   'Revolutionaries' heirs vow support for Party reforms', *Global Times*, 25 February 2016.

63   Mao Tse-tung, 'Problems of War and Strategy' (6 November 1938) in: Mao Tse-tung, *Selected Works*, Vol. II, p. 224 (see also: https://www.marxists.org/reference/archive/mao/ selected-works/volume-2/mswv2_12.htm).

64   'Communist Party "controls the gun"', PLA top brass reminded', SCMP, 5 November 2014.

65   See https://www.nytimes.com/1983/05/01/world/new-book-says-mao-ordered-lin-biao -killed.html.

66   'PLA urged to unite behind Xi Jinping and prevent "Political Liberalism"', SCMP, 12 August 2014.

67   'Chinese goldfinger general quizzed in corruption probe', *Financial Times*, 15 January 2014.

68   'Ex-PLA chief Guo Boxiong to be prosecuted for allegedly accepting bribes for promotions', SCMP, 6 April 2016.

69   'Guo Boxiong, Jiang Zemin, and the Corruption of the Chinese Military', *The Diplomat*, 31 July 2015.

70   Michel Korzec, *Het voelen van de draak*, Amsterdam, 1986.

71   'China's Xi takes up new military title as part of reforms process', Reuters, 22 April, 2016; 'Xi's China: command and control', *Financial Times*, 26 July 2016.

72   'China unveils five new theater commands', *Global Times*, 2 February 2016.

73   'Xi slams defiant cliques within Party', *Global Times*, 4 May 2016.

74   'Why General Fang Fenghui Was Purged', *The Diplomat*, 18 January 2018.

75   Cheng Ki, 'Xi Jinping's Inner Circle: the Shaanxi Gang', *Brookings Institute*, 30 January, 2014.

76   'PLA general who helped Xi battle graft in military retires', SCMP, 30 December, 2015.

Chapter 5

1   'China's Hu Jintao warns congress corruption could cause fall of state', *The Guardian*, 8 September 2012.

2   *Ibidem.*

3   'China's Xi Jinping supports "democracy", but not in the Western sense', SCMP, 24 September 2014.

4   C. Chen and S. Bennett, 'China Smog at Center of Air Pollution Deaths Cited by WHO', *Bloomberg Business*, 25 March 2014.

5   'The Victims of China's Soil Pollution Crisis', 3 July 2014 (www.chinafile.com/reporting -opinion/environment/victims-chinas-soil-pollution-crisis).

6   'China cuts poor population to two thirds', *Xinhua*, 5 January 2018.

7   After decreasing slowly for years, China's Gini-index (which measures income inequality) went up again in 2016 https://www.statista.com/statistics/250400/inequality-of-income -distribution-in-china-based-on-the-gini-index. See also 'Despite China's Fast-Growing Wealth, Millions Still Remain Poor', 4 February 2018, *Forbes*, https://www.forbes.com/ sites/ralphjennings/2018/02/04/why-tens-of-millions-remain-poor-in-china- despite-fast-growing-wealth/#5dde544e7e9e.

8   'Marketing to China's Middle Class', *China Business Review*, 1 June 2014.

9   Vogel, *Deng Xiaoping and the Transformation of China*, p. 342.

10   M.W. Frazier, 'Narrowing the Gap: Rural-Urban Inequality in China', *World Politics Review*, 24 September 2013.

11   'Evaluating the Urban-Rural Wealth Gap', *China Digital Times*, 5 May 2017.

12   'Carrying out a new type of people-centered urbanization' from the 'Full text: report in the work of the Government', *Xinhua*, 14 March, 2014, http://www.chinadaily.com.cn/china/2014npcandcppcc/2014-03/14/content_17348344_4.htm.

13   'Don't worry about China's slowing economic growth', Li Keqiang tells Davos', SCMP, 23 January 2015.

14   '3,500 new districts built to house 3.4 billion', *Global Times* 17 May, 2016.

15   'Can China's President Xi Jinping realise his "perfect' city" dream?', SCMP, 27 April 2017.

16   'Architect envisions a smog-free Beijing', *The International New York Times*, 7–8 February 2015.

17   See note 12.

18   'China releases earthquake death toll of children', *The Guardian*, 7 May 2009.

19   'Without the Communist Party, There Would be No New China' (https://en.wikipedia.org/wiki/Without_the_Communist_Party,_There_Would_Be_No_New_China).

20   'Charter 08', for an English translation see *The New York Review of Books*, at: http://www.nybooks.com/articles/2009/01/15/chinas-charter-08/, in addition to: http://www.chinafile.com/library/nyrb-china-archive/chinas-charter-08#sthash.GgtidwTb.dpuf.

21   R. Reagan, 'Inaugural Adress', 20 January 1981 (www.heritage.org/initiatives/first-principles/primary-sources/reagans-first-inaugural-government-is-not-the-solution-to-our-problem-government-is-the-problem).

22   'Don't worry, be happy', *The Economist*, 17 March 2011.

23   *Ibidem*.

24   M. Jacques, *When China Rules the World: The End of the Western World and the Birth of a New Global Order* (New York, 2009).

25   M. Jacques, 'We see Chinese governance in western terms', *The Globe and Mail*, 18 March 2013.

26   Lin Yutang, *My Country and My People* (Singapore, 2001), p. 76.

27   Lin Yutang, *op. cit.*, p. 109.

28   D. Hume, 'Idea of a Perfect Commonwealth', cited in: M. Church, 'Scottish Founding Fathers & Early Promotors of [r]epublicanism', 29 November 2013.

29   'Positive and Negative Liberty', *Stanford Encyclopedia of Philosophy* (2003); see: https://plato.stanford.edu/entries/liberty-positive-negative/.

30   J. McGregor, *One Billion Customers: Lessons from the Front Lines of Doing Business in China* (New York, 2005), p. 9.

31   'What is the Beijing Consensus', *The New York Times*, 28 January 2011.

32   'Wen Jiabao says no democracy in prc for 100 years', *Taipei Times*, 28 February 2007.

33   Shirk, *China: Fragile Superpower*, p. 53.

34   B. Anderson, *Imagined Communities: Reflections on the Origin and Spread of Nationalism* (London, 1991).

35   J.K. Fairbank, *The United States and China* (Cambridge, MA, 1958), pp. 191–193, 308.

36   For the song lyrics, see: Mao Zedong, 'Dongfang Hong' (lyrics.wikia.com/Mao_Zedong:Dongfang_Hong).

37   B.S. Clark, *Political Economy: A Comparative Approach* (Santa Barbara, 1998), pp. 57–59.

38   G. Orwell, *Animal Farm* (London, 1945).

39   G. Raby, 'Third Plenum Decision, a reform manifesto', http://www.corrs.com.au/thinking/elsewhere/third-plenum-decision-a-reform-manifesto/.

40   Quote from Leon Trotsky, who used it to dismiss his political opponents, the Mensheviks, as a movement that had played out its role. See: P. Sonne, 'The Dustbunnies of History', *The Oxonian Review* 8:9.7 (2009).

41   Constitution of the People's Republic of China. The version of 2004 and its amendments made in 2018; http://www.npc.gov.cn/englishnpc/Constitution/node_2825.htm; https://npcobserver.com/2018/03/11/translation-2018-amendment-to-the-p-r-c-constitution/.

42   'The permanent party', *The Economist*, 17 July 2010.

43   'Communist Party's Western xenophobia is more opportunism', SCMP, 14 February 2015.

44   'Beijing pledges to get tough on state security, raising fears NGOs and activists may suffer', SCMP, 13 March 2016.

45   'Chinese university revives research on official ideology to head off suspicious values', *Global Times*, 1 June 2015.

46   'Reform unlikely, says China expert Roderick MacFarquhar', SCMP, 31 October 2012.

47   'Party must embrace Mao spirit to survive, Xi Jinping quoted as saying', SCMP, 28 September 2014.

48   Ryan Mitchell, 'The Rise of Wang Huning', *Foreign Affairs*, 4 December 2017 and 'Meet the mastermind behind Xi Jinping's power', *Washington Post*, 6 November 2017 'https://www.washingtonpost.com/news/theworldpost/wp/2017/11/06/wang-huning/?utm_term=.35ff4194edb0.

49   'Liu still China's invisible man two years after Nobel', *Bangkok Post*, 11 October 2012.

50   'Tie Liu Revealed Liu Yunshan Is The Shackle On China's Press', ndt.tv, 30 August 2014 (www.ntd.tv/en/programs/news-politics/china-forbidden-news/20140830/203411-tie-liu-revealed-liu-yunshan-is-the-shackle-on-china39s-press---.html), https://www.youtube.com/watch?v=KR1Q7T5rtWg.

51   'China Detains Writer Tie Liu for "Provoking Trouble"', *China Digital Times*, 22 December 2014.

52   Liu Yunshan, 'Five dimensions in understanding the CCP', *China Insight*, 7 July 2014 (http://english.cccws.org.cn/archiver/cccwsen/UpFile/Files/Default/20140708162532187779.pdf).

53   Interview by the author on 1 July 2014, with Frank Pieke, professor of sinology at Leiden University, who had attended this conference in Copenhagen.

54   'Xi stresses core socialist values', China Daily 26 February, 2014, http://usa.chinadaily.com.cn/china/2014-02/26/content_17305163.htm.

55   'The historical struggle of the working people against Confucius/Confucianism' (http://
      chineseposters.net/posters/e13-785.php).

56   'Confucius Statue Vanishes Near Tiananmen Square', *The New York Times*, 11 April 2011.

57   W.J. Dobson, 'The East is Crimson', *Slate.com*, 23 May 2012.

58   'Why Beijing has the authority to lead', SCMP, 18 July 2012.

59   'Real meaning of the rot at the top of China', SCMP, 23 April 2012.

60   See D.A. Bell, *China's New Confucianism: Politics and Everyday Life in a Changing Society*
      (Princeton, 2010); and D.A. Bell, *The China Model: Political Meritocracy and the Limits of
      Democracy* (Princeton, 2015).

61   'China's government may be communist, but its people embrace capitalism', Pew
      Research Center, 10 October 2014 (www.pewresearch.org/fact-tank/2014/10/10/chinas
      -government-may-be-communist-but-its-people-embrace-capitalism).

62   https://www.transparency.org/country/CHN.

63   Cited in T. Saich, 'Controlling political communication and civil society under Xi Jinping',
      MERC Papers on China (June 2016).

64   'All the president's men: Xi Jinping tells Communist Party Politburo to unite behind
      him in thought and action', SCMP, 9 January 2016.

65   'Control, on the shores of China's dream', China Media Project, 22 May 2013 (http://cmp
      .hku.hk/2013/05/22/33193/).

66   Fairbank, *East Asia: The Great Tradition*, p. 382.

67   'China journalist arrested after exposing corruption', BBC.com, 10 October 2013.

68   'Jailing of Xu Zhiyong a disgrace', SCMP, 29 January 2014.

69   'The "cancer" of corruption in China', *The Globe and Mail*, 8 January 2014.

70   'Xi echoes Mao's era with plans to send artists to live in rural communities', SCMP,
      2 December 2014.

71   'China's internet users grew in 2016 by the size of Ukraine's population to 731 million',
      SCMP, 22 January 2017.

72   'A Giant Cage', *The Economist*, 6 April 2013.

73   'China says internet security necessary to counter "hostile forces"', SCMP, 18 May 2014.

74   'China Social Media Jail Rumours', *The Guardian*, 10 September 2013.

75   'F-F-Fear and Loathing on the Chinese Internet', *Wall Street Journal*, 12 September 2013
      https://blogs.wsj.com/chinarealtime/2013/09/12/f-f-fear-and-loathing-on-the-
      chinese-internet/.

76   'China adopts new security law', *Financial Times*, 1 July 2015.

77   'China defends state control over internet at technology forum', *Financial Times*,
      3 December 2017.

78   See: https://freedomhouse.org/report/freedom-net/freedom-net-2015.

79   'The Social Credit System in 2020: is black mirror coming true in China?' *Dareasia*,
      10 March 2018. https://dareasia.com/en/social-credit-system-in-china/.

80   'Burgeractivisten opnieuw in de verdrukking', *de Volkskrant*, 31 May 2014.

81   J. McGregor, *No Ancient Wisdom, No Followers: The Challenges of Authoritarian Capitalism* (Norwalk, 2012), p. 16.

82   D. Shambaugh, *China's Future* (Cambridge, 2016), p. 24.

83   'China stresses authority of Constitution, pledges judicial reform', SCMP, 29 October 2014; 'Rules of the Party', *The Economist*, 1 November 2014.

84   'China stresses authority of Constitution, pledges judicial reform', Xinhua News Agency, 29 October 2014; see: http://en.people.cn/n/2014/1029/c90785-8801273.html.

85   'Chinese rights lawyer Tang Jinglin dealt maximum 5-years jail sentence for subversion', SCMP, 30 January 2016.

86   'Prominent Chinese rights lawyer Xia Lin, who defended artist Ai Weiwei, sentenced to 12 years' jail for fraud', SCMP, 23 September 2016.

87   'China's top judge denounces judicial independence', *Financial Times*, 17 January 2017.

88   'China's Xi Jinping supports "democracy" but not in the Western sense', SCMP, 24 September 2014.

89   'Interview with Wang Yi', *Financial Times*, 29 January 2014.

90   Shambaugh, *China Goes Global*, p. 66.

Chapter 6

1   Shambaugh, *China Goes Global*, pp. 26–43.

2   See, e.g., Leonard, *What Does China Think?*, pp. 32–70, for the 'economists' debate'; and Hu Angang, *China in 2020: A New Type of Superpower* (Washington, 2009).

3   VPRO (i.e. Vrijzinnig Protestantse Radio Omroep, or 'Liberal Protestant Radio Broadcasting Corporation'), *Tegenlicht*, 28 March 2011.

4   'CCP Central Committee Resolution Concerning Some Major Issues in Comprehensively Deepening Reform', China Copyright and Media, 15 November 2013.

5   'Party paper invokes Xi's father while lauding reform', SCMP, 10 August 2013.

6   'Two Years in Jail for Calling Xi Jinping a "Steamed Bun"', *The Newslens*, 14 April 2017 https://international.thenewslens.com/article/65955.

7   Constitution of the People's Republic of China (following the 2004 amendment). (www.npc.gov.cn/englishnpc/Constitution/node_2825.htm).

8   *Ibidem*.

9   Spence, *The Search for Modern China*, p. 315.

10   Wang Zhenmin, 'The road to permanent peace and stability', *Tsinghua China Law Review* 6 (2013), p. 3.

11   A. Nathan and P. Link (eds.), *The Tiananmen Papers* (London, 2001), p. 379.

12   Cited in: *Liberty Monthly*, December 1988 (https://en.wikipedia.org/wiki/Liu_Xiaobo).

13   See 'Charter 08' at, again, *The New York Review of Books*, (http://www.nybooks.com/articles/2009/01/15/chinas-charter-08/), in addition to: http://www.chinafile.com/library/nyrb-china-archive/chinas-charter-08#sthash.GgtidwTb.dpuf.

14   *Ibidem.*

15   'China: Q and A on Nobel Peace Prize Winner Liu Xiaobo', Human Rights Watch, 8 October 2010; see: https://www.hrw.org/news/2010/10/08/china-q-and-nobel-peace-prize-winner-liu-xiaobo#_How_has_the.

16   Liu Xiaobo, 'I have no enemies: my final statement', speech for the Nobel Peace Prize, 23 December 2009 (for the complete text, see: www.nobelprize.org/nobel_prizes/peace/laureates/2010/xiaobo-lecture.html).

17   'Live on well': fury, farewells and Nobel laureate Liu Xiaobo's last words to his wife', SCMP, 14 July 2017.

18   *Ibidem.*

19   'China tells world to stay out of its 'domestic affairs' over Liu Xiaobo's death', *The Guardian*, 14 July, 2017.

20   'Liu Xiaobo raises questions for China in life and in death', *Financial Times*, 14 July 2014.

21   Fareed Zakaria, interview with Wen Jiabao, CNN, 3 October 2010 (http://transcripts.cnn.com/TRANSCRIPTS/1010/03/fzgps.01.html).

22   'Hu Deping talks political reform', Before It's News, 15 November 2014 (http://beforeitsnews.com/china/2014/11/hu-deping-talks-political-reform-2450264.html).

23   For Zhao Ziyang's ideas about political reforms, see: A. Ignatius (ed.), *Prisoner of the State: The Secret Journal of Premier Zhao Ziyang* (New York, 2009), pp. 247–272.

24   'Resolution on certain questions in the history of our party since the founding of the People's Republic of China', 27 June 1981 (for the complete text, see: www.marxists.org/subject/china/documents/cpc/history/01.htm).

25   'Party liberal stirs reform pot by calling for greater democracy', SCMP, 5 October 2011.

26   'Danger ahead', SCMP, 2 September 2011.

27   See 'Toe the Communist Party's red line on Cultural Revolution, state paper warns', SCMP, 31 March 2016; and 'China declares cultural revolution a total mistake', *Financial Times*, 17 May 2016.

28   'Defying the silence on Mao's dark past', *The New York Times*, 24 January 2017.

29   'China's top party mouthpieces pledge "absolute loyalty" as president makes rare visit to newsrooms', SCMP, 20 February 2016.

30   'China's Maoists rue decline of the left', *Financial Times*, 14 September 2012.

31   *Ibidem.*

32   'Bo Xilai's City, a Legacy of Backstabbing', *Caixin Online*, 12 July 2012 (http://english.caixin.com/2012-12-07/100470022.html).

33   'China Leaders Laud "Red" Campaign', *The Wall Street Journal*, 22 June 2011.

34   'Bo Xilai sentenced to life in prison for bribery, embezzlement, power abuse', *People's Daily*, 2 September 2013 (http://en.people.cn/90785/8406344.html).

35   'Gu Kailai poured poison into Heywood's mouth', SCMP, 7 August 2012.

36   'Coup plotters foiled: Xi Jinping fended off threat to "save Communist Party"', SCMP, 23 October 2017.

37   Cited in Lee Feigon, *Mao: A Reinterpretation* (Chicago, 2002), p. 41.

38   Dikötter, *Tragedy of Liberation*, p. x.

39   '"Political reform doesn't need blueprint", says academic Fang Ning', SCMP, 1 November 2012.

40   'Danger Ahead', SCMP, 2 September 2011.

41   'Full Text of the Oxford Consensus 2013', *The New York Times*, 18 October 2013.

42   'Q. and A.: Yang Fenggang on the "Oxford Consensus" and Public Trust in China', *The New York Times*, 18 October 2013.

43   'China on course to become world's "most Christian nation" within 15 years', *The Telegraph*, 19 April 2014.

44   The state councilor Dai Bingguo, the country's highest-ranking diplomat until 2013, had already formulated these principles in 2009. See: 'Dai Bingguo: The Core Interests of the People's Republic of China', *China Digital Times*, 7 August 2009.

45   'Constitutional Politics: The Road to Permanent Peace and Stability On How The Communist Party of China Can Escape From the Historical Cycle', *Tsinghua China Law Review 6* (Autumn 2013).

46   Zhao Tingyang, *The Tianxia System: An Introduction to the Philosophy of a World Institution* (Tianxia Tixi: Shijie zhidu zhexue daolun 天下体系：世界制度哲学导论), Nanjing: Jiangsu Jiaoyu Chubanshe, 2005, 160 pp.

47   Full title: 中国不高兴：大时代、大目标及我们的内忧外患 (*Zhōngguó bù gāoxìng: Dà shídài, dà mùbiāo jí wǒmen de nèiyōu wàihuàn – Unhappy China: The Great Time, Grand Vision and Our Domestic Disturbances and Foreign Aggression*), Nanjing, 2009.

48   Zhu Caifang, *The Ordinary Mind in Chan/Zen Buddhism and its psychological significance*, PHD-thesis, 2010.

49   Hu Angang, *China in 2020*, p. 162.

50   W.A. Callahan, *China Dreams: 20 Visions of the Future* (Oxford, 2013), pp. 76–77.

51   'Foreword' in Hu Angang, *China in 2020*, p. xvi.

52   '"New left" scholar Hu Angang for strident defence of party line', SCMP, 19 August 2013.

53   Lin Yutang, *The Wisdom of Confucius* (New York, 1938), p. 182.

Chapter 7

1   'The Unconscious Mind & The Iceberg Metaphor', Process Coaching Centre (see: www.processcoaching.com/unconscious.html).

2   *Ibidem.*

3   Duyvendak, 'The last Dutch Embassy to the Chinese Court (1794–1795)', pp. 76–79.

4   F. Wood, *The Silk Road: Two Thousand Years in the Heart of Asia* (Berkeley, 2004), p. 50.

5   'US takes a tougher tone with China', *The Washington Post*, 30 July 2010.

6   'The dragon's new teeth', *The Economist*, 7 April 2012.

7   Ryan Mitchell, 'Xi Jinping and Han Feizi', https://u.osu.edu/mclc/2015/01/16/xi-jinping
        -and-han-feizi/, 16 January 2015.

8   Communique of the Fourth Plenary Session of the 18th Central Committee of the
        Communist Party of China, October 23, 2014: http://www.china.org.cn/china/fourth
        _plenary_session/2014-12/02/content_34208801.htm.

9   Paul A. Cohen, *History and Popular Memory: The Power of Story in Moments of Crisis* (New
        York, 2014), p. 68.

10   D. Chau (ed.), *China and International Security: History, Strategy, and 21st-Century Policy* (Santa
        Barbara, 2014), p. 46.

11   B. Gill, J. Chang and S. Palmer, 'China's HIV crisis', *Foreign Affairs* (March/April 2002).

12   'Bursting for Change', SCMP, 20 June 2012.

13   'On the source of the phrase "half-colonial, half-feodal society"', *People's Daily*, 18 February
        2009.

14   P. Hopkirk, *The Great Game* (Oxford, 1990), pp. 348–349 and p. 410.

15   See, among others, H.E. Richardson, *Tibet & Its History* (Boston, 1984), pp. 91–107.

16   'Anti-Qing Sentiment' (see: https://en.wikipedia.org/wiki/Anti-Qing_sentiment).

17   *China's Destiny*, discussed in Fairbank, *The United States and China*, pp. 191–193.

18   Cf. 'Ancient Chinese maps debunk Beijing's sea claims, says Philippine judge', SCMP,
        10 June 2014.

19   'China Unveils New Map of South China Sea', *The New York Times*, 25 June 2014.

20   Mongolian and Tibetan Affairs Commission (see: www.mtac.gov.tw/emain.php).

21   'China's six wars in the next 50 years', *The Strategist*, 26 November 2013.

22   For a discussion of recent analysis, see: Judith Shapiro, 'America's Collision Course with
        China', *NYTimes Book Review* (15 June 2017) https://www.nytimes.com/2017/06/15/books/
        review/everything-under-the-heavens-howard-french-destined-for-war-graham-
        allison.html.

23   'Taiwan Relations Act' (see: www.ait.org.tw/en/taiwan-relations-act.html).

24   'Anti-Secession Law' (see the entire text at: http://en.people.cn/200503/14/eng20050314
        _176746.html).

25   Comment made at a forum of the Cross Strait Relations Research Centre, as cited in:
        'Taiwan secessionism "the common enemy of all Chinese"', *China Daily*, 12 July 2005.

26   'Taiwan not fully sold on "1992 consensus": ARATS', *The China Post*, 7 March 2014.

27   'China's Xi and Taiwan's Ma balance delicate diplomacy in Singapore talks', SCMP,
        8 November 2015.

28   'Losing Hearts and Minds', *The Economist*, 6 December 2014.

29   'What Qian Qichen and Deng Xiaoping could teach today's Chinese leaders', SCMP,
        14 May 2017.

30   For an excellent the history of the Taiping Rebellion, see: Spence, *God's Chinese Son*.

31   *Xinhua News Agency*, 6 October 2000.

32   'Cracks in the atheist edifice', *The Economist*, 1 November 2014.

33   See 'Chan teachings of Huineng' by Venerable Master Xing Yun, Fo Guan http://www.fgsitc.org/wp-content/uploads/2014/08/itc-chan-teachings-of-huineng.pdf?g Shan International Translation Center, 2014.

34   'China's spat with Japan: Deng's heirs ignore his advice', Chennai Centre for China Studies, 1 October 2012.

35   'Normalization of relations: China claims it agreed with Japan to shelve the dispute in 1972, Japan denies', *The Asahi Shimbun*, 26 December 2012 (http://ajw.asahi.com/article/special/Senkaku_History/aj201212260103).

36   '1978: Deng Xiaoping Visits Japan', China.org.cn, 22 October 2007 (see: www.china.org.cn/english/congress/229174.htm).

37   Yoshihisha Komori, 'Time to move on from Japan's History', *Asian Wall Street Journal*, 4 May 2005.

38   D. Sneider, 'Textbooks and Patriotic Education: Wartime Memory Formation in China and Japan', *Asia-Pacific Review* 20:1 (2013), p. 48.

39   Sneider, *op. cit.*, p. 48.

40   Sneider, *op. cit.*, pp. 39–40.

41   Sneider, *op. cit.*, p. 35.

42   See: http://en.wikipedia.org/wiki/Devils_on_the_Doorstep.

43   'Truth about Japan's atrocities', *China Daily*, 7 April 2014.

44   'Tiananmen Mothers urge China's government to bear responsibility for "historical crimes"', SCMP, 2 June 2015.

45   B.W. Tuchman, op. cit., pp. 150–151.

46   'China's Foreign Ministry curtails access to declassified historic archives', SCMP, 9 August 2013.

47   'Abe's Yasukuni visit: the view from Japan', East Asia Forum, 24 January 2014 (see: www.eastasiaforum.org/2014/01/24/abes-yasukuni-visit-the-view-from-japan).

48   'About Yasukuni Shrine', Yasukuni.or.jp (see: www.yasukuni.or.jp/english/about/index.html).

49   'Japan's Abe visits shrine for war dead, China, South Korea angered', *The Telegraph*, 27 December 2013.

50   'Ishihara seeking to buy Senkaku Islands', *Japan Times*, 18 April 2012.

51   'Anti-Japanese protests flare in China over disputed islands', *Business Week*, 17 September 2012.

52   'Mao comes back to life amid widespread anti-Japan protests in China', Offbeat China, 16 September 2012 (see: http://offbeatchina.com/mao-comes-back-to-life-amid-wide-spread-anti-japan-protests-in-china).

53   'China denies putting radar-lock on Japanese warship', CNN, 9 February 2013 (see: http://www.cnn.com/2013/02/08/world/asia/china-japan-tensions/index.html).

54   'Japan defence white paper warns of China "force"', BBC.com, 9 July 2013.

55   'Joint Press Conference with President Obama and Prime Minister Abe of Japan', The White House, 24 April 2014 (see: www.whitehouse.gov/the-press-office/2014/04/24/joint-press-conference-president-obama-and-prime-minister-abe-japan).

56 'Chinese jets intercept US military plane over East China Sea', SCMP, 19 May 2017.

57 'Japan must bear fallout of Miyako tensions', *Global Times*, 11 December 2016.

58 Shirk, *China: Fragile Superpower*, p. 144.

59 Shirk, op. cit., p. 158.

60 Shirk, op. cit., p. 159.

61 Shirk, op. cit., pp. 166–167.

62 Cited in Joshua A. Vogel, *Articulating the Sinosphere – Sino-Japanese relations in space and time* (Cambridge, MA, 2009), pp. 13 f.

63 Cited in Shirk, *China: Fragile Superpower*, p. 180.

64 Lin Yutang, *My Country and My People*, p. 355.

65 A. Walder, *'China under Mao, a Revolution derailed'* (Cambridge, MA, 2015), cited in: 'An awkward occasion beckons as China gears up to commemorate victory over Japan', *Financial Times*, 9 June 2015.

66 '[B]etween the people and the troops... [t]he former may be likened to water, the latter to the fish who inhabit it', On Guerrilla Warfare (1937) https://www.marxists.org/reference/archive/mao/works/1937/guerrilla-warfare/.

67 'Modern Chinese History IV: Japanese Invasion and World War II 1937–1945', *Chinafolio* (see: www.chinafolio.com/modern-chinese-history-1937-1945/).

68 See 'Good News, Bad News', SCMP, 11 May 2011.

Chapter 8

1   Preamble of the Constitution of the People's Republic of China (following the 2004 amendment). (www.npc.gov.cn/englishnpc/Constitution/node_2825.htm).

2   Shambaugh, *China Goes Global*, p. 60.

3   Kissinger, *On China*, p. 188.

4   For a Chinese perspective see 'The Bandung Conference of 1955', *China Daily*, 20 April, 2005 http://www.chinadaily.com.cn/english/doc/2005-04/20/content_435929.htm.

5   'Border dispute exposes faultline in China-India relations', *Financial Times*, 9 May 2013.

6   'Modi ready to do business with China', *Global Times*, 19 May 2014.

7   'Modi, Japan and Diplomatic Balancing', 3 September, 2014.

8   'Japan, India agree to boost ties, fast-track defense talks', *Global Times*, 2 September 2014; 'India's Narendra Modi chides China as he embraces Japan', *Financial Times*, 2 September 2014.

9   'Modi-Abe intimacy brings scant comfort', *Global Times*, 2 September 2014.

10 'U.S. Proposes Reviving Naval Coalition to Balance China's Expansion', SCMP, 2 March 2016.

11 'No progress on Sino-Indian border dispute during Xi Jinping visit, analysts say', SCMP, 21 September 2014.

12   'Chinese State Media Video Mocks India In Bizarre Propaganda On Doklam', NDTV, 17 august 2017.

13   'Chinese arms sales surge 143% in 5 years', SCMP, 16 March 2015.

14   'Comment on the Open Letter of the Central Committee of the CPSU (IX)', editorial departments (i.e. Mao Zedong) of *Renmin Ribao* (People's Daily) and *Hongqui* (Red Flag), China (14 July 1964), as published in a pamphlet by Foreign Languages Press (Peking, 1964); see also: https://www.marxists.org/reference/archive/mao/works/1964/phnycom.htm.

15   A. Osborn and P. Foster, 'USSR Planned Nuclear Attack on China in 1969', *The Telegraph*, 13 May 2010.

16   '1991 Sino-Soviet Border Agreement' (see: https://en.wikipedia.org/wiki/1991_Sino-Soviet_Border_Agreement).

17   T. Weiner, 'Stalin-Mao Alliance was Uneasy, Newly Released Papers Show', *The New York Times*, 10 December 1995.

18   F. Dikötter, *Mao's Great Famine* (London, 2010), p. 3.

19   Cited in Hopkirk, *The Great Game*, p. 9.

20   D. Trenin, *The End of Eurasia: Russia on the Border Between Geopolitics and Globalization* (Washington, 2002), p. 205.

21   Weiner, 'Stalin-Mao Alliance Was Uneasy'.

22   'Chinese president's trip to fortify military ties with Russia', SCMP, 7 May 2015.

23   'Putin pivots to the East', *The Economist*, 24 May 2014.

24   T. Cliff, 'China-Russia: The Monolith Cracks', Marxists' Internet Archive (see: www.marxists.org/archive/cliff/works/1963/xx/split.htm).

25   'Natural gas deal boosts Vladimir Putin', *The Economist*, 24 May 2014.

26   'Economic interests attract China to Russia, not imperialist policies', *The Nation*, 5 February 2015.

27   'Xi and Putin present united front in Moscow ahead of massive military parade', SCMP, 9 May 2015.

28   'Island dispute dominates as Japan pins hopes on Russia summit', *Financial Times*, 6 May, 2016.

29   'Enemy of world peace', Chineseposters.net (see: http://chineseposters.net/posters/pc-1960-001.php).

30   Cited in Shambaugh, *China Goes Global*, p. 313.

31   'Toasts of the President and Premier Chou En-lai of the People's Republic of China at a Banquet Honoring the President in Peking', The American Presidency Project, 21 February 1972 (see: www.presidency.ucsb.edu/ws/?pid=3748).

32   For the complete text, see: https://history.state.gov/historicaldocuments/frus1969-76v17/d203.

33   See: https://www.law360.com/articles/922201/us-report-finds-little-interest-in-china-finance-markets.

34   'China Makes Biggest Play', *The Wall Street Journal*, 30 May 2014.

35   'Trump talks by phone with Taiwanese president, risking major row with Beijing', SCMP, 3 December 2016.

36   '"One China" policy cannot be used for bargaining', *Global Times*, 12 December 2016; for another version, see: http://rachelcritelli.com/blog/listen-up-trump/.

37   'Trump reaffirms one-China policy in surprise phone call with Xi Jinping', SCMP, 10 February 2017.

38   'Beijing, US reach trade deal to boost American imports to China in wake of Xi-Trump summit', SCMP, 12 May 2017.

39   'Trump tells Xi of Syria missile attack over Thursday night dinner in Mar-a-Lago', SCMP, 8 April 2017.

40   See: https://www.weforum.org/agenda/2017/01/full-text-of-xi-jinping-keynote-at-the-world-economic-forum.

41   'US Policy in Asia: Assessing the Obama Administration's Efforts to Manage a Rising and Increasingly Assertive China', Clingendael, 28 September 2011.

42   'America and China are rivals with a common cause', *Financial Times*, 16 April 2015.

43   Waldron, 'How China Was Lost', *The Weekly Standard*, 28 January 2013.

44   'Revising U.S. Grand Strategy Toward China', Council on Foreign Relations, April 2015.

45   'Donald Trump to call China, Russia competitors in national security strategy speech', SCMP, 18/ December 2017.

46   'China: Opinions of the United States', Pew Global Attitudes Project, 2014 (see: www.pewglobal.org/database/indicator/1/country/45/).

47   'Views of China and the Global Balance of Power', Pew Global Attitudes Project (see: www.pewglobal.org/database/indicator/24/survey/all/) and 'Americans OK with China but not with Xi, according to poll', SCMP, 5 April 2017.

48   'Further Explanatory Note on the Progress of China', Suzhou Industrial Project (see: www.sipac.gov.cn/english/zhuanti/fnotpoc/fnotpoc_nmoic/).

49   Bandung Conference (Asian-African Conference), 1955 (see: http://history.state.gov/milestones/1953-1960/bandung-conf).

50   'Full Text: Diaoyu Dao, an Inherent Territory of China', Xinhua, 25 September 2012 (see: http://news.xinhuanet.com/english/china/2012-09/25/c_131872152.htm).

51   S. Myšička, 'Chinese Support for Communist Insurgencies in Southeast Asia during the Cold War', Academia.edu (see: www.academia.edu/9668512/Chinese_Support_for_Communist_Insurgencies_in_Southeast_Asia_during_the_Cold_War).

52   See: http://meetville.com/quotes/quote/mao-tse-tung/55686.

53   'Tao Guang Yang Hui (韬光养晦) as a strategy – is China a threat?', see http://sun-bin.blogspot.fr/2005/07/tao-guang-yang-hui-as-strategy-is.html.

54   'China's Peaceful Development Road', *People's Daily*, 22 December 2005.

55   'List of Chinese administrative divisions by GDP per capita' (see: http://en.wikipedia.org/wiki/List_of_Chinese_administrative_divisions_by_gdp_per_capita).

56   See: http://southseaconversations.wordpress.com/2012/08/30/more-doing-required-ding
-gang-brings-the-taoguang-yanghui-debate-to-the-south-china-sea/.

57   H.W. French, *Everything under the Heavens – How the past helps shape China's push for global power*, New York 2017, p. 169.

58   D. Tretiak, 'China's Vietnam War and its consequences', *The China Quarterly* 80 (1979), pp. 740–767.

59   Taiwan Relations Act, Section 2, 2.4 (see: www.ait.org.tw/en/taiwan-relations-act.html).

60   'Mao and the Atom Bomb' (see: http://claudearpi.blogspot.nl/2013/03/mao-and-atom-bomb.html).

61   'China able to attack Taiwan by 2020', *Taipei Times*, 9 October 2013.

62   'Xi tells Kerry: Pacific Ocean big enough for China and US', *Yahoo News*, 17 May 2015, https://www.yahoo.com/news/xi-tells-kerry-pacific-ocean-big-enough-china-164047724.html.

63   Song Qiang, Zhang Zangzang and Qiao Bian, *China Can Say No: The Choice Between Politics and Emotion in the Post-Cold-War Period* (Beijing, 1996).

64   See: http://english.gov.cn/official/2005-08/17/content_24165.htm.

65   'President Xi Jinping vows peace, as PLA top brass talks tough and with Vietnam ablaze', SCMP, 18 May 2014.

66   Shambaugh, *China Goes Global*, p. 28.

67   R. Cottrell, 'How Mrs Thatcher Lost Hong Kong', *The Independent*, 20 August 1992.

68   'China's state-run newspaper backs "non-peaceful" steps against Vietnam', SCMP, 18 May 2014.

69   Leonard, *What Does China Think?*, p. 85.

Chapter 9

1   G. Segal, 'Does China matter?', *Foreign Affairs*, September/October 1999.

2   Wu Jiao, 'Peace Quest Spurs Defense Push', *China Daily*, 5 March 2014.

3   'Benigno Aquino Compares China's Leaders to Hitler, New York Times Reports', *The Huffington Post*, 5 February 2014 (http://www.huffingtonpost.com/2014/02/05/benigno-aquino-china-hitler-philippines-president_n_4727887.html).

4   'Xi outlines his vision of "dream and renaissance"', SCMP, 18 March 2013.

5   'US Congress report warns American interests at risk in China's military rise', SCMP, 21 November 2014.

6   'China's "Core Interests" and the East China Sea' and 'Is the South China Sea, like Taiwan, a core national interest now for China?'; see: www.cfr.org/china/south-china-sea-like-taiwan-core-national-interest-now-china/p31159.

7   Dikötter, *Mao's Great Famine*, p. 80.

8   'Human Rights Watch Reporters' Guide to covering the Beijing Olympics', June 2008,

https://www.hrw.org/reports/2008/china0608/HRW_Beijing%20Olympics_
Reporters%20Guide.pdf.

9   'Olympic torch relay cut short amid Paris protests', *The Guardian*, 7 April 2008.

10   'Olympic-Torch Protests Ignite Chinese Indignation', *The Wall Street Journal*, 8 April 2008.

11   '660 Held in Tibetan Uprising, China Says', *The New York Times*, 27 March 2008.

12   'Security Council Fails to Adopt Draft Resolution on Syria as Russian Federation, China Veto Text Supporting Arab League's Proposed Peace Plan', United Nations, 4 February 2012 (see: www.un.org/press/en/2012/sc10536.doc.htm).

13   'UN Security Council resolution 1973 (2011) on Libya – full text', *The Guardian*, 17 March 2011 (see: www.theguardian.com/world/2011/mar/17/un-security-council-resolution).

14   Peter Ford, 'China to Russia: You're putting us in a tight spot', *Christian Science Monitor*, 7 March 2014.

15   'China opposes proposed EU sanctions against Russia', *Reuters*, 1 September 2014.

16   'Fear of conflict with Japan as China sets up air defense zone', SCMP, 23 November 2013.

17   R. Kaplan, *Monsoon* (New York, 2010), p. 287.

18   'Japan PM Abe calls for new defense law interpretation', BBC.com, 15 May 2014.

19   '"Pandora's Box" fear as Japan passes bills empowering its military to fight overseas', SCMP, 20 September 2015.

20   'Japan and China really don't like each other', *The Diplomat*, 26 August 2013.

21   UNCLOS, Part VII, Article 121 (see: www.un.org/depts/los/convention_agreements/texts/unclos/part8.htm).

22   'Own shoal', *The Economist*, 28 January 2017.

23   For the complete text, see: www.asean.org/asean/external-relations/china/item/declaration-on-the-conduct-of-parties-in-the-south-china-sea.

24   'China's land reclamation in South China Sea grows: Pentagon report', *Reuters*, 21 August 2015.

25   'ASEAN deadlocked on South China Sea, Cambodia blocks statement', *Reuters*, 25 July 2016.

26   'Vietnam vs. China: The Captain Who Went Down With His Ship', *The Huffington Post*, 22 May 2014.

27   'China creates new islands', ABC, 3 November 2014 (see: www.abc.net.au/lateline/content/2014/s4120861.htm).

28   'The US Will Open Massive Philippine Bases Not Occupied Since The Cold War', *Business Insider*, 8 June 2012 (see: www.businessinsider.com/the-us-is-reopening-massive-philippine-military-bases-not-used-since-the-cold-war-2012-6).

29   'Vietnam walks a thin line after oil rig exit', *Thanhnien News*, 7 August 2014.

30   'Vietnam's communist party meets to elect new leadership', SCMP, 12 January 2016.

31   B. Hayton, *The South China Sea: The Struggle for Power in Asia* (Yale, 2014), p. 154.

32   'Beijing warns all outside ASEAN against involvement in the South China Sea', SCMP, 10 August 2014.

33   'Hanoi should give up on opportunism', *Global Times*, 4 September 2014.

34   H.W. French, *Everything under the Heavens* (New York, 2017), p. 149.

35   Monroe Doctrine (see: http://www.digitalhistory.uh.edu/disp_textbook.cfm?smtID=3& psid=161).

36   'Will a rising PLA Navy end of Deng Xiaoping's dictum?', China Defense Mashup, 1 April 2004 (see: www.china-defense-mashup.com/will-a-rising-pla-navy-end-of-deng -xiaopings-dictum.html).

37   'China charts course for blue-water navy, extending reach into open seas', SCMP, 26 May 2015.

38   'Sea Power and China's Strategic Choices', *China Security* (Summer 2006), pp. 17–31; here: p. 22.

39   B. Hayton, *The South China Sea: The Struggle for Power in Asia.* (Yale, 2014).

40   '"Ancient Chinese maps debunk Beijing's sea claims", says Philippine judge', SCMP, 10 June 2014.

41   'The, https://pca-cpa.org/wp-content/uploads/.../PH-CN-20160712-Award.pdf Republic of the Philippines v. The People's Republic of China' and 'China reiterates refusal of Filipino sea arbitration', *Global Times*, 16 December 2014.

42   'Chinese and US think tanks agree South China Sea situation needs to be cooled down', *Beijing Review*, 8 July 2016.

43   'Beijing claims "indisputable sovereignty" over South China Sea', *The Washington Post*, 31 July 2010.

44   'Chuck Hagel: "China territorial claims destabilize region"', *Politico.com*, May 2014.

45   UNCLOS, Article 60, lid 8 (see: www.un.org/depts/los/convention_agreements/texts/ unclos/part5.htm).

46   'China warns US not to send warships to disputed South China Sea waters', SCMP, 13 May 2015.

47   'Mattis sticks to his guns', *The Washington Post*, 5 June 2017.

48   'Philippines' Rodrigo Duterte announces "separation" from US', *Financial Times*, 21 October 2016.

49   'Beijing charm offensive curbs Philippine protests', *Financial Times*, 3 April 2017.

50   For Deng Xiaoping's South China Sea policy statement, see http://news.xinhuanet.com/ english/china/2016-07/13/c_135509153_5.htm.

51   'Duterte will have to change tune on China and the US', SCMP, 29 October 2016.

52   'Did Duterte go back on his word after Beijing visit?', *Global Times*, 24 October 2016.

53   'America's Pacific Century', *Foreign Affairs*, 11 October 2011.

54   'China's foothold in South China Sea: analysts reveal endgame to Beijing's reclamation efforts', SCMP, 30 May 2015.

55   See: www.58pic.com/psd/12208988.html.

56   'Patriotic songs sing more individualist tune', *China Daily*, 17 March 2005.

57   See: www.hollywoodreporter.com/news/china-screens-48-episode-documentary- 724552.

58   'Ignoring Lei Feng: China's Failed Revolutionary Biopics', *The New Yorker*, 13 March 2013.

59   See: www.constructionweekonline.com/article-10012-shanghai-expo-cost-60b-ten-times-original-budget.

60   'Is China's next moon probe a preparation for a lunar landing?', *Wired.com*, 7 November 2014.

61   'China's Manned Space Program', *The Atlantic*, 9 July 2013.

62   'China plans manned moon mission', *The Guardian*, 30 December 2011.

63   'China foreign trade reserves 1980–2015', *Trading Economics* (see: www.tradingeconomics .com/china/foreign-exchange-reserves).

64   'China Criticizes U.S. Economic Policy and Requires Security of Investments', http:// thechinatimes.com/online/2011/08/991.html.

65   'China rises to forefront of global development', *Global Times*, 11 August 2014.

66   'AIIB plays to China's powerful strengths as good institutional citizen', *Global Times*, 15 April 2015.

67   McGregor, *No Ancient Wisdom, No Followers: The Challenges of Authoritarian Capitalism*, p. 23.

68   McGregor, *op. cit.*, p. 4.

69   'What China's Political Crisis Means for U.S. Business', *The Wall Street Journal*, 1 May 2012.

70   'Xi: There is no gene for invasion in our blood', *China Daily*, 16 May 2014.

71   'Full Text: China's Peaceful Development', see: http://www.china-embassy.org/eng/ gdxw/t856287.htm.

72   Cited in Callahan, *China Dreams: 20 Visions of the Future*, p. 48.

73   According to the *Encyclopedia of Genocide and Crimes Against Humanity*: 'Under Article II of the United Nations Convention on the Prevention and Punishment of the Crime of Genocide, the Qianlong Emperor's actions against the Zunghars constitute genocide, as he massacred the vast majority of the Zunghar population and enslaved or banished the remainder, and had "Zunghar culture" extirpated and destroyed' (see: https://en .wikipedia.org/wiki/Dzungar_genocide).

74   G. Wade, 'The Zheng He Voyages: A Reassessment', ARI Working Paper No. 31 (2004), cited in: B. Hayton, *The South China Sea: The Struggle for Power in Asia*, pp. 24–25.

75   Callahan, *China Dreams: 20 Visions of the Future*, p. 106.

76   Mao Tse-tung, 'A study of physical education' (April 1917), *Selected works*, Vol. VI (see also: https://www.marxists.org/reference/archive/mao/selected-works/volume-6/mswv6_01.htm).

77   Cited in *The New York Times*, 9 September 2004.

78   F. Dikötter, 'Racial Theories in The China Critic', *China Heritage Quarterly* 30/31 (2012).

79   'Chinese challenge to "out of Africa" theory', *New Scientist*, 3 November 2009.

80   See: http://roberts-report.blogspot.nl/2009/07/information-war-over-urumqi-riots-and .html.

81   'A Glimpse Into Chinese Nationalism', *The Diplomat*, 7 November 2014.

82   'Chinese state leader Zhang Dejiang announces Beijing's plans to tighten grip on Hong Kong', SCMP, 28 May 2017.

83   'Vietnam asked Philippines to form pact to counter China, Aquino reveals', SCMP, 21 April 2015.

84   'Stapled visa for Arunachal residents a "goodwill" gesture, says Chinese Foreign Minister', *The Indian Express*, 10 June 2014.

85   'Arunachal Pradesh visa row: CM condemns China's act; BJP writes to Prez', *Zee News*, 11 October 2013.

86   'Xi says China respects Mongolia's independence, but stresses joint development', SCMP, 22 August 2014.

87   'World Hegemony', SCMP, 17 February 2011.

88   Shambaugh, *China Goes Global*, p. 234.

89   'Danger in Mainland Media's Rabid Nationalism', SCMP, 26 December 2012.

90   'What does Xi Jinping's China Dream mean?', BBC.com, 6 June 2013.

91   Kissinger, *On China*, p. 521.

92   Cf. Kissinger, *op. cit.*, p. 521; see also Callahan, *China Dreams: 20 Visions of the Future*, pp. 58–62.

93   Callahan, *op. cit.*, p. 59.

Chapter 10

1   'Where China outpaces America', *The New York Times*, 1 May 2011.

2   D. Bell, *The China Model: Political Meritocracy and the Limits of Democracy* (Princeton, 2015), p. 198.

3   'Quánguó lǐngdǎo gànbù jiāng lúnxùn guóxué bāokuò zhìguó lǐ zhènghé dàodé xiūyǎng' ('Country's leading cadres will take turns receiving instruction in National Studies, including governance and ethics'), *Beijing News*, 16 June 2015; and 'China Prepares "Traditional Culture" Textbooks for Its Officials', *Caixin*, 18 June 2015.

4   'Organic Law of the Villagers Committees of the People's Republic of China' (see: www.npc.gov.cn/englishnpc/Law/2007-2/11/content_1383542.htm).

5   Essay placed in the *Yanhuang Chunqiu* and cited in 'Party liberal stirs reform pot by calling for greater democracy', SCMP, 5 October 2011.

6   'Tocqueville's advice on French revolution captures Chinese leaders' attention', SCMP, 22 January 2013.

7   'Vow to step up corruption battle', SCMP, 12 January 1996.

8   Mao Tse-tung, 'Report to the Second Plenary Session of the Seventh Central Committee of the Communist Party of China' (5 March 1949), *Selected Works*, Vol. IV, p. 374 (see also 'Quotations from Mao Tse-Tung – Chapter 24': www.marxists.org/reference/archive/mao/works/red-book/ch24.htm).

9   Dikötter, *Mao's Great Famine*, p. 163.

10   'Xi's Corruption Crackdown', *Foreign Affairs*, May/June 2015, p. 37.

11   'China launched an anti-corruption campaign last year. So why is its reputation getting worse?', *The Washington Post*, 2 December 2014. In 2017 China ranked 77th, see https://www.transparency.org/country/CHN.

12   'After Bo Xilai, corruption as usual', SCMP, 29 September 2013.

13   'Chinese ex-leader Zhou Yongkang charged with corruption', SCMP, 5 December 2014.

14   C. Walter and F. Howie, *Red Capitalism: The Fragile Financial Foundation of China's Extraordinary Rise* (New York, 2012), p. 22; also cited in *Financial Times*, 7 July 2012.

15   'A Year in a word: Princeling', *Financial Times*, 26 December 2012.

16   'Bloomberg: "Revolution to Riches"', *China Digital Times*, 26 December 2012.

17   'The family of Wen Jiabao holds a hidden fortune in China', *The New York Times*, 26 October 2012.

18   Minxin Pei, *China's Crony Capitalism* (Cambridge, (MA), 2016), as discussed in 'Too big, too Leninist', *Financial Times*, 13 December 2016.

19   'China must defeat "all enemies that dare to offend", President Xi tells troops at military parade', SCMP, 30 July 2017.

20   'Retired generals point to "horrible" graft in PLA', SCMP, 10 March 2015; '16 major generals, many of them newly promoted, under investigation for military corruption', SCMP, 2 March 2015.

21   'Rank and Vile', *The Economist*, 14 February 2015.

22   'China's People's Liberation Army told to learn from Japan's 1894 victory', SCMP, 23 March 2015.

23   'Is Xi Jinping protecting himself from an internal threat? China president reshuffles elite security unit', SCMP, 11 March 2015.

24   'Invited to farm, but forced off the land', SCMP, 6 August 2011.

25   'The emperor does know', *The Economist*, 12 May 2012.

26   Confucius, *The Analects*, Book 12, Ch. 1.

27   'A secret weapon in the battle to save the snow leopard?', *The Economist*, 16 September 2013.

28   Confucius, *The Analects*, Book 13, Ch. 3.

29   Zeng Qinghong, address delivered at the Fourth Plenary Session of the Sixteenth Central Committee (2004) (Cited in David Shambaugh, *China's Future*, (Cambridge, 2016), p. 114).

Chapter 11

1   See: www.pages.drexel.edu/~cp28/marx.htm.

2   S. Shirk, *Changing Media, Changing China* (Oxford, 2011).

3   Mao Tse-tung, 'On Contradiction' (August, 1937), *Selected Works*, Vol. I, p. 333 (see: www.marxists.org/reference/archive/mao/selected-works/volume-1/mswv1_17.htm).

4   Hammering Shield, *Permanent Revolution: The Rise And The Ruthlessness of Chairman Mao*

(see: http://hammeringshield.wordpress.com/2014/03/18/permanent-revolution-the-rise-and-the-ruthlessness-of-chairman-mao/).

5   Plato, *The Republic*, Book IX, transl. Desmond Lee (Harmondsworth, Middlesex, 1974).

6   Cited in K. Popper, *The Open Society and Its Enemies: The Spell of Plato* (Princeton, 1971), p. 37.

7   Fukuyama, *The End of History and the Last Man*, p. 56.

8   Fukuyama, *op. cit.*, p. 64.

9   Passage from Yan Fu, *Learning from the West*, see: http://afe.easia.columbia.edu/special/china_1750_reform.htm.

10   Cited in Spence, *God's Chinese Son*, p. 116.

11   'The World of Da-Tong (*Dah-Tong*)' (see: taousa.org/classic-texts/4The-World-of-Da-Tong.pdf).

12   'Xi marks Confucius anniversary', *Global Times*, 25 September 2014.

13   'China's top philosophy scholar and "sinology master" Tang Yijie dies at 87', SCMP, 10 September 2014.

14   Cited in Callahan, *China Dreams: 20 Visions of the Future*, p. 158.

15   E.g. 'Tu Weiming – The World's Leading Confucian Scholar' (see: www.east-west-dichotomy.com/tu-weiming-the-worlds-leading-confucian-scholar).

16   For the following discussion, see: 'Beyond the Enlightenment Mentality', in: M. Evelyn Tucker and J. Berthrong, *Confucianism and Ecology: The Interrelationship of Heaven, Earth, and Humans* (Cambridge (MA), 1998); Tu Weiming, *Global Significance of Concrete Humanity: Essays on the Confucian Discourse in Cultural China* (New Delhi, 2010).

17   Confucius, *The Analects*, Book 6, Ch. 28.

18   Cited in Tu, 'Beyond the Enlightenment Mentality'. See also: Wang Yangmin, '*Inquiry on The Great Learning*', in *Instructions for Practical Living, and Other Neo-Confucian Writings*, transl. Wing-tsit Chan (New York, 1963), pp. 217–280; here: p. 272.

19   Jiang Qing, D.A. Bell, et.al. (eds.), *A Confucian Constitutional Order: How China's Ancient Past Can Shape Its Political Future* (Princeton, 2012), p. 41.

20   Jiang Qing, *A Confucian Constitutional Order*, p. 86.

21   Yuri Pines, a visiting Professor at the Beijing Normal University, School of History and the Michael W. Lipson Professor of Asian Studies at the Hebrew University of Jerusalem, contend that Jiang Qing draws on the Qing-dynasty (1644–1911) version of the Gongyang Zhuan, which bears little resemblance to the original text that was composed in the Warring States period (453–221 b.c.e.). *China Review International*: Vol. 19, No. 4, 2012, see http://yuri-pines-sinology.com/files/review-of-jiang-qing.pdf.

22   'Canada confirms new millionaire migration scheme will be tiny, costly and strict', SCMP, 17 December 2015.

23   See e.g. 'Why money and prestige aren't enough to lure foreign scientists to China', SCMP, 17 November, 2016.

24   Amy Chua, *Day of Empire: How Hyperpowers Rise to Global Dominance and Why They Fall*, p. 295.

25   See: https://en.wikipedia.org/wiki/List_of_countries_by_ median_age.

26   'Chinese ideologues' wrong tilt on universal values', SCMP, 7 October 2013.

27   https://freedomhouse.org/report/freedom-world-2018-table-country-scores.

28   VPRO, *Tegenlicht*, 28 March 2011.

29   H. Kissinger, *World Order* (New York, 2014).

Chapter 12

1   'Country pushes for Code at Sea', *China Daily*, 14 November 2014.

2   'China says land reclamation projects in disputed South China Sea territory to finish "within days"', SCMP, 17 June 2015.

3   'Own shoal', *The Economist*, 28 January 2017.

4   'Xi personally behind island-building the South China Sea', SCMP, 28 July 2017.

5   'Full Text: Work Report of NPC Standing Committee' (2014) (see: http://www.npc.gov.cn/ englishnpc/Speeches/2014-03/18/content_1856663.htm).

6   'US obsession to maintain hegemony', *China Daily*, 11 November 2014.

7   *Ibidem.*

8   Shambaugh, *China Goes Global*, pp. 133–136.

9   'Regional free trade zone an elusive goal to accomplish', *ChinaDaily*, 10 November 2014.

10   'Jointly Shoulder Responsibility of Our Times, Promote Global Growth', Keynote Speech by Xi Jinping (see: https://america.cgtn.com/2017/01/17/full-text-of-xi-jinping-keynote -at-the-world-economic-forum).

11   'President Xi's Davos speech receives warm applause', *The Telegraph*, 24 January 2017.

12   'China stakes a claim for globalism without liberalism', *Financial Times*, 27 January 2017.

13   Confucius, *The Analects*, Book 13, Ch. 16.

14   'Full text of Hu Jintao's report at 17th Party Congress' (see: http://www.straittalk88.com/ uploads/5/5/8/6/55860615/full_text_of_hu_jintaos_report_at_17th_party_congress__ qiushi_journal.pdf); cf. 'Hu Jintao calls for enhancing "soft power" of Chinese culture' (see: http://en.people.cn/90002/92169/92187/6283148.html).

15   'Americans have grown more negative toward China over the past decade', Pew Research Center (see: http://www.pewresearch.org/fact-tank/2017/02/10/americans-have-grown -more-negative-toward-china-over-past-decade).

16   'Hostile Neighbors: China vs. Japan – View each other as arrogant, violent; disagree on WWII legacy', Pew research Center, http://www.pewglobal.org/2016/09/13/hostile -neighbors-china-vs-japan/.

17   Cited in Shambaugh, *China Goes Global*, p. 215.

18   Shambaugh, *op. cit.*, p. 212.

19   Fukuyama, *The End of History and the Last Man*, p. xx.

20   'China, Burma sign $7.8 bn of deals', Irrawaddy.org (see: www.irrawaddy.org/burma/ china-burma-sign-7-8-bn-deals-china-daily. html).

21 'Did China Just Re-enact the Famous "Birdie" Scene from Top Gun with US Plane?', *Foreign Policy*, 22 August 2014.

22 'China's President Talks Trade in India as Troops Face Off at Border', *The Wall Street Journal*, 18 September 2014.

23 'US, China reach landmark pacts', *China Daily*, 13 November 2013.

24 'The U.S.-China Incidents at Sea Agreement: A Recipe for Disaster', 7 March 2012 (see: www.phisicalpsience.com/public/Tumblehome_Hull_ddg-1000/us_China).

25 'Kunming rail station attack: China horrified as mass stabbings leave dozens dead', *The Guardian*, 2 March 2014.

26 'China and US recognize truths of power', *Global Times*, 28 July 2014.

27 Graham Allison, *Destined for War: Can America and China Escape Thucydides' Trap?*, Scribe Publications, 2017.

28 'The Koguryo Controversy, National Identity, and Sino-Korean Relations Today' (see: www.ou.edu/uschina/gries/articles/texts/Gries2005Koguryoeaiq.pd).

29 See e.g. 'Rising China, sinking Russia', *The Economist*, 14 September 2013.

30 Cf. Jane K. Leonard, *Wei Yuan and China's rediscovery of the maritime world* (Cambridge (MA), 1984).

31 See e.g.: http://www.businessinsider.com/historical-view-global-gdp-shares-2015-9?IR=T.

32 'Chinese contractors grab lion's share of Silk Road projects', *Financial Times*. 24 January, 2018.

33 'China looks to economy, countering US', *The Nation*, 3 February 2015.

34 'Silk Road initiatives to restore lost glory', *China Daily Asia Weekly*, 6 February 2015.

Works Consulted

Allison, Graham T., *Destined for War: Can America and China Escape Thucydides' Trap?* (Boston: Houghton Mifflin Harcourt, 2017)

Anderson, Benedict, *Imagined Communities: Reflections on the Origin and Spread of Nationalism* (London, 1991)

Barrow, John, *Travels in China, Containing Descriptions, Observations, and Comparisons* (London, 1804); reprint ed., Ch'eng Wen Publishing Company (Taipei, 1972)

Bary, Wm. Theodore de, ed., *Sources of East Asian Tradition, Volume 1: Premodern Asia,* (New York 2008)

Bary, Wm. Theodore de, and Richard Lufrano compiled by, *Sources of Chinese Tradition,* Volume Two, (New York, 1999)

Bell, Daniel, *The China Model: Political Meritocracy and the Limits of Democracy* (Princeton, 2015)

Bell, Daniel A., *China's New Confucianism: Politics and Everyday Life in a Changing Society* (Princeton, 2010)

Bor, Jan, *Een nieuwe geschiedenis van de filosofie* (Amsterdam, 2011)

Bor, Jan, *De verbeelding van het denken* (Amsterdam, 2014)

Boxer, Charles Ralph, *Fidalgos in the Far East, 1550–1770* (The Hague, 1948)

Boxer, Charles Ralph, *The Dutch Seaborne Empire* (London, 1977)

Brady, Anne-Marie, *Making the Foreign Serve China: Managing Foreigners in the People's Republic* (Lanham, MD, 2003)

Butterfield, Fox, *Alive in the Bitter Sea* (London, 1982)

Callahan, William A., *China Dreams: 20 Visions of the Future* (Oxford, 2013)

Chau, Donovan C. (ed.), *China and International Security: History, Strategy, and 21st-Century Policy,* (Santa Barbara, 2014)

Chow, Gregory C., *China's Economic Transformation* (Malden, MA, 2007)

Chua, Amy, *Day of Empire: How Hyperpowers Rise to Global Dominance* (New York, 2007)

Confucius, *The Analects,* in: *Confucian Analects, the Great Learning, and the Doctrine of the Mean,* transl. James Legge, revised, 2nd ed. (Oxford, 1893)

Xiaoping Cong, *Teachers' Schools and the Making of the Modern Chinese Nation-State, 1897–1937* (Washington, 2007)

Constitution of the People's Republic of China (Peking, 1987)

Dikötter, Frank, *The Age of Openness: China Before Mao* (Hong Kong, 2008)

Dikötter, Frank, *Mao's Great Famine: The History of China's Most Devastating Catastrophe, 1958–1962* (London, 2010)

Dikötter, Frank, *The Tragedy of Liberation: A History of the Communist Revolution, 1945–1957* (New York, 2013)

Drege, Jean-Piere, *Marco Polo et la Route de la Soie* (Paris, 1989)

Economy, Elizabeth, *River Runs Black* (Cornell, 2010)

Joseph Esherick, *Empire to Nation: Historical Perspectives on the Making of the Modern World* (Lanham, MD, 2006)

Fairbank, John K., *The United States and China* (Cambridge, MA, 1958)

Fairbank, John K., *East Asia: The Great Tradition* (London, 1960)

Fairbank, John K., *East Asia: The Modern Transformation* (London, 1965)

Fenby, Jonathan, *Chiang Kai-Shek* (New York, 2004)

Fitzgerald, Charles Patrick, *The Horizon History of China* (New York, 1969)

Fung Yu-lan, *A short history of Chinese philosophy*, ed. Derk Bodde (New York, 1948)

Fukuyama, Francis, 'The End of History?' *The National Interest* 16 (1989)

Fukuyama, Francis, *The End of History and the Last Man* (New York, 1992)

George, Henry, *Progress and Poverty* (New York, 1879)

Gibson, James R., *Otter Skins, Boston Ships, and China Goods: The Maritime Fur Trade of the Northwest Coast, 1785–1841* (Montreal, 1992)

Gries, Peter H., *China's New Nationalism: Pride, Politics and Diplomacy* (Berkeley, 2005)

Guo, Fei and Zhongwei Zhao, *Transition and Challenge: China's Population at the Beginning of the 21st Century* (Oxford, 2007)

Haar, Barend J. ter, *Het Hemels Mandaat. De geschiedenis van het Chinese keizerrijk* (Amsterdam, 2009)

Halbertsma, Tjalling, *De verloren lotuskruisen* (Haarlem, 2002)

Hansen, Valerie, *The Open Empire: A History of China to 1600* (New York, 2000)

Hayton, Bill, *The South China Sea: The Struggle for Power in East Asia* (New Haven, 2014)

Hill, John E., transl. and ed., *Through the Jade Gate to Rome: A Study of the Silk Routes During the Later Han Dynasty, 1st to 2nd centuries CE* (Charleston, SC, 2009)

Hopkirk, Peter, *The Great Game: On Secret Service in High Asia* (Oxford, 1991)

Hu, Angang, *China in 2020: A New Type of Superpower* (Washington, 2011)

Huntington, Samuel P., *The Clash of Civilizations and the Remaking of World Order* (New York, 1997)

Jacques, Martin, *When China Rules the World: The Rise of the Middle Kingdom and the End of the Western World* (New York, 2009)

Jenner, W.J.F., *The Tyranny of History: The Roots of China's Crisis* (London, 1992)

Jiang Qing, D.A. Bell, et.al. (eds.), *A Confucian Constitutional Order: How China's Ancient Past Can Shape Its Political Future* (Princeton, 2012)

Kaplan, Robert D., *Monsoon: The Indian Ocean and the Future of American Power* (London, 2010)

Killion, Ulric, *A Modern Chinese Journey to the West: Economic Globalization and Dualism* (New York, 2006)

Kissinger, Henry, *On China, with a new afterword* (New York, 2012)

Kissinger, Henry, *World Order* (New York, 2014)

Lattimore, Owen, and Eleanor Silks, *Spices and Empire* (London, 1973)

Lee Feigon, *Mao: A Reinterpretation* (Chicago, 2002)

Leeuw, Karel van der, *Het Chinese denken. Geschiedenis van de Chinese filosofie in hoofdlijnen* (Amsterdam, 1994)

Leonard, Jane K., *Wei Yuan and China's Rediscovery of the Maritime World* (Cambridge, MA, 1984)

Leonard, Mark, *What Does China Think?* (New York, 2008)

Legge, James, ed., *The Great Learning* [The Text of Confucius], Ch. 1, transl. James Legge (Oxford, 1893)

Legge, James, ed., *The Sacred Books of China. The Texts of Confucianism*, Pt. III, incl. the Lî Kî, transl. James Legge (Oxford: Clarendon, 1879)

Legge, James, ed., *The Sacred Books of China. The Texts of Confucianism*, Pt. I, incl. the Hsiâo King, transl. James Legge (Oxford: Clarendon, 1879)

Legge, James, *The Sacred Books of China. The Texts of Tâoism*, Pt. II, incl. the Writings of Kwang-ze [i.e. Zhuang Zi], transl. James Legge (Oxford, 1891)

Levathas, Louise, *When China Ruled the Seas* (New York, 1994)

Leys, Simon [pseud. Pierre Ryckmans], *Ombres chinoises* (Paris, 1974); *Chinese Shadows* (New York, 1977)

Li Zhisui, *The Private Life of Chairman Mao* (London, 1994)

Liang Zhang, Andrew Nathan, et al., *The Tiananmen Papers* (New York, 2002)

Lim, Louisa, *The People's Republic of Amnesia* (Oxford, 2014)

Lin Yutang, *My Country and My People* (Singapore, 2001)

Link, Perry, 'China after Tiananmen: Money, Yes; Ideas, No'. In: *The New York Review of Books* (31 March 2014)

Lovell, Julia, *The Opium War: Drugs, Dreams and the Making of China* (London, 2012)

Macartney Robbins, Helen H., *Our First Ambassador to China: An Account of the Life of George, Earl of Macartney, with Extracts from His Letters, and the Narrative of His Experiences in China, as Told by Himself, 1737–1806* (Cambridge, 2011)

McGregor, James, *One Billion Customers: Lessons from the Front Lines of Doing Business in China* (New York, 2005)

McGregor, James, *No Ancient Wisdom, No Followers* (Westport, CT, 2012)

McGregor, Richard, *The Party: The Secret World of China's Communist Rulers* (New York, 2010)

Meisner, Maurice, *Mao Zedong: A Political and Intellectual Portrait* (Cambridge, 2007), (New York, 2012)

Miller, Tom, *China's Urban Billion: The Story Behind the Biggest Migration in Human History* (London, 2012)

Mitter, Rana, *Modern China* (Oxford, 2008)

Mitter, Rana, *China's War with Japan, 1937–1945: The Struggle for Survival* (London, 2013)

Morgan, David, *The Mongols* (Oxford, 1986)

Naughton, Barry, 'Shifting structures and processes in economic policy making at the centre'. In: *China's Core executive. Leadership styles, structures and processes under Xi Jinping*, eds Sebastian Heilmann and Matthias Stepan (Berlin: 2016)

Nietzsche, Friedrich, *Jenseits von Gut und Böse. Vorspiel einer Philosophie der Zukunft* (1885)

Patten, Chris, *East and West* (London, 1998)

Pieke, Frank, *The Good Communist: Elite Training and State Building in Today's China* (Cambridge, 2009)

Pinker, Steven, *The Better Angels of Our Nature* (New York, 2011)

Plato, *The Republic*, transl. Desmond Lee (Harmondsworth, Middlesex, 1974)

Polo, Marco, *The Travels*, transl. and with an introduction by Ronald Latham (London, 1958)

Popper, Karl R., *The Open Society and Its Enemies: The Spell of Plato* (Princeton, 1971)

Putten, Frans-Paul van der, *Corporate Behaviour and Political Risk: Dutch Companies in China 1903–1941* (Leiden, 2001)

Putten, Jan van der, *China wereldleider? Drie toekomstscenario's* (Amsterdam, 2013)

Richardson, Hugh E., *Tibet & Its History* (Boulder, 1994)

Schipper, Kristoffer, *Zhuang Zi. De volledige geschriften. Het grote klassieke boek van het taoïsme* (Amsterdam, 2007)

Schipper, Kristoffer, *Lao Zi. Het boek van de Tao en de innerlijke kracht* (Amsterdam, 2010)

Schipper, Kristoffer, *Confucius. De gesprekken, gevolgd door Het leven van Confucius door Sima Qian* (Amsterdam, 2014)

Schulte Nordholt, Henk, *De Chinacode ontcijferd. Economische grootmacht ja, wereldrijk nee* (Amsterdam, 2006)

Seagrave, Sterling, *The Soong Dynasty* (London, 1985)

Seagrave, Sterling, *Dragon Lady: The Life and Legend of the Last Empress of China* (London, 1992)

Seagrave, Sterling, *Lords of the Rim* (New York, 1995)

Senger, Harro von, *Strategemen. Listen om te overleven* (Rotterdam, 1988)

Shakya, Tsering, *The Dragon in the Land of Snows* (NewYork, 1999)

Shambaugh, David, *China Goes Global: The Partial Power* (Oxford, 2013)

Shambaugh, David, *China's Future* (Cambridge, 2016)

Shirk, Susan L., *Changing Media, Changing China* (Oxford, 2011)

Shirk, Susan L., *China: Fragile Superpower* (Oxford, 2008)

Spence, Jonathan D., *Chinese Roundabout: Essays in History and Culture*, (New York, 1993)

Spence, Jonathan D., *God's Chinese Son: The Taiping Heavenly Kingdom of Hong Xiuquan* (New York, 1996)

Spence, Jonathan D., *Mao* (London, 1999)

Spence, Jonathan D., *The Search for Modern China* (New York, 2013)

Sun Tsu, *The Art of War*. Edited and with a foreword by James Clavell (London, 1989)

Szuma Chian, *Records of the Historian*, transl. Yang Hsien-yi and Gladys Yang (Peking, 1979)

Trenin, Dmitri, *The End of Eurasia: Russia on the Border Between Geopolitics and Globalization* (Washington, 2002)

Tu Weiming, *Humanity and Self-cultivation: Essays in Confucian Thought* (Fremont, CA, 1978)

Tu Weiming, *The Living Tree: The Changing Meaning of Being Chinese Today* (Stanford, 1994)

Tu Weiming, *Confucian Traditions in East Asian Modernity* (Cambridge, MA, 1996)

Tu Weiming, 'Beyond the Enlightenment Mentality', in: Mary Evelyn Tucker and John

Berthrong, eds, *Confucianism and Ecology: The Interrelation of Heaven, Earth, and Humans* (Cambridge, MA, 1998

Tuchman, Barbara W., *Stilwell and the American experience in China* (New York 1971)

Verstappen, Stefan, *The Thirty-Six Strategies of Ancient China* (San Francisco, 1999)

Vogel, Ezra, *Deng Xiaoping and the Transformation of China* (Cambridge, MA, 2011)

Vogel, Joshua A., *Articulating the Sinosphere – Sino-Japanese relations in space and time* (Cambridge, MA, 2009)

Walder, Andrew G., *China under Mao, a Revolution derailed* (Cambridge, MA, 2015)

Walter, Carl, and Fraser Howie, *Red Capitalism: The Fragile Financial Foundation of China's Extraordinary Rise* (New York, 2012)

Wang Yang-Ming, *Instructions for Practical Living, and Other Neo-Confucian Writings*, transl. Wing-tsit Chan (New York, 1963)

Wasserstrom, Jeffrey N., *China in the 21st Century: What Everyone Needs to Know* (Oxford, 2010)

Weatherford, Jack, *Genghis Khan and the Making of the Modern World* (Jack Weatherford Foundation, 2012)

Wood, Frances, *The Silk Road* (Berkeley, 2002)

Wood, Frances, *The First Emperor of China* (London, 2008)

Yang Guobin, *The Power of the Internet in China: Citizen Activism Online* (New York, 2009)

Yu Hua, *China in Ten Words*, transl. Allan Barr (London, 2012)

Zhao Ziyang, *Prisoner of the State: The Secret Journal of Premier Zhao Ziyang*, transl. Bao Pu (New York, 2009)

Illustration Credits

Index of persons

Abe, Shinzo   92, 200, 212, 238, 295

Adams, John Quincy   59

Ai Weiwei   139

Allison, Graham   303

Anderson, Benedict   122

Annan, Kofi   281

Anson, George   52

Anti, Michael   137

Antoninus Pius   23

Aquino III, Benigno   4, 234, 247

Armstrong, Neil   251

Augustine of Hippo   277

Bacon, Francis   28

Barrow, John   55, 59

Bayan   25

Bell, Daniel   132, 290

Berlin, Isaiah   120, 133

Bertolucci, Bernardo   71

Black, Dora   78

Blackwill, Robert   221

Blaeu, Joan   32

Bo Guagua   154

Bo Xilai   103, 108–109, 141, 153–154

Bo Yibo   103, 108–109, 153

Bodhidharma   193

Buddha   39, 168, 193, 197

Bor, Jan   35

Borodin, Mikhail   80

Bos, Hendrik   2

Braam Houckgeest, Andreas Everardus van   17, 54–56, 178

Brezhnev, Leonid   3

Bush, George H.W.   227

Bush, George W.   221

Butterfield, Fox   2

Cai Hesen   185

Cai Julan   271

Cai Mingchao   61

Cai Qi   94

Cai Yingwen   190, 219

Cao Cao   42

Cao Jianming   124

Carpio, Antonio   245

Carter, Jimmy   114, 190, 223, 227

Castiglione, Giuseppe   47, 60

Chang Ping   78

Chang Wanquan   112, 234

Charlemagne   29

Charles II   20

Chen Duxiu   146

Chen Feng   168

Chen Guangcheng   271

Chen Shuibian   190

Chen Xi   94

Chen Yuan   108, 124

Chen Yun   91, 105, 108–109

Chen Zhong   89

Chen Zuyi   255

Cheng Li   171

Chiang Ching-kuo   145, 287
Chiang Kai-shek   67–68, 81–85, 87, 121–122,
    145–146, 187, 189, 191, 199, 204, 221, 261
Chow, Gregory   85
Christ, Jesus   10, 195, 278
Chua, Amy   285
Churchill, Winston   67
Ci Xi   63–64, 66, 71, 73
Clausewitz, Carl von   42
Clinton, Bill   122, 136, 202, 227, 241
Clinton, Hillary   8, 246, 249
Coen, Jan Pieterszoon   51
Columbus, Christopher   31
Confucius (Kong Zi; Master Kong)   33–39,
    119, 130–131, 143, 162, 173, 175, 178, 261, 263,
    272–273, 277, 279–280, 283–284, 288–289,
    297
Cui Tiankai   141, 209

Dai Bingguo   246, 248
Dai Qing   127
Dai Yi   196
Dalai Lama   24, 48, 91, 136, 149, 169, 192–193,
    210, 236, 272–273
Deng Xiaoping   2–3, 13, 40, 82, 85, 93, 95, 99–
    101, 104–105, 108–109, 114, 117, 119, 121–122,
    124–125, 128, 137, 143–144, 153, 173–174, 177,
    183, 193, 197–199, 202–207, 222–230
Dewey, John   78
Dikötter, Frank   91, 214
Ding Gang   259
Ding Li   166–168, 175, 257, 289, 311
Du Chunhua   236
Du Yuesheng   83
Duterte, Rodrigo   248

Einstein, Albert   78
Elvin, Mark   32
Engels, Friedrich   88

Fairbank, J.K.   16
Fang Fenghui   112, 187, 230, 237
Fang Ning   155
Feng Youlan   40
Feng Yuxiang   77
Franz Ferdinand   302
Friedman, Milton   144
Friedman, Thomas   98
Fu Chai   181–182
Fu Ying   234
Fukuda, Takeo   198
Fukuyama, Francis   6–10, 12, 183, 277, 298

Gaddafi, Muammar   237
Gan Yang   7
George III   53, 59
George, Henry   72
Glaser, Bonnie   221
Glenn, John   251
Gorbachev, Mikhail   121
Gordon, Charles   195
Gou Jian   181–182
Grotius (Groot, Hugo de)   239
Gu Junshan   110–112
Gu Kailai   154
Guan Yu   112
Guo Boxiong   110, 111, 112, 270
Guo Qijia   131

Hagel, Chuck   247
Hai Rui   10
Han Deqiang   287
Han Feizi   163, 179
Han Zheng   95, 111
Havel, Václav   146, 150
Hayton, Bill   245
He Lu   41
He Ping   108
He Shen   57
He Weifang   153

Hegel, Georg Wilhelm Friedrich   1, 6–7, 277
Henry VIII   196
Heywood, Neil   154
Hirobumi, Itō   66
Hirohito   198
Hitler, Adolf   4, 234, 289
Hobbes, Thomas   163, 180
Hong Wu see Zhu Yuanzhang
Hong Xiuquan   195, 278
Hu Angang   171–173, 175–176, 242, 279, 311
Hu Deping   151
Hu Jintao   74, 80, 92–93, 95–96, 98, 104, 113–
    114, 120–121, 124, 126, 133–134
Hu Muying   108
Hu Qiaomu   108
Hu Sen   240
Hu Weiyong   98
Hu Yaobang   117, 121, 151, 165
Hua Guofeng   101
Hume, David   119
Huntington, Samuel   10, 59
Hussein, Saddam   227

Ibsen, Henrik   78
Ishihara, Shintaro   201

Jacques, Martin   118
Jenner, William John Francis   77
Jia Qing   57
Jiang Jieshi see Chiang Kai-shek
Jiang He   246
Jiang Ping   155
Jiang Qing (Neo-confucianist)   283–284,
    290
Jiang Qing (wife of Mao Zedong; Lan Ping)
    2, 85–86
Jiang Zemin   93, 95–96, 98, 104, 110–112, 121,
    126–128, 159, 203, 227, 229, 264, 271, 289
Jin Canrong   237
Jin Yongming   307

Jing Hui   170–171, 193–194, 197
Jones, Bruce   301

Kabat-Zinn, John   168
Kang Sheng   127
Kang Xi   26
Kang Youwei   73–74, 146, 279, 289, 293
Kant, Immanuel   1, 164
Kaplan, Robert   238
Kelly, John   229
Kertanegara of Singhasari   244
Ketteler, Clemens von   63
Khan, Genghis   25, 187, 215, 258
Khan, Kublai   25, 244
Khrushchev, Nikita   119, 213–214, 216, 227
Kim Dae-jung   203
Kim Jin Hyun   258
Kissinger, Henry   43, 190, 210, 217–218, 259,
    290
Koizumi, Junichirō   200
Kong Zi see Confucius
Kosygin, Alexei   214
Koxinga see Zheng Chenggong
Kristof, Nicolas   261

Lam, Carrie   258
Lan Ping see Jiang Qing
Lao Zi (Master Lao) 37–38, 40, 157, 275, 290
Lawick van Pabst, Albert van   311
Lawrence, D.H.   135
Ledeen, Michael   71
Lee Kuan Yew   105
Lee Wei Lin   105
Lee Tenghui   226
Leeuw, Karel van der   42
Lenin, Vladimir   88, 140, 208
Leonard, Mark   231
Leys, Simon   2, 176
Li Datong   65
Li Hongzhang   28, 66, 69, 166, 195

Li Keqiang   93–95, 101, 109, 114–115, 138, 199, 294
Li Peng   309
Li Qun   271
Li Xiannian   109
Li Xiangyang   211
Li Yufu   266
Li Zhanshu   95, 264
Li Zhuang   153
Liang Qichao   12–13, 70, 77, 184, 289
Lin Biao   109–110, 130
Lin, Justin   31
Lin Yutang   1, 9, 39, 119, 204
Lin Zexu   58
Lincoln, Abraham   148
Liu He   131
Liu Mingfu   259–260
Liu Shaoqi   108, 112
Liu Shiyu   105
Liu Xia   150
Liu Xiang   256
Liu Xiaobo   117, 143, 145–150, 156, 176, 184, 271–272, 286, 289, 300
Liu Yuan   108, 112
Liu Yunshan   113, 126–129, 132, 134, 152, 184, 253, 261, 272, 311
Liu Zuoming   253
Locke, John   7, 183
Lorenzana, Delfin   248
Louis IX (Saint Louis)   25
Louis XIV   20
Luo Guanzhong   42
Luo Yuan   270

Ma Yingjiu   190, 192
Macartney, George (Earl)   53–55, 58–60, 303
MacFarquhar, Roderick   126
Mahan, Alfred Thayer   244
Mandela, Nelson   149–150, 287
Mao Yushi   253

Mao Zedong IX   2–3, 5, 11, 20–21, 39, 43, 71, 80–89, 91, 94–95, 98–102, 104, 108–112, 118–119, 121–124, 126–127, 129–130, 133, 135, 139–140, 143, 146, 148, 150, 152–155, 160, 165, 173, 177, 185, 187, 193, 195–196, 199, 201–205, 207–218, 224, 227, 230, 235, 250, 256, 261, 263, 266, 268, 270, 272, 275–276, 284, 286, 288, 291
Marshall, George   84, 146
Marx, Karl   6, 11, 72, 88, 108, 123–126, 145, 148, 156, 208, 275–277
Mattis, James   67, 202, 247, 295, 303
McCarthy, Joseph   217, 221
McGregor, James   120
Mencius (Meng Zi)   19, 33, 35–36, 121, 183
Merkel, Angela   125
Metternich, Klemens von   230, 290
Minxin Pei   269
Mo Yan   265
Modi, Narendra   211–212
Mohammed   10
Monroe, James   243
Montesquieu, Charles de   73
Moses   36

Nanninga, Johan   310
Needham, Joseph   28, 31, 305
Nehru, Jawaharlal   210–211, 224
Nguy Văn Thà   145, 241
Ni Lexiong   270
Nietzsche, Friedrich   1
Nixon, Richard   190, 211, 217–218, 221, 226
Nye, Joseph   297

Obama, Barack   67, 181, 202, 219, 247–249, 294–296
Obama, Michelle   41
Orwell, George   10, 123, 135, 137, 177

Palmerston, Lord (Henry John Temple) 58–59
Pan Shiyi 136
Pan Wei 281
Pan Xueqing 149
Pedrozo, Pete 300
Peng Liyuan 41, 100
Peng Zhen 109
Pelosi, Nancy 147
Perry, Matthew C. 65
Pieke, Frank 128, 311
Pinault, François-Henri 61
Piontkovsky, Andrey 216
Plato 164, 276–279, 281, 289
Pliny the Elder 17
Pol Pot 226
Polo, Marco 25, 31, 223
Popper, Karl 281
Protagoras 8
Pu Yi (Xuan Tong) 68, 71
Putin, Vladimir 215–216, 221, 237–238, 262

Qi Fanhua 263
Qian Long 15, 17, 26, 45–48, 52–57, 59, 134, 178, 187, 254, 275, 302–302
Qin Gang 236
Qin Shi Huangdi 15, 19, 21, 118
Qin Yaqing 157–159, 175, 258, 311

Raby, Geoffrey 252
Reagan, Ronald 117, 227
Ren Yuling 267
Rho, Jerónimo 51
Ricci, Matteo 33
Rogers, William 217
Roosevelt, Franklin D. 67
Ruan Zongze 295
Rubruck, William of 25
Ruffijn, Hans 51
Russell, Bertrand 78

Saint Laurent, Yves 61
Sarmento de Carvalho, Lopo 51
Schell, Orville 275
Scheffer, Paul 311
Schutten, Arjen 311
Schwab, Klaus 296
Segal, Gerald 233
Seneca, Lucius Annaeus 17, 23
Shambaugh, David 141, 143, 229, 233, 296–297
Shen Dingli 212
Shi Lang 52
Shirk, Susan 121–122, 202
Siddhartha 46, 197
Sima Qian 41
Smith, Adam 53
Sneevliet, Hendricus 80–81
Snow, Edgar 83
Song Jiaoren 76
Song Meiling 146
Song Qiang 229
Song Qingling 72
Song Renqiong 109
Song Xiao 61
Speelman, Tabitha 311
Spence, Jonathan 69
Spencer, Herbert 74
Stalin, Joseph 84, 88, 102, 187, 189, 209, 213–215, 290
Stilwell, Joe 199
Störig, Hans Joachim 1
Streicher, Julius 259
Suiko 23
Summers, Larry 9
Sun Chunlan 102
Sun Yatsen (Sun Zhongshan) 71–73, 75–76, 80–81, 87–89, 97, 121, 166, 174, 186–187, 208, 256–257, 289, 298
Sun Zi (Master Sun) 40–43, 80, 92, 180, 225, 228–229, 272, 286

Tagore, Rabindranath   78
Tan Zuoren   139
Tanaka, Kakuei   205
Tang Jinglin   139
Tang Yijie   280
Tasman, Abel   238
Temür, Toghon   25
Thatcher, Margaret   230, 272
Thein Sein   299
Thornton, John   171
Thucydides   5–6, 11, 301–302
Tian Chunsheng   216
Tie Liu   127
Tillerson, Rex   150
Titsingh, Isaac   54–55
Tocqueville, Alexis de   266
Trajan   285
Trenin Dmitri   217
Trotsky, Leon   123
Truman, Harry S.   189
Trump, Donald   100, 181, 219–222, 247, 285, 296
Truong Tan Sang   241
Tsang, Steve   88
Tu Weiming   9, 12, 144, 169, 281–284, 289–291
Tuchman, Barbara   68

Ullmann, Liv   149

Ven, Hans van der   200
Voltaire   254

Wade, Geoff   255
Wang Dan   150
Wang Hou   42
Wang Huning   95, 111, 126, 136
Wang Jiangfeng   145
Wang Jun   108
Wang Lijun   153–154

Wang Qishan   94, 96, 266
Wang Wei   235
Wang Xiaodong   164–166, 176, 229, 244, 257, 284, 311
Wang Xuedong   125
Wang Yang   94, 95, 265
Wang Yangming   283
Wang Yi   140, 242, 265
Wang Yiwei   216, 307–308
Wang Zaixi   191
Wang Zhen   108–109
Wang Zhenmin   159–162, 176, 192–193, 278, 311
Watt James   28
Wei Yuan   305
Wen Jiabao   121, 151, 154, 264, 268
Wu, emperor of the Han dynasty   38
Wu Han   10–11
Wu Liangyong   115

Xi Jinping   5, 11–12, 41, 57, 74–76, 91–113, 115, 121–126, 129, 131, 133–136, 139–140, 144–146, 150–154, 160, 165, 168, 179, 181, 192, 212, 215, 219–222, 229, 234, 251, 254, 257, 262, 264, 267, 270–271, 275, 279–281, 287, 294, 296, 300
Xi Zhongxun   43, 91, 266
Xia Lin   139
Xiang Lanxin   259, 286
Xin Yun   197
Xu Caihou   107, 119–111, 270
Xu Ming   103
Xu Zhiyong   134
Xuan Zang   30, 174–175, 191, 257, 293, 311

Yan Fu   74–75, 184, 256, 259, 278
Yan Xuetong   297
Yan Yuan   272
Yang Fenggang   156, 196
Yang Jiechi   101, 197

Yang Jisheng 152
Yang Liwei 251
Yang, Philip 249
Yang Shangkun 109
Yang Yuanqing 265
Yang Zhifa 22
Yao Ming 265
Yao Mingle 110
Yasay, Perfecto 248
Ye Jianying 174
Yong Le 255
Yongjin Zhang 297
Yu Gong 291
Yu Xian 64
Yu Zhengsheng 144, 265
Yuan Guiren 124
Yuan Shikai 76, 261, 281
Yuan Weishi 65
Yudin, Pavel 215
Yun Tang 184

Zeng Guofan 69, 166, 183, 195
Zeng Qinghong 274
Zeng Zi 37
Zhang Baoyi 40
Zhang Dejiang 258, 294
Zhang Dongsun 94
Zhang Qian 30
Zhang Rongye 149
Zhang Wei 251

Zhang Weiying 152
Zhang Wenmu 244, 249
Zhang Xiaogang 6
Zhang Xizhen 307
Zhang Xueliang 84
Zhang Yimou 16
Zhang Zhijun 192
Zhao Leji 95
Zhao Tingyang 124, 162–164, 175, 278–279, 311
Zhao Ziyang 93, 117, 121, 151
Zheng Bijian 254
Zheng Chenggong 51–52
Zheng He 49–50, 165, 238, 249, 254–255, 296, 302, 305
Zheng Jing 52
Zhou Enlai 83, 157, 203, 209–211, 217
Zhou Qiang 139
Zhou Ruijin 152, 263–264
Zhou Yongkang 105–107, 110, 141, 154, 268
Zhu Caifang 168–171, 176, 197, 311
Zhu Rongji 138, 233, 253
Zhu Xi 119
Zhu Yuanzhang 97–98
Zhuang Dehui 108
Zhuang Zi 38
Zhuge Liang 42–43
Zi Gong 35
Zi Si 119
Zoellick, Robert 298